People of Kituwah

The publisher and the University of California Press
Foundation gratefully acknowledge the generous support
of the Peter Booth Wiley Endowment Fund in History.

People of Kituwah

The Old Ways of the Eastern Cherokees

John D. Loftin and
Benjamin E. Frey

UNIVERSITY OF CALIFORNIA PRESS

University of California Press
Oakland, California

© 2024 by John Loftin and Ben Frey

Parts of chapter 1 have been reprinted from "Eastern
Cherokee Creation and Subsistence Narratives: A
Cherokee and Religious Interpretation," *American
Indian Culture and Research Journal* 43, no. 1, by
permission of the American Indian Studies Center,
UCLA. © 2019 Regents of the University of California.

Library of Congress Cataloging-in-Publication Data

Names: Loftin, John D., 1955- author. | Frey, Benjamin
    E., 1983- author.
Title: People of Kituwah : the old ways of the eastern
    Cherokees / John D. Loftin and Benjamin E. Frey.
Other titles: Old ways of the eastern Cherokees
Description: Oakland, California : University of
    California Press, [2024] | Includes bibliographical
    references and index.
Identifiers: LCCN 2023040953 (print) | LCCN
    2023040954 (ebook) | ISBN 9780520400313 (cloth ;
    alk. paper) | ISBN 9780520400320 (pbk ; alk. paper) |
    ISBN 9780520400344 (ebook)
Subjects: LCSH: Cherokee Indians—North Carolina—
    Religious aspects. | Cherokee Indians—North
    Carolina—History.
Classification: LCC E99.C5 L635 (print) | LCC E99.C5
    (ebook) | DDC 975.600497/557—dc23/eng/20231025
LC record available at https://lccn.loc.gov/2023040953
LC ebook record available at https://lccn.loc.gov
    /2023040954

Manufactured in the United States of America

33 32 31 30 29 28 27 26 25 24
10 9 8 7 6 5 4 3 2 1

In honor of the Ancestors

Contents

Preface

This book embodies a collaborative effort between John D. Loftin, a historian of religions and a lawyer, and Benjamin E. Frey, a linguist and an enrolled citizen of the Eastern Band of Cherokee Indians. Utilizing a Cherokee-centered methodology, our work embodies religious theory primarily insofar as it helps uncover meanings related to the old ways of the Eastern Cherokee. Although there are undoubtedly aspects of any culture that seem incomprehensible to an outsider, there are also elements common enough to be understood and shared. In this book, we address Cherokee spirituality over time from the perspectives of both the Cherokee people and religious studies to unveil an understanding that does justice to the Cherokees.

John, who has been hanging around Indian Country and interviewing old-timers for more than forty years, has taught widely and written in the field of American Indian spirituality. A third-generation North Carolina lawyer, he has also represented the Eastern Band of Cherokee Indians since 2003. John, as an ally and student of the Cherokee, both advocates for their sovereignty and seeks a respectful understanding of Cherokee traditions and customs.

A few years ago, John had the good fortune to meet Ben Frey, an assistant professor of American Studies at the University of North Carolina at Chapel Hill. Ben teaches courses in Cherokee language, philosophy, and worldview, and he reads, writes, and speaks the Cherokee language. He is the great-grandson of Ollie Otter Jumper, a healer, who was married to a medicine man named Amoneeta "Doc" Sequoyah. Their daughter, Mabel Sequoyah, Ben's great-aunt, was like a second grandmother to him; they were quite close, and she taught him a lot about Cherokee culture and language. Ben also learned from his uncle, Jim Eller, his mother's brother. Ben remains engaged with a number of Cherokee elders and speakers and is actively involved in the revitalization and preservation of the Cherokee language.

As Ben puts it: I have long roots with the Eastern Band of Cherokee Indians. I have been a citizen of the nation since birth, but I really started working in earnest with the tribe and its language programs in particular around the summer of 2003. I knew that my grandmother's experiences at boarding school had meant that she did not pass the language on to my mother or her siblings, and so I had missed out on learning it at home. After a meaningful trip to Germany in high school, I asked my mother if I could stay with my uncle on the Qualla Boundary for the summer in an attempt to learn our people's language. Fortunately, my mother told me our cousins Eddie and Jean Bushyhead were in charge of the language program—at that time located within the tribe's Department of Cultural Resources—and would likely be able to help me.

I met with my cousin Eddie, who provided me a copy of *Cherokee Language Lessons*, the grammar book his father, Robert Bushyhead, had coauthored with Dr. Bill Cook while Cook completed his doctoral dissertation, *A Grammar of North Carolina Cherokee*. I based my senior honors thesis in linguistics on that book, then worked as a teaching assistant for Tom Belt's Cherokee language classes at Western Carolina University, in Cullowhee, for a year. Each summer for the next decade I returned to the Qualla Boundary to work on the language.

In 2005, the tribe launched a comprehensive survey to assess how many first-language speakers of Cherokee remained. I coordinated the surveyors' efforts and helped to edit the survey. During the remaining years, I helped annotate Cherokee texts for linguistic analysis, taught courses in Cherokee grammar, and helped lay the groundwork for the Eastern Band's online Cherokee language engine. I focused my doctoral dissertation on the process of language shift, comparing the shift from German to English in eastern Wisconsin with the shift from Cherokee to English in western North Carolina. Throughout the years, I have had the honor of working with many influential figures in Cherokee language revitalization, from Gil Jackson and his sisters Shirley Oswalt and Lou Jackson to Myrtle Driver Johnson.

John D. Loftin
Benjamin E. Frey
2023

Introduction

This is a story about the old ways of the Eastern Cherokees who live in the Great Smoky Mountains in North Carolina. What might non-Indigenous peoples gain from reading a detailed religious interpretation of traditional Eastern Cherokee worldviews and lifeways? First, as the historian of religions Charles Long liked to say, "understanding carries its own virtue." Questions concerning the meaning, purpose, and value of life have gripped humans since they first came into being. Rather than examining such age-old questions in the abstract, this deep dive into the Cherokee spiritual cosmos explores religious experience and expression from the standpoint of a Native American community that is alive and well in the twenty-first century. In learning about the Cherokees, the reader will better apprehend an often eclipsed but worthwhile aspect of their own humanity. That is so because our ancestors were once Indigenous, and most Indigenous folk perceived and engaged the world as a reality that transcends them. Therefore, studying traditional Eastern Cherokee worldviews and lifeways will reward the reader with a better understanding of themselves. Humans do not live by bread alone and an examined life is worth living. This study of a fascinating Native American people will enhance the depth and breadth of the reader's apprehension of the world we share.

Moreover, understanding the Cherokee way of life may bring useful, everyday benefits to post-Enlightenment Westerners who have created a polarized society that is environmentally unsustainable. Many people might promote their own survival by realizing that the world is our Mother, not an "other." This is not simply a matter of engaging in a lifeway that seeks to preserve finite natural resources; rather, it is a matter of respecting the cosmos as a relative. Folklorist Barre Toelken once inquired of a Hopi, "Do you mean to say, then, that if I kick the ground with my foot . . . nothing will grow? He said, 'Well, I don't know if that would happen or not, but it would just really show what kind of person you are.'"[1] At the risk of grossly oversimplifying the Cherokees' narrative, the world makes us more than we make the world and nature is not simply material. In other words, Cherokees help us understand that we live in a cosmos that embodies a spiritual power on which our lives depend.

For Cherokees, according to Cherokee co-author Ben Frey, it is good to know these things because it helps Cherokees make sense of the cosmology and worldview from which their spiritual and cultural thinking and understanding arise. Traditionally when Cherokees asked elders why they did things a certain way, they were told: "Because we have always done this; this is who we are. This is what our ancestors did; it would please them to know we are still doing it." The book paints with a broad brush the larger context of customs, traditions, and practices that a number of Cherokees hold on to and sometimes embody at an almost unspoken level. Many Cherokees grow up with a foot in both worlds, and knowing the spiritual foundation of their own lifeway gives them a sense of meaning, value, and purpose.

This volume represents a consolidation of many disparate sources on Cherokee spirituality, with special emphasis on Eastern Cherokee spiritual ways. In so doing, we offer a new and fresh interpretation refracted through a spiritual lens. We contend that Cherokee economic, social, and political traditions are fundamentally animated by deep-rooted spiritual feelings. Rather than maintaining a Western European–style separation between spiritual and everyday life, Cherokees have historically viewed all significant aspects of their lifeways as sacred. Such an outlook, we argue, has long informed Cherokee people's actions in a variety of spheres, and it continues to do so today. Because of the shared history of Cherokee people, this adherence to spiritual roots is not isolated to Eastern Cherokees. Consequently, although we pay special attention in this volume to what has become known as Eastern Cherokee spirituality, we do not shy away from outside academic sources, as they have much to tell us about the common inheritance of Cherokee spiritual tradition.

Our work has, in effect, two parts. Part 1, chapters 1–4, focuses on traditional Cherokee spirituality by interpreting beloved stories, community, ceremonies, and medicine. We realize that we address those topics in a somewhat structural and timeless manner. The truth is that Cherokee religion has never been completely static, but the internal and external historical change experienced by aboriginal Cherokees was fundamentally different from the forced change occasioned by European invaders. Contact with the West and with Christianity shocked the Cherokees and at times overwhelmed their old way of incorporating novelty into their worldview. Thus, part 2, chapters 5–12, wrestles with Cherokee religious experience and expression after contact and during colonialism. Cherokees often creatively appropriate Western and Christian influences in ways that are ultimately meaningful. Sometimes Cherokees incorporate outside influences and events into their old religious orientation, and other times they affirm and embrace them outright. Whether they adopt these ideas in part or in whole, Cherokees maintain their identity as Cherokees, a people with a strong spiritual foundation.

As scholars such as Chris Teuton, Sara Snyder, and Sandra Muse Isaacs have shown, storytelling and oral performance are among the primary tools for this investigation within Cherokee epistemology.[2] Eastern Cherokee sacred (ᏍᏓᎤᎶᏗ, *galvquodi*, "beloved") narratives concerning creation are still told and their ultimate significance is still experienced and embodied by contemporary Cherokees. But Cherokee narratives do not exhaust the range of meanings in traditional Cherokee spirituality. As Osage scholar and pastor George Tinker says, "what we call spirituality is, for us as it is for most indigenous peoples, a way of life more than a religion."[3] Because Cherokee spirituality informs and grounds their worldview and way of life, we not only examine and interpret traditional stories, symbols, metaphors, dances, rites, medicine, and ceremonies, but we also look at kinship patterns, food production, and communities.

While some argue that comparisons between religious traditions are fruitless due to the differences in personal experiences, we contend that there are also deep similarities that deserve consideration. By the same token, we disagree with the premise that scholars should consider religion solely through a theological or essentialist lens. Instead, we seek a nuanced view that gives proper attention to similarities as well as differences, and to structural continuities as well as to historical transformations.

Cherokee tradition says that time is not linear; it cycles and echoes back on itself. Therefore, understanding the past can shed light on what is happening now and what will happen later. Spirituality was woven into Cherokee life so seamlessly that there is no word for *religion* in the Cherokee language. As such, we examine their old worldviews and life-ways to focus on those aspects that might be properly called, in English, *religious* or *spiritual*. To fully consider the strands of thought that weave together to create Cherokee religion, it is necessary to consider the fundamental impact of language and thought upon one another. Translating Cherokee to English, for example, sometimes presents challenges. A term in religious studies as common as *sacred* is not easily matched in Cherokee. As co-author Ben Frey notes, in talking about the Cherokee term *beloved* as a term for *sacred*, using it with a set *a* prefix, as in *galvgwodi*, gives more of a nominal sense, as in "the beloved." This also comes up in the name of the Oconaluftee River—*egwona galvgwodi* or "beloved river." It's not too far a stretch to also extend this meaning to "sacred" or "hallowed" as it is used in the Lord's Prayer: *ogidoda, galv-ladi hehi, galvgwodiyu detsado'v'i*—"our father, heaven dweller, hallowed be your name." As we shall see, some Cherokee terms translate well into English but some do not; the two languages contain some very real differences that defy a 1:1 correspondence. At the same time, despite linguistic differences between English and Cherokee and between Cherokee and other Native American languages, it is fair to say that the English term *sacred* makes sense to most Cherokees.

Throughout the book we use the terms *Cherokee* and *Cherokees* interchangeably, depending primarily on the context, sentence structure, and the way it reads. Generally, we refer to the Nation as the Cherokees rather than the Cherokee, primarily to avoid representing them as monolithic. The most formal name for Cherokees is ᏗᏂᏱᏍᎬᏯ (*anigiduwagi*, "Kituwah people"). Another more formal name for Cherokees is ᏗᏂᎥᏬᏗ (*aniyvwiya*, "real human beings"). (This is probably more akin to "the kind of human beings that we tend to see around the most"—that is, "us." The term can be used not just for Cherokees but also for other Native Americans.) While this volume concentrates primarily on the Eastern Cherokees, we often use Western Cherokee sources. Prior to the migrations and removal that occurred from the 1780s to 1839, the Cherokees lived for thousands of years throughout the Appalachian Mountains as one people. During that time, they shared a mostly common spirituality, and many of those meanings and values continue to abide among all Cherokees, wherever they live today.

Spiritual meanings and values permeate and animate the old ways of Eastern Cherokees. Stories and legends, ceremonies, medicine, and rites of passage constitute part of their religious orientation, but so do subsistence activities, kinship patterns, community life, politics, and warfare. In other words, Eastern Cherokees ground their traditional worldviews and lifeways in a spiritual understanding of—and an engagement with—the cosmos.[4]

PART ONE

Before Contact

CHAPTER I

ᏗᏃᏍᎩᏯᎬ ᎤᏂᏃᏢᏫ

*Eastern Cherokee Creation and
Subsistence Narratives*

Tucked away in the beautiful Great Smoky Mountains of North Carolina—Land of the Blue Smoke, ᏌᎪᏂᎨ ᏃᏒᏍᎤᏗ ᏤᎤᏴᏓᏒᎢ, *sakonige tsuksvsdi tsunvdasvi*; literally "blue smoke mountains"—live the Eastern Band of Cherokee Indians.[1] Driving through the largest section of the Cherokee homelands, the Qualla Boundary, the casual visitor or tourist sees several businesses and government buildings, lodging facilities, restaurants, and churches, which at first glance look similar to some of the surrounding mountain towns. But soon one notices that many of the signs contain a script that is mysterious and very different from the English language. It is the Cherokee syllabary, invented by Sequoyah in 1821, and its appearance throughout "the Boundary" is the first indication that one has entered another cultural world. This is the home of a proud and ancient people who have inhabited the Appalachian Mountains of the United States since time immemorial.

At the same time, Eastern Cherokees have adapted much of American culture, and many of their citizens are practicing Christians and have been since sometime after the Civil War.[2] But to describe the Eastern Cherokees as Christian Americans is to say too little and too much at the same time. First—and we realize this is a general argument subject to refinement and criticism—Cherokee Christianity embodies many aspects of traditional Cherokee religious experience and expression.[3] It is an overgeneralization to characterize either Cherokee spirituality or Christianity as intractably uniform; group and individual differences have always existed within the Cherokee community. The same is true of how they practice Christianity. That said, Cherokees experienced the introduction of Christianity in 1799 as something new that was often in conflict with their traditions and customs.

The widespread presence of Christianity among the Eastern Cherokees has not erased their old ways, despite James Mooney's dire prediction in 1890 concerning the loss of Cherokee religion. Eastern Cherokees still speak the language, tell sacred/beloved stories and narratives, play the ball game, practice traditional medicine and conjuring, hunt, farm, gather wild plants, weave baskets and mold pottery, observe ancient birth customs, help one another according to community tradition (ᏍᏊ, *Gadugi*, "people coming together as one and working to help one another), obscure their private names, and participate in various ritual performances and dances.[4] Moreover, traditional Cherokee narratives link religious life with nature's forms and rhythms, history, and modes of subsistence in a way that does not reduce one to the other. This chapter concentrates on Cherokee sacred narratives (myths) related to creation, hunting, and farming. These stories, often called legends, embody the meanings, values, and purposes that help form Eastern Cherokee identity at a fundamental level.

ALWAYS

The principal written source of spiritual stories comes from James Mooney's *Myths of the Cherokee*, published in 1890 when traditional Cherokee religion had declined considerably due to devastation by Old World disease, numerous wars with the British and Americans, and the influence of Christianity. Nevertheless, Swimmer (a well-known Cherokee conjuror) and a handful of other elders, including medicine people, shared with the American ethnographer well over one hundred different myths. Interestingly, the majority of the myths that Mooney collected describe why various plants, animals, and birds look the way they do. Another large group of narratives involve rabbit, the Cherokee trickster, who often fools and is fooled by other animals, and occasionally saves the world from an evil monster. After reviewing the voluminous corpus of Cherokee myths, including those still told today, we found that one point became clear: Cherokee people often discuss their origins in mythical, as opposed to historical or scientific, terms. It should go without saying that Cherokees are aware of time as a linear unfolding of events; however, in the old Cherokee way, the historical concept of time, which stresses sequential events, exists alongside a mythical perception of eternity, which can be experienced periodically. Cherokees, at times, "forget" the historical past literally to remember a timeless meaning.[5]

The beloved founding Cherokee narrative on which all others are based may be described as an "earth diver cosmogony." Many Cherokee myths reference ᏔᎳᎩ (ilvhiyu, the "long ago") or ᎠᏐᎸᎥᎦᎬ (analenisgv, "the beginning").[6] The myths often explicitly state that, at that "time," people and animals could all communicate freely with one another. It was in this timeless time that Cherokee origins took place. Then, "in the beginning," nothing existed but water and animals who lived above in the highest (seventh) heaven, above the arch of the sky vault, which was made of stone. The animals wanted to know what was beneath the water, and at last they got the little water beetle to dive down and see what was below. He brought up a small piece of soft mud, which began to grow and eventually became the island that is now called ᎡᎶᎯ (elohi, "Earth" or "the middle world.")[7]

The Great Buzzard created the mountainous land of the Cherokees on his quest to find dry land. He flew all over the earth, low to the ground, while the earth still consisted of soft mud. When he reached Cherokee, he became tired and his wings began to strike the ground each time they flapped. When his wings struck the ground, he created a valley, and when his wings turned up, he created a mountain. At first, the sun was so low in the sky that it made everything hot, and eventually various animals raised the sun until it was placed just under the sky arch, where they left it. The Cherokees understand that there is another world below this one, and that it is similar in every way, except that the seasons occur at opposite times. One can reach the underworld by streams, which ultimately flow down.

Earth diver myths like the Cherokees' are common in North America and in other parts of the world such as India, Central Asia, Eastern Europe, and Siberia.[8] While each myth is tied to a particular people and a historical situation, earth diver myths share many common elements: some creature, usually not human, dives into a primal body of water and retrieves from the bottom a small piece of matter that grows into the cosmos. As historian and religious studies scholar Charles Long notes, water in these myths serves as the "unformed, unstable and pregnant reality out of which the universe comes";[9] in other words, water is the symbol of precreation, of chaos. The ancient water of chaos is totally uninhabited; it is a formless mass representative of potential creation and potential life, as opposed to life itself. In earth diver myths, primordial water is passive and must be penetrated to yield life. In the case of the Cherokees, it was the little water beetle who successfully dove to the bottom of the waters to retrieve a small piece of mud that became a great flat island, floating on the surface of primeval waters, suspended from the vault of the sky by four cords attached at each of the four cardinal directions—east, west, north, south. The Cherokees existed on that island at the center of the world. The sky above was seen as a bowl of solid rock, which rose and fell twice a day, at dusk and dawn, so that the sun and moon could rise and set.[10] The earth was suspended from the vault of the sky attached at the four cardinal directions.

Cherokees traditionally introduced a few important mythical narratives by stating: "This is what the old men told me when I was a boy."[11] However, only two of the 125 myths and narratives Mooney collected began with this statement. The two myths are ᎦᎾᏘ (*Kanati*) and ᏎᎷ (*Selu*), and ᏅᎧᏄᏫ (*Nvyunuwi*, "Stone Clad"), two of the most basic Cherokee stories, as they pertain to the religious and practical activities of hunting, farming, and healing.

Kanati was the spiritual ancestor who taught Cherokee men how to hunt. Selu was and is the corn who taught Cherokee women how to plant and harvest corn. Traditionally, Cherokee men were hunters and women were agriculturalists, and this legend was fundamental to the establishment of Cherokee subsistence modalities as well as the division of labor by gender. Nvyunuwi, or Stone Coat (Stone Clad), was a mythical being who killed people. Eventually, the power of seven menstruating women weakened him to the point where he could be staked to the ground. Stone Coat was a great ᎠᏓᏪᎯ (*adawehi*, or "supernatural being"). Once subdued, he instructed Cherokees to burn him, and as he was dying, Stone Coat taught Cherokees a wide variety of medicinal songs to cure illness and hunting songs to call up deer, bear, and other game animals. Hence, Kanati, Selu, and Stone Coat are those mythical beings who are most responsible for giving Cherokees instructions on how to hunt, farm, and properly communicate with the gods.

By following their instructions, Cherokees transcended everyday time and experienced cyclical moments of eternity. As Cherokee author Robert J. Conley writes, "The American Indian concept of time is cyclical as opposed to the European/white American concept of linear time".[12] We see this connection deeply rooted in the culture, as the Cherokee word used for *eternity* is ᏂᎪᎯᎵᏛ (*nigohilvi*, "always"). This word uses the partitive *ni-* prefix attached to the *-gohi-* root, used to indicate a measure of time. It is related to ᎪᎯᏯ (*gohiya*, "a short time"); ᎢᎪᎯᏓ (*igohida*, "a long measure of time"); and probably even ᎪᎯ ᎢᎦ (*gohi iga*, "today"). The word *nigohilvi* uses the simple past (otherwise known as the completive) aspect suffix and adds the nominal *-v'i* suffix to make it a noun. Interestingly, this is very close to the construction ᏂᎪᎯᎸᎾ (*nigohilvna*), which uses the partitive *ni-* in addition to the *-vna* (negative) construction to indicate "not very long." By analyzing the connection between Cherokee words for time we get a closer view of how these concepts are linked in Cherokee thought.

As anthropologist Heidi Altman and Cherokee Tom Belt put it, "Cherokee speakers conceive of time (or life) as a room one enters through one door at birth and leaves through another at death. All of the possible events that have happened, are happening, or will happen exist in this room."[13] To use the language of Cherokee Alan Kilpatrick, when Cherokees replicate their old ways taught them in the long ago, they not only honor their traditions, but they also "conflate" past and present and relive the creation of their world and their ancestral way of life. This fundamental religious experience was and is also practical because that is "when" Cherokees learned how to live an ultimately meaningful life.[14] When asked about their origins, Cherokees make reference especially to the two myths of Kanati/Selu and Stone Coat. After creation, they became specifically Cherokee when Kanati and Selu taught the men how to hunt and the women how to farm. However, Cherokees became fully human only after Stone Coat brought death to the first Cherokee, and then taught them various medicinal songs and hunting songs. Compared to Western historical accounts, which prioritize "facts," the Cherokee stories of their origin and history emphasize religious meaning, value, and purpose.

THE MIDDLE

According to tradition, Cherokees live at the center of the world, where creation took place. By standing in the "middle" (ᎠᏰᎵ, *ayehli*) of the world, Cherokees experience unity with heaven, earth, and the underworld—the three vertical regions—and similarly stand situated between the four cardinal directions. Cherokees place great importance on the fact that they reside at the pivot of the cosmos, the place where the sky world (ᎦᎸᎳᏗ, *galvladi*), middle world (ᎡᎶᎯ, *elohi*), and underworld (ᎡᎶᎯ ᎭᏫᎾᏗᏣ, *elohi hawinaditsa*) meet. In that place, they feel a spiritual unity with the world; hence, they overcome their separation from the rest of the world. Indeed, as Ben notes, the Cherokee term for "the meaning" or "the purpose" is ᏍᎩᏓᎥᎩ (*gadvgvi*), which he translates as "it's sticking to the center." In so doing, traditional Cherokees seek a state of being that simultaneously connects with nature and transcends it.

According to Cherokee religious tradition, the place of creation is ᎩᏚᏩ (*giduwa*, "Kituwah, the Mother Town"), the location of the most sacred and oldest of all beloved or mother towns.[15] The Cherokee consider it to be located at the center of the world (as are the other mother towns, and, in fact, all the Cherokee village sites). Just by entering Kituwah, or indeed any village site, Cherokees reexperience the creation of the world, when the water beetle first surfaced with a piece of mud that later became the island on which they lived. The fundamental significance of Cherokee cosmogony is not lost on Cherokees today, and such cyclical repetition of mythical narratives remains essential to the old ways of Cherokees. For example, at the December 3, 2020, Tribal Council meeting, a Cherokee spoke about the significance of the center by saying, "time seems to move slower at Kituwah. Myrtle [referring to Beloved Woman Myrtle Driver Johnson] is right: It is so spiritual. You just feel it." On May 21, 2022, all three federally recognized Cherokee Nations—the Eastern Band of Cherokee Indians, the Cherokee Nation, and the United Keetoowah Band—came together for a celebration at Kituwah, which the Eastern Band recovered in 1996. Getting Kituwah back sparked a "renaissance of our culture, of our language, our customs for future generations," noted former EBCI Principal Chief Joyce Duggan, who led the way to purchase this sacred place. Vice Chief Alan Ensley added, Kituwah has "existed from 'time immemorial. . . . We all celebrate this as our Mother Town. We all celebrate this area as our homeland.'"[16]

In 1979, the Tennessee Valley Authority condemned the old Cherokee village of Chota, one of the traditional mother towns and peace towns, along with various other village and burial sites. A few Cherokees, including medicine man Amoneeta "Doc" Sequoyah, brought suit in an attempt to enjoin the damming of the Little Tennessee River. One Cherokee plaintiff, Richard "Geet" Crowe, signed an affidavit which stated that the lands in this valley, including the village site of Tellico, were sacred because "this is where we began." Similarly, Tom Belt, a Cherokee Nation citizen, said in 2012, "This is where we began as Kituwah people."[17] Tellico is also a beloved village and sacred center for Cherokees.

A review of the First Amendment Free Exercise of Religion cases brought by Native Americans through the years makes it clear that the American court system, however sympathetic and empathetic to the Indian cause, has a difficult time understanding the fundamental part that the sacred center plays for Native American people.[18] Indians are not just attached to the land merely because they love it and because their ancestors are buried there. They love their land most fundamentally because it is linked to the creation of the world and to their ability to relate to the world in the way made necessary and proper by enduring religious custom. It is this understanding that makes the Cherokee Trail of Tears that much more heart wrenching and tragic because the Cherokee people, by being forcibly removed to the Oklahoma territory in 1838, were not simply being stripped of their land and the place where their parents and grandparents had lived and existed for some time. They were also forced to abandon their traditional access to ultimacy and transcendence; or to put it another way, the forceful removal of Cherokees from their sacred center in 1838 disrupted and hindered their ability to relate properly to the Creator.

It is important to note that sacred centers cannot be reduced to geographical points on a compass or a map. Indeed, there may be several centers within any sacred territory. This is true fundamentally because its meaning is spiritual. Each Cherokee village was a sacred center, and within each traditional village there existed a council house, which was also considered a ceremonial center. Traditional Cherokees would experience unity with the world simply by being present in their village, and when entering the council house during ceremonial events, they would reexperience that unity even more deeply. Furthermore, within the townhouse certain sections were designated as more sacred than others. Anthropologist Christopher B. Rodning argues that the fire, kept perpetually burning in some villages, was the "center place."[19] Among Cherokees, as with many other Native Americans and traditional peoples all over the world, this experience of unity occurs on many different levels and in many different places.

This is a concept that can be difficult for Westerners to understand because they often view land and place as intrinsically homogeneous and secular. For example, while many Westerners feel that cemeteries contain a sacred significance, as do churches, cathedrals, and other houses of worship, they are not considered cosmic and geographic sacred centers. Moreover, there is no place where Western Christians feel, as do Cherokees, that they are located at the center of the world. To this very day, a Cherokee medicine man or woman, a conjuror, is perceived as standing in the center of the world when they invoke the seven levels of heaven, the four directions, and the underworld. They are able to cure disease, find lost children, and bring people together precisely *because* they are located in the "middle world" (DᏏC RGᎯ, *ayehli elohi*). It is only because Cherokee conjurors are situated "here in the center" that they are able to ascend to the seventh heaven to communicate directly with OᏋᏁᏓOᏉᎯ (*unetlanvhi*, "the Creator" or "the Apportioner"). Moreover, the healer's efforts are directed at the "middle" or "very middle" of the patient. Indeed, all Cherokees seek a habitus where they are "standing in the middle"—DᏏC ᏕVET (*ayehli gadogvi*).[20]

CREATOR

The Cherokee word for Supreme Being is sometimes translated as "Apportioner," "One Who Provides," or "Provider."[21] Several Cherokee Indians use the term *Provider*, in contrast to Mooney and ethnologist Frans Olbrechts, who both translated the word OᏋᏁᏓOᏉᎯ (*unetlanvhi*) as "the Creator" or "the Apportioner," perhaps linking the Creator with the sun. However, some Cherokees think Apportioner, as one who apportions the blessings of creation, is fine. Cherokees sometimes referred to the Creator as "The Ancient White One" in some sacred formulas; that and "Ancient One" were one and the same with the Provider.[22] While it is true that many sources refer to the sun as "The Great Spirit" or "Supreme Being" of the Cherokees, numerous elders have made it clear that the Cherokees possessed an all-powerful spiritual being prior to the arrival of Christian missionaries, and that this god was not the sun, the thunders, fire, the river, or any other of the many gods in the Cherokee pantheon.[23]

Nevertheless, Cherokees place great emphasis on the importance of the sun and the sun's earthly incarnation, fire, which receives many prayers in a large number of situations. In 1776, naturalist William Bartram referenced Cherokees ritually smoking tobacco and offering it first to the sun and then to the four directions.[24] Indeed, the historian of religions Wilhelm Schmidt argued that Cherokees were sun worshippers.[25] There exists some evidence for Schmidt's view, given the numerous references to the sun in Cherokee ritual and prayer. However, those comments are contrasted with clear references to one supreme being. As long ago as 1725, statesman Alexander Longe wrote, "They own a one Supreme Power that is above the firmament, and that power they say was he that made the heavens and the earth and all things that is therein and governs all things according to his will and pleasure . . . and this great king, as they called him, has four messengers that he has placed in the four winds: East; West; North; and South."[26]

In many religions, the sky god withdraws into the background after he creates the world. He becomes a *deus otiosus* (hidden god), and several lesser deities more concerned with the existential needs of humans come into focus.[27] The sky god is largely inactive and passive. He gives birth to the world and then withdraws, after which there is a progressive descent of the sacred into the concrete.[28] In some cases, the sky god comes back as a sun god, a process called the solarization of the sky god. Among the Cherokees, there seems to be some oscillation between a recognition of a sky god who is in the seventh heaven, withdrawn from the world, and a more active sun god who at times seems to be recognized as the supreme being. This may account for the apparent conflicts in the literature concerning the Cherokee sky god.[29]

For Cherokees, there existed in the beginning only the upper world or heaven and the lower world, the world of water. The upper world was the world of order and stasis, while the lower world was the world of disorder and change. The resulting world today, *Elohi*, is a blend of both order and chaos, of stasis and change. Indeed, creation itself requires inherent dichotomies in the natural world. The world embodies a multitude of oppositions, such as order-chaos; sky-underworld; fire-water; male-female, and harmony-disharmony. It has been argued that if there is a single word that characterizes the southeastern belief system, including the Cherokees, it is order.[30] Observing that southeastern Indians had an almost obsessive concern with purity and pollution, one interpretation holds that most of their rituals were means of keeping their categories pure and neutralizing pollution whenever it occurred.[31] While there is, of course, some truth to such a view, it would be a bit reductionist to limit Cherokee religion to merely a concern for purity and order. Rather, traditional Cherokee religion is concerned primarily with a proper balancing of cosmic tensions related to order and chaos, since both order and chaos were necessary for the creation and maintenance of the world. Cherokees recognize that reality is paradoxical and that the world exists precisely because of the interplay between the various oppositions that are in constant flux. This understanding is manifested most clearly in the trickster, who helps keep this world going by keeping the oppositions alive. For now, it is sufficient to say that Cherokee spirituality seeks harmony by balancing order and chaos.

But Cherokee material concerns for this world are only one part of the story. It is clear from reviewing descriptions of Cherokee tribal ceremonies such as the Green Corn Dance, as well as individual sacred formulas and prayers chanted and sung by Cherokee conjurors, that Cherokees also seek to transcend the world and to experience the ultimacy and infinite height of the Creator. Cherokee healers transcend the purely human realm and ascend to the highest (seventh) heaven where they communicate directly with the Provider to meet the needs of their patients.[32] Cherokee medicine people are able to bring people together, find lost children, bring forth rain, win wars and disputes, and heal the sick—to solve everyday, real-life concerns—precisely because they are able to relate directly to the sacred.

There are other levels of meaning in Cherokee religion as well. In the "long ago," there existed among the Cherokees a dangerous being called Stone Coat (Stone Clad).[33] John Loftin has in his possession a wood carving of Stone Coat by Cherokee artist and healer William Lossiah, whom Lossiah referred to as "Stone Coat Witch."[34] Stone Coat, among other things, taught Cherokees various medicinal cures. When a Cherokee conjuror recites, chants, or sings a sacred formula—a medicinal cure—he is performing a prayer act that Stone Coat taught to the Cherokee people in the beginning. By repeating those acts, the conjuror transcends time and space and thereby cures his patient.

CHEROKEE SUBSISTENCE: INTRODUCTION

Cherokee Indians traditionally were hunter-gatherers and farmers, and these duties were performed, by and large, according to gender. In Cherokee society, men hunted and women farmed, and those divisions still exist symbolically. The Cherokee people traditionally inhabited no less than 125,000 square miles of mountainous land in what eventually became western North Carolina; eastern Tennessee; the northern portions of Georgia, Alabama, and South Carolina; and parts of Virginia, West Virginia, and Kentucky. Their core area consisted of about 40,000 square miles.[35] Historically, Cherokees were divided into four regions: the Overhill, located in eastern Tennessee; the Middle in western North Carolina; the Valley in southwestern North Carolina; and the Lower in northern South Carolina. The Lower settlements consisted of a rolling plateau area, while the Middle, Valley, and Overhill settlements consisted of mountainous terrain. All settlements were linked with rivers and streams: the Lower with the Savannah River; the Middle with the

Little Tennessee and Tuckasegee rivers in North Carolina; the Valley with the Nantahala Valley and Hiwassee rivers; and the Overhill with the Upper Tennessee and Lower Little Tennessee rivers.

It is difficult to know exactly how many Cherokees existed at the time of first contact with Europeans. Historian James Adair mentions sixty-four villages in 1775, and Bartram mentions forty-three villages in 1790.[36] Most observers of early Cherokees place the total number of their tribe at somewhere around twenty thousand people, but it should be noted that there is some evidence that the Cherokees had been decimated by an epidemic—probably smallpox—after the Spanish came near their settlements in the middle part of the sixteenth century. Indeed, this was when Hernando De Soto explored parts of the Southeast (1540) and Juan Pardo went up into the foothills of the North Carolina mountains (1566–1568). It seems that, even though little to no direct contact was made between the Spanish and Cherokee, disease nevertheless entered Cherokee villages and reduced the population substantially by the time the English entered Cherokee territories during the first part of the eighteenth century.[37]

Cherokees traditionally subsisted upon a wide variety of foods, including many different wild and domesticated foods. At one time, wild food was more common than domesticated foods for the Cherokees and other southeastern Indians.[38] Some Cherokees continue to utilize ancient hunting, fishing, and gathering techniques. The bow and arrow was the most important hunting tool for Cherokee men. They continue to make bows out of a variety of hardwoods, especially honey locust and black locust. Bows were traditionally strung with bear gut, Indian hemp, or strips of buckskin that had been stretched and twisted. Arrow shafts were made out of a variety of mountain cane, and the arrowheads were flaked from flint.[39] Cherokee accuracy with the bow and arrow can still be seen today at the annual Cherokee Fair. The Cherokees continue to use the blowgun to hunt squirrels, birds, and other small game. The blowgun is constructed from a hollow piece of river cane, cut seven to nine feet long. Darts are about ten to twelve inches long and made of hardwood and then flexed with thistledown. The blowgun is generally accurate up to about fifty feet.

Although women helped skin the animals killed by hunters, hunting was and remains today almost exclusively a male activity, and the winter is the primary time of the hunt. Cherokees divide the year into two seasons: winter (ᎪᎳ, *gola*) and summer (ᎪᎨ, *gogi*). Each of these seasons is associated with the sexes: winter is the time of hunting (and war), and therefore the time of men, while summer is the time of farming and therefore women. Among the Cherokees, men and women often kept separate. Before and after the hunt, Cherokee men abstained from sex, just as women stayed away from men before giving birth and during menstruation. Cherokee women traditionally were secluded in a menstrual hut during the time of their menses.[40]

Like other important activities in Cherokee life, hunting embodies much spiritual significance. For Cherokees, hunting in and of itself is a religious activity. Long before the emergence of sacred narratives that describe the origin of hunting and prescribe its proper modalities, hunting occasioned an experience of the sacred through action. In the hunt, men exercise their wills against animals, which embody and are metaphors for the spiritual. Animals are similar yet different from human beings and often serve as concrete manifestations and symbols of the sacred. Put differently, many Cherokees experience the sacred as related yet distinct from themselves, and the same can be said of the human experience of animals. In the simple act of killing an animal, a Cherokee forces his will against the "beloved" to achieve some material gain such as meat, furs, and skins. While killing an animal is a transgression against the sacred, its purpose is for survival, thus Cherokees approach the hunt with great humility, reverence, thanksgiving, and a certain amount of guilt.

Cherokees traditionally hunted primarily white-tailed deer, which counted for some 70 percent of their meat diet. According to Cherokee tradition, all deer are led by a single small, invisible albino deer called Little Deer. Cherokees feel that upon killing a deer, Little Deer immediately visits the slain animal and asks whether the hunter offered proper prayers of apology and thanksgiving. If not, Little Deer might inflict the hunter with rheumatoid arthritis as punishment for his haughtiness and lack of respect. Thus, to a degree, a Cherokee hunter feels responsible for the kill and is apologetic for his transgression.

More fundamentally, a Cherokee hunter is thankful, for he recognizes that on several levels a successful hunt is primarily due to the spiritual beings. First, the Provider creates and Kanati controls the deer and other animals. Without the spiritual, there would be no animals to hunt, and hence no meat to eat and no skins and furs to keep people warm. Second, a Cherokee can only successfully hunt a deer or other game animal if the right hunting conditions exist and if he possesses the requisite skill, both of which are seen as god given. Third, all Cherokee hunters traditionally used certain prayers for a successful hunt, and many of these hunting prayers were taught in the long ago to aid Cherokee hunters who properly sought game. Cherokee medicine people also possessed additional knowledge of sacred rites that could help secure a successful hunt.

To reiterate, Cherokee hunting exemplifies a man's life. Cherokee hunters engage in an activity that is considered the opposite of essential female activity, which is giving birth. Cherokee men revere and respect Cherokee women and particularly their ability to participate directly in the divinely creative process of childbearing. In giving birth, Cherokee women embody the power of creation and sacrality. Because Cherokee women can create human life internally through the blood of their own wombs, Cherokee men acknowledge the sacred power of their blood.

In some academic circles, the blood of women has often been discussed as polluting and, therefore, is prone today to a recurrently negative connotation. However, although Cherokee hunters avoid menstruating and pregnant Cherokee women, it is not because they view them as unclean. Rather, Cherokee hunters avoid menstruating and pregnant Cherokee women because the blood of women related to childbirth conflicts with the blood that Cherokee hunters shed through the act of killing an animal. Cherokee men shed blood external to themselves while hunting in the world, whereas women give birth through their own blood. In one sense, through hunting, men participate symbolically in an act of birth (by producing meats and furs), while women participate in birth directly. Historian Theda Perdue rightly notes that prior to the advent of the commercial deerskin trade, Cherokee hunting was more symbolic than economic.[41]

Male taboos surrounding menstruating women are not based on a view of menstrual blood as dirty or unclean but rather as a potent force that is more powerful than male blood and capable of overcoming evil. For example, in the Stone Coat myth, menstruating women destroyed Stone Coat (a being whom the male hunters had sullenly failed to conquer), which gave Cherokees access, through Stone Coat's dying revelations, to many ceremonies.[42] Still, it is not so much that female blood is destructive (indeed, the blood of women is the blood of birth and life, as opposed to the blood of the hunt and of warfare, which is the blood of destruction and death), but rather, the blood of women, by embodying creative powers, exists in direct opposition to the blood brought forth by male hunting and warfare. Hence, men about to embark on hunting activities are precluded from having contact with menstruating and pregnant women. In fact, men are not allowed to have sex prior to the hunt because that type of intimate contact with women is thought to weaken the ability of men as they undertake specifically male activities.[43]

Not only should men to avoid women prior to the hunt, but traditionally (and even today in some cases) women ought not associate with men while farming. Indeed, Molly Sequoyah, a consultant for Raymond Fogelson, confided to him that women did not want Cherokee men in the fields because growing corn was a sacred activity involving specialized spiritual knowledge, and that young men were often bloody and their presence in the corn fields endangered growing crops, a conception which clearly distinguishes the destructive blood of the hunt and warfare from the life-giving blood of childbirth and farming.[44]

Adair wrote in 1775 that wounded warriors, particularly those with open wounds, were required to stay in small huts outside the settlement for some period of time, where they were attended to only by medicine men and by postmenopausal women.[45] Adair saw a parallel between the menstrual hut and these warrior huts, as both involved the shedding of blood. Even though all evidence of the menstrual hut had disappeared on the Cherokee reservation in the twentieth century, as late as 1930, Cherokee women were still not allowed to cook during their menstrual periods.[46] Thus menstrual huts secluded women for shedding internal blood while the townhouse secluded men for shedding external blood.

It is not just that male and female bloods conflict: the blood of women is, in the end, more powerful than the blood of hunting and warfare. No hunter or warrior could bring down Stone Coat in the "long ago" when he was engaged in systematically killing the Cherokee people. It was women and women alone who could overcome the power of this supernatural being with their blood force. Although there is more than one Cherokee myth about the origin of death, in one version it was Stone Coat who brought about the first Cherokee death. To that end, he represents the evil of witchcraft, which is destructive and deadly, and only the power of female blood was strong enough to destroy this evil being.[47] As he died, Stone Coat imparted important ceremonial knowledge to Cherokee men, teaching them how to cure certain illnesses and to successfully hunt various animals. He also left an important crystal, which Cherokee medicine men traditionally used for ritual power.

The difference between the sexes was also reflected in divergent rituals at an early age. Traditionally, Cherokee boys were wrapped in a mountain lion skin and fur, while girls were traditionally wrapped in a deerskin. Boys were thus linked at birth with hunting and death, while girls were symbolized by the passive and docile deer. Today if Cherokees are asked why men hunt and women farm, they would say it's because they were taught to do so in the beginning.

One of the traditional Cherokee myths, alluded to earlier, is the myth of Kanati and Selu, which lays out the origin story for Cherokee hunting and farming. Mooney notes that this narrative was the best-known sacred myth of the Cherokee, and that anyone who heard it was obliged to "go to water."[48] It is a long narrative and a number of different versions exist. The myth takes place in the "long years ago, soon after the world was made." One might say that there are two levels of creation stories, *cosmogonic* and *existential*.[49] The first primordium is the time of the creation of the world itself; the second primordium comes after creation. The Cherokee earth diver myth, when the world and its creatures were first formed, occurs in the first primordium. The myth of Kanati and Selu is a narrative that takes place in the second primordium, after the world is created but before the Cherokee way of life has been established. This myth creates the Cherokees' hunting and farming way of life through the actions of supernatural beings Kanati and Selu, whose sons are the first Cherokee ancestors. Part of the myth represents the Cherokees' rupture from the primordial paradise, which existed soon after the creation. Just as the story of Stone Coat tells the origin of Cherokee death, the myth of Kanati tells of the loss of paradise in the beginning, which forces Cherokee men to work by hunting for a living.

The Cherokees ultimately learned to hunt by watching Kanati, a supernatural being, and by gaining songs from DhBЬIGᎧy (*aniyvdaqualosgi*, "the Thunder Boys, the children of Kanati and Selu"), ancestors of the Cherokee people. The Cherokees are able to secure deer (and other game) by repeating the actions taught in the long ago by Kanati and the Thunder Boys.

FARMING

Traditionally, the primary subsistence activity of Cherokee women was farming. The Cherokees farmed three main plants: corn, beans, and squash, with corn being the most important. In addition to hunting and gathering, the Cherokees were traditionally small-scale farmers who grew these things to supplement wild nuts and other vegetables they gathered. Women originated agriculture. They gathered wild plants while men hunted, and through observation and experimentation, they discovered the secrets of domesticating plants, which undoubtedly amazed men. Women not only gave birth, but they also generated large amounts of food through horticulture. Cherokee men understood that women created corn from their bodies just as they gave birth to Cherokee babies, which struck the men as auspicious proof that the women embodied the creative powers of the Provider. In hunting, men had to seek wild animals in the forest, an area Cherokees did not control, and as such, hunting was very unpredictable and sometimes ended in failure. Cherokee men clearly did not create the wild animals that they hunted, and they always experienced a successful hunt as being ultimately dependent on the favor of the gods; thus, much prayer surrounded the hunt.

Women, on the other hand, gave birth to babies and did so only through reliance on their own bodies. Cherokees also noted a natural connection between all plants and women, as both were linked to the earth. Cherokee women seemed to magically produce crops from the earth in a way that connected them to it. Given this apparent miracle, Cherokee men probably viewed early agricultural success by women with a tremendous sense of awe and fascination. It appeared that women literally grew these plants from their own essence, as the myth of Selu teaches.

Cherokee tradition says that corn grows directly from the blood of Selu. That is, corn is considered directly born from the womb of the ancestral mother of the Cherokees, Selu. Indeed, corn is sometimes called "our mother" or "old woman."[50] Cherokees perceive a direct blood link between Selu and the corn, just as they see a direct link between Cherokee mothers and their children. In the myth, Selu creates corn and beans directly from her body. She gives birth to corn and beans no differently than she gives birth to people. On the other hand, Kanati does not give birth to wild animals; he simply knows where they are located and secures them for the people. Later, the Thunder Boys teach the Cherokees various hunting songs, which they use to call up deer, but never are Cherokee men credited with creating wild animals through their own blood. Cherokee men must shed the blood of animals to create meat and skins for the tribe. By contrast, Selu gave birth to corn directly from her own body.

Selu is a somewhat unique story because in general, most agricultural narratives concerning grain describe the primordial theft of seeds, not the killing of a deity. The latter theme most often shows up in tuber mythologies. The Cherokees, however, defy this classification because corn is a grain, not a tuber, and in the Cherokee myth, the Goddess of Corn, Selu, is killed by her sons and her blood produces corn. Thus, the Cherokee story of corn structurally resembles tuber rather than grain mythology.

Viewed on one level, Cherokee hunting and farming myths oppose one another. In the story of Selu, Cherokees kill a deity and secure more corn—that is, human volition results in material gain. How different is Kanati's story, where rolling back the cave stone ultimately results in less game, not more. This difference helps account for how hunting is, in a spiritual manner, a more passive activity than farming—as game is collected, not created.[51]

These divisions were, however, not absolute. Traditionally, for example, while women cultivated and harvested small kitchen gardens, men would nonetheless help occasionally, particularly in the larger communal plots that seem to have been present in most Cherokee villages.[52] Theda Perdue has written that while theoretically the sexual division of labor was very rigid, in reality men and women often helped one another.[53] They especially worked in tandem when clearing fields and harvesting crops. In 1835, it was common for whole towns to plant a large field in which each family got its share, and men and women often worked together in that field.

The Cherokees grew at least three types of corn: a short corn, a flint or hominy corn, and a white-grain bread corn.[54] Traditionally, they planted these in mounds about three feet apart, and into each hole they dropped seven grains. Selu gave the Cherokees seven grains in the beginning. In general, the number seven was significant: seven was the number of clans, the levels of heaven,[55] and a symbol of the cosmos. In between these corn hills Cherokees grew traditional crops of squash, gourds, pumpkins, and sunflowers. They also adopted potatoes, peas, watermelons, and other crops from Europeans. Perdue notes that at the first harvest of plants, either a priest or head of the household stood at the edge of the field (at each of the cardinal points) and wept loudly, perhaps for the death of Selu, whose sacrifice made agricultural life for the Cherokees possible.[56] Then when all the crops were gathered, the owner of the field, perhaps accompanied by a medicine man, would build an enclosure in the center of the field and sing prayers to the Spirit of the Corn.

Between planting and harvest, Cherokee men traditionally withdrew from farm work and women did all the tending work. Women cultivated and hoed the fields with a sharpened stick or a stone mattock. Because Cherokee women are thought to be the descendants of Selu, who is corn, they identify themselves with the very corn that they grow and feed to the people. In other words, Cherokee women are corn, and corn is Selu. By virtue of being women who engage in the act of farming, Cherokee women relive the long ago and experience identity with corn and with Selu.

Beloved narratives such as the cosmogony, Kanati and Selu, and Stone Coat orient the Eastern Cherokee's lifeway and establish fundamental elements of their worldview.[57] Methods and theories employed to understand traditional Eastern Cherokee spirituality should discuss myth and history, as well as constitutive relationships and diachronic differences. While it is accurate to say that Cherokee religious experience and expression cannot be separated from historical conditions and changes, it is also true, as Cherokee Sean Teuton argues, that Cherokee religious experience and expression creates their historical identity.[58] Their deep-rooted spirituality and their stories orient their daily behavior as much as their everyday life bears on their tradition.

CHAPTER 2

DhYSGY ᏬᏚᏚᎩ

Cherokee Community

Eastern Cherokees reside mostly in the following communities scattered over some 68,000 acres (once 135,000 square miles): Big Cove, Snowbird, Wolftown, Birdtown, Painttown, Yellowhill, and Cherokee County, as well as other communities, like Big Witch, Big Y, Hanging Dog, Whittier, and the 3200 Acre Tract. Also, communities may be further referenced in smaller sections, often related to the nearest creeks, such as Bunches Creek, Galimore Creek, Straight Fork, Stoney, the Cove, Wright's Creek, Swimmer Branch, Tooni Branch, Stillwell Branch, Old Soco Road, Rich Farm, Lambert Farm, "Birdtown Road," Goose Creek, Cooper's Creek, Adams Creek, McCoy Branch, and Lambert Branch. Sometimes Cherokees will say that they live "along the highway," "across the river," or "across the bridge." Many other Cherokee citizens are scattered throughout the Unites States and, indeed, over the entire earth.

Whether one lives on federal trust land in North Carolina or in a city like Chicago, Eastern Cherokees feel a vital connection with other Cherokees. Community today may not be as unified as it once was, but it would be fair to say that the Cherokees were always unified through their divisions. Cherokees embodied the community value ᏕᏣᏓᏝᏲᏎᏍᏗ (*detsadatliyvsesdi*): "the struggle to hold on to one another or cling to one another." This value conjures the image of people in a circle holding hands. Just as each individual has the responsibility to stand on their own, each also has the assurance that they will be helped up if they should stumble and fall. As a unit, Cherokees each have subjectivity, and within the universal, their inflections may differ. Hence, Cherokees seek to make sense of the world and each other by exploring both inter-relatedness and contrast, both essence and indeterminacy.

Traditionally, Cherokee social life was multifaceted and complex but their identification as members of a clan was basic. In fact, the rela-tionships between clan members allowed Cherokees to connect between villages and was, at times, almost as important as membership/citizenship in the tribe/nation. Cherokees were composed of seven matrilineal clans known as Wolf (DhᏳᏭᎠ, *aniwaya*); Deer (DhᏯᎡ, *anikaw*); Bird (DhᏂᏍᏫᏓ, *anitsisqua*); Paint (DhᏋᎫ, *aniwodi*); Twister or Long Hair (DhᎩᏳᏟ, *anigilohi*); Blind Savannah or Wild Potato (DhᎠᏫᎢᎡ, *anig-otagèwi*); and Blue or Holly (DhᎤᎢᏂ, *anisahoni*).[1]

There is little consensus concerning the translation of the last three clans. Jack and Anna Kilpatrick, the latter a direct descendent of Sequoyah, state that *Anigilohi* is invariably translated as "Twisters" or "Long Hairs," but that knowledgeable Cherokees insist the name means something like "They just became offended."[2] Ethnologist William H. Gilbert lists one clan as Anigotigewi (Wild Potato)[3] and, in fact, a number of sources say that one clan is Wild Potato rather than Blind Savannah. On the other hand, William Lossiah once said that there is, in reality, no Wild Potato clan. However, he may have been simply ref-erencing the fact that the Cherokee word for *potato* does not appear in the Cherokee term for Wild Potato clan. Most Eastern Cherokees today list their clans as follows: Wolf, Deer, Bird, Paint, Long Hair, Blue, and Wild Potato.

For the most part, the names of Cherokee clans referenced aspects of the natural world, showing that they naturalized humanity more than they humanized nature. The Wolf Clan used to hunt much like wolves, and members of this clan were said to be fond of wolves and often raised them in captivity. Although killing a wolf is generally taboo for all Cherokees, there were professional wolf killers who were provision-ally allowed to hunt wolves.[4]

Deer Clan members were likened to the deer for swiftness. They also were said to have kept deer in captivity and were especially skilled in hunting and killing deer.

Bird Clan people were considered to be especially fond of birds and kept captive crows and chicken hawks. They were noted for successful use of snares and blowguns, and Bird Town is named after this clan.

Red Paint Clan members were formerly noted for their magic with red iron oxide paint, which is a sacred formula designed to protect people from illness and evil and to attract the opposite sex. Red Paint Clan medicine people were considered especially adept at those matters. The Cherokee community of Paint Town is named after them.

Blue Clan is named after a bluish plant, which was gathered from swamps for food and medicine. The plant is called *sakoni* or *sahoni*. It was said that children were traditionally bathed every new moon in a concoction of this plant to protect them from disease.

The Wild Potato Clan was known for gathering plants called in English "wild potatoes," which grew in swampy places along the river. It is said that many Cherokees still eat them. Mooney says the clan term has no meaning and has been absurdly rendered Blind Savannah from an incorrect idea that the name is derived from swamp or savannah, and blind.[5]

The Twisters, or Long Hair Clan, supposedly derived their name in two ways. One refers to the fact that these people were very proud and that they strutted when they walked and twisted their shoulders in a very haughty manner. According to another version, the name is derived from long hair, which refers to the love of adornment, which was once characteristic of this group. Mooney thinks the word comes from an archaic term denoting wearing the hair long or flowing loosely and is usually recognized as applying more particularly to women than men.[6] Clans are, after all, matrilineal. Still another tradition says that this was the clan that adopted Cherokees belonged to.

Traditionally, clans were exogamous. In fact, it was a capital offense to marry a member of one's own clan. Accordingly, Cherokees would never commit incest by marrying within the clan.[7] The two most important social functions of clans were to regulate marriage and to exact revenge for murders committed against clan members. A *Cherokee Phoenix* article from 1829 describes the clan as "the grand work by which marriages were regulated, and murder punished."[8] Traditionally, it was just as important to be a member of a clan as it was the tribe, and some have argued that it was more important.[9] Indeed, clan membership made one a Cherokee. Clans were also important economic units because they were the landholding segments of Cherokee society; moreover, each clan was allotted garden space used by clan women.[10]

Membership in a clan was itself a religious experience. First, the clan was regarded as being idealized with the mother's blood.[11] Cherokees traditionally said that clans originated "in the beginning when Stone Coat was killed." When Stone Coat died, he gave Cherokees their songs, dances, sacred formulas, hunting prayers, and other aspects of their tribal culture. Therefore, simply being a member of a Cherokee clan occasioned the experience of the mythical time when the Cherokee way of life came into being.

Clan membership was sacred, and perhaps its paramount importance in Cherokee society was demonstrated, paradoxically, by the lack of information found in the historical record about clan life. Although a number of popular articles exist on clan membership, some of which were put together by Cherokees, it is important to note that early observers of the Cherokee were able to learn important aspects of clan functioning but little about the clans themselves, other than their names. Either these early observers did not ask questions about the clan or the Cherokee consultants simply withheld details about the sacred meanings and workings of the clan. It was probably the latter because it is clear that a number of early observers of Cherokee life asked many, many questions and compiled a tremendous amount of information about the Cherokees. It seems plausible that early outside observers asked questions about clans for which they received no answers.

BEAR PEOPLE

In many Native American tribes, knowledge of important ceremonial functions is held by specific persons and groups who embody certain powers related to their origin and ancestry, and it is difficult to believe the Cherokees were any different in that regard.[12] The Cherokees say that in the "long ago," there was a clan called Anitsaguhi. According to a clan myth, there was once a boy in this clan who used to leave home and stay gone all day in the mountains. He started going more often and staying away longer, until he began to leave at daybreak and not come back at night. Eventually, his parents noticed that the boy began to grow long brown hair over his body and did not eat when he came home. The boy explained that "he found plenty to eat there and it was better than corn and beans that we have in the villages."[13] His parents began to worry but he informed them that "it was better there than here and invited his parents to come with him." After hearing that there was plenty to eat and that one did not have to work for it, the clan got together and decided that they would go with him because "here we must work hard and have not always enough. There he says there's always plenty without work. We will go with him."[14] They fasted seven days and then began their migration into the woods to live. People from the other towns heard about this and headed out to meet them to try to talk them out of leaving; however, they noticed that the people were already beginning to be covered with hair because they had not eaten human food for seven days. The Anitsaguhi told them that they were going where there was always plenty to eat and that afterward they would always be called Yona (Bears).

These Bear People instructed the Cherokees that "when they were hungry they should come into the woods and call us," at which time bears would come to sacrifice their own flesh for food. They also said that Cherokees should not be afraid to kill bears because bears would always live. Then they taught the Cherokee messengers certain hunting songs, which Cherokees possess to this day. The Cherokees say that one can still hear mother bears singing Cherokee lullabies to bear cubs in a few mountain places.[15] According to the Cherokees, there are four mountains under which the bears have a townhouse where they hold a dance before they retire for hibernation in the winter. The White Bear, chief of the Bear tribe, is said to reside at Kuwahi (Mulberry Place), which is located near a sacred lake where wounded bears go to be bathed and cured.

This is a narrative fraught with spiritual meaning. First, this story does not take place in the "long ago," although it happened in the distant past. At the time of this story, the Cherokees no longer lived in paradise but were fully human, having to work to have enough food to eat. In other words, this story takes place after the paradisal period of perfection had already come to a close and the Cherokees had become fully human. The Cherokee Bear People, arguably, is a clan that originated from bears, given their ability to turn back into bears. Here, a segment of the Cherokee population seeks to transcend the human condition and turn into the animal ancestor from which they sprang, understanding the animal mode of life to be superior to the human way of life with all its many problems.

The great medicine man Swimmer (Ayunini) recited to James Mooney another story in which a Cherokee man went hunting in the mountains and came across a black bear, which he wounded with an arrow. As it turned out, the bear was a medicine man who stopped and began to converse with the Cherokee hunter, stating that he could not be killed. The black bear invited the Cherokee to his townhouse, which was full of all types of bears, all headed by a large white bear who was chief. The bears commented on how bad the human smelled. Staying with the bears, the hunter began to eat their food until he started to grow hair all over his body and act like a bear. His bear friend told him one day early in the spring that his people would come down and kill him and take his clothes from him—meaning his skin—and that he should, therefore, try to reintegrate himself back into the Cherokee community. He tried but was unable to do so and eventually died because he had taken on a bear's nature and could not live like a person. However, Swimmer maintained that if the Cherokees had isolated him and made him fast for seven straight days, he would have become a man again and lived.[16]

These stories show the special relationship between bears and Cherokees and demonstrate how each can be transformed into the other with proper ritual precautions, including a seven-day fast, seven being the most sacred of all Cherokee numbers. Some would argue that these Cherokee stories show an attempt to overcome their separation from nature and return to a state of being that has been called the "paradise of animality."[17] Others insist that "nature is never simply natural" for human beings and, therefore, that Cherokee transformation into animals refers to a process whereby humans become one with the sacred, which has manifested itself—in this case—in the form of a bear. That is to say, the bear symbolizes the distance and relationship of the sacred to the Cherokees, which distance the Cherokees, through proper ritual procedures, can overcome to restore the unity they had with the sacred prior to their loss of paradise in the beginning.

Socially, clan relationships determined how Cherokees behaved toward one another.[18] Clan membership transcended village association. Traditionally, each Cherokee village was considered autonomous, and yet any traveling Cherokee would see clan kinfolk whenever they visited another village. Those relationships superseded the differences between villages and helped link people from separate parts of Cherokee country to one another.

Clans played a very important part in Cherokee justice. Whenever one Cherokee killed another, clan relatives would seek out the offender and slay him in retaliation for the death of their own kin.[19] At that point, "all was straight," the Cherokees would say.[20] Clans also contributed to the political structure of each Cherokee village. When the Cherokees met in the council house for important political matters, each of the clans had an important say. In fact, the Cherokee council house was divided into seven sections, each of which was occupied by one of the seven clans, all of whom had at least one major spokesperson who would represent the clan's interest at the meeting.[21]

WARRIORS AND PRIESTS

Cherokee men were divided into two main factions or moieties: priests and warriors. Each of these was associated with a color: red with war and white with peace. In traditional times, Cherokee villages were considered to be either white or red, although both warriors and priests lived in each.[22]

Both red and white political divisions ultimately unfolded within myths and religious ritual.[23] Ritual surrounded the political activities of peace and war, and more importantly, all activities were understood as ways of life that were set down in the beginning of time. It is important to recognize that when speaking of Cherokee white and red moieties and of Cherokee peace and war activities, one is talking primarily about activities related to men. However, as important as men were, the essentials of Cherokee life were bound up with the activities of women because it was women who gave birth, raised children, cooked meals, owned rights to fields and houses, and cared for the sick.[24] Outside of these basic essential activities, men served as priests or warriors (and hunters). As hunters, Cherokee men were gone for many days at a time, especially in the winter; the same was true whenever the Cherokee men went on the warpath, which was a common activity right through the eighteenth century.

Politically, the Cherokees were a tribe composed of relatively autonomous villages, which traditionally contained anywhere from two hundred to five hundred residents.[25] The village was organized by the seven clan sections and a body of elders whom the Cherokees called "Beloved Men" (ᏗᏂᎬᏩᎵ ᎠᏂᏍᎦᏯ, *tsunilvquodi anisgaya*). The foremost officials were the Priest Chief, who was linked with three other priests and one secular officer. These five men lived near the council house and probably acted without reference to clan affiliation. Seven Beloved Men formed a second level of leaders who were regarded simultaneously as clan representatives and members of the village-wide body of elders. These composed the Priest Chief's inner council. One man was drawn from each clan to compose the second level; the third order of officials was the remaining body of the elders or Beloved Men. The village met as a whole, and the white standard was raised for both political and ceremonial councils. The Priest Chief and his immediate council sat on benches toward the center, as did the seven-clan second council. The rest of the population sat around the sides of the council house, some of which were built with seven sides, and everyone sat with the clan to which they belonged. Any male villager could express an opinion on important matters. There is some evidence that the Priest Chief, at special ceremonial times, dressed in all white clothing and may have symbolized the Great White Being Above, which was another name for the Supreme Being.[26]

At one time, Chota was called, at least by some Cherokees, the grandmother town of all, the home of the first Beloved Man.[27] It is not clear if the Chief Priest at the time was ever seen as an incarnation of the "Creator Who Dwells Above."[28] It seems that the great high priest did officiate ceremonies, which were understood to unite Cherokees with the Creator in Heaven. In any event, it is clear that the political function of the Cherokee peace chief was fairly well organized and founded on important religious concepts.

The war organization seems to have been a much looser structure.[29] When the village council decided for war, the red standard was raised and a new combination of organized officials went into operation. Beloved Men remained organized as a body of elders, but four Beloved Men with esoteric ritual knowledge necessary for war became major village war officials: the War Chief, War Priest, Speaker for War, and Surgeon.[30] The warriors elected these four figures, and these four figures appointed some eight officers for each war activity. There was also a seven-man council for war with one prominent warrior from each clan. The war parties were generally small and consisted of between twenty and forty men.[31] Cherokee warriors ranged in age from twenty-five to sixty.

Much ritual surrounded warfare, and prior to going to war, men would fast and abstain from contact with women anywhere from four to seven days.[32] One observer notes that there were different levels of military titles: the first or lowest military title was Slave-Catcher, the second Raven, the third Man-Killer, and the highest Great Warrior. Before receiving titles, warriors were simply called men or boys.[33] A 1764 source mentions Raven, Slave Catcher, Mankiller, and the Highest Skyagusta or War Captain.[34]

Another source states that the Great Red War Chief, or High Priest of the War, who was sometimes called Raven, was the principal scout when the army was on the march. The Raven wore a raven skin about his neck. Next in line was The Great War Chief's second or right-hand man, then the Seven War Counselors who ordered the war. After them came the Beloved Women or War Women, who chose the fate of captives, and then the Chief War Speaker, Flag Warrior, and Chief Surgeon. Some elders said that Killer was the highest name obtained as a warrior, followed by Raven, Owl, Wolf, and Fox.[35] Upon meeting the enemy, Raven gave a signal and the whole army gave a war cry and rushed forward to the attack. In general, warriors ran forward on the right and left in two wings, so as to enclose the enemy, while warriors in the center marched directly forward. They used other strategies too, of course. Following war, the Cherokees might sue for peace by approaching an enemy village carrying a swan's wing painted with white clay.[36] At that time, the Cherokee Chief assured the enemy that he came as a "friend in the name of the Great Spirit."[37]

A warrior who killed a person or who had touched a dead person or a grave was considered unclean for four days. On the first day after assembly for war, some of the warriors would "go to the water" and be purified in the river. In the evening, the war standard—a pole painted red with a red pelt or skin four to five yards long—was erected and a war dance was celebrated during the night. A little before dawn, all went to the river and plunged in seven times. Then the red priest, appointed for war, took some of the sacred war fire, fed it with some fresh wood, and then sacrificed a deer's tongue.[38]

After sunrise, the Red Wolf Priest then used beads to divine the outcome of the war. He prayed in successive stages to the first Heaven, the second Heaven, the third Heaven, the fourth Heaven, the fifth Heaven, the sixth Heaven, and culminated with a prayer to the seventh Heaven, each time raising his hand higher. Also, beads were used to divine victory or failure, and a crystal was also set in the sun to refract the sunlight to forecast the likely outcome. So important was the role of the conjuror that success in a war was attributed more to his power than to the ability of warriors.[39] Next, the Red War Priest made a new fire with basswood and goldenrod. This fire was regarded as a guide and a helper in the upcoming battle and was designated implicitly as the principal priest of the war. The fire was placed inside a sacred ark. Gilbert notes that the ark was a rectangular clay object about a foot long with a lid, and it contained only sacred fire. There were always two arks: one kept in the council house for peace and one for war.

Upon returning from war, the warriors stayed at the council house for up to twenty-four days to purify themselves before going home or associating with their wives. Each night a Scout Dance and a Snake Dance were celebrated and performed. On the twenty-fourth day, all fasted and the War Priest offered a sacrifice and again consulted his crystal. Finally, a priest sacrificed a deer tongue.

During aboriginal times, warfare was extremely small scale, although the Cherokees were often at war with the Creek, Choctaw, Chickasaw, and Shawnee. Many times, a skirmish would end with the wounding or killing of a single enemy warrior. The taking of a scalp sealed a symbolic victory, proving that the Cherokees' gods were more powerful than the enemy's on that particular day. European soldiers and observers, upon first seeing aboriginal Cherokee warfare, called it little more than a manhunt and did not consider it true war. The Cherokees did not get involved in large-scale warfare until after the arrival of Europeans, who pitted various tribes against each other i to further their own political, military, cultural, and ideologically religious aims.

CHEROKEE RITES OF PASSAGE
Conception and Birth

In Cherokee, "she is pregnant" is rendered "she is carrying it."[40] Cherokee women would tell their husbands as soon as they felt that they were pregnant, and news would spread quickly through the village.

Traditionally, a pregnant Cherokee woman was subjected to many taboos and ritual observances related to her condition, including "going to water."[41] Cherokee elders made it clear to James Mooney that "going to the river to pray and to be prayed for and to bathe is the outstanding ceremony in Cherokee religious life."[42] It was customarily vital that a pregnant Cherokee woman go to the water during the new moon once she knew she was pregnant. Some Cherokees say this ritual should occur after the third month of pregnancy; others say during the last three months of pregnancy. Still another Cherokee shared that the ceremony took place every new moon once the pregnant woman felt the motion of the child within her, which usually occurs after the fifth month following conception.

For this ritual, a medicine man accompanied the pregnant woman to the river, took either two white beads or two red beads and a white thread, all of which was put on the ground on a yard of white calico cloth. In this ritual, white symbolized life and red symbolized success.[43] The pregnant woman and healer were usually accompanied by the woman's husband or mother or some other relative who acted as the assistant. While the woman stood at the bank of the river facing the water, the medicine man recited a prayer while holding a red (or white) and a black bead between thumb and index finger of both hands, which he used to divine information concerning the child's health and sex. Prior to undergoing this ceremony, the woman drank a concoction of slippery elm, spotted touch-me-nots, speedwell, and pine. Slippery elm was ingested to make the inside of the woman slippery so the child would slide out easily. The spotted touch-me-not frightened the child and enticed it to "jump down quickly." Through prayer, the last two plants, evergreens, conveyed their properties of longevity and good health to the infant.

Standing near the water, the woman induced vomiting to purify herself by ridding herself of any latent disease germs and flushing from her system any ᎣᏏᏬ ᎦᏟᏫ (*uyotsv watsila*, "spoiled saliva").[44] Slippery elm does not cause a Cherokee child to be born more easily because of the slippery qualities of the plant any more than evergreens cause Cherokee children to live a long time. Those plants are not the power that brings about the desired result, but rather the means through which the power is employed. Or to put it another way, the Cherokees anchor their prayers to the sacred through concrete forms and rhythms, which symbolize the object of their prayer.

Sir James George Frazer, in his classic work *The Golden Bough* (1890), wrote an early scholarly discussion of the theory of contagious and sympathetic magic. Although an old work, some scholars continue to make use of his theories of magic when discussing Indian prayer and ritual. In short, Frazer's theory of magic holds that "like produces like, or that an effect resembles its cause; and, second, that things which have once been in contact with each other continue to act on each other at a distance after the physical contact has been severed."[45] Sympathetic magic, according to some, is very common among traditional peoples and has been used in many contexts. It has two separate but related branches, according to Frazer: homeopathic and contagious.[46] Homeopathic magic is based on "the association of ideas by similarity"; that is, it assumes that "things which resemble each other are the same."[47] Contagious magic, somewhat differently, is based on "the association of ideas by contiguity" and holds that "things which have once been in contact with each other are always in contact."[48]

Frazer argued that humans first appropriated the world magically and that magic was an early attempt at modern science that failed due to its barren and false logical underpinnings. Magic, said Frazer, was correct in assuming that one event follows another necessarily and invariably in nature without the intervention of any spiritual or personal agency, but incorrect in attempting to decipher those immutable laws through the principles of similarity and contact. According to him, religion, strictly speaking, did not emerge until humans repeatedly failed through magic to control the world.[49] Eventually, humans began to feel there must be another agent involved in the workings of the world, and they began to supplicate this being with prayer. At that point, the religious phase of human evolution gave way to the advance of modern science, where empirical and rational experimental techniques assured success in manipulating the world for some desired result. A number of scholars since Frazer have employed his theory of magic in one way or another in interpreting various aspects of Cherokee religion.

James Mooney referenced magic by saying that Cherokees employed a "theory of resemblances" as the basis for treatment in medicine by homeopathy.[50] Gilbert concurred that Cherokee culture can be interpreted in terms of Frazer's theory of magic and on a comparative basis with other cultures in the world.[51] Even the Cherokee Alan Kilpatrick, son of Jack and Anna Kilpatrick, cited Frazer's notion of imitative and contagious magic when discussing Cherokee prayer formulas.[52] He noted that there is considerable proof that Cherokee witches and sorcerers employed "magical sympathy, which is supposed to exist between a man and any severed portion of his person, such as his hair or nails; so that whoever gets possession . . . may work his will at any distance upon the person for whom they were cut."[53]

However, Gilbert rightfully qualified Frazer's theory by stating that each Cherokee prayer consists of two parts. The first part contains specific directions for bringing about certain results, such as the use of plants and herbs to cure certain diseases. The second part of the prayer embodies an invocation: a spell designed to invoke supernatural forces that will bring about the desired effects.[54] Similarly, a fuller examination of Alan Kilpatrick's writings shows that he understands that Cherokee prayer acts presuppose a spiritual reality that is contacted to bring about the desired end, whether good or evil.[55] Strictly speaking, Frazer's theory of magic involved a rudimentary scientific theory of the world that was based on false assumptions and did not involve any sacred reality. Nothing could be further from the truth for Cherokees. Among the Cherokees, healers and sorcerers always appeal to and participate in a spiritual reality to affect either a cure or a harmful effect.

This is not to say that there are no examples in Cherokee medicine where Cherokees have an understanding of medicinal qualities of plants that parallels Western scientific understanding. In fact, Cherokee healers have vast knowledge of the medicinal properties of plants, despite criticisms by James Mooney and others. In particular, Cherokee women, having been the primary gatherers of plants and being closely connected to the earth, were formative in the development of traditional Cherokee plant medicine. The Cherokees recognize a number of plants that have medicinal and curing properties. At the same time, it is also true to say that, scientifically speaking, the Cherokees are not always correct in their observations concerning the medicinal properties of plants. The Cherokees, like everybody, make mistakes. However, when healers administer slippery elm bark to a pregnant woman so that the baby may slip out quickly at birth, they are not practicing "the bastard sister of science," which involves an "association of similar ideas, that is necessarily false and barren."[56] Rather, they are wishing and willing with a pure and humble heart by and through a symbolic, material medium to supplicate and participate in the sacred power that created and sustains the cosmos.[57] Moreover, these prayers were arguably felt before they were formalized and articulated.[58]

Cherokee men are very careful not to eat the food that a menstrual or pregnant woman has prepared, to touch whatever object she has used, or even to walk along the trail that she has traveled, for fear of becoming ill.[59] Stone Coat, a supernatural being, was slain when he walked down a path, passing seven menstruating women.[60] This story, more than any other, demonstrates the power of women's blood, which is considered to be in direct opposition to the power of male hunters and warriors. By 1931 such understandings were beginning to decline as compared with just two or three generations before. Traditionally, menstruating women retired to the menstrual hut (Dʃ, *asi*, "hot house" or "winter lodge"). One observer noted that there was not one *asi* left on the reservation and not even the oldest people had remembered ever seeing one by 1931. Therefore, menstruating Cherokee women by the 1930s no longer retired from the dwelling but simply abstained from cooking meals and other duties.

While pregnant, a woman should not eat squirrel because a child will not come down when he or she is about to be born but will "go up as a squirrel climbs a tree when frightened." A pregnant woman should also avoid speckled trout so that the child will not have birthmarks and should not eat rabbit because the child might sleep with eyes open or have large eyes.[61] A pregnant woman should not eat salt any more than possible, although the reason for this was not clear. The Cherokee word for *salt* is spelled exactly the same as the word for *water*: DᏉ (*ama*); it contains two syllables. The pronunciation for *salt* places emphasis on the first syllable, while the pronunciation for *water* emphasizes the second. Salt absorbs water (and blood) and dries out the moisture of pregnancy. It is, in many ways, the opposite of water, which is essential to birth. One consultant said that salt makes flesh swell.[62] A pregnant woman should not wear neckerchiefs or a belted cloth, nor should she have an apron tied around her waist because this may cause the umbilical cord to wrap itself around the neck of the child and suffocate it. She should not see a corpse because her thoughts should be those of life and happiness. Furthermore, a man whose wife is pregnant should not dig graves or help in any way with burials. Again, a man's thoughts should be focused on life and creation rather than on death.[63]

Traditionally, upon feeling the first pains of labor, a woman retires to the menstruation lodge and remain there for some twelve to twenty-four days even after delivery; however, today it is all done in the house or the hospital. Traditional Cherokees today may summon a healer, who walks to the eastern corner of the cabin, recites a prayer, and calls upon the child "to jump down." He or she then slowly walks to the north side of the house, repeats the formula, and does the same for the west side and south side of the residence. Sometimes if deemed necessary, the conjuror will also walk around the house once more to ward off the activity of any evil spirits. Raven Mockers (powerful evil witches), in particular, are understood to prey on the weak; infants and laboring women are considered particularly easy marks.

Taboos play a vital role in traditional Cherokee religious life and Cherokees take their violation to heart. Simply put, taboos are inviolable rules that were revealed in the beginning by the great power that creates, sustains, and withdraws life. Cherokees experience most taboos as fundamental "givens" that protect them from misfortune, sickness, and death. No right-thinking Cherokee would dare violate these taboos. In fact, they once viewed some taboos so seriously that breaking them warranted shame, physical punishment, or even death.

If asked why a taboo is followed, a Cherokee will respond that it either assures something good, like health or food, or it prevents something bad, like sickness or starvation. Traditional Cherokees generally do not feel that the violation of most taboos triggered punishment from the gods; rather, the transgression occasioned the manifestation of sacred power in a harmful way. The reason that Cherokees do not articulate long explanations for taboos is not because they have forgotten the underlying mythical narrative. Rather, it's because they live and inhabit the taboos long before they conceptualize them. Taboos are always prohibitions against doing something that brings one too close to the presence of sacred power. The performance of certain acts is felt to bring about a connection with a "powerful something" that invokes an event dangerous to the community or to individuals.

Cherokee taboos, including those surrounding pregnancy, cannot be reasonably interpreted as moral transgressions, as they do not involve dishonesty, violence, or any other social vice. Cherokees understand that acts embody feelings and, therefore, a pregnant Cherokee woman will not tie a handkerchief around her neck because she does not want to invoke the sacred to wrap the umbilical cord around the child. Some outsiders are quick to dismiss such taboos as "superstition," but traditional Cherokees say they are humbly avoiding a dangerous manifestation of sacred power.

The positions taken by women giving birth vary, and some may have been learned from whites. In one position, a woman stands, with assistance by two women, and leans backward in a slanting position with her legs wide apart. In a second position, the woman kneels on the ground with her legs wide open. She sits in the lap of her husband in the third position, and in the fourth she lies down, which was very rarely done traditionally. If the child is scared to be born, a formula may be recited in which the child is told to hurry as Flint, a "dreadful being" held in great fear, is said to be approaching.[64] If a medicine man is present, he applies a concoction by standing near a laboring woman and blowing it through a reed tube so that it goes over the head of the woman and lands on her stomach and abdomen.[65]

Traditionally, Cherokees name a child four or seven days after birth.[66] In this context, four symbolizes the four cardinal directions, and seven symbolizes the four cardinal directions plus above, below, and "in the center."[67] On either the fourth or seventh day, a healer takes the newborn child to a creek or river and prays to the Creator that the baby might enjoy a long and happy life. The healer then plunges the newborn into the water seven times and returns the child to his parents.[68]

Cherokees are affectionate toward children and very nurturing. Mothers nurse their children unless the mother is unable to provide sufficient milk, in which case the baby is fed the liquid part of corn hominy.

According to Cherokee tradition, some parents raise children, particularly twins, to become witches.[69] If twins are born and the parents want them to become witches or sorcerers, they feed them no mother's milk for twenty-four days. During this time, they are fed only corn hominy liquid and only at night. They are also kept secluded from all visitors for twenty-four days. Twins raised like this are said to have supernatural powers. They are able to fly through the air, dive underground, walk on the rays of the sun, and take any human or animal shape.[70] Moreover, they are able to make events happen just by thinking them. It is also said that twin witches can see and talk with the mythic DhBϴ ᏠhꭶᎫT (ani-yvwi tsunisdii, "Little People"). One informant in about 1930 reported that a community once suspected that parents were raising a witch; the community members had a menstruating woman cook some food and slip it to the infant, thereby nullifying the process.[71] The mythic origin of this cure was the story of Stone Coat, who was a very powerful witch destroyed by seven menstruating women. Again, female blood powers are able to overcome the power of evil as well as the power of men to kill through hunting and warfare. In the end, it is not so much that that the power of female blood is dangerous, but that it's dangerous to the powers of evil and death.

Marriage

Much has been written about Cherokee marriage rituals or, more accurately, the apparent lack of rituals surrounding this important rite of passage. A number of early observers of the Cherokee commented on the apparently casual manner by which Cherokee men and women married, separated, and divorced. Author John Payne noted that some Cherokees claimed they seldom married a second time, as second marriages were not considered honorable.[72] However, Payne was writing in the 1820s and 1830s, some twenty years after Cherokee contact with Christian missionaries, who may have influenced tradition. By then, some Cherokees were amalgamating and incorporating a number of Christian elements into their religion.

In any event, if a young man wanted to marry, he approached the woman's parents to gain consent. The time was appointed and a priest was obtained to officiate over the ceremony. Early in the morning, the priest got two roots and laid them on his hand a little distance from each other. Then, facing the east, he prayed to divine whether they would live a long, happy life together. If the couple were not meant to be together, the roots would stay still. If they would live well together for a short time until one died, the roots would move together but one would quickly wilt. In either case, the priest would forbid the marriage and nothing more was said about it. However, if the roots came together and continued to do so for some time or until the priest put them down, the marriage was consummated. The priest then prayed to God that they might live happily together for a long time and warned them about adultery.

Alexander Longe, writing in 1725, observed that "as soon as the child is born, if a boy, the oldest of the husband's relations is sent for to name the child. The grandfather looks for the name of a deceased ancestor with a good reputation and thus names the boy."[73] For a female, the

oldest female relative was sent for and she too was bestowed an honor-
ific name from a deceased family member. Longe noted that the parents
of a young couple seeking marriage consulted with one another. If the
parents agreed to the marriage, the next morning the young man cut
some wood and laid it at the young woman's door. The marriage was
confirmed if the young woman took the wood, made a fire, and called
him in and fed him. At that point, the husband's parents brought a big
load of wood, and the parents of the bride held a big feast. Longe also
noted that men never married a woman of their own family, thinking of
them as sisters. Here, he was no doubt referring to the fact that Cherokees traditionally would not marry within their own clan.[74] Marrying a
woman within one's own clan was considered incest and, like murder,
was traditionally punishable by death. This prohibition against marrying within one's clan eventually broke down sometime in the twentieth
century as a result of the influence of European patterns of descent.

Two other brief traditional Cherokee marriage ceremonies have been
observed. According to one, the groom sent the bride a deer ham, showing that he was a good hunter who could supply ample food, and she in
turn gave him an ear of corn to show that she was a good farmer.[75]
Another ceremony existed in which the groom simply approached the
bride's mother and, receiving her consent, he was admitted to the bride's
bed without further ceremony.[76]

In many Native American tribes there exists some ritual initiation that
marks the transition from child to adult. Among many tribes, these ceremonies are quite elaborate. However, the Cherokees had no such adult
initiation ritual, and very little ceremony surrounded marriage.[77] Traditionally, Cherokees generally married when a girl reached the age of fifteen and a boy the age of seventeen, although earlier marriages were
known.[78] The groom sometimes gave a wedding feast, which was attended
by the relatives on both sides. In the past, a woman signified her acceptance of a marriage proposal by grinding up and baking bread from a
stack of corn left at her door. Despite the lack of formal ceremony, much
religious significance was attached to marriage. The very act of marrying
outside of one's clan acknowledged the Cherokee structure of society laid
down in the beginning by Stone Coat. Moreover, Cherokees also reaffirmed the difference between male and female sacralities and approaches
to the sacred. Following marriage, men left their mother's clan and moved
in with their wives, but both retained their own clan affiliation.

Outside observers might question why so little formal ceremony
marked such an important transition in Cherokee society. Some might

be tempted to say that Cherokees did not surround marriage with much ceremony precisely because it was considered a flexible social institution that was easily entered into and easily dissolved. Numerous outside observers noted how quickly some Cherokees got married and divorced. At the same time, until the twentieth century, marriage within one's own clan was strictly prohibited. One might get married and separated but one never, upon threat of death, married into one's own clan. Given the fact that marriage inside one's own clan was punishable by death, it is far too simple to say that Cherokee marriage was not an important rite of passage. Moreover, given the foundational importance of religion and the prohibition against incest, it would seem that the Cherokee understanding of marriage was deeply spiritual.

Indeed, marriage may have functioned as an initiation ritual into adulthood for both men and women. Still, the lack of ceremony surrounding marriage seems puzzling at first glance. However, little ritual and myth surrounded Cherokee marriage, not because it was unimportant, but because it was so fundamental to the Cherokee way of life as to be embodied at an almost unconscious level, what Pueblo scholar Gregory Cajete calls the "the mind without or before Words."[79] One might say that Cherokees inhabited their marriage and incest mythology—they lived it—and therefore did not talk about it. This may be especially true because relationships are often established at an emotional and spiritual level before they are formulated as traditions.

All Cherokees share a spiritual substance that connects them with the world and one another in a primordial manner. By being receptive to the spiritual reality that pervades all of life's vibrations, rhythms, and forms, Cherokees embrace the sacred source that connects everything. In so doing, they do not control the world; instead, they are permeated and enveloped by it. This occurs on an affective, not an intellectual, level and the relationship between Cherokees is well described as mythological, not epistemological. At the moment Cherokees "find" a mate, or rather are found by one, they are not an individual opposing another; rather, they are a relationship that exists at the juncture of the two.

Death

Death, of course, is the final rite of passage in all human communities. Cherokees, like other traditional Native Americans, observed certain funerary rites upon the passing of a member of the community. The Cherokee people were traditionally buried in the flexed, or fetal, position in both straight-walled and chambered pits, which were found mostly in either house floors or in the floors of mound structures. By placing burials at or near houses and townhouses, Cherokees linked death with sacred centers. Most burials had grave goods, including marine shell beads, gorgets, and ear pins and spools, along with fancy clay pipes, polished stone disks and celts, and chipped stone projectile points.[80] Although we do not have any direct ethnographic evidence about Cherokee burial practices, we do know that many traditional peoples all over the world have buried their dead in pits in a flexed position. Like a number of other traditional peoples and Native Americans, ancient Cherokees perhaps understood this burial to be symbolic of rebirth into the next world. In that case, Cherokee burial chamber pits were likened to the womb of Mother Earth, and the deceased were placed into the pit (the womb) in a fetal position like an embryo in its mother's womb. Until contact with Europeans, it seems that most Cherokees practiced flexed burial in various types of pits.

Some Cherokee burials included the use of uncut conch shells, some of which were filled with red ocher.[81] In Cherokee culture, red is associated with east, life, and success. Red, of course, is the color of blood, and in the context of burial, symbolized that death was birth into the next life. It is interesting that Cherokees apparently traded for conch shells and used them from time to time as grave goods. Belief in the spiritual virtues of shells is found all over the world, from prehistoric times to the present.[82] Seashells tend to be linked to origin from waters and to lunar symbolism. The Cherokee cosmogonic narrative speaks of the emergence of the world from primordial waters. Cherokee religion considered the moon a major deity, and many prayers are linked to the moon. However, most of all, seashells such as conch shells are linked with the vulva and are used symbolically as prayers for fecundity and fertility.[83] Seashells are used by many indigenous peoples in funeral customs.[84] Therefore, the Cherokee use of conch shells in burials probably represented a ritual for rebirth into an eternal mode of existence.

Originally, Cherokees were quite careful to avoid coming into physical contact with corpses. James Adair noted in 1775 that Cherokees took great precautions to avoid touching the bodies of their deceased nearest relatives and that they would not bury them.[85] In the 1920s, Cherokees did not place the body in the coffin until a few hours before burial. The body was kept in the house for two to three days, and there is some indication that it once was four to seven days, until the government no longer permitted it.[86]

Cherokees traditionally appointed a single individual to bury a corpse, and after burial the same individual destroyed the personal belongings of the deceased and made a fire of cedar boughs and goldenrod to purify the house.[87] Another source says Cherokees purified the house by smoking the house with pine branches, the evergreen being associated with eternal life and able to ward off more death.[88] A conjuror then took the person charged with burial to a river or stream, where he administered medicine to make him throw up and then ritually immersed him in the water seven times while facing first east then west.[89] The funerary person then dressed in new clothes but stayed separated from the rest of the community for an additional four days.[90]

By the 1920s, almost all funeral songs were Cherokee Christian hymns, usually sung in Cherokee, but some traditional practices long endured.[91] While the corpse was in the house, friends and relatives kept a constant watch, probably a vestige from the past to prevent witches from "stealing the liver" (ᎤᏪᎳ ᏚᏂᏃᏍᎩᏍᏗ, *uwela duninosgisdi*) of the deceased. Up until the 1950s a dance took place seven days after the burial both to send the spirit on its journey and to lift the family's sorrow.[92] This dance was sanctioned by the myth "The Daughter of the Sun."[93] In that story, several young Cherokee men and women danced before the Sun to cheer her up after her daughter died.

Cherokee cultural historian Will West Long shared much information about Cherokee funeral practice and beliefs concerning death.[94] Long apprenticed under respected Cherokee conjurors Charley Lossiah, Lawyer Calhoun, and Morgan Calhoun, although he himself never became a very accomplished doctor by his own admission. At the same time, he never became a Christian despite the fact his father was a Baptist lay preacher and a number of people pressured him to convert to Christianity. He remained until his death a conservative, traditional Cherokee.

Long explained that Cherokees understood a person to have four souls and go through four stages of death. With respect to funerals, he said they should be carried out by one's neighbors and that the ᏍᏕᎳ (*Gadugi*, "people coming together as one and working to help one another"), a community organization, could be involved. No payment was involved in a traditional Cherokee funeral. The Gadugi made coffins and draped them with a black cloth. Traditionally, burial occurred the day after death, and Long said that in earlier times the corpse was covered with a special shroud that had been interlaced from apocynum cord (or Indian hemp). Molly Sequoyah, mother of renowned potter

Amanda Swimmer, was still able to spin the two-strand cord on her thigh, as she had been taught by her mother. Long said that this practice was the final survival of traditional Cherokee weaving.[95]

Death, of course, is a Western concept that implies the end of life. Long called all four souls ᎠᏕᎭᎾ (*askina*, "spirit being"), which unfortunately gets translated as "devil" in the New Testament in a number of English translations.[96] Of the four souls possessed by Cherokees, the first is described as the soul of conscious life, which leaves the body immediately at death, continues its individual life, and sometimes hovers around the area for a short time as a harmless ghost. This soul eventually follows the "trail of Kanati" to the Night Land in the west. Some say that this soul goes into the river and follows it up to the spring head, where it goes down into the underworld.[97] One tradition says that only the evildoers are swept to oblivion in the water below.[98] This soul is located in the head, directly under the front fontanelle, and the act of scalping was directed against this soul. Will West Long related that this soul was conscious and self-conscious, and it had personality, memory, and continuity after death. This soul was responsible for the secretion of the water fluids of the body, such as saliva, phlegm, spinal fluid, lymph, and sexual fluids. Cherokee witches sometimes "spoil the saliva" of victims, and those witch attacks are directed against this particular soul.

The second soul, which is located in the liver and is associated with physical life, carries primary importance in Cherokee conjuring and medicine. This soul is considered substantive, is not anthropomorphic, and has no individuality. Witches attack the liver-soul to lengthen their lives. This soul begins to die at the moment of death, when the conscious life leaves the body. Long said that the liver is gradually diffused back into nature as a life force. It takes about a week for this life force to dissipate if the death has been normal and not caused by witches who hover around dying persons and, if possible, attack the liver-soul at the time of death or soon thereafter. A conjuror who is protecting a dying person guards against witch attacks at night just before death, the first night after death, and soon after burial. When a person is about to die, the conjuror sits in front of the fireplace and stays awake all night reciting prayers, which invoke the spirit of the fire, who is referred to as Old Woman. He performs a number of ceremonies to listen for witches and to ward them off if he detects their presence.

The third soul is located in the heart, which secretes blood. This soul is also nonhuman and takes about a month to die. Apparently, it is of no use to witches after death.

The fourth soul is located in the bones. Its life force takes a year to die before it gradually returns to nature, where it contributes to the growth of crystals in the ground, especially quartz crystals used in divination and conjuring.[99] Because the life force lingered, Cherokees traditionally mourned the deceased for about a year and tended the graves during that time. At the end of a year, the Cherokees understood that the process of separating the deceased from the living was completed.

Long disclosed that the most dramatic conflicts between conjurors and witches occurred in the context of Cherokee funerals.[100] He expressed ambivalence in talking about conjurors and witches—sometimes revulsion and other times admiration. However, the classification of conjurors and witches based on Long's information seems to be somewhat garbled. The categories get blurred at some point because one man's enemy is another man's friend. However, it seems clear that one group of conjurors works to support and extend the health and life of patients and to harm enemies of the patients. The other group seems bent on extending their own lives by stealing the liver-souls of others. The greatest example of the latter is AWOᏧ DᏝᎮᏍᎠᎩ (kolanv ayelisgi)— "Raven Mockers," who are considered the most powerful and evil of all Cherokee witches. In fact, extending one's own life by shortening another's is a very common notion in witchcraft throughout Native North America.

In one sense, despite the prevalence of Christian concepts of afterlife among some Eastern Cherokees today, saying it takes a year for Cherokees to separate the dead from the living draws too large a distinction between life and death. Instantaneous termination of life is a very secular Western concept that has no meaning among traditional Cherokees. For Cherokees, both the living and the deceased possess a spiritual life that is eternal, so it is more accurate to say that in the Cherokee worldview, death is simply the end of the body. Using such expressions as "this life" and "next life" does not accurately describe Cherokee views, because "they look upon life and afterlife as different lives in space, rather than as successive lives in time."[101] As Cherokee Hastings Shade once said, "There's no ... it don't end, you know? It's just one more step in who we are. ... There's no end."[102] For Cherokees, the body is the repository of souls, which, strictly speaking, never die.

However, the most visceral of the souls, and really the most essential, is located in the liver, which partakes of the spiritual essence that undergirds, permeates, and supports all life. The liver stores the eternal soul that is not distinct from the Creator. When a Cherokee individual dies, it takes about a week for the life force that inhabits the liver to seep back into the universal sacred essence that aboriginal Cherokees referred to as the Provider or the Creator. The same is also true, at a certain level, of both the heart and bones. After death, they remain inside the physical organ or structure that houses them during life, and gradually they merge into the spiritual essence of the cosmos. It is only the soul located near the top of the head that immediately leaves the body at death to travel to the Night Land.

Death is a transformative state that separates a Cherokee individual from the community, in terms of most day-to-day relations, but the essence of life does not cease to be. Death does not signal nothingness, but rather the passage from embodied life into transcendent spiritual life.[103] The soul is a spiritual substance that Cherokees share with all other living beings and which is part and parcel of the spiritual reality that undergirds all rhythms and forms. This understanding is not a matter of anatomy based on observation; it is a given feeling and an emotional connection. The concept of the personal soul located in the head, which escapes the body at death and lives in heaven, represents a later development in Cherokee religious thought compared with the feeling of the liver-soul, which does not clearly separate body and soul but rather connects them in a very primal manner.

CHAPTER 3

ᎤᎳᏏᏅ ᏔᎦᎣᎹᎾᏗ

Cherokee Ceremonial Life

The Cherokees traditionally celebrated an annual cycle of complex rituals, periodic dances, and rites associated with major life events such as birth, marriage, and death. In addition, Cherokee healers regularly practiced their craft for various individuals by curing the sick, finding lost people, protecting and purifying warriors, fighting off witches and other evil forces, assisting pregnant women, and helping the Kituwah People in many other ways. Cherokee ceremonies and rituals embodied a spiritual dimension that brought about practical results. For example, the annual Green Corn Ceremony and Dance thanked the Creator and Selu for a bountiful harvest and re-created the cosmos for another year. Dances such as the Beaver Dance were prayers for a successful hunt, the Eagle Dance was a solemn rite to bring about peace, and there were rituals to ensure a healthy birth and to protect the soul(s) of the dying. This chapter describes and interprets traditional Cherokee ceremonialism with a focus on their spiritual meanings and purposes.

Coauthor Ben Frey fondly recalls the crispness of the air during autumn on the Qualla Boundary and how the slight cool of the evening begins to creep in, letting everyone know the Cherokee Fair will be coming soon. Cycles typify Cherokee life even today, and the collective energy on the Boundary changes its timbre based on those cycles' ebbs and flows. Elders talk about their childhood days and how part of knowing about the changes in season was expecting what you would be eating next. Now, there's a palpable feeling of excitement in the air whenever ramp season comes around, and people try to protect the knowledge of which spots are best for gathering the wild mushrooms called ᏫᏏ (*wisi*, "hen of the woods mushroom"). Ben's uncle used to joke that he ought to plug in the spots on his GPS, but Ben suspects that would have just taken all the fun out of it. There is, after all, still something very magical about these small ceremonies. Although they may not be the same as the old ones that Cherokees practiced since time immemorial, they still represent modern Cherokees' marking of time, place, and the eternal tides of change.

Cherokee elders told Daniel Butrick in the early nineteenth century that their ceremonial cycle contained six major rituals: the First New Moon of Spring, a Preliminary or New Green Corn Feast (ᎢᏤ ᎠᏕᏘᏱᏍᎬ—*itse adetiyisgv*, literally "new year"), the Mature or Ripe Corn Feast, the Great New Moon, the Propitiation or Reconciliation Festival, and the Exalting or Bounding Bush Festival.[1] In saying "traditionally," we refer to the time prior to 1794, which marks the waning of the old ways, according to some scholars and Cherokee consultants.[2] At least one source said that each village acted independently with respect to the ceremonial cycle in the mid-1780s, at least in the case of the Green Corn Festival.[3] This was a departure from earlier times. Cherokees in the late eighteenth century also pointed to the decade of the 1780s as a time when the last great medicine people died.[4]

For traditional Cherokees, religious ritual and dance are often synonymous. Indeed, the *Payne-Butrick Papers* noted that, for the Cherokees, "most of the religious feasts or festivals are called dances, as they are accompanied with dancing."[5] Davy Arch, a contemporary traditional Cherokee artist and storyteller, succinctly asserts, "Our dances are a form of prayer." This was a common indigenous understanding. Lame Deer, a Lakota, once explained, "All our dances have their beginnings in our religion. They were sacred. Dancing and praying—it's the same thing."[6] It is helpful in this context to remember R. R . Marett's observation that religion is first emotional, not logical, and is first danced, not intellectualized.[7] One of the oldest forms of dance was circular, and it is interesting to note that Cherokee dancers often moved in a circle, counterclockwise. They still do that today at their Green Corn Dance.

The earliest account of the Cherokee Green Corn Feast was written by Alexander Longe, who lived with the Cherokees from 1714 to 1724.[8] The Preliminary Green Corn Feast was also discussed in the *Payne-Butrick Papers*, which contains material from multiple Cherokee elders from 1789 to removal (1838). This ceremony occurred at the time when the corn was in the ear and involved a command from the priests for people to avoid polluting themselves by eating the first fruits before they delivered some to the "high place," where a priest offered it to the "most high god," with prayers of thanksgiving.[9] A high priest of the ceremony recited a speech, reminding the people that this was a timeless ceremony, first performed in the "long time ago."[10] Mothers were warned to restrain their children from eating green cornstalks and that if they did, they must be brought to the "high place" to be purified by scratching. Later, a priest declared a general prohibition against polluting the feast or themselves and informed the people that it was important for them to keep themselves pure during this ceremony, or else when they died, they would not be held in high regard in the other world. Young men were told to stay away from women for four days, purge themselves with an emetic, and "go to the water."

The priests fasted four days without eating anything, other than drinking a certain concoction made from a root, and every day after sundown, they drank a little bit of hominy juice. Neither priests nor elders took anything at all on the last day of the feast. Old priests told Alexander Longe that they fasted for the "Great King of Heaven" and to rid themselves of the old corn before they ate the new corn. One elderly priest declared that this ceremony had been performed ever since the Cherokees were a people and that this was essential to Cherokee survival. Without it, the Supreme Being would withhold corn and other fruit of the fields.

NEW GREEN CORN FEAST

The Preliminary or New Green Corn Feast, was held when the young corn first became fit to eat.[11] The Cherokee term is ᏎᎷ ᏧᏂᏍᏗᎩᏍᏗᏱ (*selu tsunistigistiyi*, "Green Corn Feast"), which is roughly translated "roasting ears time" and literally translated "corn, where they eat them, rigid."[12] Cherokees told one outside observer in 1856 that, until the harvest feast had taken place, the corn was exclusively the property of the Great Spirit.[13] Some say that the ceremony occurred in mid-summer or August, others on the night of the full moon, nearest the period when the corn became ripe. The ceremonial name for new corn is ᎠᎦᏪᎳ (*agayvlige*, "Old Woman"), who is said to reside in the center, located above the four cardinal directions.[14] Corn is associated with women, who cultivate it; in fact, a number of references addressed the highest power as female and located her in the above. Purification rituals surrounded the Preliminary Green Corn Feast. Council members fasted during the six days the hunters were out gathering game for the ceremony, and villagers drank a liquid in connection with a number of sacred ceremonies to purify themselves.

All observers mentioned that a great feast took place. On the seventh day, seven ears of corn were delivered to the Chief, a new fire was made from the bark of seven selected trees, and the seven ears of corn were placed in the fire with a piece of deer's tongue, all of which was offered as a sacrifice. Charles Hicks, a Cherokee Chief, wrote in 1818 that a conjuror took grains from seven ears of corn and sacrificed them to the fire, and then drank a tea of wild horehound, after which each Cherokee was allowed to cook and eat corn.[15] Hicks may have been talking about green corn medicine, which was prepared prior to the first corn eaten and was followed by going to the water. Moreover, the villagers danced a number of animal and social dances, lasting all night. Conservative Eastern Cherokees were still making and administering green corn medicine in the 1940s and found that this medicine was generally made from four or more different plants, including volunteer corn and bearded wheat grass.[16]

In the 1830s, seven counselors, each from a different clan, fasted seven days, and on the seventh morning, when the festival began, the first order was given to bathe.[17] A prayer was recited to cleanse all the pollutants and impurities from the preceding year.[18] When the feast began, the seven counselors threw small pieces of meat in every direction in order to share it with the spirits,[19] and everyone was again ordered to the river, where they were plunged entirely under water seven times. They then returned to the council house, where the women performed an important religious dance.

MATURE GREEN CORN FEAST

The Mature or Ripe Green Corn Feast was held some forty to fifty days after the Preliminary Green Corn Feast, in middle or late September when the corn had become hard and perfect.[20] Elders told John Howard Payne, who visited the Cherokees from 1835 to 1836, that the ceremony was set down by the "Being who dwells on high" in "the beginning of time." More specifically, Molly Sequoyah, mother of Beloved Woman Amanda Swimmer, told John Witthoft in the 1940s that the story of Selu was the origin of the Green Corn Festival.[21] An arbor of green boughs was framed in the sacred square of the seven-sided council house. A beautiful shade tree was cut down, a place was dug, and it was put in the very center of the beloved square.[22] The next day, the men danced a ceremony around the sacred square, each bearing in his right hand a green bough. They danced with great energy, joy, and singing. All movements were done in accordance with a long-settled rule and guided by a leader who conducted the entire party seven times during each dance around the tree that was set in the center. This festival continued for four days, and women were excluded from entering the sacred square until the boughs were put away after the fourth day. Payne noted in the 1830s that it was this festival which had outlived all the rest, being the same known to this day as the Green Corn Dance. Chief Charles Hicks, in 1818, explained that the Cherokee National Council met at this time and that a person spoke each day in an archaic and mysterious language.[23]

Traditionally, during the Green Corn Ceremony a long migration myth was recited, which was nearly lost by the time John Haywood wrote about it in 1823.[24] Chief Hicks told Haywood that Cherokees came from the seacoast where "whales and sea snakes abounded" and that the Cherokees still retained the names of the monsters of the deep. According to this migration narrative, the Cherokees came from the rising sun and were placed upon this land by the divine orders of the Four Councils sent from Heaven.[25] In this version, Cherokee migration stories were part and parcel of the earth diver cosmogony and centered Cherokee creation and migration in the Great Smoky Mountains, where they have always been. For Eastern Cherokees, the water beetle surfaced the primeval waters with a piece of earth at Kituwah, the center of their world.

Lieutenant Henry Timberlake's memoirs from 1756 to 1765 made note of the Green Corn Dance, which he says was performed in a very solemn manner in a large square before the townhouse. The motion of the dance was very slow and involved a song that thanks the Creator for providing corn to the people.[26] Throughout the nineteenth century and later in some communities, fire in the settlement was extinguished just before the Green Corn Dance and a new fire known as "the honored or sacred fire" was made in the townhouse and distributed to all the people.[27] Cherokee elders told missionary Daniel Butrick of three vertical cosmic levels: heaven, earth, and the underworld. The tree represented the juncture of the three, "the place of uniting," and allowed Cherokees to transcend space and experience unity with the world.[28] The Green Corn Dance was established by the Creator in the "long ago." The old Cherokee way viewed ritual time as cyclical and space as centered. The

Green Corn Dance, the most sacred of all ceremonies, allowed Cherokees to experience timelessness and unity with their world.

The Green Corn Dance made multiple references to a Supreme Being
who was said to provide the Cherokees with corn and other foods.
Alexander Longe, who wrote of the Cherokees in 1725 after living some
fifteen years among them, observed that they worshipped "one supreme
power."[29] Numerous names for the Creator have been noted. It is hard
to know if some of these were influenced by outsiders, although several
of these names were apparently translated from Cherokee. Given the
fact that these observations took place after contact, it is difficult to
know how much or to what extent Europeans had, by then, influenced
Cherokee religious understandings or how much Cherokees were
amending their own indigenous religious concepts either unconsciously
or to please their European visitors. Or it may be that English settlers
recording Cherokees failed to fully understand the offered lessons and
took license to translate concepts into those they understood.

An extract from the diaries of Moravian brethren at Spring Place Mission, in Georgia, discussed a Green Corn Dance on August 26, 1803, at
the townhouse in the village of Estanelly.[30] Moravians noted that the
Cherokees had five different kinds of dances, which were simple but very
orderly. They were all very different from one another, except that in
each dance, one or two men shook rattles filled with small pebbles and
sang. The brethren could recognize only four words: *Hanji, Hanjo,
Hanani*, and *Johani*, which were repeated over and over. A Moravian
named Steiner asked about the meaning of the song the Cherokees sang
during the Green Corn Dance and discovered that none knew what any
of the words meant, even those well versed in the language. Cherokees
also told him that one song was sung exclusively at the Green Corn
Dance—a song that expressed their joy and gratitude for the new corn.[31]

Major John Norton, who claimed Cherokee descent, left a valuable
journal of his visit to Cherokee, North Carolina, in 1809. A forty-year-
old Cherokee who accompanied Norton revealed that when he was a
boy, a very respected Cherokee spoke at the Green Corn Dance in a
poetic voice and in a strange dialect. As a boy, he understood only a few
words. However, he specifically remembered this statement, "We are
immigrating into a strange country, and now move our encampments."[32]
Note the use of the present tense; Cherokees are "conflating time" (Alan
Kilpatrick) and reliving their migration. At the completion of the ceremony, they extinguished all fires and then lit them again by rubbing two
pieces together in a very ancient manner. Norton's Cherokee companion

also noted that the man who extinguished the fire sang and said these words: "I have been to the country above, and have now returned from thence, with the commands of the Great Spirit whose abode is there." After that, he directed the participants to perform several ceremonies, dances, and purifications. Norton's journal seems to reference a group of priests among the Cherokees who perhaps spoke an archaic or esoteric religious language known only to them. These folks were called DhJWh (*anigutani*, "Anikutani").

The Cherokees have a tradition about an ancient priesthood, the Ani Kutani, who were the people who once directed many religious affairs for the Cherokees. However, oral tradition holds that they became quite corrupt and evil and that the people rose up against them and slayed them. Some have argued that the archaic language spoken at the Green Corn Dance was a holdover from the Ani Kutani.[33] Another possible explanation is that the Cherokees, especially after contact and colonialism, simply lost knowledge of certain ancient religious traditions and ceremonies.[34]

However, another theory seems more plausible. For the Cherokee people, the Green Corn Dance was the most sacred of all ceremonies. It was a classic example of a New Year festival, typical of many traditional Native Americans and other archaic peoples. At this annual New Year festival, the old world was destroyed symbolically and a new world created for another year. Thus, the Cherokees consumed the food from the old year and extinguished the fires of the old year, representing the end of time and of the world. Then they lit a new fire that represented the primordial fire. At that point, the world was created anew. After going to water several times, Cherokees considered themselves purified of all evil as they were at the time of creation. By plunging under water, the Cherokee people reexperienced the beginning of time when the water beetle dove underwater and brought up a little mud that became the earth. An act of death and resurrection, whose ultimate model is the myth of creation, the symbolism here is well known.[35] This was a time of joy and happiness; much giving and sharing took place and all wrongdoings except murder were forgiven.[36]

The earliest expressions of the experience of the sacred (numinous) were arguably inarticulate sounds, which were not part of grammar and were nonrational.[37] The most profound religious utterances, which hark back to the time of creation, are sounds that attempt to express the inexpressible. Hence, the reference by both Cherokees and outsiders to an archaic language no longer understood by the people perhaps refers to an ancient language, which is symbolic of the primordial experience of the sacred at the time of creation.

SUPREME BEING

Ancient Cherokees worshipped a Supreme Being, but the assertion that the Supreme Being was the sun has little support.[38] Mooney translated ᎤᏁᏢᎥᎯ (*unetlanvhi*, "the Creator" or "the Apportioner"), the most commonly used term for Supreme Being, as "He has apportioned, allotted, divided into equal parts," which he likened to the "time-dividing role of the sun." However, the term may come from the verb *to provide*.[39] Accordingly, the Cherokee Supreme Being may be better translated as "Provider" or "Creator," rather than "Apportioner." Another term sometimes used for the Supreme Being is "Ancient White One."[40] This term is used occasionally in sacred formulas chanted by Cherokee medicine men and women. The Wahnenauhi transcript (1889) makes it clear that Cherokees worshipped one high god, whom they called by various names, including ᎤᏁᏢᎥᎯ (*unetlanvhi*, "Maker of all Things") and ᏍᏏᏩᏗ ᎡᎯ (*galvladi ehi*, "The One who lives above" or "heaven dweller").[41]

The term *galvládi éhi* (*galvladi*), "Resider [or One Who Properly Belongs] Above, He [or She],"[42] is also interpreted as "Above, On High"[43] (a reference to Heaven and especially the Seventh Heaven). The Provider resides in the Seventh Heaven.[44] Another related term, ᏍᏏᎥᏳᎩ (*galunkw'ti'yu*), is interpreted as "Honored, Sacred."[45] Mooney also noted that the same term in the Bible means "Holy or Hallowed." A Cherokee named Ta-ka-e-tuh told the Missionary Cephas Washburn that there were two creator beings: ᎤᏁᏢᎥᎯ (*unetlanvhi*, "Author of All Things") and ᏍᏏᏩᏗ ᎡᎯ (*galvladi ehi*, "Governs and Disposes of All Things").[46] Washburn's Cherokee consultant went on to say that in the end there is only "one God who sustains different relations to us, and is spoken of in terms indicating those relations." A *Cherokee Phoenix* article in 1829 written by Samuel Worcester, who knew the language, reported that the Cherokees had only two names for God: ᎤᏁᏢᎥᎯ (*unetlanvhi*, "Creator") and ᏍᏏᏩᏗ ᎡᎯ (*galvladi ehi*, "He Who Dwells Above").[47]

Observers of the Cherokees often distinguish the Christian term *God* from the Cherokee *Great Spirit* and, indeed, Cherokee elder Goingback Chiltoskey translates "God" or "Father" as ᏑᏛ (*edoda*) and "Great Spirit" as ᎤᏓᏅᏙ (*adanto*).[48] One Cherokee dictionary translates "God" as ᎤᏁᏢᎥᎯ (*unetlanvhi*), a term very much like the 1829 Cherokee

Phoenix term for "Creator."[49] The *Payne-Butrick Papers* reference ᎤᎯᎦ (*yihowa*, "God" or "Jehovah") as the most sacred name of God.[50]

Much more work needs to be done in this area, and this is the sort of material that can ultimately only be sorted out by knowledgeable Cherokees who are willing to discuss this subject with outsiders. At the same time, the Cherokees, like many other Native Americans, may have many expressions for that which is anonymous, autonomous, and ultimately inexpressible. In other words, the lack of orthodoxy may represent religious sophistication rather than a need for precision. What does seem clear is that Cherokees traditionally understood that the Creator "resides" and "dwells . . . in the centre of the sky, directly overhead . . . in the centre of the four points" (four cardinal directions).[51]

In 1887, Cherokees in North Carolina performed the Green Corn Dance, in its long form, for the last time, according to some Cherokees.[52] There were four separate periods of the dance. During the first period, men with guns danced counterclockwise in a circle several hundred yards from the main dance ground behind a leader who sang and shook a gourd rattle. At various intervals throughout the morning, the dancers discharged their guns. Traditionally, a medicine man made an incantation and struck a "big white rock" sprinkled with a certain powder, which caused an explosion, symbolizing thunder.[53] The loud noise symbolized thunder on two separate levels: male and female. On one level, thunder is a prayer for rain to fall to grow wild plants that feed the animals that Cherokee men hunt. Thunder is also a prayer for the crops and wild plants, which women traditionally grew or gathered. Additionally, thunder sounds symbolize the Thunder Beings, who are said to be the children of Kanati, the primordial hunter, and Selu, who is the corn.

According to the myth of Kanati and Selu, the primordial Cherokee ancestors had two children, named the Thunderers, or the Little Men.[54] In the 1880s, Swimmer, the medicine man, revealed that when the Thunderers talk to each other, Cherokees hear low-rolling thunder in the west. According to him, the Thunderers taught the Cherokees seven songs to call the deer, all of which had been forgotten except two, that Cherokees still sang.[55] The Thunderers are important deities associated with the Cherokee ball game. Moreover, the Thunderers are important deities, involved in a number of Cherokee narratives. Alexander Longe noted that "the thunder and lightning is God's Great Guns."[56] One observer around 1835 made a distinction between the Thunder and the Little Men, who are the Thunderers,[57] and another nineteenth-century text observed that the Thunderers are the two sons of Kanati, who live above the sky vault. The Great Thunder should be distinguished from his two sons, the Two Thunder Boys, who live far in the west above the sky vault.[58] The Thunder and his two sons are the enemies of the Darkening Land in the west, and Thunder is the friend of Cherokee Indians.[59] Finally, the Thunderers are the most powerful beings in the Cherokee pantheon—except for perhaps their aloof father, Kanati.[60]

The Cherokee name for Thunder Beings, or Thunderers, should never be used in everyday conversation.[61] The name is so sacred that it is only pronounced by a Cherokee medicine man who is engaged in conjuring. Historian of religions Michael Zogry noted that it was only after several years of fieldwork in the Cherokee community that certain Cherokee consultants even saw fit to mention them.

During the first stage of the Green Corn Dance, as recorded and described in the late nineteenth century, the women dancers performed a Meal Dance on the main plaza while the men discharged their guns. During this dance, the women acted as though they were preparing cornmeal. This ritual reactualized the role of women as laid down in the beginning by Selu; it was also a prayer that there be plenty of corn to grind in the coming season.

Later, around noon, the men dancers moved to the plaza, circled it, and then merged with the women before moving back to their original position. This second stage of the ritual symbolized the fertilization of grain and reaffirmed the respective labors of men and women.[62] More fundamentally, at a religious level, these actions symbolized the roles of Cherokee men and women laid down in the second primordium in the story of Kanati and Selu. Following the dance, a feast was held for everyone, including strangers and visitors.

The third stage, the Green Corn Dance, occurred prior to sundown. Men and women danced in separate groups, as in the first stage. Here, a man, singing for the women dancers, used a gourd rattle. The lead woman dancer shook a turtle shell rattle. This stage, some have said, symbolized the harvest. Perhaps more importantly, however, this stage showed reverence for Selu and Kanati and reaffirmed traditional Cherokee gender roles in which women ground meal and men prepared for hunting and war. This stage also expressed thankfulness, especially to Kanati, the great hunter.

The fourth stage opened with the Friendship, or Stone Coat, Dance, in which men and women alternated. Following the conclusion of the Friendship/Stone Coat Dance, the participants performed dances with sexual connotations related to fertility. Next, the dancers performed various animal dances, including the following: beaver, buffalo, pigeon, groundhog, horse, pheasant, chicken, frog, raccoon, deer, and turkey. The Booger, Eagle, and Bear dances were never performed at this time because they were linked to the winter season and were held only after the first frost. Performing a Booger, Eagle, or Bear dance in connection with the Green Corn Dance could shorten the growing season by bringing on winter too soon.

In the Beaver Dance, the dancers carried sticks, which they used to strike at a beaver skin, representing a beaver. In this dance, the hunters symbolically engaged in beaver hunting with sticks representing beaver clubs (or guns).[63] This dance traditionally lasted about half an hour and presumably foreshadowed hunts—successful or unsuccessful. Striking the beaver skin many times with their sticks predicted a good hunt. Missing often forecasted an unlucky hunt.

Interestingly, the Buffalo Dance persisted along with these other dances until about the 1930s, although the buffalo disappeared from the Smoky Mountains perhaps two centuries before. Despite scant archeological evidence for the existence of buffalo, some observers noted their presence, and Cherokee tradition asserts the existence of buffalo in their homeland and their use of buffalo meat and skins.

The last dance performed in the Green Corn Dance was the Round or Running Dance, which symbolized going around the mountain to reach home. The next-to-last dance was the Corn Dance. Taking place in the morning, the dance forecast early spring planting and made the corn grow fast. During the Corn Dance, men and women danced counterclockwise around a mortar that was set in the center of the dance area. As they circled the mortar, the dancers acted as though they were dipping and pouring corn and meal into a basket or bowl that was held in the other hand. In so doing, the dancers simultaneously asked for abundant corn crops and thanked God for corn crops.[64]

Most importantly, the Green Corn Dance was a classic New Year ritual during which the origins of Cherokee life were relived. The lighting of a new fire marked the re-creation of the world and the establishment of the Cherokee way of life. This ceremony affirmed the sacred foundation of Cherokee culture and society and revealed the importance of spirituality in orienting Cherokee men and women to the world. In the ceremonies, one can clearly see the influence of Cherokee religion on society. Indeed, historian Tyler Boulware argues that the Green Corn Ceremony was the most important ceremony for alleviating tensions between Cherokee clans, towns, and regions.[65]

CHEROKEE BALL GAME

DꞂK (*anetso*), the Cherokee stick ball game, is both recreation and ritual, as early Europeans observed. Outsiders such as Henry Timberlake made numerous references to the ball game and its importance to Cherokee culture, identity, and religion.[66] Today the ball game, which is similar to lacrosse, is mostly played during the Fall Festival, the first weekend in October. The authors have witnessed a number of Cherokee ball games during the Fall Festival and can personally attest to the players' skill and ferocity. The players use one or two sticks to scoop a ball made of rawhide or deerskin from the ground, after which they may carry it with their hands.

A close connection existed between the Cherokee ball game and warfare.[67] Indeed, one of the names for the ball game, ᏝᎾᏩ ᎤᏍᏗ (*danawa' usdi'*), translates as "little war."[68] The game normally took place in midsummer through late fall, and several games might be played over the course of the season. Traditionally, respected elders from villages would meet and negotiate when and where the games would be played, and then return to their villages and relay the news to the young men who would be playing. At that point, the team employed the services of a conjuror or medicine man to conduct various rituals thereby enhancing his village's chances for victory.

The ball game is a sporting event that takes on ritual dimensions couched in religious terms.[69] It is important to remember that "in the eyes of many Cherokee the outcome of the game was less a function of the athletic ability of the players as it was a power struggle between opposing conjurors."[70] While it is easy to make the facile statement that Cherokees and other Native Americans understand everything important in their lives as embodying a religious dimension, it is quite something else to argue that the Cherokees understand success in the ball game as being primarily the work of the team's medicine man. Many outsiders find it difficult to understand that the spiritual dimension plays a more significant role in day-to-day activities than does the material.

Traditionally, the players practiced daily for two weeks in preparation for the game under the direction of a conjuror, which, again, shows the important part that a spiritual leader played in this activity. A number of important taboos surrounded preparations for the ball game, and the players honored these or risked loss and ridicule by fellow players.[71] Cherokees recognized the essential importance of the sacred in determining the game's outcome, which made the conjuror "the most important actor in the play."[72] The significance of conjuring in the ball game is furthermore shown by the unwillingness of those steeped in ball play traditions to discuss this aspect of the game. Michael Zogry, who did field research from 1993 to 2007 among Eastern Band Cherokees, observed that information about conjuring remains very guarded. Some sources told him that discussing or revealing sacred formulas and rituals would compromise their power.[73] At the same time, Lloyd Sequoyah, a respected and knowledgeable elder from Big Cove in North Carolina, disclosed a number of formulas used in the ball game.

To this day, the most important part of pregame preparations is the all-night dance that occurs on the eve of the game.[74] Men and women dance during the night in separate dances, as the sexes are kept strictly apart. Participants dance until daybreak; during the course of the night, the men dance seven times, with each dance lasting about twenty minutes. Prior to each dance by men, the players form two parallel lines facing the opposition's town. A man designated as *talala*, or redheaded woodpecker, runs between the two lines and makes sharp war cries. The players then dance around the fire with their ball sticks in imitation of the game. The dance leader circles the players and keeps time with a gourd rattle, which often is decorated with the rattle of a rattlesnake to make the players fierce. At different times, the players face the opposition village and utter various war whoops and cries. Between dances, the men retire to the riverbank to undergo additional ritual, and at those times, women dancers will move back and forth in front of the structure that holds the ball sticks while keeping time with a male drummer. The women sometimes sing songs, but often with subdued and almost solemn voices that sharply contrast with the spontaneous singing and war cries of men.

The medicine man who acts as a singer uses a gourd rattle, which may be decorated with an eagle or hawk feather, as a prayer medium gives the players speed and strength.[75] The players form parallel rows, and a man selected by the conjuror runs back and forth between the lines. As he faces the opposition's village, he shouts formal cries of defiance and makes a certain war cry seven times. He alternates between the lines and ends with a jump and a shout, which means, "weak, unsuccessful, to no purpose."[76] This man embodies the woodpecker's attributes of strength and flight. As the men dance, they repeatedly refer to the "flycatcher," which is a bird of speed, accuracy, and sight, and is able to seize an insect in flight.[77] In one of the songs, the WWW (*talala*, "redheaded woodpecker") imitates the cry of the flycatcher, and during this chant the dancers go through the motion of catching and throwing the ball. During the dances the men are purified by the smoke from the fire, and, indeed, the last dance before morning is performed in heavy smoke caused by pinewood, which is intended to increase their strength.[78]

At one point, seven women representing the seven clans take part in dances, which they're expected to do all night. They, too, face the opponent's community, and they finish with ritual steps that symbolize "stepping on the players of the opposite town."[79] The women's final dance takes place just before daybreak, and after its conclusion a conjuror takes them to water. On the way, their singer chants the flycatcher song that was sung earlier on behalf of the men. The women also step on a rock under which black beads have been placed. The beads represent specific players on the other team and this is done to weaken the other team and to help promote victory.

The link between the ball game and birds figures prominently in a major Cherokee myth concerning the ball game. Cherokee elders told Mooney a narrative entitled "The Ball Game of the Birds and Animals," which is set in the "long ago, before humans existed." This is an important myth and continues to be widely repeated.[80] Furthermore, depictions of hawks, eagles, and woodpeckers appear throughout the prehistoric Southeast.[81] Although there is no specific ethnographic reference to the Cherokee use of an ornamental bird feather assemblage on ball players, old drawings of other southeastern Indian ball players wearing feather tails link the players with animals. Indeed, the Cherokee name of the ball game dance is ᏓᎤᏪ ᏍᎭ (*datsela nuni'*, "things transformed") and ᏓᏁᏍᏲᏃᏔᏂ (*daneksinotani*, "they are going to put things on their buttocks").[82] Arguably then, the Cherokee ball game dance is ritually linked with the mythical narrative that Cherokee ball players reenact, homologizing themselves with the victorious birds. The game is deeply mystical, as Cherokees are transformed into the victorious birds who played before humans inhabited the earth. By becoming the birds of legend, Cherokee ball players help ensure their victory against the opposing team.

The players observe a number of food taboos. For example, players do not eat rabbit for seven days prior to the game because rabbits are easily confused and scared. Players also abstain from eating frog or frog bones. They eat no sucker fish, which would make them sluggish, and no young animals because they would become sluggish or easily scared. Also, they observe the general ritual of avoiding hot food or salt. Above all, the ball player must not touch a woman for seven days prior to the ceremony. Again, the ball play was and is symbolic war, and the blood of war conflicts with and is overpowered by the blood of birth, which women embody.

Traditionally, on the morning of a game, the men ritually bathed four times in the river. Cherokee Indians still go to water in connection with the ball game. There are many references in the literature to this ritual, which indicates that it has been part of the Cherokee ceremonial life for quite some time. Alan Kilpatrick, a Cherokee, wrote that Cherokees see victory as determined solely by the skill of the conjuror, ᏗᏓᏅᎦᏫᏍᎩ (*didanvwisgi*, "curer of them").[83] According to Kilpatrick, the most common of all Cherokee purification rituals is ᎠᎼᎯ ᎠᏤᏍᏗᏍᎠᏗ (*amohi atstesdi*, "going to water").[84] Lunar events, ceremonial dances, the ball game, and protection against the outbreak of disease or witchcraft prompt this ritual. It is also used to combat the problems of old age. Moreover, the word *going* is traditionally connected with pregnancy, birth, and healthy child-rearing, as well as funeral rites and, traditionally, going to war. Generally, a conjuror conducts going to water and recites a sacred writing known as ᏔᏍᏉᏍᏗᎠᏗ (*igawesdi*, "to say,").[85]

James Mooney wrote that going to water was the most sacred of all Cherokee rituals and that it played a role in "every important ritual performance."[86] In the most formal ceremony, a conjuror accompanies the participants, but the ritual is so widespread that sometimes individuals go by themselves. Michael Zogry referred to these two alternatives as "being taken" versus "going" to water.[87] In the end, this ritual is so sacred and so pervasive precisely because it is a ritual reenactment of the Cherokee creation myth. It is important to note here that sometimes while going to water, conjurors merely splash participants with water, while other times they completely submerge the participants. Complete submersion usually involves being dipped four to seven times—again, those numbers being beloved for Cherokees. Being submerged completely under water reactualizes the Earth Diver creation myth and re-creates the ritual participant. By going to the water, a Cherokee located himself "in the middle" when the world was first created. Undergoing this ritual purification, a Cherokee reexperiences the long ago and resurfaces into this world free of all pollution and disorder.

The lack of any formal Cherokee initiation ritual into adulthood raises a number of questions as to why no such ceremony existed, at least in the ethnographic literature. While not in itself an initiation ritual, going to water embodies important initiatory structures and meanings for Cherokees. Among many Indigenous peoples, initiates are symbolically plunged into chaos, where they symbolically die, only to be reborn to a new mode of being.[88] Through the initiation process, participants transcend their position as a natural person and enter into a transcendental and sacred reality. Thus, going to water with a Cherokee conjuror was a particularly powerful, spiritual exercise in which the Cherokee participant was ritually plunged into chaos, only to resurface in a world of order and harmony. Perhaps Mooney was right when he said this was the most important of all Cherokee ceremonies, and it's important to note that it is still done today.

In preparation for the game, players also submit to ᏕᏥᎾᎦᏍᎫ (de'tsinuga'sku, "scratching"). Bloodletting took place in a wide variety of contexts. The oldest written reference to scratching we have found was in Alexander Longe's 1725 postscript. Discussing the sanctity of the Cherokee "temple," he noted that no one but properly appointed priests were allowed to go to the temple and that if children went there, as they sometimes were, "the priest sends for them and has them scratched all over their body."[89] In Longe's example, children are scratched because they have polluted a sacred area by improperly crossing a boundary. They may also get scratched so as to be discharmed from the power of the temple before they reenter society. That is to say, in this context, it is both a purification and a discharming ritual designed to protect both the sacrality of the temple and the youth from spiritual power.

Scratching is a preliminary ritual of the ball game and other ceremonies as well as a medicine man's mode of injection. A very painful procedure, scratches are drawn by use of a seven-tooth comb of turkey bone.[90] This comb is called a ᎧᏄᎦ (kanuga)[91] and use of the turkey bone scratcher is sanctioned in Cherokee mythology. Lloyd Sequoyah related the myth of the "Ball Game between Animals and Birds," which revealed that Cherokees used animal and bird body parts to win future ball games. By using the parts of the turkey to let blood, a Cherokee ball player acquired the power of the turkey to run fast and with great stamina. As the turkey said, scratching with his bones would, "make the fastest runner you've ever seen. I don't give up when I go running up the mountain."[92] The use of a turkey-bone scratcher originated in the long ago; by repeating this ancestral act, a Cherokee acquires the speed and endurance of turkeys. Moreover, in so doing, a Cherokee inhabits the mythical narrative, and hence transcends ordinary time.

Traditionally, a Cherokee ball player wore only a breechcloth and an ornament on the head. The piece worn in the hair is highly symbolic and consists of an eagle feather (or hawk, if eagle feathers were not available) for keen sight; deer tail for swiftness; and a rattlesnake rattle for ferocity. These animal parts serve as mediums through which the Cherokee ball players concentrate their prayers to achieve keen sight, swiftness, and ferocity. Again, however, it would be a mistake to interpret the hair ornament as an example of sympathetic magic. Cherokees do not think that wearing an eagle feather will give them superior eyesight by some magical causation. These animal parts are not the power themselves but are rather the symbols through which the powers are summoned and manifested. Each of these ornaments represents a different plane of the vertical world. Eagle feathers are symbolic of the sky; the deer tail is symbolic of this world; and the snake's rattle is symbolic of the underworld. By playing through each of these symbolic modalities, the Cherokee ball player is united with the world and therefore able to employ the sacred powers that reside within. These powers are able to be summoned precisely because the ball player is locating himself in the "middle" so that he may relate directly with the Provider.

Cherokee players also mark their bodies in various patterns with paint or charcoal.[93] Charcoal is taken from the dance fire, fueled by wood—when possible—from a tree that was struck but not killed by lightning. This type of wood is considered especially powerful, as lightning is considered a manifestation of, or close relation to, the Thunderers. Cherokees pulverize the charcoal obtained from the fire and put it into a cocoon along with a red and a black bead. This concoction serves as a ritual prayer to make players swift like lightning and as invulnerable as the tree that survived a thunderbolt. Honey locust tree ash is also used in this mixture as a prayer that a ball player will be hard and firm to the touch, like the wood of that particular tree.

Just before playing, the players also rub their bodies with slippery elm, sassafras, and some sort of grease to make them slippery. Traditionally, players also bathed their limbs with a solution made of two plants: cat gut, to make their muscles tough like the root of that plant, and small rush, as a prayer that they will always stand erect, as that plant does, even when it is stomped upon. They also bathed with a solution of wild crabapple or ironwood and stargrass because these plants are considered especially tough and remain off the ground even when heavily weighed upon. After the first scratching, players traditionally ate a bit of rattlesnake, which was killed and cooked by the conjuror. They also rubbed themselves with an eel skin to make themselves slippery like the eel, and rubbed each limb with the leg of a turtle because turtle legs are strong and stout.

Once dressed, the players are ready to go to the water for the last time. This time, the medicine man, in addition to plunging them in the water, uses beads to divine success for the hometown team. Red beads are used to symbolize the hometown; black beads are used to symbolize the opponent. An elder Cherokee told Mooney that the conjuror recounts this prayer to the River, called Long Man: "Oh, Long Man, I come to the edge of your body. You are mighty and most powerful. You bear up great logs and toss them about where the foam is white. Nothing can resist you. Grant me such strength in the contest that my enemy may be of no weight in my hands—that I may be able to toss him into the air or dash him to the earth."[94] Similarly, the conjuror prays to the Red Bat and the Land of the Sun to make him dodge the enemy; to the Red Deer to make him fast afoot; to the Red Hawk to give him excellent vision; and to the Red Rattlesnake to make him terrible to his opponents.

Continuing in a low tone with staccato accents, the conjuror mentions each player by name (and traditionally includes clan) and exclaims that he has now ascended to the first heaven. The conjuror continues to chant and to raise the Cherokee ball player to successive levels of heaven, each time raising his hands a bit higher to indicate a higher level of heaven. Finally, he raises his hands high and declares that the spirit of the ball player has now risen to the Seventh Heaven. Next, the medicine man asks the player for the name of his archrival on the other team and he then recites a number of sacred formulas to bring failure to that opponent. He prays to the Black Fog to cover him so that he may be unable to see; to the Black Rattlesnake to envelop him; and last to the Black Spider to drag him along the black trail to the Darkening Land in the West and to bury him in a black coffin under the clay. In the final prayer, the conjuror makes a hole in the soft dirt with his finger, symbolic of stabbing his opponent, drops the black bead into it, and covers it with a vicious stomp of his foot.

This conjuror invokes the aid of the bat and various birds, including the peewee, the chimney swift, and finally the white dragonfly, to make his team swift and powerful. The opposing players, on the other hand, are linked with the terrapin, the turtle, the mole, and the bear, all considered clumsy. Additionally, the opponents are connected with the color blue, which is symbolic of defeat, while the home team is homologized with red and white, metaphors of success and happiness, respectively.[95] Just before the game begins, the conjuror recites another secret formula addressed to hickory, which is done for the purpose of weakening the enemy's ball sticks.

The two teams come together in the center of the ground, facing each other, each shouting a number of war whoops, and finally, an old man approaches with the ball. He delivers a final address to the players, telling them that the Creator is looking down on them from Heaven and that they are to conduct themselves as did their fathers before them. He also implores them to keep their tempers and to return in peace once the game is over. He concludes with a long ᎣᏩᏒᎢ (hatalduqui), meaning "now for the twelve," and throws the ball in the air. The game is very violent and vigorous and may last anywhere from one hour to several hours. There are no timeouts and the first team to score twelve wins. Once the game is over, the players immediately go to the water again with their medicine men, who perform a ceremony for turning aside the incantations of their rivals.

The considerable amount of ritual and symbolism associated with this sporting activity is extraordinary. One outside observer, in an unpublished tape recording, states that *anetso* was itself a religious ritual linked with the Twin Gods or the Little Men. He argues that the ball game was a "major religious ceremony that had to do with rainmaking and with the worship of the Twin Gods."[96] It is clear that the ball game is linked in some way with the Thunderers; and because the Thunderers are associated with rain, his interpretation seems plausible. Although the Thunderers are clearly connected to the ball play ritual complex, most consultants reject the rainmaking ritual interpretation.[97] Of course, it may be that the lack of written records supporting the rainmaking theory does not in and of itself mean that his interpretation is incorrect. In other words, the absence of evidence does not necessarily mean evidence of absence.

Although it is true that there are lots of published accounts of the Cherokee way of life, none of the eighteenth- and nineteenth-century accounts, until James Mooney, were done by trained ethnographers. Mooney's work, because of Cherokee involvement, is extremely detailed and impressive, despite his occasional offensive comments about the savage, primitive, or unintelligent nature of the Cherokees. However, we should not judge Mooney too harshly, for he was, like everyone else, a product of his time, and for the most part, he gives an accurate depiction of Cherokee religious life as related to him by various knowledgeable elders in the late nineteenth century. While it makes sense to infer that a ritual game like the ball play associated with the Thunderers would have a rainmaking function, there is very little evidence in the ethnographic record to support it. It is true, for example, that the Hopi

Indians of Arizona engaged in a number of different types of foot races, which were simultaneously sporting events and prayers for rain.[98] Whether a similar meaning resides within the Cherokee ball play remains at this point inclusive.

BOOGER DANCE

At least one traditional Cherokee religious ceremony involves the use of masks in a ritual dance—the Booger Dance. It is not entirely clear how long the Cherokees have performed the Booger Dance, but we do know that references were made to it by outsiders in the late eighteenth century. At the same time, neither Longe nor Timberlake, both early observers of the Cherokees in the eighteenth century, mention this ceremony. However, that may be because it was shrouded in secrecy or they simply did not make note of it. Much speculation exists as to whether this Cherokee ceremony was aboriginal or post-contact in nature. Nevertheless, we discuss Booger Dancing here because the practice is very old, and although it may have declined in the 1950s, it continues to this day. As Big Cove elder Bernice Bottchenbaugh shared in August of 2019, "this ceremony is not just something our ancestors practiced, but a living tradition practiced by my family and others within the EBCI."[99] Furthermore, Davy Arch, Cherokee elder, storyteller, and traditional artist, participated in a Booger Dance before being deployed to the Gulf War in 1991. The Cherokee name for the Booger or Mask Dance is ᏦᏍᎠᏢ (*tsunagaduli*), which means "many persons, faces covered over."[100]

The Booger Dance was a winter dance. One observer in 1836 discussed the Booger Dance as part of the Eagle Dance, which was always done in winter. Three Big Cove men, Lawyer Calhoun, Deliski Climbing Bear, and Will West Long, are among those who made masks that have been photographed.[101] One mask shows an Indian in fearful apprehension, a second an Indian with black stains beneath the nose, and a third an Indian with the skin of a rabbit's head tacked on the forehead. Four masks depict white men, three masks a Black man, and one an Indian woman. A wasp's or hornet's nest sits on one mask, which was "perhaps a caricature of a diseased white man." William Lossiah has carved several Booger masks over the years, one as recently as 2020. Booger Dances were generally performed by four to ten or more masked men (sometimes accompanied by a woman), who some say represent "people from far away or across the water," meaning Germans, French, Chinese, African

Americans, or even alien Indians.[102] Daniel Butrick depicted them in the 1830s as "mendicant travelers on a long journey."[103] Described by one observer as the Witch or Booger Man Dance, the Cherokee Booger Dance has no equal among all Native American dances.

Each Booger Dancer had a name, which was usually obscene and was given when requested by the host of the dance. All dancers pretended to speak a language other than Cherokee. Boogers occasionally wore animal masks when they wanted to represent themselves as hunters. During those times, they carried weapons such as guns, bows, and clubs.[104] Sometimes they carried a gourd neck to imitate a phallus, which they periodically exposed while chasing after women and girls. In a performance in Big Cove on January 2, 1935, many of the dancers had obscene names. For example, at that ceremony, the leader of the Boogers was named German, but other names were Black (Little Man), Black Buttocks, French Man, Big Testicles, Sooty Anus, Rusty Anus, Burster (Penis), and Making Pudenda Swell. At another dance, names emphasized foreign nations or regions within the country such as Southerner, Northerner, Spaniard, and China Man.[105] A hornet's mask represented Hornet, a mean creature, which dancers frequently impersonated. Some scholars writing about the Booger Dance in the 1930s argued that there was no religious symbolism or meaning in the Booger Dance among the Eastern Cherokee.[106] They did not define what they meant by religious meaning or symbolism; in any event, they were simply wrong about this. For example, pregnant women were not allowed to look at the masks and the dance contained a curing function,[107] indications that the ceremony must have embodied some spiritual power.

The Booger Dance was done in conjunction with other night dancing and was not held as a separate ceremony. Much tension and excitement surrounded the entrance of the Boogers to the house. Forty people sat around waiting for the dance to begin. When the first dancer entered and was questioned about his nationality and identity, he responded by loudly breaking wind. Another dancer followed suit, which gave rise to much laughter. The host then conversed in whispers with the leader. Asking "who the visitors were, where they came from, and where they were going," he then "interprets their answers to the other spectators in the house." The host also asked the dancers if they came from a foreign land or if they were headed either north or south. When asked what they had come for, they decisively answered, "Girls." The Boogers next said that they also want "to fight."[108] Each Booger then gave his name and danced for about five minutes.

The dances involved many awkward and clumsy steps. Every time the dancer's name was called, the crowd applauded and yelled. The dancers did not yell or speak but generally exhibited lust by chasing women around and gesticulating toward them, sometimes pulling out a gourd phallus and thrusting it toward them. After the exhibitions were over, the host asked if dancers would like to do a dance and they generally whispered either the Bear or Eagle Dance, although the Pigeon Dance was permissible. An eagle rite generally took place either before or after the Eagle Dance or Bear Dance. This seems to confirm an 1836 observation that the Booger Dance was associated with the Eagle Dance.

Among the house party were Singers who, at this point, began to sing a song in which the word "tobacco" dominated.[109] This was a demand for tobacco as payment for their office. The Dance Leader (Driver) at that point filled and lit a pipe and took one puff himself while facing the fire with his back to the dancers. He then held the pipe to the mouth of the drummer and each of the singers for a puff of tobacco; then he put the pipe away.

If the dancers performed an Eagle Dance, the Eagle Killer received ceremonial compensation for sacrificing an eagle. After all this took place, women entered the room and danced with the Boogers. Once the women joined the dance, the Boogers began their sexual exhibitions. They sometimes approached women from the rear and feigned intercourse. The women proceeded serenely, unmoved, and the Boogers did not actually touch them. This dance movement symbolized the strength of Cherokees in the face of evil and colonialism, and their ability to maintain their way of life despite temptation and interference. The Boogers now prepared to leave, and they dashed among the women and clumsily tried to drag a struggling victim outside.

Will Pheasant hosted a Booger Dance at his house in Big Cove on the night of January 7, 1936. At that dance, the Leader (Driver) asked the dancers for their identities when they entered, and they responded that they had come from Germany in search of women and then were going back home. The dance then proceeded as discussed above and after the dance was concluded, an intermission ensued. The dancers removed their masks and joined the group, after which a number of dances were performed, including the Women's dance, taken from the second movement of the Green Corn Dance, the Horse Dance, the Beginning Dance, and a Friendship Dance. A number of social dances followed. The participants had the following names: Long Phallus, Sweet Phallus, Piercer, Big Rectum, Sooty Anus, Pudendum Has Long Hairs on It, and Bear.[110]

Boogers portrayed the Cherokee view of European invaders as awkward, ridiculous, lewd, and menacing, and whom they regarded with disdain.[111] The dance functioned to weaken the harmful powers of many Europeans, who, as living beings or ghosts, might cause sickness or misfortune. The Booger Dance could also be recommended by a medicine man as part of a cure for a sick person.[112] Curative Booger dances followed divination by beads and the sick person's family going to water.[113]

Described at times as the Bugah Dance, dancers were sometimes called "Bogies" or "Buggers."[114] In this dance, a drummer with five assistant music makers holding gourd rattles, known as "Callers, positioned themselves on one side of the room."[115] When the Callers had finished their sixth song, the Boogers entered one by one, concealed in their masks and various wraparound materials, and hobbling in very comical positions with odd motions.[116] In one tradition, there were seven Bogies and as the seventh song was played, they went around the room scaring the children who were related to them. After the seventh song, the dancers seated themselves in a comical fashion on a log at one side of the room and the organizer of the dance asked them for their names and where they came from. Replies were always ludicrous or obscene and the place of origin was some remote or fanciful locality.[117] As each individual Booger danced, his name was called out over and over and the dancer engaged in movements consistent with his name. The steps of each solo dancer were totally different from any other Cherokee dance.[118] Following the individual dances, the participants joined in a Bear Dance. Emphasizing the social function of the Booger Dance by displaying joking and familiarity between certain types of relatives, Bogies themselves were said to imitate white people, Black people, or joking relatives.

The Cherokees traditionally performed the Booger Dance in late fall or early winter after the first frost, which clearly linked it with weather because Cherokees feared that the dance could bring on a frost and harm crops if done too early.[119] Most masks represented Indians but a few caricatured whites and Blacks. Some actually had a fierce and warlike expression while others had a witless, dunderheaded look. Most dancers wore baggy suits, old rags, and tattered blankets or sheets, which they had wrapped around themselves. As coauthor Ben Frey notes, the very name Booger Dance is problematic; the word for *mask* (DSPVꞫ, *adutlvdodi*) is very similar to the word for *beggar* (DSWЛꚋУ, *aduladisgi*), and the word for Cherokee *ghost* or *spirit* (ꚋУꞀ, *sgili*) is not similar at all to the word for Booger/beggar. In fact, the similarity between the words for *mask* and *beggar* may revolve around the root word for the verb *want* (OᵒSᖴⱺᎥ, *uduliha*, "he/she wants it"). While a mask is an image one wants to convey to the world (presenting what one seems), a beggar might have been conceived of as a person who is wanting. C. C. Trowbridge (1825) and J. P. Evans (1836) wrote the earliest descriptions of the Booger Dance, and neither mentioned them as being ghosts or Boogers.[120]

James Mooney wrote in the 1880s that masks were worn by certain performers in the Feather or Eagle Dance. The wearers impersonated strangers from another tribe.[121] According to him, the masked figures should be understood as mendicants or travelers from afar rather than ghosts. The close association between the Booger Dance, Eagle Dance, and Bear Dance strengthens the argument that the masked figures represent foreign travelers rather than ghosts. Cherokees traditionally greeted visitors with sourwood wands and attached eagle feathers. This was a highly formalized greeting that is mentioned by a number of eighteenth-century white travelers and was associated with a welcoming dance that appeared to serve in part as a purifying function to neutralize any negative powers brought by the strangers.[122]

That some masks represent Europeans and Americans who carried catastrophic epidemic diseases seems clear. Thus, the Booger Dance accepts the presence of European Americans and seeks to purify their harmful effects by greeting them and sending them on their way.[123] Although it cannot be proven, masked dances among the Cherokees were arguably pre-Columbian. But it is not clear if the Booger Dance as such is an aboriginal dance that took on new meanings after contact or whether it is simply a post-contact dance. If we see the Booger Dance as an admonishment against unrestrained want or desire in Cherokee culture, we can draw parallels to the Anishinaabeg concept of the *windigo*—a being consumed by an endless hunger for human flesh. These analogues would be reasonable for cultures that valued a communitarian ethos, especially when resources could be particularly scarce at times. One scholar conducted an elaborate analysis discussing Iroquois False Face dancing and then tried to draw a connection between the Cherokees and the Iroquois—an assertion with which many Cherokees disagree.

The Cherokee Booger Dance may have originally been a curative ritual that healed disease caused by evil spirits.[124] According to this interpretation, Booger male dancers were "disease-healers" who drove evil spirits from persons. According to some, Booger men represented old people. Boogers sometimes answered that they did not know where they were from and did not know where they were going. Interestingly, in one dance, Booger men had primarily animal names, including Hoot Owl, Skunk, Weasel, Buzzard, Jaybird, Jackrabbit, Pee Wee, Bobcat, and Wall-Eyed Pike.[125] Skits were sometimes associated with the dance of the Booger men, which is quite interesting and calls to mind the clowns of the Pueblo Indians of the Southwest who often enact skits that parody the weaknesses and shortcomings of human beings.[126]

In one dance, the Booger men labored ferociously to tote short pieces of log across the room, causing the crowd to laugh. In another skit, one Booger wore a ferocious warrior mask, while a very small boy was dressed in traditional Indian dress. The Booger warrior carried a tomahawk and the boy carried a tiny bow about a foot long. As the drummer beat a medium-fast beat, the Booger hustled into the ring with quick, jerky motions, brandishing his tomahawk. While this was going on, the little boy walked in, sat on the ground, and began playing with some twigs in a very innocent manner. The Booger warrior advanced until he saw the boy and then raised his tomahawk but knocked his knees together several times, trembling with great nervousness. Then he dashed toward the boy, who stood up with his tiny bow, pulled the string, and shot him in the stomach. The Booger shrieked, turned around, and ran out with the boy running after him.

What does all this mean?

At a psychological level, the Booger masks of the Cherokees may serve to synthesize different parts of the self. Perhaps more importantly, the dance brings together young men and old men so that each participates simultaneously in the other's world. Fogelson notes that a second important feature is that it provides the audience with a ritual enactment of "their own primal and unsocialized qualities."[127] In watching the Boogers dance, Cherokees vicariously live in a non-Cherokee world. This mixing of worlds is multilayered, as it also reflects the intersection of the upper and lower worlds, invoking both duality and dichotomy. The Boogers parody what is basically unacceptable to Cherokee ethics.

In particular, the dance serves to criticize the acts of the Boogers as inimical to the Cherokee way of life, while simultaneously providing space for these kinds of impulses to take place in a controlled and prescribed way. Cherokees simply do not burst into others' houses uninvited, demand women, and perform hostile sexual acts, yet there is a cultural understanding of these impulses and an emphasis on balance between order and disorder. Socially speaking, the dance emphasizes the negative behavior of outsiders—especially Europeans and Americans, who aggressively entered Cherokee lands, took their women, fought with them, and destroyed them with diseases.[128] In other words, the dance reenacts the coming of whites to Cherokee and also serves to counteract the resulting harmful effects of the dominant society.

In the Cherokee mind, the Booger Dance was handed down by Stone Coat in the beginning of time. With respect to its link with outsiders, Stone Coat prophesized the comings of whites as well as Blacks and other Indians from the east. He gave them the Booger Dance as a way of counteracting the evil influences of outsiders.[129]

At some level, the Booger Dance is also a way of curing disease and counteracting evil, especially that brought by outsiders. The Cherokee Booger Dance is thus a curing ritual that not only drives out the evil spirits associated with outsiders but also counteracts the evil effects of witches within Cherokee society. Indeed, the Booger Dance may be prescribed as an auxiliary treatment to scare away evil spirits causing sickness.[130]

But it would be too simple to state that the Booger Dance is only concerned with parodying the negative behavior of outsiders and curing the illnesses caused by them. All human beings have shortcomings and weaknesses, and that includes the Cherokees. Like the clown ceremonies of the Southwest Pueblo Indians, the Booger Dance teaches Cherokees how they are but should not be. When Cherokees laughed at the antics of the Boogers, they did not simply laugh at outsiders. They also laughed at themselves and their own problems as human beings who failed to live up to their idealized standards.

There are also new versions of old ceremonies. For example, coauthor Ben Frey witnessed a "Miss Pretty Legs" competition at the 2016 Cherokee Indian Fair in Cherokee, North Carolina. In a 2019 personal communication, he observed: "This straightforward example of cultural continuity was interesting, but perhaps more intriguing was the Miss Pretty Legs competition. The competition, largely a Cherokee drag show, consisted of several Cherokee men wearing women's clothing and demonstrating off-the-wall 'talents,' possibly in a parody of the more standard Miss Cherokee pageants that occurred yearly alongside Miss Pretty Legs. The other noteworthy aspect of the event was the bawdy presentations and speeches of the contestants. The ribald jokes evoked laughter from the crowd, serving as reminders of the community's social norms through intentional violation of taboos." As Frey watched, he realized "that Miss Pretty Legs was extremely similar to what I had read about the tradition of the Booger Dance. Although the dance was typically written about in the past tense, the underlying spirit and performativity of it seemed to survive in the competition. By adapting the

Booger Dance into the form of a contemporary beauty pageant/drag show, Eastern Band Cherokees had both established a form of cultural continuity that reified traditions and community norms and adapted an ancient tradition to contemporary circumstances."

The ultimate lesson of the Booger Dance is that human beings are far from the perfect spiritual beings that they will become in the next life. Cherokees are not perfect: they know hunger, pain, suffering, death, greed, ignorance, lust, and laziness. By recognizing their weaknesses and limitations, the Booger Dance teaches Cherokees how they should not act. In other words, the Booger Dance simultaneously inspires Cherokees to improve their behavior while simultaneously affirming the sacredness of their humanity. Laughing at their own weaknesses and problems serves to promote humility, forgiveness, and harmony among the people, while driving away evil spirits and curing the sicknesses associated with them.

CHAPTER 4

ᎤᏪᏥ

Cherokee Medicine

Old-time Cherokee religious specialists (ᎠᏗᎾᎩᏍᎩ, *adonisgi*, "sorceror"; plural ᏗᎠᏗᎾᎩᏍᎩ, *dinadonisgi*, "sorcerors") are generally called medicine people, conjurors, physician-priests, or more recently, healers. Elder and storyteller Davy Arch uses the term *conjureman* to describe medicine men. Most sources concentrate on Cherokee men, but women were also connected to medicine. For example, to ward off disease, seven clan women might slowly step around the fire in single file, eventually joined by the other women and girls until they formed a large circle.[1] A great deal of written literature exists on Cherokee "doctoring."

James Mooney wrote the most important work on Cherokee medicine, with the help of a famous Cherokee conjuror, Swimmer, whose Cherokee name was A'yun'ini. Mooney described Swimmer, who died in 1899, as a prominent authority and medicine man of the Cherokees. Mooney started work on the Swimmer manuscript in 1887, when Swimmer was about fifty-three years of age, and he was Mooney's primary consultant on the history, mythology, and medicine of the Cherokees. As Davy Arch says, traditional Cherokee medicine has almost gone "underground." William Lossiah, whom coauthor John Loftin knew and interviewed several times, as chronicled in the epilogue, passed away in 2021. It is hard to say how many traditional conjurors exist in 2021, but a few are still around.

ETHICAL ISSUES SURROUNDING FIELDWORK

Swimmer, after several days of inquiry and investigation, finally told Mooney the myth of the origin of the bear.[2] According to Cherokee mythology, bears were formerly Cherokees who decided to abandon the human way of life and go into the forest. Prior to leaving, the bear people taught Cherokees certain songs that would allow them to hunt bears successfully. The passive, sacred nature of the hunt is denoted through Swimmer's narrative: "It is better for you that we should go; but we will teach you songs, and some day when you are in want of food come out to the woods and sing these songs and we shall appear and give you meat."[3] Swimmer thereby clearly disclosed the receptive and religious nature of hunting and emphasized that successful bear hunts occur because bears surrender themselves to the Cherokees.

Reading Mooney's work reminds one of the ethical issues surrounding fieldwork among Native American peoples. To this very day, Cherokee consultants to this work (one of whom is a conjuror) carefully guard any disclosures that they make about Cherokee spirituality, and sometimes they remain silent when approaching certain sensitive subjects. From an ethnographic standpoint, it is somewhat amazing that a traditional conjuror like Swimmer, from Raven's Place, commonly called Big Cove, would have relayed such detailed information to James Mooney. It is clear that he was hesitant to give much information at first. After telling the bear story, Mooney asked Swimmer if he knew any bear songs, and Swimmer replied that he did. Mooney then requested Swimmer to sing one of the songs, but Swimmer "made some excuse and was silent."[4] Mooney observed that it would do no good to press for more information that day, especially since there were other Cherokees present. The next day, Mooney told Swimmer that he would have to employ someone else as his consultant if he continued to refuse to communicate openly with him. Furthermore, it was unfair for the conjuror to produce an incomplete cultural history when he was paid to tell all that he knew. Swimmer's response was that "he said he was willing to tell anything he knew with regard to stories and customs but that these songs were part of a secret knowledge and brought high prices from hunters who sometimes paid as much as $5.00 for a single song." Swimmer went on to say that hunters were willing to pay that much "because you can't kill any bears or deer unless you sing them."[5]

At first glance, there was more going on here than meets the eye. Mooney eventually was able to get Swimmer to talk by stating that he would record the songs and thereby preserve them, in the end showing the world just how much the Cherokees had known. Swimmer finally agreed to talk freely but only on condition that no one else was present when secret matters were discussed and that nothing should be discussed when other Indians were present. Other conjurors tried to persuade Swimmer to cease communicating with Mooney and hinted that they would damage his reputation by saying that he was giving inaccurate information. These conjurors also argued that this information would ultimately be taken to Washington, DC, and locked up, thereby depriving the Cherokees of sacred knowledge. Mooney noted that this objection was the most difficult of all to surmount because he could think of no argument against it.

Swimmer worried greatly about talking to Mooney, as he was extremely sensitive about his reputation among Cherokees. Finally, however, Swimmer relented and produced some 240 pages of medicinal cures for all kinds of diseases; love charms to attract women; and an array of prayers, including ones for fishing and hunting, growing crops, driving off storms and witches, success in the ball game, and long life and safety. There were prayers to many different gods, among whom Mooney emphasized Long Man, Ancient White, Great War Wind, and Yellow Rattlesnake.[6] Still, despite the fact that many Cherokees acknowledge the significance of Mooney's work in chronicling some of the old Cherokee ways, some Cherokees say that Swimmer "held back" certain powerful spiritual secrets.

The *Payne-Butrick Papers* also detail ethical issues that arose in the course of communications and conversations with a number of important Cherokee consultants. While containing much ethnographic information and serving as a valuable source for traditional Cherokee customs and practices, the papers are nonetheless weakened by their lack of a clear ethnographic theory and methodology and by the attempt to prove that the Cherokees are one of the long-lost Tribes of Israel.[7] The efforts to link Cherokee religion to Judaism at times influenced not only the data collected but the way those data were interpreted. Notwithstanding those limitations and biases, the *Payne-Butrick Papers* are all the more remarkable because of their detailed discussions of the ethical considerations concerning fieldwork.

Cherokee Principle Chief John Ross tried hard to convince John Payne that the very old priestly men, who were little influenced by white culture and Christianity, provided the parallels with Judaism. There are at least three very different possible interpretations of Ross's position. Ross may have been deliberately and consciously trying to draw parallels between aboriginal Cherokee religion and Judaism to show that the Cherokees had a close spiritual relationship with Americans and therefore should be treated as brothers rather than others. However, it may very well be the case that John Ross was sincerely interpreting the syncretistic Cherokee narratives as aboriginal because the Cherokees, by that time, had incorporated parts of the Judeo-Christian tradition into their own. The mythic embodiment of historical change is nothing new to Native Americans, and Cherokees periodically incorporated religiously meaningful new events into their mythic worldview. Finally, it may be the case that in the 1830s there existed some parallels between Cherokee and Judaic religion, which Cherokees understood as connecting the two.

One very impressive letter from Reverend Butrick to John Payne dated December 12, 1840, outlines sophisticated, ethical considerations concerning the information gleaned from Cherokee consultants. Butrick correctly notes that it was very difficult to get any correct information from Cherokees concerning "their ancient religions, customs, and traditions."[8] He mentions several reasons for this difficulty, all of which warrant closer examination. First, Butrick notes that only a few Cherokees were knowledgeable about ancient religious customs, even among the elderly. Second, those who possess knowledge of Cherokee religion received this knowledge in trust and would rather die than betray their people and gods. Third, disclosure of ceremonial secrets can result in death by the gods. Fourth, Cherokees do not wish to offend or fall out of favor with their fellow Cherokees by sharing ceremonial secrets with outsiders. Fifth, Cherokees hold some white people in contempt and consider them irreligious, unprincipled, and crude. Finally, Cherokees do not always tell the truth to outsiders. All the above arguably reflect a defensive cultural strategy designed to protect and preserve the Cherokee way of life.

To Butrick's list, we would add the old ethnographic principle: "Those who know do not say; those who say do not know." Oftentimes in the field, Cherokees too eager to speak to outsiders may, in fact, be persons who are not steeped in knowledge and tradition, whereas conjurors, in particular, are very slow to speak about important spiritual matters, and even then only after they have gotten to know their interviewer. Despite all these difficulties, in the nineteenth century James Mooney was able to acquire a tremendous amount of material from Swimmer and other Cherokee conjurors, as were John Howard Payne and Daniel Butrick.

CHEROKEE CONJURORS

The first point that should be made about Cherokee conjurors is that, traditionally, Cherokees recognized them as a distinguished group called DᏏᏬᎯ (adawe'hi). Mooney defines adawe'hi as "a magician or super-natural being."[9] In other words, there existed at one time among the Cherokees a group of religious specialists who were considered so close to the sacred powers that they were called by the same name as certain supernatural beings. It is not clear when the last Cherokee to achieve this status lived, but by most accounts it was probably sometime in the eighteenth century. At the same time, the term was used by a Cherokee to describe a healer as recently as 2017. Jack and Anna Kilpatrick define adawe'hi as "wizard."[10] The Kilpatricks write that an adawe'hi is a being "spiritual or human of boundless powers and that that is a state that is very rarely achieved by any Cherokee in this world."[11] A common term for medicine man, according to Mooney, is DᏏZᏔᏯ (adanowski, "he cures anyone"), plural ᏗᏏZᏔᏯ (didanowski, "he cures people").[12] The correct word for Cherokee conjuror, described as a physician and priest, is ᏗᏏᏫᏔᏯ (didahnvwisgi), "curer of them."[13] The opposite of a conjuror is a witch, which in Cherokee is denoted by the term ᏗᏏᏁ4Ꮿ (didanesesgi, "putter-in and drawer-out of them").[14]

The distinctions between a witch and a conjuror are blurred at times and, moreover, there are different types of witches. However, at the risk of oversimplification, it might be said that a curer is one who uses their powers in some socially approved manner, whereas a witch does not. A Cherokee conjuror uses their power to support life and to do good, while a Cherokee witch utilizes their articular powers to destroy life and to do evil. More than that cannot be said at this point because of the difficulty in separating these two types of spiritual specialists at their juncture. If pressed, both conjurors and witches would state that they owe their craft to the teachings of Stone Coat, who perished in the long ago.

Raymond Fogelson astutely noted in the 1960s that, although the North Carolina Cherokee at first glance seemed to be quite accultur-ated, Cherokee conjuring still continued in "a vital but atrophied condi-tion."[15] Paradoxically, Cherokee writing using the Sequoyah syllabary, which was originally viewed as a step toward acculturation, has instead promoted conservative traditionalism. This is especially true in North Carolina, where conjurors tend to follow the old formulas written in notebooks in a more rigid fashion than is done in Oklahoma.[16]

Whereas the Cherokees, like other Native Americans, were traditionally an oral culture that did not employ written communication and passed along traditions by word of mouth, the use of the Cherokee syllabary to preserve certain traditions has actually promoted the continued existence and use of a number of spiritual and religious practices. These written formulas have made their way to the written page and are concerned with various aspects of Cherokee life. Interestingly, some of the most esoteric, powerful, and numerous of the spiritual formulas used by healers are love incantations, which are of two basic types: those that attract members of the opposite sex and those that cause the opposite sex to reject other potential suitors.

Cherokees are very careful to repeat the ritualistic language of various sacred formulas and prayers. According to Frans Olbrechts, "whether these are conjurations, incantations, or conventional prayers, a Cherokee conjuror pays more attention to form than content." He goes so far as to say that "the desired result is held to be brought about, not by the meaning of the words used, but merely by strict adherence to the wording and the form."[17] Cherokee conjurors often utilize archaic expressions. Early accounts of Cherokee ritual activities from the eighteenth and nineteenth centuries refer to the use of archaic language, the meaning of which has been lost with time. It is not clear that these are archaic words, which have been repeated in a formulistic way without any meaning, or that the meaning of these terms, taught to them in the beginning, is highly symbolic. Again, the conjuror uses words and techniques that originated soon after the world was formed, and it is for that very reason that they are mysterious. No medicine man would dare change a prayer that was, in effect, learned when the Cherokee way of life was established. The Creator, Stone Coat, and especially Cherokee ancestors taught the Cherokees how to cure illness, find game, bring people together, find lost children, control the weather, and fight evil and witchcraft. Cherokee healers told Olbrechts that "this was the way it was said by the people who lived a long time ago."[18] Hence, Cherokees should strictly follow those ancient ways.

Some prayers are directed to the main beings of Cherokee stories such as the Creator, the Thunderers, Long Human Being (River), Kanati, and Sun. However, many Cherokee sacred formulas contain references to spiritual beings that are never mentioned in the vast corpus of published mythology. Perusing Mooney and Olbrechts, one encounters references to the following (mostly animal spirits linked with a directional color), for example: Red Dog, Blue Dog, Black Dog, White Dog, White Terrapin, Red Spider, Blue Sparrow Hawk, Red Spider, Blue Spider, Black Spider, White Spider, Black Raven, Red Raven, Blue Raven, White Raven, Brown Rock, Little Whirlwind, Black Snake, Yellow Chat, Yellow Frog, Yellow Small Fish, Little Frost, Little Fog, Red Otter, White Fawn-Imitator, White Fish, Little Flint, Little Snow, Purple Blue-Catfish, and White Squirrel. Western Cherokee sources include additional spirit beings whom conjurors invoke in prayer.

Perhaps North Carolina Cherokees are more concerned with form than content. While it is correct in one sense to say that strict adherence to the form brings about the desired results, it is also incorrect in another sense. The Cherokee conjuror is able to do good in the world because he is located in the center of the world. Indeed, both the Eastern and Western Cherokee medicine texts show that the spirits are invoked from the "very middle" of their being to come and aid the healer.[19] In addition, the conjuror directs his prayers to the middle of the sacred's essence and asks that the supernatural spirit direct his power to the center of the patient's souls.

Alan Kilpatrick, a Cherokee, has outlined the very state of being centered spiritually, denoted by the Cherokee term DꞵCG (*ayehliyu*, "the very middle").[20] The middle denotes equilibrium in an ultimate sense and is considered the spiritual goal of all Cherokees. Heidi Altman and Cherokee Tom Belt describe the Cherokee cosmos in its normal state as *tohi*, which means smoothly flowing, not rushed; fluid and peaceful. The word OⱱGVAꝋƠ° (*nvwatohiyadv*) is rendered as peace, health, well-being, and harmony. A common Cherokee greeting is VAꝺ (*tohitsu*), which literally means "Are you at peace?"[21]

THEORIES OF DISEASE

The Cherokees have a number of different theories for the cause of disease, but almost all involve a spiritual power. A primary Cherokee myth involving the origin of disease held that in the old days, all animals, plants, and people lived together in peace and harmony. However, people began to expand so quickly that they infringed on the land of others, and they also began to slaughter various animals for food and clothing, while smaller creatures were simply crushed by people as they walked about. The bears held a council led by the old White Bear and they decided to use bows and arrows so that they could defend themselves against humans. One bear sacrificed himself so that his gut could be used for the string. However, bears could not shoot bows and arrows because of their long claws and decided that it was better to use their god-given teeth and claws. At that point, the bear council was dismissed. Next, the deer held a council and decided that whenever a hunter killed a deer, Little Deer would quickly run to the spot and ask the spirit of the slain deer if the hunter had prayed for forgiveness. If the answer was no, Little Deer would invisibly strike the hunter with rheumatism. Snakes and fish devised their own forms of disease, and so did birds, insects, and other small animals. When the plants heard what was happening, they decided to help human beings, and so the trees, shrubs, herbs, grasses, and mosses devised cures to remedy the diseases caused by vengeful animals.

In Cherokee eyes, disease is caused, first and foremost, by animals killed by humans. Plants offer cures for many of these diseases, and Cherokee medicine people are very knowledgeable in observing and "listening" to plants that offer themselves for medicinal purposes. Cherokee doctors and other knowledgeable elders possess great knowledge of the local plants in their area.[22] J. T. Garrett, a Cherokee who worked for several years with a renowned Cherokee medicine man, has published some popular works in which he discusses a number of Cherokee medicinal plants (while carefully preserving ceremonial secrets).[23] Medicinal plants are primarily the province of conjurors who guard this information carefully and are slow to share it with anyone, especially outsiders. Cherokee conjuring is shrouded in great mystery, although there are a number of publications regarding medicinal chants and prayers taken directly from the notebooks of Cherokee conjurors in North Carolina and Oklahoma.[24]

This notion of vengeful animals carries more of a religious meaning than might appear at first glance. Animals are symbolic of the sacred, and the act of hunting is itself considered an exercise of human volition over and against the sacred. When a Cherokee hunter asks forgiveness from a deer, he is asking forgiveness from the sacred as manifested through the deer. It is not the animal per se that creates disease, although that is the way the myth frames it. Rather, disease is caused by human transgression against the sacred. This is a common theme.[25] In other words, at times Cherokees understand disease to be fundamentally the result of divine retribution.[26]

There are other causes of disease, but it's ultimately caused by spiritual, not material, forces. Even when discussing obvious physical injuries that result from incidents like breaking a leg when falling, Cherokees may come to the conclusion that "the Little People" or "the

Mountain People" are angry with them and caused them to be injured.[27] Perceiving a spiritual force behind a physical injury is typical of a number of Native American peoples and should always be taken into consideration when studying Cherokee disease and medicine. Anglos and Cherokees may view the same event very differently. For example, if someone slipped from a ledge and fell several feet onto hard rocks, breaking a leg, an Anglo might be quick to interpret that in very physical terms. They would likely say that the impact of falling several feet against a hard object caused the victim's leg to break. All that is true, and Cherokees are certainly aware of those sorts of physical dynamics. However, a Cherokee, upon reflection, might inquire why the person fell from the ledge, likely ascribing causation to some spiritual force. For that reason, it is fair to say that in many cases, traditional Cherokees understand disease to be caused by some supernatural power, which requires a supernatural remedy.

The list of disease-causing spirits among Cherokees is quite long. The Swimmer manuscript contains a chart several pages long, listing the spirit, where it resides, and the disease it causes and cures.[28] The Sun, whom Mooney and Olbrechts interpret to have been the Creator or Great Spirit of the Cherokees, which is itself a very debatable assertion, nevertheless was clearly an important god among the traditional Cherokee. He is rarely the cause of disease, but appears to cause headaches in those who disrespect him. One myth states that the Sun causes fever because she hates to see her grandchildren twist their faces when looking at her.[29]

Fire, an important deity, is closely linked with the Sun and was perhaps traditionally seen as an incarnation of the Sun. Fire is known sometimes as Ancient White or Ancient Red.[30] Although some outside observers seem confused about the gender of Fire, Fire is sometimes referred to as DSBᏢᏂ (agayvlige, "Ancient Lady").[31] Fire is generally invoked as a cure against all diseases caused by cold-blooded animals and is used in conjunction with a number of cures.

The Moon, which probably played an important part in Cherokee religion through the nineteenth century, is associated with going to water, since that ritual was traditionally performed with every new moon. Moreover, the Moon often figures prominently in the religious orientation of hunting cultures, and it is clear that Cherokees surrounded the hunt with much ritual and religious meaning. To a Cherokee, the Moon is male and seems to have been the cause of very few diseases except blindness. It is interesting to note that the Cherokee language does not have separate words for Sun and Moon. The Sun is simply, "the luminary that is (that lives in the daytime)" while the Moon is "the luminary that is (that lives in the nighttime)."[32]

The Cherokees call the River by several names: EΘЛႦ DᎥᏚᏍᏫ (*gvnahida asgaya*, "Long Man") or EΘЛႦ BΘ (*gvnahida yvwi*, "Long Human Being"), or sometimes EΘЛႦ TΘႦ (*gvnahida inada*, "Long Snake").[33] The River sends disease to those who disrespect it by dumping garbage or urinating in it. When ceremonies are performed by conjurors at the river, efforts are made to choose a spot at a bend in the river where the patients can face east.[34]

Thunder, who is also called Red Man, has two sons who are called the two Little Red Men. A heavy, rolling crash of thunder is said to be the voice of Thunder himself, whereas softer claps of thunder are said to be his sons.[35] The Cherokees say that Thunder is their friend and that few Cherokees have ever been struck by lightning. Having said that, there is one Cherokee conjuror who has been struck by lightning and who attributes some of his healing powers to that event. Thunder does not cause disease but rather expels it. Indeed, thunder is considered to be the enemy of the Black Man, who is said to reside in the Black Land or Darkening Land or Abode of the Dead.[36] The only time that Thunder causes disease is when the Cherokees violate taboos related to him.

Spirits or spiritual people live in each of the various directions. The Black Man, living in the west, is associated with death. In the north live both the Purple Man associated with witchcraft and evil, and the Blue Man associated with cold. All three are opposed to the Red Man who is linked with the east and victory. There is also a group of small spiritual beings that the Cherokees call the Little People.[37] Accounts of them vary greatly but generally speaking, they live in different groups, reside in settlements like humans, and are usually invisible, although some persons can see and communicate with them. They are very mischievous and can both help and hurt humans.

Another cause of disease among the Cherokees is human ghosts. Many of these are deceased persons who are very lonely and miss contact with their family and friends. Lonesome ghosts attempt to make their friends sick and die so that the newly deceased will come visit them. Animal spirits are responsible for most diseases. Human ghosts tend to "spoil the saliva" of victims, which results in more psychological symptoms, whereas animal ghosts tend to cause more physical symptoms such as rheumatism, dysentery, swelling, and headache.[38]

Witchcraft, the most feared and dreaded of all disease causes, is widespread among Native Americans and is the subject of many myths.[39]

Arguably, the most famous of the Cherokee witches is Stone Coat, who killed many Cherokees until the power of the blood of seven menstruating Cherokee women destroyed him. In some accounts, Stone Coat was responsible for bringing death among the Cherokees, but he was also responsible for creating much of Cherokee culture. Generally speaking, witches in Native American societies are human beings who seek to prolong their own lives by taking the life of others.[40] Swimmer referred to witches as ᏥᏍᎩᎵ (*tsikili*, "they walk about during the night").[41] Witches are "powerful wizards" and are always associated with concepts that express baseness, meanness, slyness, and an activity that is insidious, nefarious, and deleterious.[42]

Raven Mocker (Ravenmocker), the most feared type of witch, is especially associated with a purplish light flying through the night sky. Cherokees say that Raven Mocker literally steals the breath of his victims.[43] This powerful witch probably bears some relationship to the ancient Cherokee war title of Raven, whose duties involved scouting the enemies at night.[44] John Haywood, in 1823, described witches that can take the form of a bird or beast but are generally seen as cats or owls.[45] Cherokee witches today are especially associated with the owl. Some translate the one Cherokee word for *witch* (ᏥᏍᎩᎵ, *tsisgili*) as "hoot owl."[46] Alan Kilpatrick implies that this may be a linguistic oversight because both the hoot owl and the barn owl are known as ᎤᎫᎦ (*uguku*). He notes that his own parents translated *tsisgili* as "long-eared owl" because that bird was so hated and feared.[47] However, he also notes that Cherokee witches have been known to carry out their activities in the guise of the screech owl (ᏩᎤᎯ, *wahuhi*), and so it would seem that all classes of owls now are identified by the term *tsisgili*.

Another class of humans bent on harming others are called "Man Killers" (ᏗᏓᏁᏎᎩᏍᎩ, *didanesegiski*). Whereas the evil process of witches is not clearly understood, Man Killers are said to "change the food in a victim's stomach" or "cause the food to sprout," thereby making someone very sick. Above all, Man Killers are said to shoot invisible arrows into the bodies of victims to make them sick.[48] Very few people achieve this status, which requires many years of study.

Jack and Anna Kilpatrick observed that there is another form of witch called ᎠᏁᎵᏍᎩ (*anelisgi*), which is translated as "those who think purposely" or, more simply, "thinkers."[49] These are people who project evil onto other human beings through their own thought processes. Thinkers may exist only among Western Cherokees, although Eastern Cherokees call one group ᎤᏲ ᏣᏪᏍᎩᏴ (*uyo igaweskiquu*, or "imprecator").[50]

An Eastern Cherokee informant in 1959 said that this term means "bad talker, bad conjuror, or curser." Accordingly, the Western Cherokee term "thinker" and the Eastern Cherokee term "imprecator" may refer to the same kind of people.[51]

The Eastern Cherokees live by a set of customs that Robert Thomas called the "Harmony Ethic."[52] Although there does not seem to be a particular Cherokee term corresponding to Thomas's brilliant observation, Jack Kilpatrick discussed a term referring to the Cherokee commitment to proper human relations. Cherokees use the term SGAᎢ (duyugodv), which defies precise translation but connotes terms such as just, right, straight, honest, true, and upright—in essence, "the right way."[53] The sense of propriety in Cherokee relations has led to the classification of two types of persons. A Cherokee is either OᏏᏬᎫ (udanvti), meaning a person with soul, heart, or feeling, whose behavior is summarized as kind; or they're OᎥᎵᎫKᎢ (unegutsodv), which means "evil" or "mean." This classification does not distinguish between good and evil but rather between kind and evil. Interestingly, after contact, the Cherokees, traditionally looked at white people as "being more than anything else, mean people."

RITUAL SMOKING

The Cherokees, like most Native Americans, ritually smoked native tobacco in a wide variety of contexts, including several different religious ceremonies.[54] The Cherokees used tobacco aboriginally, but the available evidence suggests that smoking, while spiritually significant, was not performed routinely. Early observers rarely report tobacco use among the Cherokees, and when they do, the references are scant.[55] Nevertheless, Cherokees did use tobacco in a wide variety of contexts, many of which were religious. For example, the Cherokees used tobacco as a sacred incense, to seal solemn oaths in many important functions, to send a warrior off to war against the enemy, to ratify peace treaties, and to confirm business transactions.[56] Spiritually, tobacco was used to predict success or failure in hunting, to drive away witches and evil spirits, and to prepare for herbal medical practice and in medicine involving prayers. Cherokees did not roll tobacco into cigars. Instead, they either smoked it in a pipe or threw it onto a fire. The Cherokee name for ancient tobacco is KW (tsola, "tobacco"), or KW DSBᏝ (tsola agayvli), literally, "tobacco old woman." Mooney attempted to translate it from a Tuscaroran cognate, which essentially meant "fire to hold in the mouth," but it is fair to say that the word cannot be translated today.[57] Cherokee native tobacco today is called "ancient tobacco" and differs from commercial tobacco.

In Cherokee mythology, tobacco is most often mentioned in a medical context.[58] In one myth, a Cherokee became friends with a group of strangers who lived at Pilot Knob inside a cave that opened up to a regular countryside with bottomland and hundreds of people. At one point in the myth, the Cherokee protagonist took a Cherokee friend with him to prove that the people existed, but his companion's legs died as they entered the cave door. The companion staggered and fell to the ground. A medicine man from the mysterious group brought him "old tobacco," rubbed it on his legs, and had him sniff it until he sneezed. At that point, the man was able to stand again and went with his friend and others to watch a dance that included a drummer.[59]

The Cherokees have myths about the origin of tobacco, which Mooney entitled "How They Brought Back The Tobacco."[60] Interestingly, the first version of the myth begins "in the beginning of the world, when people and animals were all the same."[61] Everyone shared a sole tobacco plant until certain geese stole it and carried it far to the south, an act that caused much suffering. The geese killed every animal that tried to rescue the plant. Eventually, however, Hummingbird was able to dart down and grab the top of the plant and fly off before the geese were able to respond. Equipped with tobacco, Hummingbird returned home, where he blew tobacco smoke into the nostrils of a sick old woman, bringing her back to good health.[62] In a second version, a conjuror turns himself into a hummingbird and recovers tobacco.[63]

The lack of evidence of Cherokee tobacco use does not mean that they failed to avail themselves of it. Pipes were regularly included in grave goods in early Cherokee burials, and tobacco is still used by medicine people in a number of curing ceremonies.[64] For example, tobacco is used for treating snake bites, faintness, headache, back pains, and blackening of the areas around the eyes and lips.[65] Furthermore, it was used to cure children who constantly cried, and provided a treatment for boils and ringworm as well as toothaches.

For the Cherokees, tobacco in and of itself contains no spiritual qualities and therefore must be "remade" by a medicine man. The remaking of tobacco begins with planting. Traditionally, a medicine man prepared a small patch of ground with a piece of wood struck by lightning. In Cherokee religious orientation, such wood carries great spiritual power. It is considered an especially good omen if it thunders on the day the tobacco is planted. Tobacco for ceremonial usage is planted in a secret place and great pains are taken to hide the small patch from any visitors.[66] When harvesting this old tobacco, a medicine man says or sings a prayer over it four to seven times to infuse the plant with spiritual power. Done at dawn, if possible, the ceremony takes place on the bank of a stream facing east.[67]

To remake tobacco, a medicine man first chews and then blows upon it. In the Cherokee view, saliva and breath contain the spiritual essence of a person and this essence is imparted to the tobacco through chewing and blowing. The medicine man then places the tobacco in his left hand and kneads it with four fingers of the right hand, rolling it in a counter-clockwise motion.[68] Sometimes other ingredients are added, depending on the ritual purpose at hand. For example, cedar leaves turn away witches and threaded grapevine attracts a mate. Remade tobacco must be shielded from the powers of pregnant or menstruating women, as well as dead people or persons who have been in contact with the dead.[69] The mere presence of those people weakens the spiritual power of sacred tobacco. Traditionally, Cherokees who handled or were in contact with the dead had to be ritually purified before reentering the community.

Tobacco serves as a medium through which one addresses the spiritual powers at the four corners of the world. Usually, Cherokees blow the tobacco smoke toward the four cardinal directions by pivoting around in one place. Each of the four directions has various important associations: east symbolizes success, power, red, blood, life, sacred fire, direction of the sun, and home of Thunder, while west connects to the souls of the dead, black, death, moon, and oblivion. North signifies cold, blue and purple, trouble, defeat, failure, and spiritual depression; and south symbolizes warmth, white, peace, purity, and happiness.[70]

Several ritual uses of tobacco included connecting to the east. Before rekindling the sacred fire during the Green Corn festival, the Chief Beloved Man would place a few roots of the button snakeroot, some leaves of the tobacco plant, and seven ears of new corn into the bottom of the hearth.[71] Tobacco was also used in times of too much rain. On those occasions, Cherokees would offer tobacco to the Woman of the East (Sun) along with a prayer for her to stop the rain.[72] Members of war councils often smoked tobacco in pipes.[73] Before war or when traveling long distances, medicine men held remade tobacco in both hands, at dawn, while extending their arms slowly up and down, across the face of the rising sun.[74]

One hunting divination ritual involves sweeping ashes into a cone and sprinkling some tobacco dust on top. Dust bursting into flames predicted big game.[75] Tobacco was—and still is—used during the ball game. Placing remade tobacco on the field where the opposing players are likely to walk serves as a prayer for their bad luck and misfortune. Also, players blow smoke upon themselves four times as a ritual to nullify the opponent's attempts at magic.

Tobacco has also been ritually used in connection with the west. Ancient tobacco smoke was blown in the direction of the enemies to destroy them. For centuries, Cherokees used pipes as grave goods, and it is understood that at death Cherokees travel west to the Nightland or the Darkening Land of the West.[76] Tobacco is thus linked with the west and the afterlife.

The south—associated with peace, purity, and happiness—has also figured into purity rituals with tobacco. For example, on the second day of the Green Corn Festival, one of the beloved old men placed ancient tobacco outside of the sacred square ground so that all the men unable to enter the sacred ground due to illness, impurity, or lack of stature could take it.[77] Also, the head priest, during his four-day fast prior to the Green Corn Festival, ate only button snakeroot and ancient tobacco for purification purposes.[78] Medicine men who performed the ritual of "going to water" for relatives of a deceased person chewed tobacco and sprayed the juice over the next of kin as they stood facing east at the water's edge.[79]

Tobacco is also used in a number of rituals associated with the north and with loneliness and spiritual depression. Spiritual depression can lead to death if it is not treated properly. In one ritual, a medicine man "goes to the water" at dawn while remaking tobacco, or infusing it with new spiritual power. Once he gets to the edge of the river, he faces east, washes his face, and gathers a small amount of debris from the river, which he burns, rubbing the ashes on his forehead and chest. He uses coals from the fire to light the tobacco in a pipe, which he smokes on his way home, blowing four clouds of smoke in the direction of the woman he wishes to make lovesick. Tobacco is also used to force an undesirable person to move out of the community. Here, tobacco is remade on four successive mornings and then smoked at dawn, mid-morning, mid-afternoon, and sunset. To separate lovers or mates, medicine people will blow the smoke of remade tobacco toward their abode at dawn, noon, and dusk for four days.[80]

North is associated with purple, which is connected with witchcraft, and especially with Raven Mockers, as they are said to be capable of taking the shape of a purple flash of light.[81] Tobacco is used to divine whether evil forces are in an area, particularly around the house of a gravely ill person.[82] To divine the presence of a Raven Mocker, ashes from the hearth are swept into a cone and tobacco dust is sprinkled on top of it. If the tobacco clings together and lands on top of the center of the ashes, it signals that a witch is in the house, although invisible. If the tobacco bursts into flames, its medicine kills any witch present. However, if the tobacco does not catch fire but only sparkles like a star, it indicates that the witch's power is stronger than that of the medicine man.[83] In one formula, a medicine man uses tobacco to bring death to a witch who lurks around the house of a sick person. Here, a medicine man drives four sharp sticks into the ground at the four corners outside the house, with the pointed ends up. At noon he fills his pipe with ancient tobacco, repeats a prayer, wraps the pipe in black cloth, and sets it aside. At dusk, he lights the pipe and circles the house in a counter-clockwise direction, praying and blowing tobacco smoke toward every trail the Raven Mocker might use to approach the house. When the witch approaches, a pointed stick shoots up like an arrow, and the witch will die within seven days.[84]

By remaking tobacco, a conjuror infuses it with his life force and soul. From there, one can communicate a spiritual message to the Four Corners by "reasserting a oneness with the Cherokee universe."[85] As Ethridge notes, "the process of 'remaking' and the ritual manner of smoking, all of which serve as my basis for the assertion that tobacco has a symbolic function to the Cherokee as an intervening substance through which one solemnly declares his spiritual continuum with the forces of the universe."[86] Ritual smoking of tobacco is very widespread in native North America. It seems to be a very old ritual prayer rite, which involves the supplication of and participation in the sacred essence that creates and sustains the cosmos.[87]

The Cherokees ritually smoked tobacco at a variety of times in a variety of settings. Cherokees refer to tobacco that has been remade as "ancient tobacco" or as "white tobacco"—КМЛE (*tsolunegv*).[88] Jack and Anna Kilpatrick state that remade tobacco is made more effective if it is done facing east by a stream at dawn and if it is powdered with KWSBP (*tsolagayvli*).[89] Oftentimes, smoking is a prayer offering to the persons or gods located in the four cardinal directions. Although directions are associated with these "persons," the anthropomorphism of the cardinal directions references a later stage in ancient Cherokee life. When a Cherokee medicine man offers tobacco to each of the four directions, he is reestablishing the Cherokees' position in the center of the world.

A conjuror sometimes goes through a series of incantations exclaiming that he is "in the middle of a great lake, in the middle of a great brush land, in the middle of a great sun, in the middle of a great mountain." In one prayer, a conjuror says, "I can see my white feet there in the middle."[90] Kilpatrick emphasizes the psychological calm of this state, as being located in the center more fundamentally embodies a specifically spiritual dimension.

Tobacco smoke is used by the Cherokees both as a supplication of the divine and a medium through which a Cherokee concentrates and focuses his soul to establish unity with the Creator. It is the latter understanding that has been erroneously referred to as "magical" in the sense of James Frazer. Cherokees may participate in the sacred to the extent that they align their breath with the Provider or the sacred essence of the cosmos. Many Cherokee myths begin by discussing how all was the same in the beginning, and how humans and animals, for example, could communicate freely with one another and could even transform themselves into one another. In this timeless period, Cherokees lived in very close relationship with the sacred and could thus bring about certain results by properly relating the spiritual essence of themselves to the spiritual essence of the universe. By using tobacco, a medicine man "strengthens the spiritual umbilical cord to the universe, thus linking his power of thought and being to the overwhelming and omnipotent universal powers."[91] A traditional Cherokee followed age-old instructions that were given in the beginning of time, which allowed him to communicate directly with the Provider to bring about important results.

Interestingly, there is no ethnographic evidence in the published literature that states tobacco was used to produce rain for the Cherokees. There were rainmaking rituals, but none involved the use of tobacco.[92] Ironically, unlike a number of Native American tribes for whom tobacco smoke was seen as a microcosmic image of rain clouds, which were used as a prayer for rain, Cherokees apparently used tobacco only to stop torrential rains. For the Cherokees, it seems rain was associated especially with the Sun, and she was offered tobacco if the village was flooded. Thus, when a Cherokee Indian ritually smoked tobacco to help the crops, to ensure success in war, or to defeat an evil conjuror, he simultaneously wished for the desired results. Cherokees prayed often through some material mode, such as tobacco, precisely because they discerned that nature contains a spiritual essence.[93]

Cherokees regard the life and forms of their cosmos as revelations or manifestations of the sacred. It is not that Cherokees perceive their world and then logically infer that the world contains a spiritual undergirding; rather, their perception embodies the experience of the spiritual. Cherokees discern their gods whenever and wherever certain cosmic events, such as rain, lightning, thunder, birth, and death, are manifested. Cherokees do not hear thunder and infer that it is caused by either the Little Men of the North or the Greater Man of the West. Instead, where thunder reveals itself—when Cherokees hear thunder—they experience the presence of the Thunders or the Thunder. The Cherokees have many gods, but they are not polytheistic. Rather, Cherokees understand that the sacred manifests itself through the various forms and rhythms of the cosmos. Cherokees are well aware that there is one sacred principle that reveals itself in many modes of manifestation.

Cherokee prayer involves a ritual act and a particular way of thinking. When a Cherokee prays, he utilizes activities taught at the beginning of time, thereby reactualizing creation.[94] A Cherokee medicine man smokes tobacco or performs some other ritual act to make good crops, find a lost person, heal the sick, or repel an enemy. He places himself in the middle of the universe, in the time before there was time. Alan Kilpatrick refers to this as "time conflation" and notes that generally most Cherokee incantations used the curious verb suffix -iga ("the subject has just come [to do something]").[95]

For example, in performing a number of different spells, a Cherokee medicine man will say something such as "You have just come to untie it," or "You have just come to wrap around it," or "You have just come to strike it."[96] By using this -iga suffix, a speaker signifies that "at the time of speaking the action has just been performed."[97] In other words, "this ritualistic moment is now being actualized by the speaker's presence."[98] Therefore, as Kilpatrick puts it, the medicine man is able to "conflate" time and bring about the prayer's goal instantaneously. If one reads a large number of Cherokee medicine and spiritual texts, it becomes apparent that the conjuror more often *wills* the desired result than he *wishes* for it. That is to say, he unifies himself with the very spiritual essence that brings about the sought-after effect. At the same time, medicine people both supplicate and participate in the sacred, and both prayer acts show the sacred to be both immanent and transcendent. In either case, their acts show that they experience the sacred passively—that is, as creating them before they project themselves in the world. In saying this, it is important to remember that when a Cherokee healer directs the gods to heal the sick, it is not them, strictly speaking, who participates in the sacred, but rather their breath and saliva, which are part and parcel of the Supreme Being.[99]

The paradoxical nature of Cherokee prayer acts might be uncovered by distinguishing prayer from conjuration.[100] In one group of formulas, a Cherokee voices a desire to a power that is clearly superior and upon whom the supplicant feels dependent. Here, it is important that the supplicant express the desire humbly; the desired result cannot be forced or extorted from the spiritual being. In such a case, the Supreme Being cannot be commanded or compelled to act. Such prayers are different from conjurations, in which one addresses a power—not necessarily superior—by command, coercion, or even threats and insults. In conjurations there is "absolute certainty that the desire will materialize if the ceremony is performed properly."[101] Prayers refer to requests of the Creator, who is perceived as transcendent and distant from Cherokees; in this case, Cherokees pray with a humble heart and ask that God bless them by granting their requests. On the other hand, conjurations refer to prayer acts in which a medicine man, utilizing techniques taught "ever since the time of long ago,"[102] participates in beloved power according to their will and volition. In this case, it is not the conjuror as a human being who makes his wish come true, but the soul within him, who is raised to the seventh heaven, where it is unified with the Supreme Being.[103]

PART TWO

After Contact

CHAPTER 5

The Contact Era

1540–1760

Up to this point, the book has concentrated on aboriginal and traditional Cherokee religious experience and expression. Examining the essential patterns of traditional Cherokee religion, previous chapters took a more structural view of Cherokee religious practice. In reality, all religions unfold in history and none remain the same for very long. Even prior to the arrival of and brief contact with the Spanish in 1540, the Cherokees were undergoing historical change and transformation. No doubt Cherokees borrowed from other Native American tribes around them, and they also experienced internal modifications to their culture and traditions. But those changes did not call into question, in a fundamental way, core Cherokee values and traditions.

A different kind of change occurred with the arrival of Europeans. English and American settlers and their governments brought about unprecedented, and at times devastating, threats to the Cherokee way of life. The next chapters, 5–11, concentrate on the religious significance of contact with the newcomers from across the great water and the various creative spiritual strategies the Cherokees embodied to make their world meaningful.

ENGLISH CONTACT

English contact with Cherokees brought about a new order in at least three distinct and overlapping stages.[1] First, Old World diseases killed large numbers of natives who had no immunity to such diseases. Next came traders who exchanged European goods and technologies for Native American products and brought those people into the developing "world market."[2] Finally, overwhelming numbers of settlers arrived to occupy and develop the land according to a European vision.[3]

Early European documents say very little about how disease and slave raiding affected the Cherokee in the late 1600s and early 1700s. For example, there is no written record of the effects of the 1696 smallpox epidemic among the Cherokees.[4] However, the Cherokee population may have been reduced by some 50 percent, from 32,000 in 1685 to 16,000 in 1700.[5] Colonial censuses in 1708 and 1715 show that the Cherokee population continued to decline to about 11,000. There exists little documentation concerning the number of Cherokee enslaved between 1670 and 1715, but the number is likely in the hundreds, perhaps a thousand—a small number compared to other surrounding tribes. There is some evidence that, by 1690, the first South Carolina traders were entering the lower Cherokee villages and that Cherokees were beginning to abandon their settlements north of the Little Tennessee Valley and consolidate their villages along the Little Tennessee and Hiwassee Rivers to the Southeast.[6]

Much has been written about the deerskin trade established between Europeans and various Native American groups in the late seventeenth and early eighteenth centuries. The Cherokees were little known compared to the other large southeastern Indian tribes, such as the Creek, Chickasaw, and Choctaw. In fact, most of the Cherokee villages were able to maintain some distance from the English until the beginning of the Yamasee War in 1715, whereas tribes such as the Westo, Savannah, and Yamasee suffered terrible consequences during the early contact period with South Carolina in the late seventeenth and early eighteenth century.

European maps during the late seventeenth and eighteenth centuries show that the Cherokee territory was relatively unknown by both French and English mapmakers. The two earliest maps referencing Cherokee were drawn in 1682 and 1701 by French cartographers.[7] These maps suggest the Europeans were beginning to understand that the Cherokees represented a large population in the pre-Yamasee War years. Compared with the Chickasaw, Choctaw, and Creek, Cherokee participation in the deerskin trade from 1670 to 1715 occurred on a much smaller scale. Cherokees had some contact with Europeans, and by 1670, evidence points to a century-long chain of trade with Europeans. Spanish iron tools, brass ornaments, and glass beads have turned up in a number of archaeological sites in eastern Tennessee and western North Carolina.[8] Also, historical and archaeological evidence suggests that some Cherokee villages traded with Virginians at least indirectly during the last half of the seventeenth century.[9] By 1690, South Carolinians appear to have begun trading with the Cherokee.[10]

Nevertheless, European traders seem to have largely forsaken Cherokee settlements during this early contact period. Some English accounts seem to show contempt for the Cherokee, who did not offer quick riches in the way other tribes did.[11] Indeed, as late as 1713, English trader Pryce Hughes commented that "of the many nations I've seen . . . these (Cherokee) keep up their old customs in their greatest purity."[12] Moreover, Cherokee involvement in the Indian slave trade seems minimal when compared with groups like the Westo, Savannah, Yamasee, Tallapoosa, and Chickasaw. In fact, prior to 1700, the Cherokees were more likely victims rather than active participants in slavery.

Cherokees, by and large, stayed out of the Yamasee War, although a few towns did get involved. However, the Cherokee and Creek, traditional enemies, fought for years between 1716 and 1727.[13] This prolonged warfare hurt trading in the area to such an extent that the governor of South Carolina, in 1727, convened peace talks in Charleston between Cherokee and Creek representatives. The two promised to cease their raids and to pledge their friendship to the English.[14]

The Yamasee War brought the Cherokee fully into the European trade network. From that point forward, South Carolinians aggressively sought trade with the Cherokee and initiated more vigorous diplomatic strategies. It is not clear whether Cherokees actively sought the South Carolinians or whether they simply found themselves confronted with them at every turn, but the Yamasee War certainly changed life for the Cherokees in a fundamental way. The Cherokee alliance with the English in the Yamasee War and their protracted raiding against the Creeks brought the Cherokees into sharp European focus. Whereas in 1713 trader Pryce Hughes lamented that the Cherokees were little known, by 1720 the colony had produced a substantial body of knowledge regarding the Cherokee, including accurate and comprehensive maps depicting the locations of individual towns, town censuses, and numerous records related to the deerskin trade.[15]

In less than a century, the Cherokees had begun to participate dramatically in the deerskin trade and became important to England's colonial ambitions. The Yamasee War was devastating in the minds of South Carolinians because it brought about the cessation of trade in Indian slaves and the loss of trade with the Creek and Yamasee, two of the most prolific suppliers of deerskins. These losses created a vacuum, which the Cherokees were called upon to fill, since they were the only friendly Indian group large enough to replace Creek and Yamasee trade. Although they could no longer maintain an isolationist strategy, Cherokees recognized their own need for firearms and ammunition to compete against enemy tribes and to participate in the deerskin trade. In 1716, South Carolina's government gave hundreds of guns to both the Upper and Lower Cherokee settlements. Cherokee participation in deerskin trading at that point exploded. Between 1716 and 1718, Cherokee trading factories generated more deerskins than all the other trading factories combined. Cherokees also received twice as many trading privileges as the other groups during the same period. At the same time, Cherokees sought to befriend the Virginians to have another trading partner who could benefit them. This caused South Carolina to lower prices for the Cherokees, which effectively eliminated the Virginians as a serious trading partner.[16]

South Carolina conducted two major diplomatic missions to Cherokee in 1715 and 1725. They discovered some factionalism among the Cherokees, which ran along regional and generational lines.[17] The Cherokees, as noted earlier, were not a unified nation but a loosely held confederation of some sixty autonomous villages that were not controlled by any national political body. South Carolinians were very concerned about competition with French traders at that time, and the English were determined to be the Cherokees' trading partners, beating out the French.[18]

Much to the frustration of South Carolina diplomats, the Cherokee remained, from 1715 to 1740, a people whose government rested on consensus but was divided along regional and generational lines. Nevertheless, in 1730, under considerable pressure, the Cherokees agreed to elect an emperor named Moytoy to effectually centralize the government and give the appearance of a nationalized government with whom the English could trade and negotiate treaties. Then in 1738, just when it seemed that Cherokees were beginning to adjust to their newfound relationship with the English, smallpox ravaged the community.[19] This epidemic caused the Cherokees to rethink their political, social, economic, and religious ties to Europeans. Interestingly, conjurors reported that smallpox was caused by divine anger at widespread adultery by young married people over the course of the previous year.[20] The 1738 smallpox epidemic was so severe and the conjurors' efforts to stop its spread so unsuccessful that many conjurors discarded their gear and several committed suicide in utter despair. By the seventeenth and eighteenth centuries, as Charles Hudson observed, southeastern Indians were no longer simply Mississippian chieftains operating within an aboriginal world. As he put it, "They were a new kind of people in a new kind of world."[21] In short, the Cherokees, like other southeastern Indians, were introduced into the modern world-system.[22]

RELIGION AND THE COMMERCIALIZATION OF THE DEERSKIN TRADE

No one can seriously doubt that the combined forces of European contact, warfare, colonization, disease, Christian missionization, and commercial fur and skin trade vigorously challenged the meaning, value, and purpose of aboriginal Native American spiritual life.[23] Epidemic diseases such as smallpox decimated native populations and called into question the efficacy of traditional healing, at least with respect to those diseases. Dependence on European trade goods, especially guns and ammunition, became widespread. Commercial hunting of deer for the European skin trade resulted in their depopulation. Since deer provided most of the meat and skins for the Cherokee diet and material culture, this decline in game during the course of the eighteenth century had a major effect on Cherokee lives, including their religion.

Within this context, Christian missionaries made their greatest mark on Native people including, to a degree, the Cherokees, although the impact was minimal until the early nineteenth century. Cherokee missionary activity did not begin in earnest until 1799, approximately five years after the Cherokees finally surrendered once and for all to the United States of America.[24] At that point, Cherokee numbers had been dramatically reduced by disease and warfare, which Cherokee medicine seemed unable to stop. Furthermore, they had ceded much of their land in various treaties. Factionalism became severe and problematic for the cohesion of the community. Their old way of life was beginning to change.

The aboriginal roles of Cherokee men as warriors and hunters declined, if not were eliminated altogether, and it was at this point that the Cherokees invited missionaries into their nation, beginning with the Moravians in 1799. Cherokees wanted missionaries primarily to set up schools so that Cherokees could learn the ways of Europeans in order to survive in this new world. Epidemic disease and the loss of game did not in and of themselves cause the Cherokees to shirk their traditional religion and turn to Christianity; in fact, most Cherokees were quite slow to adopt the religious worldview of the Europeans. By 1838, at the time that most Cherokees were removed from the Southeast to Oklahoma, only a small percentage had formally rejected traditional religion and converted to Christianity.[25] Moreover, most of the Cherokee Christians of the first half of the nineteenth century merged Christianity with their traditional religious orientation in some unique way, rather than outright rejecting the old ways for the new.[26]

It is true that Native Americans were fascinated by European trade goods, but often they got more joy from shiny trinkets and baubles than from metal tools and guns. Initially, trade seemed fair, as Europeans were willing to trade their European goods for Indian skins and furs, of which there was a great abundance. The introduction of European goods in and of themselves had little effect on early Native American communities, including the Cherokees. Cooking with a kettle and chopping wood with a metal axe did not initially change cultural meanings, values, and purposes. The judicious borrowing of certain material goods simply made life more convenient at some level. Native Americans were not interested in the gross accumulation of material surplus to enhance their wealth. Indeed, too many material goods became a hindrance and a cumbersome burden rather than a convenience for Native Americans and other Indigenous peoples. As historian Calvin Martin notes, Native Americans were interested in borrowing materials from Europeans to achieve "enhanced convenience—without material encumbrance."[27] Indeed, Theda Perdue observed that the Cherokees traditionally sought little economic surplus.[28]

Indians were the primary agents responsible for overhunting, and yet, paradoxically, the Cherokees believed that hunting was a holy occupation and that there were sanctions against overkilling wildlife, including a firm belief that animals could inflict arrogant hunters with disease. Several Indian tribes, including the Cherokees, believed animals were the primary cause of disease, and one theory holds that unexplained epidemics of European disease were experienced as aggressive acts by the animal kingdom against Indians. In essence, some Indians were said to blame disease epidemics on animals and responded by declaring war on animals, killing them off in large numbers to protect themselves against the enemy, while simultaneously engaging Europeans in trade.[29]

One of the primary Cherokee theories of the origin of disease is retaliation by animals who were hunted in a haughty or disrespectful manner.

However, the Cherokees also have other theories of disease origin. Cherokees could fall ill as the result of the actions of a Raven Mocker or simply by violating a taboo governing ritually correct behavior.[30] Also, violating certain moral taboos could offend the gods, causing further illness.[31] Cherokees told Butrick about a ceremony that he called the "Smallpox Dance" and said Cherokees also performed a modified version of the Propitiation or Cementation Ceremony to avert contagious diseases and epidemics. Butrick also linked the physic dance to the Cherokees' efforts to cleanse themselves and obtain pardon from the Supreme Beings above who might punish bad conduct with smallpox, which, as noted earlier, had already taken roughly 50 percent of the population.[32]

Unfortunately, little documentary evidence exists concerning early Cherokee understandings of European epidemics like smallpox, and a single reference by Adair and Butrick is not enough to settle the issue. While Adair and Butrick did make a number of important observations of southeastern Indians, including the Cherokees, their viewpoints were skewed by the lack of an ethnographic perspective and by their attempt to relate Cherokee religious life to Jewish religious life, given how they believed that the Cherokees were one of the Lost Tribes of Israel. Still, there is little evidence to support the view that Cherokees blamed smallpox on the animals they hunted commercially. The 1738 smallpox epidemic occurred more than ten years after the large-scale hunting of deerskins for commercial sales had declined. Although there was much written about the Cherokees in the Colonial period, very little of that material utilizes a Cherokee perspective or even attempts to gain a Cherokee viewpoint. Moreover, with respect to European diseases, the Cherokees may have had little to say, at least to Europeans. The Moravians did describe a smallpox outbreak in 1842, which Cherokees attributed to a giant serpent with a foul odor, probably a reference to the supernatural *uktena*.[33] Three of Mooney's informants clearly blamed white people for epidemic diseases such as smallpox but did not give many details concerning its spread.[34] They did, however, mention a smallpox outbreak near the end of the Civil War, which was supposedly caused when two captured Cherokees were forced to look at a fish.

Cherokees probably incorporated European disease into their aboriginal mythical system. Epidemic disease did not occasion a new religious vision, although it paralleled the loss of traditional religion among some Cherokees, including conjurors. However, with respect to commercial hunting, it seems that the Cherokees became involved in a new economic and political order; this required them to undergo a fundamental transformation that forced them act in ways that bore little relationship to their traditional values and customs.[35] In actuality, despite epidemic disease, loss of land, military defeat, and dependence on European goods, Cherokee religion remained very much alive and well throughout the eighteenth century. Some Cherokee medicine men despaired, and a few abandoned their practice following the 1738 smallpox epidemic; but traditional "doctoring" continued largely as usual. Cherokee medicine men still held great power among the people, and the Cherokee people highly valued their healing rituals. There exists little evidence that the traditional religious system had changed, although it may have been in a somewhat steady state of decline.

By 1751, Skiagunsta, the chief of the Lower Towns, explained that he had told his people they could not live independent of the English and that they relied on the English for clothes, guns, and ammunition: "I am an old man, and have been a warrior, and am a warrior still, and have always told my people to be well with the English for they cannot expect any supply from anywhere else, nor can they live independent of the English. What are we, red people? The clothes we wear we cannot make ourselves, they are made for us. We use their ammunition with which we kill deer. We cannot make our guns, they are made for us. Every necessary thing in life we must have from the white people."[36]

The Cherokees found themselves in a new economic and political situation, which required that they engage in commercial hunting to survive. When the English settled in an area, Indians had a choice of either buying guns to defend themselves or being killed or enslaved.[37] In short, southeastern Indians slaughtered deer and each other because they were positioned on the outer fringes of an expanding modern world-system.[38] Indians in the Southeast, by and large, had no chance of surviving in the end, but they could postpone their extermination, assimilation, or removal by aligning themselves with the most powerful European country and by buying guns from them to provide vital deerskins to make the aggressors happy.[39]

As European settlement expanded, cattle husbandry had a negative impact on Indian settlements. Cattle got into Indian cornfields and essentially assisted the English in moving west through Indian country. Indians, like the Cherokees, had to stay out of the way of cattle, forestry, and agriculture, and they had to produce a commodity that was valuable enough to put them on friendly terms with the English. Since European powers vied with one another for possession for the Southeast, Indians tried to align themselves with one European power or another in exchange for the receipt of European goods.[40]

All this helps explain the Cherokee war with the British in 1760. By 1760, it became clear that the uneasy alliance with England that had existed for little more than half a century was unsustainable in the long run. Accordingly, the Cherokees were faced with two choices: either voluntarily remove themselves or go to war. They chose the latter, with devastating consequences. Nevertheless, Cherokee traditional religion remained alive and strong, and likely served as the backbone of their determination to live life on their own terms. Their land, their life, and their religion were all closely interrelated, and competing European powers attacked all three. The commercial trade in deerskins in the first half of the eighteenth century no doubt paralleled some sort of religious reflection on the part of the Cherokees, but the evidence does not support the view that Cherokees blamed the deer. The Cherokees blamed Europeans, and to a degree themselves, for commercial deerskin hunting. When it became clear to them that they could not sustain such an economy in the long run, they decided to say no more, take a stand, and fight for their old way of life.

CHAPTER 6

Contact, Colonialism, and Christianity

1725–1799

The Cherokees were the largest Indian tribe on the Anglo-American frontier in the eighteenth century, occupying at least sixty villages scattered throughout the Appalachian Mountains. By 1755, the Cherokees numbered more than ten thousand persons.[1] Each village maintained autonomy but the villages themselves were organized into three regions, each of which spoke its own dialect. There were five or six Lower Towns in South Carolina and Georgia; a number of Middle Towns in the mountain valleys of North Carolina, segregated into four village clusters; and nine Overhill towns in present-day Tennessee. When Alexander Longe wrote his brief account of the Cherokees in 1725, they were little influenced by English culture and were still a militarily and politically powerful people. Between 1750 and 1799, the Cherokees got caught up in the world market, fought wars with both the English and the Americans, and saw Christian missionaries come into their lives.

By 1750, deer hunting was the chief industry of the Cherokees, who depended on trading their skins for European manufactured goods.[2] By the time Lieutenant Henry Timberlake arrived in the Overhill villages in 1761, the men were wearing woolen match coats and flaps of British make rather than furs or deerskins.[3] Although the women still wore short deerskin skirts, they increasingly demanded calico material for dresses. Glass beads had replaced shell beads and glass earrings were common. Glass arrowheads, metal axes, hoes, kettles, and steel knives had replaced flint points, stone tools, and earthen pots. They still made bows and arrows, but there was great demand for guns and ammunition. All the above articles were acquired by trading deerskins to the Charleston merchants in South Carolina. By the middle of the eighteenth century, the Cherokees were supplying Charleston merchants with more than fifty thousand deerskins annually. South Carolina traders lived in some thirty of the Cherokee towns, and often had marriage ties with chiefs.[4]

The extent of Cherokee dependence on European goods can hardly be overstated. The Warrior Chief from one of the lower towns lamented the loss of self-sufficiency in 1751.[5] At the same time, the Cherokees were still a powerful tribe with a large army of warriors. Governor Glen of Virginia made clear the necessity of remaining friends with the Cherokees, who had about three thousand gunmen.[6] Colonel George Washington, in 1756, wrote that Cherokees "were very numerous and had never been conquered." Washington also noted that "the Cherokees should be shown great respect because much depended upon good relations with them."[7]

One important observation made by Lieutenant Timberlake in 1758 concerned the large number of buffalo, bear, deer, beaver, turkey, and other game present in Cherokee country.[8] This is an important observation, for it shows that although Cherokees had been involved in large-scale commercial deer hunting for about half a century, game was still abundant in the area. The Cherokees, although hurt by the smallpox epidemic of 1738, lived in some sixty villages, had around three thousand warriors, and were still a force to be reckoned with.[9] At the same time, the relationships between the mother towns of Chota and Tellico were showing signs of rivalry and discord.[10]

In 1755, Cherokees were very much politically autonomous and sovereign; however, things were to change very rapidly.[11] Cherokee difficulties were exacerbated by the fact that Cherokee history was bound up inextricably with European history in America. As the French and English battled for possession of the eastern United States, both sides attempted to use Indians to further their own political and economic agendas. Mislabeled the French and Indian War, this war lasted for almost eight years (1755–1763). At the beginning, the French and English competed for Cherokee loyalty. However, the Cherokees wished to remain neutral and to live on their own terms. But that was not possible. The Cherokee ultimately sided with the French, a decision that proved devastating. From 1759 to 1761, the Cherokees found themselves at war with the British.

In June of 1761, Colonel Grant, with an army of about 2,600 men, descended on fifteen of the Middle Settlement towns, burning homes and fields. Estimates suggest that five thousand Cherokees fled into the mountains where they suffered greatly for lack of food and shelter. While in principle the Cherokees retained their sovereignty following the Anglo-Cherokee War, the conflict disrupted their subsistence cycle and caused widespread hunger, in some cases leading to starvation. Kituwah lost about half of its population and was permanently abandoned, no doubt a painful blow to the Cherokees' worldview. At the conclusion of the war, Attakullakulla sat down with Colonel Grant, smoked a peace pipe, and reached a temporary resolution that the Cherokees felt they had to accept.[12]

After the war, settlers began pouring into Cherokee country. The intrusion prompted the Cherokees to seek help from the British to preserve their lands. Another series of treaties with the British resulted in major land cessions and loss of hunting grounds. In 1770, the Cherokees ceded their hunting grounds in Virginia and present-day West Virginia. They surrendered hunting grounds east of the Kentucky River in 1772, and in 1775, in a fraudulent land transaction, Cherokees lost their land west of the Kentucky River.[13]

The American Revolution demanded Cherokee participation, despite their wish to remain neutral. Choosing between the lesser of two evils, Cherokees aligned with the British, who ultimately lost the war to the upstart American colonists. In 1776, General Griffith Rutherford commanded North Carolina troops to attack the Cherokee Middle Towns. The soldiers killed and scalped women and sold children into slavery.[14] Surviving Cherokees fled into the mountains, where they almost starved. American soldiers destroyed almost fifty towns, leaving the Cherokees largely without food or shelter. Although the Cherokees managed somehow to get back on their feet economically, they never truly recovered from Rutherford's "scorched earth" campaign. Twenty years after the American Revolution, US Indian Agent Benjamin Hawkins noted that Cherokee women became silent with fear and children ran screaming in terror at the mere sight of a white man.[15]

After the American Revolution, the majority of Cherokees favored peace and agreed to give up all their lands east of the Appalachians, except for a small band of warriors called Chickamaugas, who moved their families to northeastern Alabama and the area around Chattanooga, Tennessee. They fought the Americans until 1794, at which time the Cherokees finally surrendered to their European invaders.[16] The years

1760–1794 were devastating to Cherokees. Not only did they lose lives and land, they also lost much of their traditional religion and culture. Numerous priests and medicine men died during this time. Because the Cherokees were in such turmoil, much of their ancient religion was simply not passed down by word of mouth as it had been. As the Cherokee elder and anthropologist Robert Thomas noted, Cherokees faced a foreign presence that completely disrupted the traditional dynamics of the division of Cherokee society into peace (white) and war (red) functions.[17]

Despite having adapted many European goods and some of their ways, the Cherokees preserved their language, maintained some of their traditional land base, and continued to practice traditional Cherokee religion.[18] Marriages between Cherokees and whites did not take place at a steady rate until well into the nineteenth century.[19] Intermarriage occurred in waves that, in the end, did not have an appreciable impact on Cherokee traditional culture or society. Technically speaking, by the beginning of the nineteenth century many Cherokees had some European ancestry, but whites did not bring about fundamental cultural change. Loss of unity escalated during the Cherokee War, as evidenced by the Overhill towns such as Chota and Tellico. Those divisions are well documented. Again, however, it was not intermarriage that created blocs as much as it was Cherokee response to European colonists bent on conquest and the acquisition of Cherokee land.

DIVISION AND RELIGIOUS IDENTITY

In many ways, Dragging Canoe's movement represented a turning point for Cherokees.[20] After the American Revolution was over, Dragging Canoe moved away and created a town of Cherokees called the Chickamaugas. He later moved his followers to a new town south of the Hiwassee River in Tennessee in anticipation of staging Cherokee attacks against Virginia. However, the Cherokee National Council vetoed that idea and sent peace envoys to the Americans. Cherokee Beloved Men declared Dragging Canoe an outlaw and offered to surrender him to American forces. Dragging Canoe left with large numbers of Cherokees and a few white loyalists, and they continued to fight with the Americans until the 1790s. He died in 1792 and his followers formed the nucleus of the "Old Settlers" who were living in what is now Arkansas and Oklahoma, before the removal of the rest of the tribe in 1838.

Dragging Canoe's determination to keep whites from stealing any more Cherokee land tore apart the Red and White councils that characterized traditional Cherokee political life.[21] When the White or National Council overrode Dragging Canoe's activity as a war leader, they essentially performed a legislative rather than a judicial function, thereby marking another fundamental change in Cherokee politics. Dragging Canoe's movement was not simply political, however, as the spirit of his movement, although not clearly nativistic, contained religious elements. In effect it was, to borrow a term from Joel Martin, a "sacred revolt."[22] Dragging Canoe's movement established a perspective that was clearly nationalist and anti-American and survived through the Redbird Smith movement in early-twentieth-century Oklahoma.

What was most significant about Dragging Canoe's movement was that a number of Cherokees willingly migrated from their sacred homeland to a largely unknown region. Native Americans migrated prehistorically before they arrived at their traditional homelands, but those migrations were generally done on their own terms and according to revelations from the sacred. In other words, Native American people settled in places where the sacred revealed itself to them. Fundamental to any traditional Cherokee settlement was the existence of a sacred center, a place where heaven, earth, and the underworld, as well as the four cardinal directions, were united. A very aged elder, named Sickatower, told John Payne in 1835 that a spiritual Woman (Selu), who "in the beginning . . . had been brought down from the skies," instructed Cherokees that "you are to make your invocations first toward the east, and secondly towards the north, and thirdly towards the west and fourthly towards the south. Then you are to stand in the centre of the four points and to call me, above."[23] Given that message, it is difficult to imagine the pain a Cherokee like Dragging Canoe felt when migrating to a strange and uncentered place.

Dragging Canoe took with him the war fire when he and his followers relocated to the Chickamauga towns.[24] Moreover, the Chickamaugans who went west established a ceremonial center in northeastern Oklahoma, which has since fallen into disuse but was apparently used as a site for war ceremonies among Cherokees who fought in the Civil War. Nevertheless, much was lost by relocation in terms of both religion and kinship. The Cherokees had been a matrilineal, matrilocal society, but Chickamauga warriors took with them their wives, an act that disrupted the kinship system and set the stage for bilateral rather than matrilineal inheritance. In other words, this move involved a migration of nuclear families rather than matrilineal clans, thereby challenging the traditional Cherokee kinship system.

In Philadelphia on June 26, 1794, the secretary of war and thirteen principal men of the Cherokees negotiated and signed a treaty intended to supplement the Treaty of Holston of 1791.[25] Four skirmishes broke out, and finally, on November 18, 1794, Hanging Maw, Head Chief of the Nation, and Colonel John Watt, Principal Chief of the hostile towns, met with Governor Blount at Tellico and reached a final resolution on friendly terms. At that point, the long Cherokee War came to an end.[26]

As the Cherokees began to move into the nineteenth century, fundamental questions surrounding their identity emerged. Who were the Cherokees and what did it mean to be a Cherokee Indian in 1794? What was the defining principle of Cherokee identity: kinship, language, or religious orientation?[27] These were not simple questions, and the Cherokee answer was multifaceted and very complex.

The religious dimension of Cherokee identity is fundamental. However, Cherokee religion is inextricably related to kinship, subsistence modalities, and the Cherokee language. Looking for a single origin or essence of the Cherokees may be like peeling back the layers of an onion to look for its center. Nevertheless, to say that Cherokee religion is related to subsistence modalities, kinship, land, and language is not to say that it is dependent upon or derived from any of those. Traditional Cherokee religious meanings, values, and purposes stand on their own and are still alive today among the Eastern Band of Cherokee Indians of North Carolina.

The American Revolution decimated the Cherokees and resulted in extensive loss of life and land, as well as the corrosion of their native religious and cultural traditions. Although they had ceded several large tracts of land, they still possessed nearly forty-three thousand square miles of land—about half in Tennessee, a little less than half equally divided between Arkansas and Georgia, and a small area in the southwestern corner of North Carolina.[28] The Cherokees had adopted much of European material life—especially guns, hatchets, knives, clothes, and trinkets. They also received peach trees and potatoes from the English, and some even kept bees and collected honey. In the treaty of 1791, the United States agreed to furnish the Cherokees with farming tools, as well as spinning wheels and cards in order that they might make their own clothing.[29]

In 1809, there were only 12,395 Cherokees.[30] The Cherokee way of life had been steadily eroding since the English made regular contact in the early 1700s, but the American Revolution directly challenged the old ways.[31] By 1800, the Cherokees had lost hunting grounds in

Kentucky and Tennessee, the fur trade had collapsed, they had suffered severe population loss, and many of their religious leaders had died, taking with them much traditional knowledge.

Whites took over the oldest villages, and subsequent land sessions following the American Revolution cut the heart out of the Cherokee homeland. Cherokee land was inseparably related to Cherokee religion, and virtually every significant topographical feature emanated sacred power and symbolized a sacred meaning.[32] Sacred narratives incorporated specific mountains, rivers, waterfalls, valleys, and other geographical features, and the loss of these places eroded Cherokee traditional religion in a fundamentally devastating manner. Moreover, the plants gathered by Cherokee medicine people grew in specific places, many of which were lost to white invaders.

Undergirding this rapidly changing lifeway was the ideology of civilization. The treaty of 1791 contended that Cherokees were being led from savagery to civilization and from hunting to farming and herding.[33] Following the American Revolution, Cherokees must have questioned virtually every aspect of their life, given the rapid decline of religion and culture, but it would be erroneous to suggest that religious ceremonies fell into disuse or became secularized by 1800. Cherokees probably questioned their ability to continue their old way of life. They had lost their land, their sovereignty, and their ability to subsist off the land. However, they still embodied much of their traditional religion, although that, too, would soon come under attack.

MISSIONARIES

By the early eighteenth century, the Cherokees had already experienced significant contact with Europeans who were self-professed Christians. Although sustained missionary activity did not begin until the Moravians arrived in 1799, Cherokees had heard about various Christian doctrines and biblical traditions and stories. Moravians had sent transient ministers to the Cherokees in 1735, 1753, and 1783, but the Cherokees showed little interest in their message. Despite the fact that the Cherokees had lost much land, sovereignty, and a number of important religious leaders, they were slow to adopt Christianity, and when they did so, they did it on Cherokee terms. From 1800 until their removal in 1838, the Cherokees were inundated by missionary activity from Methodists, Baptists, and Congregationalists, as well as Moravians, and yet no more than 12 to 15 percent of Cherokees were members of Christian

churches by 1860.[34] Even prior to the introduction of organized missionary activity, however, the Cherokee religious worldview began to reflect,
or rather, refract, contact and interaction with the Christian tradition.[35]

The European presence was significant, pervasive, and continuing,
and yet for a while, Cherokee mythology incorporated the historical
novelty of contact into their traditional religious orientation. However,
at some point, the European presence was so overwhelming and con-
tinuous as to occasion a restructuring of Cherokee religion.[36] Missionary archival records provide some evidence of Cherokee responses to
missionary activity, although it must be remembered that all these materials were written by missionaries who had a vested interest in proselytizing the people they wrote about. Therefore, most Native American or
empathetic observers who read these materials cannot help but be
struck by their biased slant. It is not that the missionaries were dishon-
est; it is that they came with a particular purpose and they, like everyone else of their time, clearly refract their own worldviews in writing
about Cherokees.

ALEXANDER LONGE

Alexander Longe's forty-five-page monograph written in 1725, only a few
years after English contact, is the first detailed description of the Cherokee
way of life. It shows that contact generated serious reflection among
Cherokees concerning religious issues. Longe breaks his discussion into
the following categories: (1) the immortality of the soul, (2) Cherokees'
opinion of the divine power, (3) the feast of the first fruits, (4) the burial
and mourning of the dead, (5) the creation of the world, (6) Indian matri-
mony, (7) the naming of children, (8) making rain, (9) the law of their
temple, (10) the eclipse of the sun, (11) Thunder, (12) their notion of
enchantments, (13) their war fire, (14) the Screech Owl, and (15) the rain-
bow. Longe begins with Cherokee notions of life after death based largely
on a discussion he had with a Cherokee priest (medicine man) whom he
describes as "one of the most sensible Indians and most wise and most
knowing that ever I saw in my life."[37] Cherokees did not compartmental-
ize religion as an aspect of life but rather as the overarching perspective
through which they understood their world.

Cherokees sought a proper relationship with the sacred/beloved
whose power was real.[38] The Cherokee word for "strong" is ᎤᎵᏂᎩᏗ
(ulinigidi), the same word Cherokees would use to describe someone
who could lift heavy objects, and ᎦᎸᏉᏗᏳ (galvquodiyu) is the same

galvquodi construction as "beloved." Perhaps further analysis would reveal that ᏇᎤ (*galv-*) is cognate with ᏇᎤᏩᏗ (*galvladi*, "heaven") or ᏇᎤᎶᎯ (*galvlohi*, "the sky"). The latter uses the locative suffix -ᎶᎯ (*-ohi*), just as a town name would—for example, ᏩᏯ (*wahya*) for "wolf" and ᏩᏯᎯ (*wahyohi*) for "wolf town."

If the -ᏉᎥ (*-quo*) piece comes from ᎤᏁᏉᏥ (*unequotsa*), "to increase something," it suggests "the one whose elevation is most increased, most high." Of course, then you often see people affixing more emphatic prefixes and suffixes. The suffix -Ᏻ (*-yu*) is indicative of emphasis, hence ᎠᎩᏲᏏᎭ (*agiyosiha*, "I'm hungry") and ᎠᎩᏲᏏᎭᏻ (*agiyosihayu*, "I *am* hungry"), as in "I really am!" Sometimes speakers add the translocative Ᏸ- (*wi-*) to superlative constructions: ᏪᏇᏉᏗᏻ (*wigalvquodiyu*), "the one far and away *most* high."

Some Native American languages use the word *mysterious* to describe the sacred. For example, in referring to spiritual power, Hopis might say *a'ni himu* ("very something") and Lakotas, *wakan tanka* ("great mystery"). However, translation of the word *mysterious* into Cherokee is challenging. Rudolf Otto wrote in *The Idea of the Holy*, "taken in the religious sense, that which is 'mysterious' is—to give it perhaps the most striking expression—the 'wholly other' . . . , that which is quite beyond the sphere of the usual, the intelligible, and the familiar, . . . filling the mind with blank wonder and astonishment."[39]

Translating *mysterious* into Cherokee is not a simple matter of forcing an English meaning on a Cherokee word, in part because no Cherokee word has the same constellation of meanings. For example, ᎤᏍᎦᏎᏗ (*usgasedi*) can have a positive connotation, like "badass" or "formidable," but it is built on the root -ᏍᎦ- (*-sga-*) as in ᎠᏍᎦᏯᎭ (*asgayeha*) or ᎠᏍᎦᎭ (*asgaha*), which means "he/she is frightened." *Usgasedi* therefore could convey the meaning "terrifying," or even "awful." One might then turn to a word like ᎤᎵᏍᎨᏗ (*ul'sgedi*), but that usually means something along the lines of "fancy," "important," "formal," or even "sacred." Words like *asgwanigohisdi* or *asgwanigohisdodi* are closer because they are built on the root *-sgwanigo-*, meaning something like "contain." That group of words translates as anything from "trash can" to "library," to "interesting/fascinating," because speakers apply a metaphoric extension to something like "it's dragging me toward it/it's captivating (to) me." This last definition is why someone might translate it as *asgwanigohisdodi*, because it's something to be wondered at or something that fascinates you and draws you in, probably because you don't really understand it.

However, Cherokees typically emphasize their relationship to, rather than their distance from, the sacred/beloved; therefore *mysterious* in the religious studies sense does seem not fit very well. Translation is difficult in Cherokee in part because it demands a cultural reconsideration of what one says in English. In other words, many of the messages we convey in English would be pragmatically and/or culturally inappropriate (if not ridiculous) in Cherokee.

When the Cherokees and other Native Americans first saw European technology, they perceived it as a manifestation of the sacred power of European gods—that is to say, in Cherokee eyes, Europeans had metal tools, guns, and an elaborate material inventory in part because their gods were very powerful. Viewing European technology as a manifestation of the same sacred power that created the world, Cherokees did so with a certain sense of awe. The interview between Longe and the Cherokee medicine man makes this point clear. Longe asked the medicine man whether he thought that the soul of human beings died with the body. When asked that question, the medicine man looked Longe squarely in the face and told him that he was a white man who knew trading and who knew how to "write and make the paper speak." He then reportedly said that "the great God above gave white people a spirit above all others and nations on the face of the world."[40] Here, the medicine man apparently referred to the English's superior material and technological developments, which he perceived as containing sacred power. But then, the medicine man immediately turned around and censured the English: "Despite the fact that the English outshine all other peoples in certain respects, they are ignorant as to whether the soul is immortal."[41] The medicine man then asserted that Cherokees sometimes actually saw the spirit of deceased Cherokees, evidence that the soul was immortal.

Longe's consultant discussed details about the hereafter that raise questions about whether Christian views of heaven and hell had made a subtle inroad on traditional Cherokee religion. Actually, the Cherokees may have had some notion of heaven and hell that predated Christianity. According to Longe, Cherokees initially buried the dead facing the rising sun, or the east. The soul rose on the fourth day and appeared to the sun, who sent a messenger to guide the soul on two paths, one to the right and the other to the left. The right path was small and led to the setting sun, where there was eternal "music, dancing and singing, and feasting."[42]

Longe then asked whether the Cherokees would renounce their own ways if the English taught them, to which the priest responded that he would turn as white as the English if the English would teach them how to make guns, powder, and cloth.[43] Longe inquired if there was a god for every nation of people, and the medicine man responded, "No . . . but we call the great God so because he loves the English best."[44] When the medicine man asked why so many of the English were wicked and immoral, given their access to divine power, Longe answered that the English had lost sight of the teachings of the priest.[45]

Longe's account gives a fairly detailed description of rituals related to the Green Corn Feast, which took place at the end of four days of fasting. All came into the high place and women brought food. The priest took a little bit of food out of each of the dishes and placed it in a new oven pan, which was painted red. He took the pan in his left hand and a white wing in his right hand and gave a long speech in a tongue that none but he understood.[46] During his speech, he periodically held his hand toward heaven, and at the end he threw the bits of food into the fire. Then he turned to the people and commanded them to go to the river and wash off all of their pollutions; they obeyed and then returned to the temple or high place.[47] The high priest or White Chief, a man described as king, held a white stick in his hand and a crown was placed on his head. The crown was painted red, blue, yellow, and purple, and on top of the crown was a bunch of white feathers with two fans of turkey feathers. For the next four days, the White Chief was carried around by four men so that his feet never touched the ground. There was much feasting and many dances, including first fruits, buffalo, clamshell, nimble, the old, the one foot, the pole cat, the pigeon, the bear, the well done, the enchant dance, and the best of all.[48] The New Corn Dance made a tremendous impression upon Alexander Longe, who called these people the most perfect he could think of, if only they professed the "Christian religion."[49]

Longe next addressed Cherokee death and burial practices. When someone was on their deathbed, many relatives came to stay with them constantly while maintaining positive spirits to encourage the dying person to live. After death, close kin joined in a mournful cry for about twenty-four hours and then buried the deceased. According to Longe, Cherokees interred their dead in the same way as white people. Perhaps this meant that they laid out their dead instead of burying them in a fetal position as in an earlier time. At some level, this reflects European influence on the way Indians lived in every respect, even the way they buried their dead.[50]

Except for the change in position of the body, Europeans had little influence on Cherokee burials in 1725, and most Cherokee traditions remained largely intact. For example, Longe notes that Cherokees buried vast quantities of goods with the deceased for their journey to the other world. Then they burned all other goods belonging to a Cherokee decedent to purify the community.[51] Interestingly, Longe observed that Cherokee burial practices provided a great advantage to traders because the burial and destruction of goods created a need for replacements. Furthermore, greedy Englishmen began early in the Colonial period to rob Indian graves to obtain goods, which they could later sell. Needless to say, grave robbing appalled the Cherokees.[52]

By 1725, Cherokees were already becoming dependent on European goods, some of which they probably buried with the dead. Traders, therefore, benefited from Cherokee burial practices since Cherokees replaced European goods with other European goods. Thus, the medicine man's earlier reference to the Cherokees' desire to produce guns, powder, and cloth reveals the important value that Cherokees placed on certain European trade items.

Longe briefly discussed the Cherokee origin narrative. He did not give a detailed version, but related an earth diver myth similar to the one Mooney collected some 150 years later. Interestingly, in the narrative Longe collected, the crawfish rather than the water beetle gathered a bit of earth and brought it to the surface to create the earth island. The earth diver myth Longe recorded reflected the influence of the English. After creating the world, god made all living creatures, except human beings. Then god took white clay and made the whites; then god made two of every other nation under the sun. The narrative placed the English first because "he has endowed them with the knowledge of making all things."[53] A migration myth is part of the earth diver creation story. Humans undertook a journey from heaven to earth because heaven became too crowded. Distinguishing between peoples as well as animals, god gave whites domestic animals like cows, sheep, and hogs, and provided the Cherokee wild animals such as buffalo, deer, and bear. The consultant told Longe that god caused a great flood to punish people for their sins, but he saved a pair of people from each nation by placing them on the tops of high mountains.

Longe claimed that the medicine man then turned to him and asked if the English knew of any such story, to which Longe responded with the story of Noah and the flood. This interesting exchange seems, in part, to reflect an unconscious adaptation of a biblical narrative by a Cherokee. At the same time, the Cherokees, like a lot of peoples, possessed an aboriginal flood story. The Cherokee migration myth does refer to a flood, but it is hard to say how much it may have been influenced by the story of Noah. Given that the English had at that time interacted with the Cherokees for only about fifteen years and that a distinguished medicine man spoke of such a flood, the Cherokees may have possessed an aboriginal flood story that later incorporated some biblical elements.

Alexander Longe observed the priest fast and pray for rain over a period of four days. The priest supposedly reiterated that "the Great King of Heaven is Lord of all things and the author of all goodness."[54] He reported that Cherokees went to the woods to fast for rain and that they threw beans toward the south to the small white god that resided there and implored the high god to send them rain. The priest furthermore told Longe that the cause of the drought was the wickedness of the people.[55] This is a significant passage because a matter as serious as a drought that spoils the crops is a matter of first importance. Cherokees in this example are not blaming drought on the coming of the English, but rather on their own immorality and misbehavior. They fasted so god might see the Cherokees' humiliation, take pity on them, and grant their request.[56] This is a clear, unequivocal Cherokee description of what we earlier called prayer by supplication. In supplication, a Cherokee endures hardship to evoke pity from the gods and receive some much-needed blessings.

Longe's monograph contains a very interesting interchange concerning a solar eclipse.[57] Upon observing the solar eclipse, the people let out a hideous cry, fired their guns, and shot bows and arrows into the sky until the eclipse ended. The Cherokee priest said that during an eclipse the great frog was trying to swallow the sun, and the gun shots scared the frog away. Longe laughed at the priest's story and proceeded to give him an astronomical explanation of the location of the sun, moon, and earth. When he finished this explanation, the priest announced that he believed that Longe was correct. A year later, there was another eclipse of the sun, and Longe claims that the priest went out among the people and reprimanded them for firing their guns into the air and screaming. The Cherokees then just stood and watched. Some Cherokees still believed that the frog was swallowing the sun, while others did not. When the eclipse ended, the priest shook hands with Longe and thanked him for illuminating the Cherokees about this subject. The priest promised that he would spread this information throughout the Cherokee Nation so that the people would never again worry about an eclipse. Once more, the priest praised the great knowledge of the English as compared with Cherokees and observed that the English even understood the very motions of the planets in the heavens.

While Longe may very well have argued for a scientific explanation of a mythological perception, it is difficult to believe that he had a nationwide impact on Cherokee understandings of eclipses. In fact, Adair, who visited the Cherokees in 1736, mentions a lunar eclipse, which prompted Cherokees to run in all directions, shouting and firing their guns to "assist the suffering moon."[58] Moreover, it is doubtful that Longe had as profound an impact on the priest as he claimed.[59] Indeed, many Eastern Cherokees described a 2017 total solar eclipse as the frog swallowing the sun.

In another section, the priest told the story of a former segment of the Cherokee Nation who went into the river and found another world that was full of food. Some ultimately migrated to this other place, and the priest showed Longe the pillars and the posts of the houses from the abandoned town. The old priest then asked Longe if he thought this was true. Longe sidestepped the inquiry and said that he believed it was a true story but that the devil had beguiled them.[60] Here we see a story that Longe viewed as false and the Cherokees as true. Longe obviously thought such a story was simply evidence of the devil's trickery. In other words, Longe believed in a spiritual reality, but not that of the Cherokees. In his mind, only the Christian god (and devil) were real.

CHAPTER 7

Christian Missions and the Ghost Dance

1799–1815

The Cherokees found themselves in a very precarious position at the end of the eighteenth century, following the American Revolution. George Washington and Secretary of War John Knox had implemented a new "civilization" policy that sought to civilize and convert Native Americans and to make them full-fledged, equal members of the United States.[1] Washington's stated civilization policy should be considered as the conscious political articulation of an ideology that had emerged with the discovery of the New World.[2] In other words, the Washington administration codified existing ideas and practices.

Americans wanted two things from Native Americans—peace and land—and the civilization policy promised to give them both.[3] Secretary Knox very quickly realized that a key to breaking down Indian traditions and customs was to introduce them to the Western concept of private property. Indian peoples held their land in common, and Knox understood that such a concept would thwart the United States' efforts to bring Indians into the mainstream. Knox wanted to introduce Indians to the love of private property, a marker of civilization.

Moravian missionaries arrived among the Cherokees in 1799 but did not commence their work until 1801, and then only to build a school, not to establish a mission post.[4] Cherokees figured out pretty quickly that their future survival depended on their ability to live alongside the newcomers, something they could do only if they better understood the settlers' ways. Cherokees initially found little appeal in Christian teachings that they did not understand or need.[5]

The Cherokees were not interested in Christian teachings but they were interested in receiving the power and knowledge that apparently came from the Christians' book, the Bible. They were attracted to the technological power of white people, which Cherokees understood in very spiritual terms. In 1799, Aarcowee, Beloved Man of Chota, responded to a Moravian missionary plan to teach Cherokees the Bible (Great Book) and convert them. His words are an important source for understanding Cherokee experience since Beloved Men were highly respected within their communities.

> Last evening I heard that you were here and were awaiting me. Then I looked toward heaven and saw my father there. I had thought all night of what I might hear today, and now I have heard great words. The Great Father of all who have breath has from the beginning made all men, the red, the white, and the black. He has placed the red men here towards the setting sun, and the white men toward the sunrise. A great day has passed since the white men came over in their great canoes and received permission to build a city. This has not been enough for them, but they have come further and further. This has caused conflict between the red and white men, which finally became war. In this both were wrong, for the Father who lives above does not like war, and would that all should be brothers. The whites are called the elder brothers and the red men are called the younger, but this naming is reversed for the red men were the first to live in the land. The Great Father of all creatures, who made all men, has given me breath, and only He can take it away, and that when He will. I am thankful to Him that so far breath has been left to me. But we were all made of earth, and sooner or later must become earth again.
>
> The Great Father who lives above sees all and knows all. He sees our present meeting and hears all that we say to one another, and rejoices to see us and hear our words. He regards our smallest affairs, and he has given many good things for our youths which we scarcely consider. We see only the water, yet we could not live without it. He made it. The fire in the fireplace, such a little thing! Yet, he has provided it for our use, and what would the poor red man do if he had it not, for he does not have much in warm clothing like the white man. Everywhere the fire lies hidden, and permits itself to be brought out of little stones, and so it is with all that man sees, all shows the power of God. White men, indeed have much more, they can make for themselves clothes against the cold. Red men can build only small canoes, and cross only small waters; white men build great canoes and cross great waters; they also have the Great Book out of which they learn all. In the beginning, when the Great Father made men, he had a great book which He offered first to the red men and bade them speak to the book (that is, reading

it,) but they could not. Then He offered it to the white men with the same command. When they saw it they could at once speak to the book, and that is the reason that the white people know so much that is not known to the red men, but the time seems to have come when the red men shall learn to do it also. When the white men first came to this land they had the great book which is the word of God, but they did not instruct the red men in it. I believe, therefore, that the great spirit has given it to you that you are willing to come to us and teach us. For my part I will welcome you; I am well content with it, and like it much.[6]

In trying to sell themselves to the Cherokees, Moravians wrestled with the relationship between teaching and preaching. Ultimately, they wanted to convert all Cherokees to Christianity, but their own records reveal that they had serious questions about whether that could be done "unless they first became more civilized, did understand English and could read."[7] The Cherokees, however, would only allow a school, and a school was very slow in arriving. In the interim, the missionaries subtly tried to spread the word of the Christian god; but the Cherokees showed very little interest.

Two intractable problems faced the missionaries and underscored a fundamental tension between Americans and Cherokees. First, missionaries were Americans of European descent. Although some missionaries, especially the Methodists, had some success in converting Cherokees and appointing Cherokee itinerant ministers, missionaries were white men who were American citizens. The Cherokees were neither. The missionaries, no matter how honorable their intentions, were part and parcel of the conquering colonial powers that killed Cherokees in large numbers, took their land and freedom, and tried to convert and civilize them. That was the fundamental, constitutive problem of the relationship between the missionaries and Cherokees. Moreover, missionaries regarded traditional Cherokee religion and culture with disdain. The American Board of Commissioners for Foreign Missions, established in 1810, explicitly announced their goal: "to make the whole tribe English in their language, civilized in their habits, and Christian in their religion."[8]

The other problem was historical.[9] Following the Indian wars, frontier whites encroached on Cherokee lands despite the government's official policy to stop illegal trespass. Moreover, frontier whites tended to see Cherokees as savages and held them in great contempt because of recent wars. As whites continued to increase their encroachment, Cherokees responded often by stealing horses and livestock. Cherokee horse thieves were condemned by the Cherokee National Council, but the Council could not control every single Cherokee. Furthermore, the Council did not necessarily speak for all Cherokees, especially culturally conservative Cherokees. Moreover, the Council began to centralize Cherokee government, which had traditionally connected autonomous villages in a loose federation. The Council, which consisted mainly of intermarried, wealthy Cherokees, tried to impress upon the United States government that the Cherokees were basically like other United States citizens and, therefore, should be allowed to remain on what was left of their land.

Cherokees had undergone very rapid and substantial change since making peace with the United States in 1794. Commercial deerskin hunting had declined rapidly because of the scarcity of the game. By 1805, overhunting had depleted much of their hunting lands of game, resulting in loss of bargaining power. This also, no doubt, helped lead the Cherokees to horse stealing.[10] The Cherokees began to develop farming methods encouraged by the United States government. Individual farms broke up the more compacted villages of traditional Cherokee settlements and dispersed Cherokees across a wider area. The result of this dispersal was a decline in communal life, although Cherokee women showed tremendous resilience in resisting the decline of village life.[11] Cherokees still came together for major religious ceremonies like the Green Corn Dance and the ball game, but this increased emphasis on nuclear families, as well as materialism and individualism, strained relationships.[12]

Cherokee "progressives," mostly the descendants of Cherokee women who married white men, became more involved in politics, and, for the most part, Cherokee "conservatives" seem to have accepted this shift as the most viable way for them to maintain some semblance of sovereignty in the face of aggressive, encroaching whites. In 1805 and 1806, the Cherokees ceded huge tracts of hunting land in a series of treaties and began the process of raising more livestock.[13] Most of the Council members were wealthy Cherokees who, in some ways, mirrored the wealthy southern plantation owners who surrounded them.[14] Because these plantation owners were often the sons of white men, the Cherokees began to adopt a number of European values and customs, which came to be seen as a critique of the Cherokees' matrilineal and matrilocal social structure. Cherokees traditionally inherited from their mothers; however, the first noticeable shifts in Cherokee social structure after intermarriage with white men was a change in inheritance laws.[15]

The power of Cherokee women waned with the breakdown of the traditional compact village structure and their loss of control over property. This change in settlement pattern, coupled with the influx of white men, brought about a shift to a patrilineal system of inheritance. Once that shift occurred, white missionaries and agents began promoting owning land in severalty according to the American legal scheme.[16]

At the beginning of the nineteenth century, the Cherokees were faced with a rapidly changing world with little time to develop an appropriate and effective cultural response. Their world saw dramatic social, political, and economic change, which also affected their religious worldview. It was all happening at a dizzying pace. This is nowhere better evident than in the rapid change in Cherokee leadership that took place between 1806 and 1810, and the rise of multiple internal divisions.

NEW RELIGIOUS MOVEMENTS

Social unrest by outsiders often generates new religious movements. Cherokees had never encountered human beings who possessed such insecurity in their identity and an insatiable appetite for land, wealth, and power.[17] Ultimately, Cherokees had to take into account that their initial impressions about European invaders were wrong and that their way of life had changed in a fundamental way.[18] Materialistic, scientific, capitalistic, and industrialized Western culture, with its religious ideology, triggered in many traditional Cherokees a longing for the return of an earlier, more pristine way of native life. In the massive cultural change which the Cherokees experienced, many tried to process the meaning of historical domination in traditional Cherokee mythical categories.

Indigenous peoples have customarily mythologized historical change. Cherokee history is replete with experiences of change that they ultimately incorporated into older mythological structures. This is not a process of rationalization, as Western logicians would have it, but rather a primal human response to that which at first appears to be novel. The fact that people articulate some myths after an event does not mean that they are ex post facto rationalizations to support one's religious view of the world. Myth often accompanies some new historical situation.[19] Mythically speaking, the historical dimension of myths does not negate the authenticity and timing of the myth's meaning. A myth embodies a timeless element, despite its historical manifestation, and it does so through two separate, but interrelated, modes.

Peoples who place great truth in myth often perceive timeless structures and unique signifiers embedded in their historical events. Meaning resides within the eye of the beholder, and peoples like traditional Cherokees and other Native Americans often apprehend phenomenons differently than those who are culturally Europeans. Historical events may evoke the remembrance of a meaning that is timeless and sacred, and therefore real.[20] Thus, forms of myth may change historically but the content of the myth remains the same. The unique historical aspect of the myth is forgotten, and what is remembered is the sacred meaning that has always been present.

Indigenous people lived or embodied myth long before they articulated it verbally.[21] The verbalization in myth represents in one sense a decline in the primordial experience of an anonymous and autonomous something. In this mythic modality, spiritual meaning is lived before it is spoken. In this sense, one could say that some historical events evoke a story, whose meaning was embodied at an almost unconscious level. In traditional Cherokee culture, prior to the coming of the Europeans, change occurred at a pace that allowed myth to incorporate historical change, and that sort of dynamic typified Cherokee traditional life. Within their mythic cosmos, life remained ultimately meaningful, and all significant forms of life were understood to be sacred and to have always existed. In the Cherokees' contact with the English and the Americans, the traditional rhythm and dynamic of myth and history was disrupted by the undeniable presence of an oppressive, encroaching culture. Although Cherokee mythology and worldview could make sense of some of the changes wrought by the West, aspects of the old myth were overwhelmed by the presence of this new military, political, economic, and social presence. Therefore, new cultural myths arose to make sense of this unprecedented and disruptive time of life.[22]

By 1806, Cherokee hunting grounds had been sold, and from 1808 to 1809, great effort was made to divide the Cherokee people among themselves. By this point, some Cherokees felt so disoriented that they essentially gave up trying to make up sense of life and sought some solace in intoxication.[23] Another alternative was for Cherokees to try and hide in the high hills and valleys of the Great Smoky Mountains of Western North Carolina. A third alternative for frustrated Cherokees was to immigrate west.

What is most significant about Cherokee factionalism was its existence. The Cherokee people were pressured and oppressed in an unprecedented manner that occasioned multiple visions of spiritual renewal.

All responses to American dominance were attempts to carve out a meaningful orientation to the world. Some Cherokees felt they could not be true unless they remained on their land, while others felt their only hope was to start over in a new place where they could reestablish a more traditional way of life. However, the great majority of Cherokees wished to remain in their own country, no matter how acculturated they became. After Agent Meigs told Bloody Fellow that the Cherokees could pursue their traditional hunting culture if they moved west, Bloody Fellow responded that "he had no inclination to leave the country of his birth." This was so, "even should the habits and customs of the Cherokees give place to the habits and customs of the whites."[24] Moreover, by and large the Cherokee people were not Christians and still practiced their ancient religion.

NEW RELIGIOUS MOVEMENT OF 1811

Interestingly, the first vision of a new religious movement in 1811 (sometimes called Cherokee Ghost Dance) preceded most of the specific problems outlined above. This is an important point and is another example of Indian religious prophecies and visions actually predating certain historical events, showing that difficult historical circumstances do not cause religious visions.[25]

Religious visions of a future paradise sometimes foreshadow rather than follow the disorganization of traditional social structures. The importance of historical, social, economic, and political forces for the birth and spread of messianic movements has been widely emphasized, and correctly so. When people are in difficult circumstances, they often await the end of the world in hopes of some cosmic renewal. However, there are also examples of such visions preceding hard times.[26] Moreover, religion is inextricably tied up with political, economic, and social structures but is not caused by them. Religion does not manifest itself separate from them but neither is it dependent upon them. In the end, there is a religious dimension where ultimate significance exists apart from the social, political, and economic realm.

For the Cherokee people, the initial spiritual vision preceded the specific political and economic problems that pressed against the Cherokees in 1811. There are several sources concerning the Cherokee new religious movement, but none are particularly detailed and almost all reflect the perceptions of government leaders or Christian missionaries, who dismissed them as either ignorant superstition or outright evil lies.[27] Thomas L. McKenney published the first account in 1838. Major Ridge, an acculturated young Cherokee chief, often referred to as The Ridge, witnessed a gathering of Cherokees in 1811 to hear a man named Charles relate a vision of the Great Spirit. Ridge, who was very much opposed to the message, related it to McKenney. At the meeting, several Cherokees assaulted him. The account begins: "[About the year 1811], some of the Cherokees dreamed and others received, in various ways, communications from the Great Spirit, all tending to discredit the scheme of civilization."[28] That single statement accurately summarizes the essence of the new religion. Certain individuals, some more charismatic than others, claimed to have received visions and direct communications from the Great Spirit, all of which, in one way or another, discredited the Cherokee adoption of the white man's way of life.

The next sentence in the account refers to the Cherokees gathered at Oostenalee town as "a large collection of . . . deluded preachers."[29] At this gathering, women participants performed a great medicine dance and an old man chanted a song from ancient times. The people were quite solemn and fixed their attention on the Cherokee man, who professed to bring a message straight from Heaven. The essence of his speech was that the Great Spirit observed that the Cherokees had adapted customs of white people. Cherokees had mills, clothes, feather beds, tables, and worst of all, books and domestic cats. This was not good, and therefore, game was disappearing. The Great Spirit was angry with the Cherokees and had withdrawn his protection of them. The Cherokees must return to the ancient traditions of their fathers, dress again as Indians, and give up their mills, houses, and all that they had learned from white people. If they did this, game would return, whites would disappear, and God would again love his people. This visionary urged the Cherokees to paint themselves, hold feasts, dance, and listen to the words of the Great Spirit, who would whisper to them in their dreams. He concluded by threatening that the Great Spirit would kill them if they did not believe this.

At the completion of this speech, many people stood up and cried out that the talk was good. Ridge, however, objected to it on the grounds that it would lead the Cherokees to war with the United States. He charged that the talk was false and not from the Great Spirit, and he stood there ready to defy the threat that any who disbelieved it would die. A big fight followed in which Ridge was attacked but ultimately saved by his followers. He then cried out that this proved that the vision was false. Nevertheless, the traditionalists founded a new Cherokee religious movement that made sense of the world they now faced.

James Wofford, a Cherokee, produced the other widely cited version of the Cherokee nativistic and revivalist movement.[30] This account began by predicting that "there would be a terrible hailstorm, which would destroy both the whites and those Indians who chose not to believe the vision. Those who chose to follow the sacred instructions from Heaven would receive warning in time to find safety in the mountains." Like Ridge, Wofford's vision involved no militant resistance against Anglos. This Cherokee prophet stated that the Great Father declared Himself to be the parent of Indians, English, French, and Spaniards, but not Americans—who were created by some evil spirit. In this vision, God asserted, "They, are numberous [sic], but I hate them. They are unjust; they have taken away your lands which were not made for them."[31]

Cherokees responded to these visions. Some in Alabama and Georgia abandoned their bees, their orchards, their slaves, and everything else that came to them through white people and began a pilgrimage to the mountains of North Carolina. James Wofford's white stepmother was able to persuade some of the migrating Cherokees that their fears were groundless. They returned home but others journeyed on to the mountains, where they waited for an appointed day, only to leave disappointed. A few Cherokees believed that the coming of the end of the world was only postponed for a time. Wofford later found other references to revitalization movements of the Cherokees in the official mission diary of the Moravians at Spring Place, Georgia, in entries from February 10, 1811, to April 30, 1812. Again, these should all be read cautiously, since Moravian missionaries believed that Native religion was false and evil and that Indians were doomed to hell unless they converted to Christianity.

Another vision occurred on February 10, 1811. The old Chief Keychzaetel (the Warrior's Nephew) related a narrative to some Moravian missionaries. He reported that he had attended the Council in Oostenalee. While there, a man with two women arrived and told them that, while on a journey, they came to an unoccupied house near a hill called Rocky Mountain and entered it to spend the night. As the sky became dark, they heard a violent noise in the air and went outside, where they saw a group of Indians descending to the hill from the sky. The Indians rode on small black horses and their leader beat a drum as he came very close to them. Frightened at first, the leader called to them to fear not and revealed that they were brothers sent by God to speak with them. The spiritual messenger then told the prophet that God was dissatisfied with Cherokees for receiving white people "without any distinction."[32]

The Cherokees could see for themselves that their hunting was gone and that they were planting the corn of white people. They must sell the white corn back to the whites, plant Indian corn, and pound it in the manner of their forebears. Moreover, the Cherokees were instructed to do away with mills, which were offensive to the Mother of the Nation (who was presumably Selu, the Corn.) She would return to the Cherokees only if they evicted white people from the land and returned to their former manner of life. The messenger then said that white people were entirely different beings from Cherokees; Cherokees were made from red clay, whites from white sand.

The messenger instructed that Cherokees must recover from whites their old beloved towns, although Cherokees were allowed to keep good neighborly relations with them. The visionary looked up at the sky and saw Heaven open, revealing an indescribably beautiful light, and in it, four white houses. The Cherokees must build houses identical to those in their beloved towns—one for Captain Blair, a white man in Georgia who had helped the Cherokees a great deal, and the rest for other white men who could be useful to the Nation. Chief Keychzaetel waited to hear the missionaries' response to this story, which he, in all earnestness, took to be true. No one contradicted the prophet at the Council except for Ridge.

Two months later, on May 10, 1811, Warrior's Nephew visited the missionaries again to bring a report from the Council. He told the missionaries that "the white people must all go out of the Nation; however, 4 smiths, some school teachers and those who are building mills for us are to be tolerated, but later they, too, must return to their own country; and no one shall put anything in their way."[33] The chief then told the missionaries that Cherokees did not consider them as white people but as Indians whom God had sent to teach their people. He also said that the missionaries did not want their land and that they were there out of love for the Cherokees.

The second version of the incident at Oostenalee contains some interesting differences from the first. For example, the vision told Cherokees to build four houses for whites who could be helpful to the Cherokees by teaching them writing. In a report by Ridge, the prophet supposedly insisted that Cherokees abandon writing and any form of communication except word of mouth.[34] Later, the old chief reported to the missionaries that all whites should leave the country except for four smiths, a few schoolteachers, and those who were building mills, and that eventually those folks must leave as well.[35]

This particular version considered some aspects of American life—specifically writing, smithing, education, and mills—to be helpful to the Cherokee people.[36] It is not clear whether the chief wanted to keep them because Cherokees intrinsically valued those aspects of Western culture or because he thought these aspects of American life would help Cherokees better deal with white people in the future. The Warrior's Nephew's version contains elements resembling Melanesian cargo cults in which European goods or cargo were actually prized and therefore sought after. Melanesian cargo cults seemed to emerge after it was evident that the old way of life had been lost forever and that Europeans were there to stay. At that point, cargo arrived, which heralded access to European goods in great abundance.[37]

The 1811 Cherokee religious movement may have contained so many variants in part because no one charismatic leader emerged to solidify a single position among the people. It was, on the one hand, a nativistic revival movement, and on the other hand, a hybrid nativistic and revival development, overlaid with a cargo cult. In the course of two months, interestingly, Warrior's Nephew had brought news of a vision in which the Cherokees learned how to smith metal and mill corn, both of which were exemplary American activities with no parallel in traditional Cherokee religion.

In the version related by Warrior's Nephew, specific instructions demanded that the Cherokees stop growing white corn and do away with all mills, which were extremely offensive to Selu, the source of Cherokee corn. Pounded and milled by hand, that particular corn was the staff and staple of Cherokee life and identity. The Cherokee prophet had described milling as offensive to the Corn Mother, who was angry with the people and withdrew her presence as a result of being disrespected and disregarded. Corn was a sacred substance that was to be planted, harvested, processed, and eaten, as taught by Selu in the "long ago." It was not a commodity to be purchased from whites, planted according to Western farming methods, and then milled by machines created by whites. White modes of farming, however efficient, turned sacred substances into mere commodities, and this change from a sacred subsistence modality to a mechanized, commercial activity represented a loss of spirituality and meaning that tore at the very identity of a Cherokee Indian.

Smithing represented an even more drastic change. There is no evidence that any North American Indian group forged and smithed metals aboriginally. A number of Native Americans, including the Cherokees, did some mining and cold hammering of copper, but there is no evidence they were ever involved in the smithing of metals.[38] The Cherokees did, however, know pottery. In some ways, pottery represented the first artificial product of humans because it is made up of clay, minerals, earth and straw, or grit. In making potter's clay, Cherokees actually created a product not found naturally and thereby participated symbolically in a creative act of the gods. Moreover, the potter baked clay and thereby transformed it into a different material. In firing pottery, Cherokees used an element (fire), which distinguished them from the animal kingdom, to transform a substance into a new material. Heated, clay became plastic; upon cooling, it retained its shape but became hard like stone. Some have argued that pottery actually represented a decisive step in the development of sedentary communities.[39]

Metallurgy, however, represented a more decisive appropriation of nature, and Cherokees did not practice metallurgy traditionally. Converting metallic ores into bronze is an authentic transubstantiation or transmutation. The metamorphosis from solid to liquid and back again to solid, which took place in metallurgy, no doubt struck traditional Cherokees as auspicious and awesome. Smiths employed skills that linked them with the mysteries of the underworld. Traditional societies where smithing did exist, such as the Dogon of Mali in Africa, saw the blacksmith as a spiritual daredevil who took ore from the earth and transformed it into something else. The Yakuts of Siberia held a similar view: "Smiths and shamans come from the same nest." The Yakut also elevated the status of women married to shamans: "the wife of a shaman is worthy of respect, the wife of a smith is worthy of veneration."[40] The prominence of smiths derived from the great heat they used to create new materials. People viewed their profession with awe and fascination. Only the gods, they believed, could take one substance and create another by heat. Most Native peoples in North America deliberately stayed away from metallurgy because they viewed it somewhat suspiciously as a haughty and aggressive activity that might rouse the ire of the gods. The Cherokees arguably once held this view. Smithing concretely exemplified one aspect of the American civilization ideology and policy and clearly differentiated American capitalistic society from Cherokee traditional society. The most significant objects that missionaries created in the first half of the nineteenth century, besides little houses, were blacksmith and triphammer shops. Therefore, it is significant that Warrior's Nephew's second vision referred to smiths and schoolteachers, as well as those who were building mills. His vision, however, did insist that once Cherokees had learned these arts, the whites who taught them must leave.

It is not clear whether Warrior's Nephew was viewing education, smithing, and milling as intrinsically meaningful activities that Cherokees were incorporating into their own way of life or as borrowed tools necessary for Cherokee survival in the face of an encroaching society. The mention of education, smithing, and milling specifically referenced in this second vision is quite telling; at some level it is clear that Warrior's Nephew was ascribing some religious or spiritual significance to those American activities.

On December 16, 1811, an earthquake shook the community of Cherokee, North Carolina, and the people wondered if the world was soon to collapse. Cherokees came up with a variety of theories about the origins of the earthquake. Some attributed the occurrence to the work of sorcerers, some to a very large snake, and some to the weakness of the earth because of its old age.[41] On February 17, 1812, a chief called The Shoeboot (*Chulioa*) came and spoke to the missionaries about the earthquakes that had occurred. He reported that many Cherokees believed that white people were responsible for the earthquakes. Whites had taken so much of the Cherokee's land and still wanted more, so God, through earthquakes, was expressing his anger at them.[42] In reply, another chief called Big Bear spoke about a vision he experienced in December of 1811, following the earthquake.

In this vision, an Indian was sitting in his house, deep in thought, while his children lay in front of the fire. A tall man approached, clothed entirely in tree foliage with a wreath of leaves about his head and carrying a small child in his hand. The man revealed that the child was God. God was not pleased that the Indians had sold so much land to whites. The loss of Tugalo (a mother town in South Carolina) to white people particularly vexed him. Tugalo was the first place God created. God had ignited a fire on a hill in Tugalo, where the white people had now built a house. If whites abandoned the place, there would be peace. The tall man revealed that the Indians no longer thanked God before they enjoyed the firstfruits of the land. They no longer organized dances before they ate the first pumpkins and other fruits and vegetables. He then gave the chief two small pieces of bark from a particular tree and told him to cook them and give them to the children. Then they would become well again. He also instructed the chief about remedies for various illnesses. Afterward he left to take God back home. The missionaries described this narration as silly; they derisively reported that one village, frightened by the visitor, fled into the hills and tried to hide among rocks to escape a coming hailstorm.

On March 8, 1812, a Cherokee woman told Moravians of another vision. An eclipse, which would last three days, was coming. During that eclipse, all white people would be carried away, as well as all Indians who had any of the white man's clothing or household articles. Indians needed to put aside everything acquired or learned from the whites so God would not mistake them for white people. Cherokees who did not believe this prophecy would die along with their stock, a fate one Indian had already met. Some Cherokees were at this point discarding their household articles and clothing.

Although interesting, none of these religious movements took hold of large numbers of Cherokees, perhaps due to the outbreak of the War of 1812. Agent Meigs did report to William Eustis on March 19, 1812, that some Cherokees were throwing their clothing into the fire to prove their rejection of "civilization." Cherokees responded that God was indeed angry, not with whites but with the Cherokee themselves. Cherokee women urged the Cherokees to quit stealing horses and drinking whiskey and to become good people if they wished to make the Great Spirit happy.[43] The Cherokees clearly faced a spiritual crisis for which they were partly responsible, but mostly it was the result of powerful invaders who would not leave them alone. Although none of these movements ever gained much momentum, the nativist and revivalist murmurings of the Cherokees reveal how restless and uncertain life was for Cherokees during this period.

Although the Cherokees wished to remain impartial, the War of 1812 and the associated Creek War drew them in. Perhaps the stark reality of war overshadowed the Cherokees' religious concerns, since they had to unify themselves politically and militarily to survive as a people.[44] On the other hand, revivalist and nativist movements never became widespread among the Cherokees and they mostly retained their traditional religious worldview. Somehow, some way, the Cherokees embodied their ancient orientation to the world. A tribe that the United States labeled "civilized" remained in the end fiercely archaic and mythic. Nevertheless, the Cherokee religious movement of 1811 was one of the early examples of a revitalization movement among Native Americans. Structurally very similar, it predated the Ghost Dance of the Plains Indians by half a century.

CHAPTER 8

Missionaries and Medicine Men

1815–1828

The 1811 Cherokee movement reflected a New World religious orientation. Simultaneously seeking to eliminate white people's values and customs from their way of life,[1] while restoring some traditional Cherokee lifeways, this creative development sought spiritual fulfillment by and through a synthesis of the old and the new.[2] However, the movement did not take, and most Cherokees, after settling down, continued to practice their traditional religion. For most Cherokees, conjurors remained respected spiritual and community leaders who rejected the teachings of Christian missionaries. Meanwhile, around 1820, missionaries became more aggressive, and their push led to vigorous and lively debates with medicine men that sometimes threatened to spill over into violent resistance. From 1824 to 1827, a traditionalist named White Path led a new spiritual movement that rejected certain newly enacted laws containing Christian elements and called for the faithful performance of Cherokee ceremonies.

Other Native American religious movements emerged in the late eighteenth and early nineteenth centuries, including one led by Tecumseh, the Shawnee leader, and his brother, Tenskwatawa, the prophet. In 1811, they traveled to the Creek Nation to share their message. A delegation of Cherokees, led by The Ridge, went to hear Tecumseh speak. Tecumseh urged to his audience to kill the old chiefs, reject everything received from the Americans, and take up the war club.[3] However, he failed to impress the Cherokees. According to oral tradition, Tecumseh visited the Cherokees at Soco at a later time. He met with Junaluska and entreated him to join his militant movement against the whites. According to this Cherokee narrative, Junaluska rejected Tecumseh's invitation to take up arms against the United States, since such a strategy would be suicidal.

Shortly thereafter, war broke out between the Creeks and the United States. The Cherokees joined the United States in a military effort to crush the Creek uprising. General Andrew Jackson led the Cherokees. In the final battle with the Creek Red Sticks at Tohopeka (Horseshoe Bend), the Cherokee fought valiantly and helped the United States crush the Creek rebellion. Oral tradition has it that Junaluska saved Jackson's life in that battle. Jackson praised the Cherokees, who felt strongly that they had shown themselves worthy of the friendship of the president of the United States.[4] Cherokees fought side by side with the Americans against the Creek in an effort to show that they could be trusted and, hopefully, left alone. In large part, Cherokee participation in the Creek War was a cultural strategy designed to enhance their efforts to remain on their sacred homeland, which was a central dimension of their traditional religious orientation.

ADAPTATION

By 1811, some Cherokees, like Charles Hicks and Lewis Ross, pushed assimilation with great vigor, but they represented a powerful minority of Cherokees. Most Cherokees at that time did not speak English and did not consider themselves Christian. It was in this context that Cherokee political reform accelerated. Between 1820 and 1823, the Cherokees passed eleven laws.[5] Under these laws, the Cherokee National Council created a bicameral legislature and a district and superior court system, duplicating the basic structure of the American political and judicial systems. The majority of the members of the Council were traditional Cherokees who must have struggled mightily with the imposition of a new political system.

Cherokee political and economic life changed and some Christian influence was present, but the old spiritual character of the Cherokee people remained the same for most of the nineteenth century. Few Cherokees in 1830 identified themselves as Christians.[6] The Cherokees were still Cherokee, and that meant, as much as anything else, a people who shared many old worldviews and lifeways. In the end, widespread and deeply felt spiritual meanings, values, and purposes tied the Cherokees together fundamentally as a people. This abiding spirituality survived in the face of rapid political, economic, and social change. But the Cherokee situation was complicated by the integral relationship of economics, politics, and society with their religion.

LOSS OF TRADITIONAL GENDER ROLES

The continued efforts of the US government to force the American model of farming on Native people unquestionably diminished certain fundamental Cherokee religious values. This happened to many Indian peoples, and Cherokees were no exception. To survive and to live on their ancestral homelands, Cherokee men gave up being hunters and turned to the work that women traditionally had done. This created a great spiritual dilemma for the Cherokees, who responded in at least two different ways. Some Cherokee men preferred to move west where they continued to hunt and embody Kanati's traditional values. Cherokees who stayed in the east suffered from the loss of a hunting way of life, but they felt that it was most critical to live where their world was created. Both views were religious responses to forced economic, political, and social change, and the choices were difficult ones for Cherokees to make. Cherokee women faced a similar dilemma. They could either stay in the east where the clan system and the matrilineal way of life were waning, or they could move to Arkansas and attempt to preserve more traditional social structures, but with the loss of family ties.

The traditional division of labor between men and women established by Kanati and Selu in the beginning of time had been fundamentally altered. Cherokee women now spent their time spinning and weaving rather than cultivating crops and dressing deer hides. Men herded cattle more than they hunted deer. Locating the nearest gristmill was more important than preparing for warfare. In the midst of all this change, friction emerged between most Cherokees and a small party of more acculturated Cherokees. The latter told President John Quincy Adams that the Cherokee people would gladly see their traditional customs and way of life extinguished if they were allowed to stay on their ancestral lands.[7] This statement shows both how acculturated certain Cherokees were and how desperate all Cherokees were to preserve their lands. Most Cherokees wanted to live on the land of their ancestors. Even a highly acculturated Christian Cherokee like Charles Hicks possessed, at least at an unconscious level, a strong spiritual connection to Cherokee lands. In other words, deep down, he may have been more traditional than even he realized.

TRADITIONALISM AND REVIVALISM

In 1820, the Cherokees were by and large a traditional people religiously. Christian missionaries had been in the area for about a generation but had made very few inroads despite the fact that Christian missionaries had spread throughout the land and were aggressively proselytizing the Cherokee people. Cherokees had already undergone significant changes, but they had been able to maintain their traditional religious orientation to a large degree. However, missionaries were now poised to a make a full-frontal assault on the old ways. Even the missionaries most sympathetic and sensitive to the Cherokees proclaimed that Christianity was the sole path to spiritual truth. In contrast, they described traditional Cherokee religion as superstitious, primitive, savage, and, therefore, false.

Aggressive missionary activity produced much resentment among some Cherokees. By 1827, religious factionalism was in many ways the most serious internal problem the Cherokees faced. Christian missionaries attempted to prevent converts participating in a host of traditional Cherokee practices, such as ball games, conjuring, and ceremonies. The evangelism of Christian missionaries became more aggressive as missionaries denounced traditional beliefs and practices, verbally attacked medicine men, and divided family members from one another. Cherokees began to resist and at least one village, as late as 1824, prohibited both schools and churches.[8]

No matter how acculturated some of the Cherokee leaders became, no matter how much their lives appeared to mirror those of non-Native plantation owners, most never gave up the idea of holding most land in common. The importance of common landholding underlay their traditional notions of religion, even among converted Christians, and set them in opposition to the ideology and political policy bent on ultimately dividing Cherokee lands in severalty. The treaties of 1817 and 1819 enabled Cherokees to become US citizens and receive private reserves of land.[9] Some Cherokees, including prominent ones, chose to accept these reserves and become citizens, but most Cherokees did not choose this option and the reserves ultimately failed.

Underlying the apparent division between Christianity and traditional Cherokee religion was a spiritual unity based on ancient symbols and meanings, which tied the people together in a way that made it possible for the various factions and competing religions to coexist. At the same time, the period from 1815 to 1838, more than any other, reflected the mounting tension between Christian missionaries and traditional Cherokee medicine men as they vied for adherence among the people.

RESISTANCE TO MISSIONARY ACTIVITY

The Cherokees had already successfully rebuffed the efforts of a dominant society to forcibly change them economically, politically, and socially. The final assault on Cherokee identity was now underway. Missionaries, who initially established themselves around 1800, became entrenched throughout Cherokee country by 1815. They established schools, which Cherokees initially saw as beneficial. However, they eventually became more aggressive in proselytizing. A handful of missionaries were sympathetic to the Cherokee cause, or at least became so after a period of contact with them.[10] Nevertheless, they brought with them the ideology of civilization and a biased understanding of Christianity as the exclusive religious truth. Historical sources are full of references by missionaries who attempted to both civilize and convert Cherokees. Some Christian denominations felt that Cherokees must be educated and civilized before they could be Christianized, while others felt that Christianity led converts down the road to civilization.[11] In any event, Christian missionaries to the Cherokees in the nineteenth century were part and parcel of an orientation and ideology bent on "converting and civilizing" the Cherokees.

The 7th Annual Report of the American Board of Commissioners for Foreign Missions (ABCFM), published in September of 1816, set forth a mission statement and goal quite clearly: "To establish rules in the different parts of the tribe under the missionary direction and superintendence, for the instruction of the rising generation in common school learning, in the useful arts of life, and in Christianity, so as gradually, with the divine blessings to make the whole tribe English in the language, civilized in their habits, and Christian in their religion."[12] In the end, all missionaries, whatever their denomination, wanted Cherokees to become civilized and Christianized.

The ABCFM, headquartered in Boston, established the Brainerd Mission, which kept daily reports from its establishment in 1818 until 1825. The mission remained open until it closed on August 19, 1838, just before Cherokee removal.[13] One journal entry on April 9, 1818, makes reference to its twofold policy of Christian civilization: "Oh how shall we white people answer when God inquires after our red brethren! Shall we use the language of some, & say, 'it is of no use to preach the

Gospel to them; they cannot be Christianized, or civilized?'"[14] Another Brainerd journal entry dated August 15, 1818, following a conversation with a fellow mission, noted, "they expressed great satisfaction in the progress of Christianity & civilization among this people."[15] On March 6, 1817, a Brainerd journal entry referred to a meeting with recent Cherokee converts to Christianity: "Here for the first time I beheld the dear sisters who are to be our associates in the arduous work of civilizing & converting the savages of our wilderness."[16]

None of this is to say that Christian missionaries did not have good intentions in doing their work among the Cherokees or that they were completely blind to traditional Cherokee religious practices. Indeed, one passage in a Brainerd journal mentions that, although most of the lower class of Cherokee people have no understanding of religion, some Cherokees have a "few correct ideas concerning a Supreme Being & a future state."[17] However, even there, the missionaries proceeded to write that they were not sure if the notion of Supreme Being existed traditionally or came about after contact with white people.[18]

Cherokees, for the most part, did not take kindly to the missionaries' attempts to convert them in an aggressive manner that denigrated their traditional religious principles. Conflict was bound to emerge, and indeed it did. In 1820, the Cherokees expressed an anti-assimilation position in several ways. First, the Council attempted to regulate mission movements. When this failed, Cherokee conjurors tried to counter the aggressive proselytizing by openly confronting missionaries whenever they arrived in a community.[19] A smallpox epidemic, which struck the Cherokee in 1824, fostered further resistance. Conjurors began openly debating missionaries; these discussions sometimes turned angry and, on occasion, violent. Where Christian missions were successful, they often became a very divisive force, splitting families and disrupting local communities.[20]

Missionaries held a religious worldview very different from that of traditional Cherokees. In one interesting interchange, a Cherokee medicine man named William engaged ABCFM missionary Daniel Butrick in a long discussion about Cherokee medicine. William told Butrick that Cherokees did not worship nature nor did they have an idolatrous understanding of God. He admitted that Cherokee medicine men called upon eagles and butterflies to help them perform cures. But he said in doing so, they did not refer to the eagles seen on earth, but to beings in heaven that shared the same names as those on earth. Butrick was not swayed and did not wish to continue the conversation, while the

Cherokee conjuror concluded that Cherokees and Christians were not even talking about the same spiritual power. The two lived in entirely different religious worlds.[21]

Missionaries objected to Cherokee ceremonies, medical practices, and the ball game. Cherokees practiced these three fundamental aspects of religious life widely and adamantly resisted change. Cherokee missionaries often discussed these activities as evil or polluting and discouraged Christian converts from participating in them. In contrast, many Christian Cherokees did not see a conflict between Christianity and Cherokee ceremonies, medicine, and stickball, and participated freely in both. In one conversation in 1822, Reverend William Chamberlain told an elderly Cherokee woman who'd inquired about traditional medicine that it was acceptable for her to administer it to the sick but that it was not okay for her to use the art of conjuring. Of course, that was nonsensical. Cherokee medicine was and is inseparably related to Cherokee religion.

During this time, Sequoyah invented his syllabary, which allowed Cherokees to write their own language. The syllabary enabled Christian missionaries, some of them Cherokee, to spread the Christian gospel in the language of the Cherokees, but it also allowed medicine men and women to preserve sacred formulas and medicine rituals. Paradoxically, Sequoyah's invention of writing enhanced both missionary activity and traditional Cherokee "doctoring." Traditionalists especially liked writing in their own language, which no doubt contributed to a revival of Cherokee traditionalism.

WHITE PATH'S REVIVAL (1824–1827)

In 1823, several chiefs called for the removal of the ABCFM missionaries and schoolteachers in the North Carolina town of Etowah (Enhalla). Most Cherokees recognized the need for free schools so they could learn English and basic bookkeeping, but the schools were linked with Protestant missions. The centralization of Cherokee government was a necessary evil, but it was moving too fast for traditional Cherokees. In 1824, the Cherokee majority participated in a spiritual movement, often called White Path's Rebellion, which can be understood best as the culmination of the antimission sentiment that had existed in Cherokee for several years.[22] Cherokees tolerated missions when they were helpful to the Cherokee cause, but most grew tired of missionaries trying to displace Cherokee religion with Christianity. The political change that took place between 1819 and 1824, including the 1825 change in inheritance laws, marked a movement away from traditional Cherokee ways and toward Christian practices. This transition culminated when the Cherokees wrote a constitution in 1827. Cherokee leaders wanted an independent Cherokee nation, but they also wanted to prove to white Americans that the Cherokees were civilized, Christian, farmers, and entrepreneurs.

James Wofford, a Cherokee Christian, called it "a rebellion against the new code of laws" and charged that White Path "preached the rejection of the new constitution, the discarding of Christianity and the white man's ways, and the return to the old tribal law and customs."[23] Several Cherokees reported visions, dreams, and spiritual messages sent by their ancestors or from the Great Spirit.[24] One vision spoke of the Cherokees' current way of life as godless, meaning lack of respect for Cherokee traditional religion.[25] For the most part, White Path's Revival was a revitalization movement of Cherokees against Christianity. Cherokees held traditional dances and ceremonies and medicine men openly practiced their craft in front of missionaries. William Chamberlain of the ABCFM called them "the heathen party" and accused them of threatening to drive out Christianity. His colleague Isaac Proctor revealed that this party spoke for the majority of Cherokees.[26] Furthermore, this movement was not an internal fight against the ruling class, many of whom paid serious attention to this affirmation of the old ways.[27]

Even many of the Christians cast a suspicious eye toward Christian missionaries. John Ross, former president of the Constitutional Convention and delegate to the 1827 Cherokee Constitutional Convention, was reportedly very cold toward the missionaries at Brainerd, calling into question the argument that only "full-bloods" opposed missions in 1827.[28] In the end, the dissatisfied parties allowed themselves to be convinced and joined in the passing of the constitution.

Unfortunately, there is no record of what took place among the Cherokees to pull the factions together. The secrecy of this resolution was perhaps deliberate and brought about because all Cherokees involved understood it to be a matter of national security, tribal sovereignty, religious freedom, and a way to preserve their sacred homeland.

US agents and Protestant missionaries exerted considerable pressure on the early Cherokee government, and Cherokee laws clearly reflected their influence. As Perdue noted, "when the Cherokees established a national police force, reordered inheritance patterns, abolished clan vengeance, extended Cherokee citizenship to descendants of intermarried white women, disenfranchised women, and made polygamy and infanticide illegal, they won the approval of these powerful forces."[29] Perdue goes on to note that many council members did in fact embrace major tenets of the civilization program, but it is doubtful whether the average Cherokee adopted such a redefinition of gender and identity. Cherokees did not reject old customs and traditions in the space of a few decades. As Perdue put it, "The evidence . . . points to remarkable cultural persistence."[30] In 1828, the North Carolina General Assembly informed US Congress that "the red men are not within the pales of civilization, they are not under the restraints of morality, nor the influence of religion; and they are always disagreeable and dangerous neighbors to a civilized people."[31]

White Path's Revival demonstrated more than merely Cherokee factionalism between a pagan party and a Christian party; it was a religious movement that rejected laws containing Christian elements and called for the continuation of traditional ceremonies. Its purpose was twofold: reject American customs while renewing commitment to traditional Cherokee values and traditions.

CHAPTER 9

Cherokees, Christianity, and Myth

1818–1830

PAYNE-BUTRICK PAPERS (1818–1838)

At the time of removal in 1838, three-fourths of Cherokees were not intermarried with whites, only 1 percent spoke English, and only 8 percent were Christians, according to the missionaries,[1] although some Cherokees had incorporated certain aspects of Christianity into the old Cherokee religion. Writer John Howard Payne and missionary Reverend Daniel Butrick chronicled in great detail the religious practices of the Cherokees, especially from 1817 through 1838, but their accounts must be read critically.[2] The authors believed that the Cherokees were one of the lost tribes of Israel, and therefore they constantly looked for connections between Cherokee religion and Judeo-Christian tradition. Moreover, at least some Cherokees, either consciously or unconsciously, had incorporated aspects of Christianity into their own religious worldviews.

Religiously speaking, the historical introduction of Christian teachings may have prompted the Cherokees to remember certain timeless traditions.[3] Decades after Payne and Butrick's accounts, James Mooney learned from traditional elders and Cherokee conjurors—many of whom were not Christian—a large corpus of Cherokee mythology that shows little Christian or outside influence.[4] In the end, the weight of the historical evidence supports the argument that the *Payne-Butrick Papers* contain biblical and Christian elements that had been incorporated or fused into traditional Cherokee religion. Because Payne and Butrick collected this material on the eve of removal, those Cherokee elders opposed to removal may have felt they could increase their chances of remaining if they appeared to embrace Christianity as well as "civilization."

Even today, a few traditional Cherokee elders and conjurors adamantly insist that the Cherokees are a lost tribe of Israel and have no qualms about practicing traditional Cherokee religion along with Christianity. At the same time, aspects of "doctoring" do create cause for concern for some Cherokee Christians. In a recent discussion with one of the book's authors, a traditional Cherokee medicine man, who was a converted Christian, made this point. Christianity, he said, has indeed influenced his practice of Cherokee traditional medicine. For example, he said that since he has become a devout Christian, he does only "good things," never "bad things," while practicing Cherokee traditional medicine.[5] The distinction between good and bad gets very gray in Cherokee conjuring, and, in fact, one man's good may be another man's bad.[6] When a group of Christian Cherokees did not approve of this medicine man's traditional "doctoring," he reported feeling pressured to move away from them. He also made the point that he no longer practices Cherokee medicine that is designed to harm another person. He did not, however, denounce love charms and said that he would only "bring two people together" after he had examined the situation carefully and made a determination that they should be together.

The *Payne-Butrick Papers* begin with a discussion of Cherokee "early unorthodox religions."[7] Payne and Butrick understood the difficulty of the problem. The oldest, most pervasive creation myth of the Cherokees described sacred beings coming down from the heavens and creating the world. These beings were eternal and always thought in unison. Payne and Butrick observed that one faction of Cherokee people described them in very general terms while another group employed three different words to express their names. Unfortunately, the three words expressing these sacred beings were archaic and obsolete by the time Payne and Butrick collected them.

The narrative structure of the Cherokee cosmogony that references the descent of sacred beings from heaven to form the world is analogous to the cosmogonic myth collected by James Mooney in 1888 from Swimmer, a famous medicine man. Interestingly, Swimmer's creation narrative contains much detail, while the entire narrative collected by Payne and Butrick consists of only a few sentences. Either Payne and Butrick's informants deliberately withheld details of the traditional

Cherokee cosmogonic myth, or being recent converts, the informants were so influenced by Christianity they did not know the myth. Or perhaps the Payne-Butrick informants, threatened with removal, were trying to curry favor with outsiders.[8]

Mooney, like a number of early ethnologists, sought the origins and purist forms of Cherokee religion, unadulterated by the influence of Europeans and Americans. However, in his quest to do so, he may have taken liberties with some content, although there is no evidence that he did. There is no pure form of Cherokee religion distinct from its historical circumstances, and myth always incorporates historical elements into its timeless structures. Mooney was impressed, however, with how contact with whites had little changed Cherokee mythology.[9] Still, he went too far when he said, "The Bible story kills the Indian tradition, and there is no amalgamation."[10]

A careful review of the *Payne-Butrick Papers* shows that this is not the case. Mooney noted that similar sacred narratives existed all over the world. He mentioned, for example, stories of a huge fish that swallowed a man and of a great flood that destroyed the people around the world.[11] The *Payne-Butrick Papers*, on the other hand, constantly drew parallels with Judaism as proof of the shared religious origins and were quite defensive about it. Payne and Butrick were aided in their enterprise by Chief John Ross, who assured them that the consultants he provided for this work were very traditional men, many of whom were carriers of ancient Cherokee tradition untouched by Christianity. Still, one has to wonder if Chief Ross sought to prevent removal by convincing Americans of an ancient, shared heritage. Or had Cherokee mythology seamlessly woven certain aspects of Judaism into the fabric of Cherokee spirituality, at least for some Cherokees?

The *Payne-Butrick Papers* discussed the obsolete archaic names that were used to describe the three primordial beings. The first, *U-ha-lo-te-qa*, means "Head of all Power," or literally "Great Beyond Expression." The second name, *A-ta-no-ti*, means "United," or literally the "Place of Uniting." The third name, *Usqo-hu-lo*, signifies "Bowels Just Below the Breast." These beings are eternal; they created all things, know all things, are everywhere present, and govern all things.[12] They determine when and how every creature dies and are enthroned in purity on "Three White Seats above." All prayers should be addressed to them, and they judge, reward, and punish. This idea of an archaic Cherokee trinity may represent some Christian influence, although the Cherokees may have originally possessed such a concept. However, for Cherokees, four and seven—not three—are the sacred numbers. Nevertheless, one contemporary Cherokee has stated that the Cherokees easily accepted and adopted the teachings of Christianity, and particularly those of the Christian Trinity, because they already had their own Trinity: the sun, the moon, and the stars. Perhaps aboriginal Cherokee religion did embody the concept of a sacred trinity.

These three terms referred to the following sacred levels: above, the center or the middle, and the below—that is to say, they referred to Heaven, Earth, and the Underworld, the cosmic regions corresponding respectively to "head," "place of uniting," and "bowels." Cherokees have always had a notion of three vertical regions. However, the matter is complicated by the fact that these terms were apparently obsolete and archaic by 1835. In other places, the *Payne-Butrick Papers* refer to the Cherokee High God as "Great Supreme."[13] Elsewhere Daniel Butrick, drawing upon various materials collected from 1817 through 1847, reports that a Cherokee named Kotiski refers to the Supreme Being as "Great White Being."[14]

There was truly no Cherokee orthodoxy, which is typical of Native American religions. Cherokees were not concerned with standardizing their religion as were the Abrahamic traditions. Different villages, classes, religious societies, and clans generated slightly different versions of religious expression, none of which caused Cherokees any real consternation. Cherokees were a traditional, mythological people whose worldview saw continuity and parallel where historical people saw contradiction.

Reverend Butrick lived with the Cherokees for more than thirty years and spoke the Cherokee language. Butrick arrived at age twenty-eight in Northern Georgia in 1817 as a representative of the American Board of Commissioners for Foreign Missions. He helped establish a station among the Cherokees at Brainerd, Tennessee, a few miles north of the Georgia state line. The complexity and beauty of the Cherokee language impressed Butrick, who concluded that "in many respects their language is far superior to ours."[15] He began to learn Cherokee, but he also retained his ethnocentrism.[16] Butrick was a very astute observer of the tensions that mounted among many Cherokees around 1824 and the growing division between those poorer Cherokees who practiced traditional religion and the wealthier Christian converts who were often more educated.[17] Although Butrick did learn the language and was somewhat sympathetic, he possessed an ethnocentric view of Cherokee culture. For example, as late as 1827 he denounced traditional medicinal practices as the "black waters of hedonism," which he said involved prayers, "to some fictitious, imaginary being who had no real existence in the universe."[18]

Chief Ross assured Reverend Butrick that the consultants he had sent to him were people almost entirely secluded from whites and steeped in ancient tradition.[19] Ross may have been entirely honest in his representation of these people, and, if so, this shows how Indigenous peoples like the Cherokees merged outside influences with their underlying older traditions. Some Cherokee traditionalists may have appropriated certain Old Testament ideas and myths to support an "anti-Christian tradition."[20] For example, when Cherokee consultants related to Butrick the stories of the flood following forty days of rain, the loss of one original language, and the parting of the great water, they in effect wove the biblical stories of Noah, the Tower of Babel, and Moses into Cherokee mythology.[21] Conversely, Butrick interpreted Cherokee stories of Selu, Kanati, and their children, the Thunder Beings, as derivations of the Biblical story of Adam and Eve and Cain and Abel.[22] There appeared to be two different, but complementary, modes of understanding in Cherokee religious consciousness during the first half of the nineteenth century. The *Payne-Butrick Papers* are full of Cherokee myths that clearly incorporate biblical and Christian elements, despite the fact that John Ross provided as Cherokee consultants those traditional Cherokees who had had minimal contact with whites.

One cannot discount the possibility that consultants related Christianized Cherokee mythical narratives to placate and favorably impress the missionaries for political reasons. Today, some Cherokees claim that these stories "were slyly manufactured to mislead or poke fun at the missionaries."[23] This argument is plausible, particularly when comparing Payne and Butrick's myths to those of James Mooney.[24] Butrick recorded myths that he believed revealed the Cherokees' Jewish ancestry, while Mooney wrote down myths devoid of any Jewish or Christian references. We should never discount the lens through which Payne and Butrick, on the one hand, and Mooney, on the other, interpreted what they heard from Cherokee informants.

A number of mythical narratives draw upon biblical narratives. For example, some Cherokee narratives, such as the story of Noah and the Tower of Babel, fused with Cherokee myths to produce a syncretistic blend Cherokees perceived as aboriginal. To use the terminology of Edward Spicer, Cherokees "incorporated" biblical events into the existing Cherokee mythology, thereby producing a narrative in which the outside influence appears native. This is a classic example of mythical thinking and typifies Native Americans as well as Indigenous peoples all over the world. That which at first glance seemed new and novel eventually became part of the existing archaic mythology so that it was ultimately viewed as timeless. To the degree Cherokees continued to think mythically at times, as they do to this very day, outsiders perceived these influences as aboriginal. Equally interesting about Cherokee religion, however, is the way in which some Cherokees did, in fact, adopt Christianity.

DEVELOPMENT OF A NEW WORLD RELIGION

How did the Cherokee people view their incorporation or adoption of this new religion brought to them by European Americans in the nineteenth century? The answer is surprising. Some Cherokees who adopted Christianity saw themselves as one of the Lost Tribes of Israel and some, conversely, said Christians must have borrowed (or stolen) their religion. In other words, they believed that conversion to Christianity did not ultimately involve the adaptation of something new and foreign. Rather, it was simply the reestablishment of the Cherokees' own ancient religion.[25] By adopting Christianity in the nineteenth century, Cherokees embraced beliefs that they perceived had an ancestry in common with their old ways.

For example, in traditional Cherokee spirituality, going to water was a widespread fundamental ritual practice. When Christian missionaries told Cherokees they must be baptized in the river be born again into the Christian faith, many Cherokees saw a common thread with going to water. At the same time, the Cherokees did not have a notion of original sin, and no doubt that concept remained very strange to them. But the important point is that many Cherokees in the first half of the nineteenth century embraced Christianity because they understood Christianity to be their most ancient religion.

Cherokees have always incorporated Judeo-Christian and Western European elements into their religion on their terms. Some of the earliest examples of this come from the diaries of the Moravian Brethren at Spring Place Mission, established Georgia in 1801. Clemens de Baillou published a diary entry from October 12, 1815, in which Chief Elk related the origin narrative reprinted below:

Moravian diaries, 1815. October 12.
Chief Elk requests Brother Gambold to write the following to Col. Migs:
You said at the Tookabatchee that the White men wanted more land from the Indians. Now I want to tell you about our origins. In the beginning there

was only one man and one woman on earth; they had two sons who had designs on the life of their mother under the pretext that she was a sorcerer because she provided them with plenty of food, yet they could not find out where she obtained it, for she did not plant anything herself. And that was her errand; she would go out and return very soon with the necessary food. Their wrongdoing was finally discovered by the mother and she spoke to them about it and asked them to refrain from it because she was not going to stay with them much longer, but would go up to heaven and they would not see her any more. She would, however, keep a watchful eye on all their actions. If they did wrong, darkness would encompass them.

Soon after this she left her sons and ascended. The father was not at home at the time. When he came back he let the sons know that he was displeased with their behavior toward their mother, told them to do better, and handed them a book from which they were to learn how to act and behave. One of the sons snatched the book violently and hurried away from his father's house with it. The father, before ascending, drew a line between the two brothers and their houses. This line is the sea. But now the two brothers got a lot of fun out of playing in the water, the one (brother) who was in possession of the book on the far side, and the other brother (who stayed in his father's house) on this side. They took canoes and followed the course of the sun, which, as they observed, always sets in the lake. Finally King George, on the other side of the line, made bigger boats and in them his people followed the course of the sun until they finally came ashore on this side. In these big boats King George sent his brothers presents. These brothers were completely naked, and the first brother was still alive, but he was old and could not run as fast as the young men, so they carried off all the presents and kept them for themselves. I . . . . Elk, am truly a descendent of the family of the first inhabitant of this side of the lake in the 7th generation. In the beginning the brothers on this side were as white as those across the lake, but did not take so much care to protect themselves from the sun. And I am the only man in the nation who knows this.

The account begins with an abbreviated version of the myth of Selu and Kanati, the ancestors of the Cherokee people. Many details are, of course, omitted from this version but the basic structure of the story is clearly demonstrated. Significantly, Chief Elk maintains that Kanati, the original ancestor of the Cherokee people, handed the two sons a book on how to act and behave. One of the sons grabbed the book and ran away. Kanati then drew a line between the houses of the two brothers, and this line became the sea. The brother who possessed the book was on the far side of the sea, and the other remained in his father's house on the Cherokee side. Eventually, according to this narrative, King George, who was on the far side, made boats bigger than canoes and followed the course of the sun until they reached Cherokee lands. Chief Elk, a descendant of the first inhabitant of this side of the lake, said that originally the Cherokees were as white as those on the other side of the lake but failed to protect themselves from the sun. Judeo-Christian religion had infused Cherokee religion, at least among some Cherokees, after only fifteen years of contact with Christian missionaries.[26]

Cherokee incorporation of Euro-American elements into their Indigenous worldview after such a short period of time demonstrates the impact that settlers had on the Cherokee way of life in the early nineteenth century. The Euro-American presence was constant and significant, and it paralleled fundamental changes in the Cherokee perception of the world. Although Chief Elk's origin narrative does not reflect conversion to Christianity, it does show the mythologizing of the Euro-American presence in Cherokee life. Settlers are not simply visitors from another land who have come to interact with the Cherokees on Cherokee terms. Rather, they are a very powerful and disruptive force whose religion Cherokees wove into their own sacred narratives after only fifteen years of interaction.

Historically novel events become embodied in the archaic mythical structures of a people. The American presence was neither temporary nor small scale. As Charles Long has noted, Western newcomers eventually became "subsumed under the structure of this mythical apprehension."[27] At one point, Cherokees perceived Euro-Americans through their own worldview; but the changes occurred too rapidly for the Cherokees to incorporate them completely into the traditional Cherokee mythical model. Change was rapid and far reaching, and it ruptured the traditional Cherokee framework in fundamental ways. Even so, Cherokees still largely apprehended the world mythically and religiously. Although the Cherokee people were unable to locate the settler presence within old mythic categories, the mythical lens through which they viewed the world remained very much alive. Cherokees, therefore, undertook the creation of a new mythology that helped them make sense of their traditional past and the historic present in religious terms.[28] This process in many ways continues to this very day.

The period of time from 1800 to 1830 saw much mixing of Cherokee traditional religion with Christianity.[29] However, Cherokee syncretism is more complex than the simple blending of Cherokee and Christian elements into a new religious vision.[30] First, the Cherokee religious orientation fused not just Christian and Cherokee narratives but also various other Euro-American cultural elements. In the first half of the nineteenth century, Cherokee religion involved the creation of mythologies that made sense of European Americans. Some of the Euro-American influences that Cherokees incorporated into their creation narratives were of Judeo-Christian origin, but some were of a more secular nature. For example, Cherokee mythology also embraced the fact that European Americans came to Cherokee country from across the sea and that their skin was lighter than that of Cherokees.[31]

Equally significant, Cherokees in the nineteenth century also remained a traditional people.[32] That is, Cherokees apprehended the world mythically more than they did historically and scientifically, and they often rejected American notions of geography and astronomy. One missionary asserted in 1821 that Cherokees discovered wonder in the creation but did not understand nature. At Creek Path the previous summer, he'd been discussing with a number of Cherokees the distances of several planets and the causes of eclipses, when an elderly Cherokee man responded that he was entirely wrong. No one knew the size of any planet, he said, or its distance from the sun. Furthermore, the stars and moon moved around the Earth, not vice versa.[33]

The Cherokee elder's response to the missionary's lecture on astronomy was not based on his ignorance of Western science but rather was part of his mythical worldview. Cherokees often emphasized a religious perception of the world more than a scientific one. Most Cherokees recognized that whites had superior technical and scientific knowledge, but they understood the superiority of American technological power in religious terms. In a blurring of categories, many Cherokees attributed this knowledge to possession of the Bible, which God gave them in the beginning.[34]

Other Cherokee myths revealed that the Great Spirit originally gave a book (the Bible) to the red man, who took it, looked at it, but could not understand it. The Great Spirit then gave the book to the white man, who understood it. The Great Spirit then presented the red man a tomahawk, bows, and arrows, and taught him to hunt, to love his friends, to hate riches, and to ban hunger. The Great Spirit also taught Cherokees to love truth, to hate a lie, to never steal, and to kill none but enemies. From the book the white man learned architecture, agriculture, fortification, and machinery. From the wampum belt given to the Indians, they learned to bear hunger, thirst, and fatigue; to endure heat and cold, poverty and misery; to bear pain without complaint; to revere the Great Spirit; to love their friends and hate their enemies; and to seek revenge.[35]

In 1829, a conjuror told Reverend Evan Jones that Cherokees originally possessed great knowledge, which they lost. The Creator first offered the book now possessed by the whites to Indians, but, being unable to read, they did not understand it. Consequently, the Creator took it away and gave it to the whites.[36] One version of the myth blamed whites for stealing the book from the Indians, but in another version, Cherokees sold the book to whites.[37] Reverend Worcester published an article in the *Cherokee Phoenix* in 1829 that discussed a Cherokee myth set in the Garden of Eden. The wicked one tempted the first man with fruit, which brought death to humankind. An older Cherokee myth depicted people multiplying in great numbers, which alarmed the beings who dwelled above about overpopulation. Therefore, they sent an evil one to bring about death.[38]

In 1824, a Cherokee had a vision after nearly dying from an illness. He had visited Heaven, where corn grew without work and deer were plentiful. He saw many Indians who were in very good health but no white people.[39] John Haywood reported in 1823 that the Cherokees believed the spirits of departed Cherokees traveled down a road to a place where the road forked. Those that had led good lives continued on a right-hand path into a pleasant country that had an eternal spring and where game was plentiful. Those who had lived wicked lives went down the left-hand road to a cold, barren country where they encountered constant danger and bad spirits.[40] Despite those stories, Cherokees did not concentrate on the afterlife the way Christians did. In the 1820s, Reverend Evan Jones stated that Cherokees did not fear death, perhaps for the reason Pathkiller revealed to the missionaries. When he was very young the elders told him that when Cherokees died, they went to another country where people lived in great towns and villages. He hastened to add that Cherokees did not talk much about this.[41]

During this period of Cherokee-Christian fusion, very few Cherokees actually converted to Christianity. Christians made up only 8 to 10 percent of the population at the time of removal, and only 12 percent of the Cherokee Nation in 1860 claimed membership in one of the five denominations among them. The Cherokee nation in 1830 still consisted largely of traditionalists, who comprised 75 percent of the population. Only 1 percent of Cherokees spoke English in 1835.[42] Christianity had made inroads at that time, but the Cherokee people, by and large, were still very traditional. At the same time, Cherokees incorporated Christian elements into Cherokee mythology. For example, several Cherokee elders told Daniel Butrick that the first woman was made from the rib of the first man.[43]

But the synthesis of Christianity with Cherokee religion was tenuous at best. Although many Cherokees incorporated certain aspects of the

Bible and American customs into their mythology and way of life, they preserved much of their traditional religion and orientation to the world. For example, nineteenth century Cherokees had serious misgivings about loving one's enemies. Cephas Washburn relates a conversation with a Cherokee named Ta-ka-e-tua, who rejected outright the idea of turning one's cheek to an enemy. The Cherokee justified revenge as an act of justice.[44] Moreover, Cherokees did not understand the Christian concepts of sin and salvation.[45] In 1830, Cherokees were still very traditional, although quite successful in adapting to the dominant society.

CHAPTER 10

Christianity and Cherokee Removal

1830–1838

Politically, by 1830, Cherokees had changed forever. The population of the United States had grown dramatically between 1810 and 1830 and encroaching settlers crowded the Cherokees and other southeastern Indian tribes to an intolerable degree.[1] The Cherokees adopted a constitution in 1827 and took great steps to centralize their government. They had demonstrated to the United States of America that they were a "civilized nation," which should be allowed to remain on their sacred homelands. However, after the 1828 election of Andrew Jackson jeopardized a decision the Cherokees had reached in 1822 to cede no more land east of the Mississippi, the federal government began to press for the removal of all eastern Indians west of the Mississippi River into Indian Country.

President Jackson announced that Indians were mere subjects of the government and should be treated as such. Accordingly, the federal government must negotiate no more treaties with Indian nations. He insisted that Indians must move away unless they wanted to live under state jurisdiction as second-class citizens.[2] Jackson delivered this message in no uncertain terms at his annual speech to Congress on December 8, 1829. Indians, said Jackson, could remain in the east only if they submitted to state law, had no tribal government, and held no land in common.

The US Supreme Court handed down three important decisions between 1823 and 1832, which became the foundation for federal Indian law. Two of those decisions involved the Cherokees as parties.

One held that the laws of the state of Georgia had no effect in Cherokee country. However, President Jackson ignored Chief Justice Marshall's decision, and in 1838, the United States began forcibly removing Cherokees west into what became Oklahoma. A few Cherokees escaped capture by hiding out in the North Carolina mountains, and some of those resistors helped form the Eastern Band of Cherokee Indians. One Cherokee, Tsali, became a spiritual and cultural hero whose defiant selflessness, in some ways, exemplifies certain values that Eastern Cherokees embody to this day.

JURISPRUDENCE: THE MARSHALL TRILOGY

In 1823, the US Supreme Court handed down an important decision concerning Indian land rights in the seminal case of *Johnson v. McIntosh*.[3] This case explicitly lays out Euro-American ideology. Justice Marshall described "the superior genius of Europe" in relation to American Indians and noted that Europeans bestowed on Indians "civilization and Christianity."[4] Furthermore, Marshall asked whether "agriculturalists, merchants and manufacturers have the right to expel hunters from their territory."[5] He cited Adam Smith, the author of *The Wealth of Nations* (1776), who wrote that human communities naturally progress through four stages: hunting, pastoralism, agriculture, and mercantilism. He considered only those who progress to mercantilism as fully human.

Justice Marshall wrestled a bit with the morality of the treatment of Indians but resigned himself to the reality of conquest and concluded that "it is not for the Courts of this country to question the validity of this title, or to sustain one which is incompatible with it."[6] Justice Marshall observed that "title by conquest is acquired and maintained by force," and then described the Indians inhabiting this country as "fierce savages, whose occupation was war, and whose subsistence was drawn chiefly from the forest."[7] Because of that, it was impossible for Europeans and Americans to coexist with Indians. *Johnson v. McIntosh*, however, noted that this situation was unique in world history, that the normal laws between conqueror and conquered could not work with Indian peoples, and that therefore some new and different rule had to be devised concerning the legal title of Indian land. According to this unique rule of law, Indians were merely "occupants." Consequently, this case took away many basic rights of Indians to their land by, among other ways, holding that Indians merely occupied their lands. Setting the stage for systematically undermining Native sovereignty, even today this case remains central to many American law school courses in both real property and federal Indian law.

Georgia passed a number of laws that terminated the Cherokees as a political society and seized their lands. Neither President Jackson nor Congress was willing to help the Cherokees, so they sought relief in the US Supreme Court. In the case of *Cherokee Nation v. Georgia*, Justice Marshall delivered an opinion concerning Cherokee sovereignty that remains an important part of federal Indian law today.[8] In this case, the Nation applied to the Supreme Court for an injunction to restrain the State of Georgia from executing certain laws that had the direct effect of annihilating the Cherokees as a sovereign nation and seizing Cherokee lands for the use and benefit of the State of Georgia.

Justice Marshall began his analysis by suggesting that if courts were permitted to indulge their sympathies, they could find no better case. The Cherokee Nation, once a powerful and populous nation, had, through successive treaties, lost much of their land. They sought relief from the Supreme Court to protect the little bit of land that they had left. The Cherokees argued that they were a sovereign nation that had entered into many treaties with the United States and were therefore immune from the political actions of the State of Georgia. Marshall, struggling to define the nature of Indian nations in relationship to the federal government and the states, held that the Cherokees no longer existed as a foreign nation. Rather, he wrote that Indian tribes were more properly labeled "domestic dependent nations," and that the Supreme Court had no jurisdiction to hear this case. Therefore, he denied the injunction.

The next year, 1832, the Supreme Court heard another case involving the Cherokees. The Georgia Assembly, in December of 1830, had passed legislation stating that "any white person living in the Cherokee Nation after March 1, 1839 was required to take an oath promising obedience to the laws of Georgia and obtain a special permit from the Governor of the State of Georgia."[9] Those who refused to obey the law were subject to imprisonment for no less than four years of hard labor. All white men, except those married to Cherokee women and certain authorized agents of the US government, were required to take the oath and follow the law. Whites had until March 1831 to sign the oath or leave the state. The law targeted missionaries, many of whom had supported the Cherokee national cause. Some missionaries took the oath, some moved out of state, and a few chose to dig in their heels and fight.

When missionary James Trott issued a written statement supporting the Cherokees' right to remain on their land, the Methodists led the way in openly opposing removal. Trott wrote that some Cherokees, desperate to stay, maintained that removal would only hurt the progress they had already made in embracing Christianity and civilization.[10]

Missionaries occupied a very difficult position during this time. Some felt that Christians should not interfere with "that which is Caesar's" and should obey the laws of the state.[11] Others felt morally bound to oppose the law. On March 12, 1831, the Georgia Guard arrested and tried a number of missionaries. William Underwood, an attorney working with the Cherokee Nation, defended them on the grounds that Georgia's law had no authority over them because the Cherokees were a sovereign nation, exempt from the laws of Georgia. Judge Clayton released the missionaries after finding that they were authorized agents of the US government and, therefore, exempt from the law. Agents of Georgia responded with a letter to the secretary of war and managed to get the postmaster general to fire Samuel Worcester, one of the missionaries, who acted as postmaster. When the news reached Governor Gilmer, he ordered all missionaries arrested again, and on July 7, the Georgia Guard took Samuel Worcester, Dr. Elizur Butler, and nine other missionaries to jail. Dr. Butler was chained by the neck to his wagon and required to walk the entire length of eighty-nine miles.[12]

A jury heard this case; after deliberating for only fifteen minutes, it found them all guilty. Following the trial, the Guard threw the ministers in jail in hopes that they would simply take the oath and leave the state. All but Worcester and Butler accepted the governor's offer and promptly appealed their cases to the US Supreme Court.[13] In the case of *Worcester v. Georgia*, Justice Marshall analyzed the treaty-making history of Indian tribes with Great Britain and with the United States.[14] Justice Marshall noted that the words *treaty* and *nation* were words that the courts themselves had used, as had both the English and later the Americans, in diplomatic and legislative proceedings. They had definite and well-understood meanings. When applied to Indians, they meant precisely the same thing. Moreover, treaties that Great Britain and the United States entered into with Indian tribes demonstrated a recognition of their "title to self-government."[15]

Justice Marshall also cited a fundamental tenet of the law of nations that a weaker power does not surrender its independence and right to self-government by simply associating with a stronger government and accepting its protection. Accordingly, the court held, "the Cherokee nation then, is a distinct community occupying its own territory, with boundaries accurately described, in which the laws of Georgia can have no force, in which the citizens of Georgia have no right to enter, but with the assent of the Cherokees themselves, or in conformity with treaties, and with the acts of Congress. The whole intercourse between the United States and this nation, is, by our constitution and laws, vested in the government of the United States."[16] The court delivered the decision on March 3, 1832, and issued a special mandate two days later.

However, Georgia officials, including the governor, announced that they would not obey the decision. The court soon adjourned. The opinion of the court and its special mandate were not self-executing, so federal marshals had to carry it out. Some have credited President Jackson with announcing that he would not enforce Justice Marshall's decision.[17] Whether he actually uttered such a statement is beside the point, because actions speak louder than words. President Jackson did not enforce the decision of the Supreme Court.

The Cherokees hoped that Henry Clay would be elected president in 1832 but Jackson won again, a victory that severely diminished the Cherokees' hopes of maintaining their lands. With Georgians clamoring for Indian lands and a gold rush booming, the state next announced a lottery to raffle off Cherokee lands.[18] The lottery made available "Gold lots" and "land lots" of 160 acres to all white adult males in Georgia who had lived there for at least four years. Thousands of whites rushed into Cherokee territory. Some found Cherokee cabins already abandoned while others forcibly removed Cherokees from their homes. In this land rush, both Butler and Worcester received pardons on the condition that they leave Georgia as soon as possible, which they did. In 1834, Georgians took Butler's mission establishment at Haweis and, in the same month, Worcester's superiors advised him to abandon his home at New Echota.[19]

By 1835, every adult Cherokee recognized the seriousness of the situation. Many felt that the only possible solution was emigration to Indian country under the best possible terms. For those in Georgia, where by 1835 half of the Cherokees lived, the reality of land loss had become all too clear and final.[20] Most of them came to favor emigration, but nationwide two major factions emerged. In 1835, both went to Washington.[21] John Ross, Principal Chief of the Cherokees, led the largest faction of Cherokees who supported resistance to removal, while a smaller faction, led by John Ridge and Major Ridge and consisting primarily of Georgia Cherokees, began to lobby for removal.

REMOVAL AND CHEROKEE PARTIES

Two parties emerged within the Cherokees during this tumultuous time. Led by Cherokee Chief John Ross, the vast majority opposed removal. The other bloc, a small minority, was led by John Ridge, Major Ridge, and a few other progressives. Both the removal faction and the anti-removal faction consisted of sincere and dedicated Cherokees who wanted what was best for their people. The Cherokee Nation at that point was clearly between a rock and a hard place. Either they could stay and fight what would amount to, in all likelihood, a losing battle, or they could leave their sacred lands and attempt to maintain some semblance of their traditional society west of the Mississippi. Neither prospect appealed to Cherokees, and both strategies were attempts to create a meaningful way of life in the face of almost total chaos. The Cherokees simply wished to live in what was left of their traditional territory where they had proven that they could live side by side with mainstream Americans.

By 1835, a few Cherokees were practicing Christians at some level. They had established a newspaper, a court system, a bicameral system of government, and a number of small family farms, all of which mirrored US society. It is here that the ideology of race becomes most telling. The Cherokee people, who had successfully adapted themselves to much of American society and culture, who had lived peaceably for the most part in the midst of white Americans since 1794, now faced the duplicity of American government and society. In the end, most Euro-Americans would not accept Cherokees as full-fledged citizens and neighbors.

In 1835, the United States and its citizens remained unable or unwilling to view Cherokees and other Indians as fellow human beings in the fullest sense. The language of civilization and Christianity that Columbus used when he first set foot in the New World was very much alive 350 years later. The novelty of the New World continued to disorient Americans as it had when their European ancestors first arrived. Cherokees like John Ross could not understand why the citizens of the United States of America sought to destroy the rights of the Cherokee people. Ross, who embraced Christianity, thought that emphasizing the Jewish and common ancestry of Indians and Euro-American Christians would help unite the two peoples. However, that did not happen. In December of 1835, a very small faction of Cherokees signed the removal treaty that forced the Cherokees to cede their ancestral homeland for five million dollars and relocate to what is now northeastern Oklahoma.[22]

In October of 1835, the Cherokee Council met at Red Clay and rejected the Treaty of New Echota.[23] In the spring of 1838, only two months before the time fixed for removal, Chief Ross presented Congress with another protest, which the Senate tabled.[24] Removal was especially hard on traditional Cherokees who still practiced the old Cherokee religion. They linked religion to their land, which was at the center of the world. Removing Cherokees, especially conservative ones, from the center was devastating. George Hicks, a Cherokee, lamented that his people were about to take their final leave to from their native land that the Great Spirit gave their fathers.[25] Approximately sixteen thousand Cherokees made the trek from the Southeast to northeastern Oklahoma in 1838 and 1839; some four thousand died along the way.

A small group of Cherokees called the Oconaluftees reached an agreement with the State of North Carolina to accept state citizenship and remained in the mountains of North Carolina, and approximately another thousand or so Cherokees escaped into the mountains to avoid capture and relocation. Those two groups, coupled with a small number of deserters, formed the people known today as the Eastern Band of Cherokee Indians.[26]

Article 12 of the Treaty of New Echota, signed on December 29, 1835, contained an article that made it possible for certain families to avoid removal west of the Mississippi if they became state citizens. In other words, a Cherokee could remain in North Carolina, Tennessee, or Alabama if he were qualified and willing to submit to the jurisdiction of state law.[27] President Jackson was confident that few would wish to submit themselves to such a condition. However, in January of 1836, trader William Holland Thomas, the adopted son of Cherokee Chief ᏯᎾᎫᏍᎦ (Yonaguska, or "Drowning Bear"), agreed to represent the North Carolina Cherokee in Washington, DC, prior to the ratification of the treaty on May 23, 1836. Thomas secured the rights of some Cherokees to remain in North Carolina. The Qualla Cherokees followed the advice of their beloved Yonaguska and agreed to stay.[28]

In addition, a few bands of Cherokees fled to the mountains and hid in caves and dense thickets along the Little Tennessee River and its tributaries. Ultimately, they became part of the Eastern Band.

TSALI: FROM HISTORY TO NEW WORLD MYTH

It is amazing how many accounts of Tsali exist. As one might expect, the accounts given by a US Army officer differ from those Cherokees relate.

Furthermore, a few Cherokee variants exist because, in almost every traditional Native American society, clans, lineages, secret societies, priesthoods, or other tribal divisions often tell their own unique version of a sacred narrative. Usually, different versions of sacred narratives do not create conflict. Cherokees do not attempt to recount a historical event in terms of what actually happened. Instead, they relive an important aspect of their relationship with the sacred. In other words, the story of Tsali is about the meaning, value, and purpose of citizenship in the Eastern Band of Cherokees more than it is an attempt to satisfy a historian's quest for the facts of the matter.

At the same time, there are some facts on which almost everyone can agree. Tsali was a Cherokee who hid from Major General Winfield Scott in 1838 in an attempt to avoid being relocated. At some point, he was involved in or was present at an incident during which at least two US Army soldiers were killed. Either Euchella or the white trader William H. Thomas later found him. After very difficult deliberation and reflection, members of his own tribe killed Tsali and two other men, perhaps his own sons.

Those basic facts give rise to the structure of a sacred narrative that most Cherokees hold dear today. According to Moses Owl's grandmother, who witnessed the killing of Tsali, a Cherokee woman named Anawaggia actually killed the two soldiers while defending herself against an attempted sexual assault. According to Molly Sequoyah's version, Tsali participated in the killing of two soldiers after they prodded his wife with bayonets. As a result, she and her newborn child fell off her horse, killing them both. In both Cherokee accounts, Tsali was protecting Cherokee women against assault by US soldiers. Moreover, he willingly faced death because the soldiers assured him that the other Cherokees hiding out in the mountains would be allowed to remain on their land if he surrendered.

William H. Thomas recorded the story of Tsali around 1848. His version contained a great deal of detail and is important for a number of reasons. First, it shows that Euchella, who reportedly found Tsali and convinced him to turn himself in, initially refused to be involved. Thomas said soldiers had hunted Euchella like a "wild deer for more than a year and that both his wife and a young boy had literally starved to death in the mountains fleeing the soldiers."[29] He buried them with his own hands in violation of traditional Cherokee burial customs. The soldiers who captured Tsali ordered Euchella and other Cherokees to execute him. Tsali willingly faced his punishment because of his broken heart and because he knew that it would help his people. Before he died, Tsali asked Euchella to tell his youngest son to never go beyond "the father of waters" but "to die in the land of his birth." Tsali also told Euchella that Cherokees who went west would never have done so if they had felt about their land the way he did.

Despite what some Cherokees might think about Tsali from a historical view, he serves as a culture hero in a sacred narrative that helps define the identity of the Eastern Band of Cherokee Indians. The story has survived among Eastern Cherokees as part of their collective memory precisely because it is remembered not simply as a historical event but because it holds deeper meanings for Cherokees. The historical character of Tsali is not in question. He did actually live, and his time on earth can be dated with relative certainty. However, his story survives not because of historical fact but because his person is transformed into a religious model and culture hero. The event holds sacred meaning. Tsali symbolizes the abiding determination of Cherokees to live a meaningful life and their willingness to sacrifice their own lives for the benefit of their people and their way of life.[30]

This story exemplifies an important aspect of the identity of the Eastern Band of Cherokee Indians, and it embodies religious meanings of perseverance and self-sacrifice. Kutsche described Tsali as a combination of the attributes of "George Washington and Jesus Christ" and recognized him as being instrumental to the identity of the Cherokee Indians as a distinct people. Tsali's significance continues to evolve. Whether Cherokees situate Tsali in the "long ago" or continue to regard him merely as a historical figure remains to be seen.[31]

For now, Tsali exemplifies Cherokee religion in a way that blends mythical meanings with historical novelty. Tsali represents a New World religion embracing traditional Cherokee spirituality, which emerged from an unforgettable confrontation with a dominant Western society. That is, Cherokees situate Tsali in historical, not mythical, time, yet his story connects Cherokees to their traditional roots and values. Tsali's life and death tell a sacred story. But unlike that of Kanati, the ancestral Cherokee hunter, Tsali lived in the nineteenth century, not in the "long ago." Tsali gives the Eastern Band of Cherokee a sacred origin but one that occurs in the undeniable context of American colonialism and conquest. Traditional mythical categories cannot describe Tsali's significance.

Moreover, Tsali's sacrifice of his life for his people is symbolically analogous to the crucifixion of Jesus. However, in 1838, at the time of Tsali's flight, surrender, and execution, most Cherokees had not converted to Christianity, although Christian missionaries had lived among them since 1801; but in 1838 few Cherokees, especially those in North Carolina, identified as Christian. In 1835, when the United States conducted a census, it was clear that the Cherokee living in the Great Smoky Mountains lived a more traditional Cherokee life and had less wealth than those living in Georgia.[32] The total Cherokee population was approximately 16,000, but only 508 were Methodists, 132 were Moravians, 167 were Presbyterians, and approximately 500 were Baptists.[33] Conversion to Christianity by large numbers of Cherokees did not happen overnight. A new Cherokee identity, including religion, evolved between 1839 and 1855.[34] And slowly a new tolerance among Christian missionaries for Cherokee traditional religious rituals and dances began to emerge.

Not surprisingly, Cherokees experienced distrust of white missionaries after the removal period, since they identified them with the government—the United States—that had dispossessed them. Christian missionaries went to prison and even removed west with the Cherokees, but most Cherokees distrusted Christianity, at least the version preached by white ministers. However, a new group of Cherokee ministers, bolstered by the translation of the Bible into the Sequoyan syllabary, helped advance Christianity. The development of Tsali's story into a sacred narrative may have made certain fundamental principles of Christianity, especially the sacrifice of Jesus, more acceptable to Cherokees. Both Tsali and Jesus sacrificed their lives for others. Moreover, the spread of Christian principles by Cherokee ministers simultaneously struck a chord with Cherokees. Perhaps Cherokees regarded Tsali's sacrifice of his life for the Cherokee people as a powerful example of Christian behavior that resonated with their own religious sentiments.

CHEROKEES AND CHRISTIANITY

Or was it something else altogether? It is probable that the Christian message spread by Cherokee ministers in the Cherokee language connected with fundamental meanings of traditional Cherokee spirituality involving self-sacrifice so that Cherokees, in embracing Christianity, in part ultimately reaffirmed values they already understood and practiced. In other words, Eastern Cherokees, in accepting Christianity after removal, did so precisely because they saw a fundamental connection between certain teachings of Christianity and principles of Cherokee traditional religion. In that sense, Cherokees did not so much change as revive principles that were part and parcel of their traditional way of life. At the same time, Christianity is a religion that offers solace and peace to troubled individuals, and its promise of salvation no doubt struck a chord with many Cherokees. It is perhaps for this reason that some traditional Cherokee healers attend Christian churches.

This is not to say that all medicine people accepted Christianity; some outright rejected it. Nor is it true that Cherokee Christianity—among those who have accepted it—is the same as ancient Cherokee religion. Far from it. In fact, many Cherokee medicine men and women say that they do not practice certain aspects of traditional Cherokee medicine that they perceive as conflicting with Christianity. Also, going to water, despite its similarities, is not identical to Christian baptism.[35] But the larger point is that there is much perceived common ground between Cherokee Christianity and Cherokee traditional spirituality, at least among those Cherokees who practice both. Indeed, some Cherokee terms represent a fusion of Cherokee and Christian concepts.[36]

The point here is that many Cherokees who embrace Christianity do so in a way that simultaneously affirms their Cherokee roots.[37] There are, of course, Cherokee Christians who subscribe to a Christian way of life that conflicts at many points with traditional Cherokee religion.[38] Indeed, one Oklahoma Cherokee minister who visited the Eastern Band admonished Cherokees present at a meeting to be careful about embracing aspects of Cherokee tradition that he said were sinful in Christian eyes.[39] Another Snowbird Cherokee has suggested that conjuring was "no good."[40]

There are some Native American Christian ministers in various tribes who do, in fact, see the conversion to Christianity as necessitating a rejection of traditional tribal religion.[41] Still, until his death in 2021, there was at least one private old Cherokee medicine man who had converted to Christianity and nevertheless considered himself both a traditional Cherokee and a Christian. Like a lot of Cherokee Christians, he was particularly moved by the Gospel of John in which Jesus showed his power in several instances through healing and by raising the dead. The teachings of Jesus Christ capture the hearts of many Cherokees because Jesus was a great healer. Quite a number of the most traditional Cherokees alive today among the Eastern Band are medicine men, and most of those are Christian. In their eyes, Jesus is the most powerful of all medicine men and his ability to heal and to raise people from the dead demands awe, fascination, and worship.

Clearly, the removal of most of the Cherokee people west of the Mississippi in 1838 was an overwhelmingly traumatic event for Cherokees that turned their religious world upside down. Traditional Cherokee religion had survived the American Revolution but removal was a much more spiritually devastating event. Old-time Cherokee religion would never be quite the same. Yonaguska, in an attempt to revive traditional religion, built a council house in Wolf Town, where he died in 1839. Charles Lanman in 1848 described it as possessing a sacred fire in the center and that it was still being used for traditional dances.[42] Built near Soco Creek, the council house was abandoned sometime around 1870.[43] Throughout the 1870s, despite the acceptance of Christianity by most tribal members at some level, the "highest power in the land" was wielded by medicine men.[44] However, despite these observations, it is clear that traditional Cherokee religion struggled and declined at some level after 1838.

CHAPTER 11

Cherokee Isolation, the Civil War, and Traditional Religion

1839–1900

Little is known about the lives of the Eastern Cherokee from removal until the Civil War (1838–1865).[1] The Great Chief Yonaguska died in 1839, exhorting the Cherokees never to part with their ancestral land. Yonaguska was succeeded by Flying Squirrel, but the de facto leader of the Cherokee people, at least with respect to their relations with North Carolina and the United States, was William H. Thomas, Yonaguska's adopted son.[2] Thomas had worked hard for the benefit of the Cherokees prior to removal and, indeed, played a part in gaining recognition rights for the Qualla Town Cherokees in the New Echota Treaty.[3] Most importantly for the Cherokees, Thomas began securing legal protection for their land in North Carolina in 1842. As the agent for the Cherokees, he used their money to purchase plots of land directly from white settlers, right up into the beginning of the Civil War in 1861.[4]

Scant ethnographic work has been done among the North Carolina Cherokees from 1838 until the outbreak of the Civil War. One of the better sources is Charles Lanman's *Letters from the Alleghany Mountains*, which chronicles certain aspects of Cherokee life in 1848. Lanman did not say much about Cherokees situated west of the Qualla boundary, and thus his remarks were generally limited to a description of Qualla Cherokees. He gave the following names of Cherokee clans: Bird Clan, Pretty-faced Clan, Paint Clan, Wolf Clan, Blue Clan, Deer Clan, and *In-e-eo-te-ca-wih*, the meaning of which he says was not known.[5]

Few Cherokees were members of Christian denominations from removal through the end of the Civil War. In fact, it appears that the majority of Eastern Cherokees did not convert to Christianity until sometime after the war's conclusion. The Civil War brought unprecedented famine, disease, and destruction to many Cherokees, which occasioned their participation in a new spiritual orientation. Christianity provided hope, peace, and strength to many Eastern Cherokees during their most trying time, and many Eastern Cherokees today consider themselves not just Cherokee, but also Christian.

QUALLA BOUNDARY: 1848

Lanman described William H. Thomas as the "business chief," which is probably an accurate way to describe his function among Cherokees. About three-fourths of the Qualla Cherokees could read Cherokee and a majority of Cherokees understood English, but very few could speak the language. Lanman also observed that the Cherokees, in 1848, could manufacture their own clothing, plows, farming utensils, axes, and guns. Stating that the Cherokees were distinguished for "their faithfulness in performing the duties of religion,"[6] Lanman described them as primarily Methodists and Baptists who had ordained ministers who preached every Sunday and had abandoned many of their "senseless superstitions."[7] Interestingly, he noted that they dressed like whites except on ceremonial days, when they dressed more "picturesquely."[8]

In reality, it is doubtful that most Cherokees were practicing Methodists and Baptists, and more likely that those were simply the two most prominent denominations among Cherokees who were practicing Christians. Thomas Donaldson's 1890 census described church buildings among the Eastern Cherokee as dilapidated, with Baptist membership at 100 out of a North Carolina population of 1,520.[9] Lanman described Baptists as extremely happy—indeed the happiest people in the South. His description of Cherokees, of course, was tainted by the biases of his own way of life, and he never praised the Cherokees on their own terms but rather lauded them because of their ability to become like white men.[10]

Lanman gave a detailed description of a Methodist church service that he attended on a Sunday, along with Will Thomas. In 1845, there was only one church in Quallatown, apparently this one.[11] In 1844, there were 103 Cherokee "Sabbath school teachers and scholars."[12] In 1860, there were still only four Cherokee ministers.[13] From 11:00 a.m.

to noon, the children were instructed from a Cherokee catechism, which was taught by "the chiefs of the several clans."[14] Women were dressed in tidy calico gowns with fancy handkerchiefs tied over their heads. They prayed on their knees and sang all but the concluding hymn while sitting in their seats. Lanman transcribed one prayer as follows:

> All Mighty Lord, who art the father of the world, look down from heaven on this congregation. Bless the Indians, and supply them with all the food and clothing they may want; bless, also, the white men, and give them everything they may need. Aid us all, Oh Lord, in all our good works. Take care of us through life, and receive us in heaven when the world shall be burnt up. We pray thee to take care of this young white man who has come to this Indian meeting. Protect him in all his travels, and go with him to his distant home, for we know by his kind words that he is a friend of the poor, ignorant, and persecuted Indian. Amen![15]

The first preacher to speak at the service was a Cherokee named Big Charley, who preached a sermon based on the first chapter of the Gospel of John.[16] The Gospel of John is the favorite among Eastern Cherokees to this very day and is often the first Gospel they learn. There are many reasons for this. Jesus performed seven miracles in John, and the number seven is sacred and beloved among the Cherokees. Also, the Gospel of John contains a lot of nature symbolism, more than any other book in the New Testament, and hence resonates with the religious sensibilities of the Cherokees. John, being the most mystical of the Gospels, is also consistent with a number of Cherokee views. John's Gospel contains no casting out of demons, no references to forgiveness of injustice, and no mention of the end of the world—all of which parallels traditional Cherokee religion more so than the Synoptic Gospels.

Big Charley preached in Cherokee and asked if he should do so through a "linguister or interpreter" for the benefit of Lanman and Mr. Thomas. Lanman told him no. The sermon was basically a brief overview of the Bible, beginning with the creation of the world, Adam and Eve, Noah's Ark, the delivery of the Ten Commandments to Moses, and the sacrifice of Jesus Christ, so that all Indians and whites "can get to heaven when they die."[17] It lasted about thirty minutes, according to Lanman. When Big Charley finished his sermon, a man named Garden of Eden explained the redemption of his life by Christ. Lanman described him as a great orator. There followed a short address on temperance and a few secular matters and then the Cherokees quietly left to go home. Lanman concluded his description of the church service by stating that he was "deeply impressed by what I had seen and heard, for my pride had been humbled while listening to the rude savage, whose religious knowledge was evidently superior to my own."[18]

Another interesting observation made by Lanman was that, despite the fact that some Cherokees had given up some of their "amusements," they still continued the ball play, a tradition very much alive and well today.[19] Ritual preparations were made the night before and some sixty young men went to a grassy area formed near the bend of Soco Creek. There they danced around a large fire and pelted out a rapid succession of whoops and shouts. The dance lasted for about an hour, and afterward the men submerged themselves in the river. The men observed certain dietary restrictions and were not to engage in any sexual activity for ten days prior to the event. The people were dressed in the Cherokee manner, displaying feathers, turbans, scarlet belts, and colorful hunting shirts.[20] This description of the game itself seems similar to games still played today. The men were extremely rough with one another during the frequent wrestling matches. After the game, the men again went to water. This is an important observation, for the ball play is a traditional Cherokee activity fraught with spiritual and symbolic significance. Also, inasmuch as missionaries condemned and criticized the ball play, Lanman's observation shows the survival of an ancient Cherokee custom.

At about 9:00 p.m. that night, a large party of Cherokees assembled at the council house, a circular structure. At the center of this they lit a large fire. Approximately two hundred men, women, and boys were present. Lanman described the dances as being of "the common Indian sort" with the exception of one, which he called "the Pilgrim Dance." The dancers came in with packs on their backs, their faces painted, and gourds hanging at their sides. Lanman claims that the dance represented Cherokee hospitality toward all strangers who visited them from distant land. This probably was a description of a Booger Dance.[21] Dancing continued until midnight, when the chief addressed everyone and sent them on their way home. Lanman then concluded his account by noting that the Carolina Cherokees gave him the name of "The Wandering Star."[22]

Lanman gave a good description of Yonaguska and his vision, his establishment of a temperance society, and his reply to the US government's request that the Cherokees move west where they would never again be bothered by whites.[23] In the presence of armed soldiers, Yonaguska gave the following speech: "The march of the white is still towards the setting sun, and I know that he will never be satisfied until he reaches the shore of the great water. It is foolish for you to tell me that the whites will not trouble the poor Cherokee in the Western country. The white man's nature and the Indian's fate tell a different story. You say the land in the west is much better than it is here. That very fact is an argument on our side. The white man must have rich land to do his great business, but the Indian can be happy with poor land. I always advise my people to keep their backs forever turned towards the setting sun and never to leave the land of their fathers. I have nothing more to say."[24]

The 1835 census shows that full bloods comprised 88.9 percent of the North Carolina Cherokees.[25] This and the fact that women still served as heads of household in 1860 may account for the traditional nature of the North Carolina Cherokees in the lead-up to the Civil War.[26] One observer, Andrew Barnard, who lived near River Valley, noted in 1840, two years after removal, that the Cherokees were actively participating in dances and the ball game and they were still erecting townhouses.[27] This observation regarding Cherokee traditionalism shows that a council house was being built one year after the death of Yonaguska, who revived the townhouse tradition by building one near Soco Creek.[28]

John Mullay also visited the North Carolina Cherokee in 1848. In contrast to Lanman, who, with the help of Thomas, tried to favorably impress the United States and the State of North Carolina with Cherokee "progress," Mullay emphasized the persistence of traditional religious and cultural practices.[29] Like many other outsiders, Mullay's descriptions do not aid our understanding of nineteenth-century Cherokee religious practice except by affirming that the old ways were far from dead. He described various dances as "wild & grotesque" and was happy that Cherokees were basically hardworking, sober, and orderly despite being "almost totally ignorant of our language."[30]

In 1848, Lanman noted that very few Cherokees could speak English.[31] In 1850, almost all Cherokees farmed but the census did mention that a few blacksmiths, gunsmiths, and wheelwrights were located on the Qualla boundary.[32] The census roll of 1851 gave more details about the makeup of the Cherokees in and around Qualla Town and increased the number of Cherokees to 883.

A perennial problem in Cherokee studies is very apparent in much of the literature dealing with the period between removal and the Civil War, 1838–1865. Indeed, most of the archival material on the Cherokees was written by Europeans and Americans with a less than sympathetic eye toward Cherokee traditional religion and culture. While it is important to write scholarly works about Cherokees based on the evidence at hand, much of the archival evidence was written by observers whose main point, either unconsciously or consciously, was to show that white culture was superior to that of the Cherokees. The observations of even the most sympathetic outside observers were colored by their own backgrounds and, inevitably, by the lens of civilization.

The lack of sources empathetic to Cherokees from the period leading up to the Civil War, coupled with William Thomas's own obvious attempts to make the Cherokees appear more like whites than they really were, leaves us with little information about traditional Cherokees during this time period. Accurate information about traditional Cherokee ceremonies was especially lacking because Thomas viewed them as vestiges of a Cherokee way of life that he hoped would fade into obscurity; however, it is obvious that Cherokee traditional religion was alive, if not well. The Green Corn ceremonies and dances were still performed regularly in 1860. Cherokees like Enola, who converted to Methodism, still continued to conjure, and Swimmer (Ayunini), later to become James Mooney's primary consultant, compiled Cherokee mythology and traditions. Born in 1835, Swimmer would go on to become the most well-known Cherokee tribal historian.

The 1860 census showed that the Cherokee population in Qualla Town had climbed to 1,063. All but eleven individuals continued to farm. At that time, there were five blacksmiths, four ministers, one mechanic, and one school teacher, although there was no school.[33] John Finger rightly noted that William Thomas and Charles Lanman tended to see the Cherokees through rose-colored glasses—Thomas trying to prove that they were Christian and civilized, and Lanman because he romanticized them. However, the reality was that most Cherokees preferred the Cherokee way of life to the American way of life. The Cherokees in 1860 clung tenaciously to their ancient traditions. Traditional Cherokee religion had survived English colonialism, the American Revolution, and removal. Few spoke English and most had not intermarried with whites. However, the Civil War would wreak havoc on the North Carolina Cherokee.

CIVIL WAR (1861–1865)

The first point to be made about the Cherokees' involvement in the Civil War is that they followed the lead of their de facto leader, William Thomas. Thomas had led the diplomatic charge on behalf of the Cherokees in pressing their rights before the US government. It was ironic that, after emphasizing the obligations the United States owed to the Cherokee, he voted for North Carolina secession in May of 1861.[34] Despite feeling bewildered by this, Cherokees trusted him and agreed to follow him and to fight with the South. In April 1862, Major George Washington Morgan, of Cherokee ancestry, enlisted Thomas in a detachment of Qualla Town Indians into Confederate service as part of the North Carolina troops. John Ross was a junior officer and Enola and Swimmer were both sergeants.[35] This was the first time Cherokees had fought in a war since the campaigns against the Creek in 1813 and 1814.

Cherokee war rituals had all but fallen into disuse, but those who enlisted consulted an oracle stone to see if they would live or die. They also participated in a traditional War Dance in the townhouse.[36] When the Cherokees from Thomas' Legion surrendered in May of 1865, they conducted the war dance around their fires all night. When they came in to surrender, they were wearing feathers and war paint. So intimidated were the Union officers that they considered renegotiating the terms even though the war was virtually over.[37] Mooney also noted that one of the sacred formulas that he collected between 1887 and 1889 had been performed by those who went out of town. According to Mooney, almost every Cherokee man who fought in the Civil War made use of this formula.[38] Cherokee Council houses were traditionally built on mounds in which a fire was built in the center.[39] A cedar log was placed on top of the fire along with a sacred crystal, an uktena scale or horn, a feather from an eagle or great tlanuwa, and beads of seven colors for protection. This fire was called "the honored or sacred fire." During the Civil War, smoke was still seen rising from the mound at Kituwah, the ceremonial center of the Cherokees.

The Civil War weighed heavily on the Cherokees. Very few North Carolina Cherokees owned slaves and some Cherokees defected to the Union side because they opposed slavery on moral and religious grounds. A Union force who captured between twenty and thirty members of Thomas' Legion in 1864 made note that many of those Cherokees learned for the first time that they were defending the right of the South to continue slavery. Some of the prisoners, having no slaves and having little sympathy for wealthy Cherokees, renounced their allegiance to the Confederacy.[40]

Most Southerners viewed Cherokees, for the most part, as second-class citizens. In fact, Cherokees had a hard time enlisting and being accepted as Confederate soldiers.[41] Union sympathizers were no different. Indeed, one East Tennessee unionist referred to them as the "wretched, ignorant, half-civilized, off scouring of humanity" and "long-haired, greasy-looking savages who could not speak a word of English or understand a plea for mercy."[42] Cherokees took scalps on one occasion when Lieutenant Astoogatogeh, a grandson of Junaluska, was killed in a battle. This occurred in Baptist Gap in the Cumberland Mountains in September of 1862.[43]

The Civil War was disastrous for the Cherokees. Cherokee families were left starving while the men were away, and one source says they were reduced to eating leaves and bark.[44] Their condition became so desperate that fifteen Cherokees deserted to the Union, which created an unprecedented sense of factionalism and disunity.[45] The war left them starving, dispirited, and divided among themselves in a way they had never been before. Worst of all, the Cherokees were ravaged by a smallpox epidemic, which killed about 125 Cherokees in 1866, apparently brought home by a warrior who had served with Union forces. William Thomas called in a physician from Tennessee but he was unable to effectively treat the disease. Desperate Cherokees returned to traditional remedies like sweat baths followed by plunges into the icy waters, none of which worked.

Christianity had influenced many Cherokees in some way prior to the Civil War but few Cherokees were members of churches. Although it is difficult to determine the precise number of Cherokee conversions to Christianity, the tribe as a whole could not be characterized as largely Christian until sometime after the end of the Civil War.[46]

In many ways the Civil War turned the Cherokees and, indeed, the entire eastern United States upside down. As Cherokees turned toward Christianity, many white Christians, disillusioned by the Civil War's destruction and death, looked to Native American religions for guidance. There are accounts of Shakers becoming possessed by Indian spirits, and Indian spirit guides enjoyed a popular resurgence during that time.[47]

Many Eastern Cherokees embraced Christianity precisely because Jesus's message harmonized with and bolstered certain principles of Cherokee life, and Christianity allowed Cherokees to find spiritual solace in the face of disorder and imbalance. Christianity offered peace and meaning to oppressed, disoriented, and marginalized people like Eastern Cherokees. Yet even as the Eastern Cherokees wove Christianity into their orientation after the Civil War, it did not displace all the old Cherokee meanings and values. The Cherokees became Cherokee Christians, not mainstream American Christians. Thus, the Cherokees did not embrace the all-out effort by the United States to "civilize" them in all respects.[48]

CHRISTIANITY, AMERICAN HISTORY, AND THE CHEROKEES

At the end of the Civil War, the United States refocused its efforts toward civilizing Native Americans. An all-out assault on Indian tradition, culture, and religion commenced as the government, often through commissioners of Indian Affairs, sought to force Native Americans to accept the dual blessings of civilization and Christianity. One Annual Report of the Commissioner of Indian Affairs on November 23, 1868, stated, "it so happens that under the silent and seemingly slow operation of efficient causes, certain tribes of our Indians have already emerged from a state of pagan barbarism, and are today clothed in the garments of civilization, and sitting under the vine and fig tree of an intelligent scriptural Christianity."[49]

The same Annual Report goes on to discuss the Cherokees of Oklahoma, but the comments could just as easily apply to the North Carolina Cherokee: "The mainsprings of Cherokee civilization were, first, the circumscribing of their territorial domain. This resulted in, second, the localization of the members of the tribe, and consequently in, third, the necessity of agriculture and pastoral pursuits instead of the chase as the means of existence; and as a logical sequence, fourth, the introduction of the ideas of property and things, of sell and barter, & c.; and hence, fifth, of course, a corresponding change from the ideas, habits, and customs of savages to those of civilized life; and, sixth, the great coadjutor in the whole work and all its progress, the Christian teacher and missionary, moving pari passu with every other cause."[50]

On November 23, 1869, a report from the Board of Indian Commissioners openly admitted the unjust treatment of Indians. "While it cannot be denied that the government of the United States, and in the general terms and temper of its legislation, has evinced a desire to deal generously with the Indians, it must be admitted that the actual treatment that they have received has been unjust and iniquitous beyond the power of words to express. The history of the government connections with the Indians is a shameful record of broken treaties and unfulfilled promises."[51] President Ulysses Grant, in response to widespread demands for reform, called for assigning religious denominations to Indian agencies. His message to Congress in 1870 affirmed that he would assign to these agencies the same religious denominations that had previously done missionary work with the Indians. As he explained it, "the societies selected are allowed to name their own agents, subject to the approval of the Executive, and are expected to watch over them and aid them as missionaries, to Christianize and civilize the Indian . . . , and to train him in the arts and peace."[52]

In 1879, the government began placing Cherokees in Indian boarding schools as part of an attempt to assimilate Native Americans nationwide.[53] In 1881, Quakers arrived at Cherokee, North Carolina, and began to set up a school at Yellow Hill, which began a new era in Cherokee education.[54] Still, Cherokees continued to struggle as change occurred rapidly. White settlers were living among them. New towns like Charleston (Bryson City) and Robbinsville were established. Quaker teachers and government agents were all around. The Cherokee way of life was now in a sea of change.[55]

The last all-night Green Corn Dance was performed in 1887, according to James Mooney, although some elders say the last real ceremony was in 1902 or 1905.[56] It was during this time that a majority of Cherokees openly embraced Christianity.

The Cherokees were very interested in gaining an education, not as a means to be assimilated into white society, but rather to learn skills necessary to maintain their own economic self-sufficiency, political sovereignty, and certain traditional values. They established a training school in 1890, but the emphasis on speaking English, rather than Cherokee, made it difficult to achieve those goals. Robert Bushyhead and Goingback Chiltoskey both told Michael Zogry in 1997 that they were required to speak only English, and Bushyhead specifically said that students were punished for speaking Cherokee: "And as punishment, if we were caught talking Cherokee, by washing your mouth out with lye soap, walking up and down in front of the school with a dress on."[57]

Quakers selected only self-professed Christian men and women as teachers in the Cherokee schools. Along with the boarding school, day schools were established in North Carolina at Soco, Birdtown, and Snowbird. The Snowbird school was discontinued in 1890, when the school contract with the Quakers was not renewed and the Quakers left, shutting down the schools by the close of 1892. Many reasons were given for this nonrenewal. Mary Chiltoskey states that Quakers exhausted the mica mines in their area, which provided a source of income, and thus felt unable to continue the schools for financial reasons. Karen Owle cites the national trend away from missionary schools to government-operated schools. In his 1929 thesis, Henry Owl cited a controversy involving factions of the Cherokee people and H. W. Spray, the Quaker superintendent, as the main reason for the closing of Quaker schools.[58]

Cherokees, despite centuries of forced contact, still remained a separate people. Agent J. C. Hart, in a report to the Indian Commissioner in 1898, referred to the Cherokees as farmers who did not use modern methods. They were described as simple people who lived in log cabins about fourteen-by-fifteen feet, consisting of one room. Most cabins included an iron pot, a bake kettle, a coffee pot, a mill, a small table, and a few cups, knives, and spoons. One or two bed stands were found in each one-room cabin. For outside work, Cherokees used a hoe and a shovel plow. Some had wagons and carts but those were not essential. The most common food was bean bread with coffee. In the fall they ate chestnut bread. They kept more hogs than cows, both of which were allowed to run wild in the summer.

The Cherokees numbered about 1,376 in 1900, of whom 1,100 lived on the reservation, with the rest living on the Nantahala, Cheoah, and Hiwassee Rivers. All the men and some of the women could read Cherokee.[59] Most were dressed like whites, although an occasional pair of moccasins was seen. Mooney observed that older people still practiced the ancient rites and sacred traditions, but he believed that the dance and the ball play were withering and that they would soon be lost.[60]

CHAPTER 12

Cherokee Traditions in the Twentieth Century

Mooney, of course, was wrong about the imminent end of Cherokee Indigenous spirituality. Cherokees continue to embody traditional values and customs to this day. They also continue to stress spiritual fulfillment and social harmony over material wealth and political power.[1] Moreover, traditional healers continue to engage in "doctoring," and the ball play lives on, although not every township fields a team as they once did. Cherokees now teach youngsters the Cherokee ball game at Kituwah, the sacred center. It is true that many Cherokee traditional dances died out in the 1950s, but Walker Calhoun and a few lesser-known elders helped revive many of them. Moreover, Eastern Cherokees continue to tell beloved stories; carve masks, form pottery, and weave baskets; help one another through community organizations like ᏐᏩ (*Gadugi*); hunt, farm, and gather edible and medicinal plants; practice ancient healing and conjuring; and conduct traditional birth customs. In fact, many Eastern Cherokees have demonstrated a renewed and revitalized interest in the old ways.

CHEROKEE FIELDWORK: EARLY TWENTIETH CENTURY

Several very important studies documented traditional Cherokee dance and medicine in the first half of the twentieth century.[2] Frank Speck began casually observing Cherokee dances and ceremonies in 1913 and resumed those observations in 1922 when he studied the Catawba. He returned at the beginning of 1928 and continued through 1931 on the recommendation of Dr. Franz Boas. In the winter of 1934–35, he returned to Cherokee with his son and began making disk recordings of all the dance songs known to Will West Long and several other elderly men in AWOᏉ (*kolanvyi*)—the Big Cove community.[3] They recorded some fifty songs that winter, and a year later, in December and January of 1935–36, more songs were recorded.

Leonard Bloom worked at Cherokee in 1935 and 1936 on a grant from Duke University and he returned in 1940 to make further studies. Speck returned again in 1937 and in 1944 and did further field research with the assistance of Robert Riggs, W. S. Hadlock, and J. G. Witthoft. Witthoft later did his own important studies with the Cherokees. On behalf of the Bureau of American Ethnology, William Gilbert visited Cherokee from September to December in 1932, and published a very detailed description of the Eastern Cherokee.

Frans Olbrechts did fieldwork in Cherokee from 1926 through 1927 and published an important revision and addition to Mooney's earlier work on behalf of the Bureau of American Ethnology (*The Swimmer Manuscript*). Despite his less than kind words about Will West Long, which have brought his work a lot of negative attention—and rightly so—the manuscript is an important ethnological work about the Eastern Cherokee in the first half of the twentieth century. Another very important series of works was written, some of which were published under the auspices of the Institute for Research and Social Science, the University of North Carolina at Chapel Hill, from field work conducted June 1956 through August 1958. A number of researchers—including Raymond Fogleson, Charles Holzinger, Harriet Kupferer, Paul Kutsche Jr., and Robert K. Thomas, under the direction of John Gulick—did field research on behalf of the University of North Carolina at Chapel Hill during that time. Utilizing that field work, John Gulick edited *Cherokees at the Crossroads*, and many papers, published and unpublished, emerged from that work.

Raymond Fogelson and Robert K. Thomas also contributed important papers. Fogelson's work on the Eastern Cherokee remains exemplary. Robert K. Thomas was an Oklahoma Cherokee, although it is not clear if he was an enrolled member. However, he was very active in Cherokee affairs and spoke the language fluently.[4] Thomas was a professor and director of the American Indian Studies Program for years at the University of Arizona and worked very closely with Vine Deloria Jr., and no doubt knew Emory Sekaquaptewa, a Hopi Indian who was the coordinator of Indian Programs at the University of Arizona.[5]

SURVIVAL OF TRADITIONAL RELIGION

What emerges from an overview of Eastern Cherokee religious life in the first half of the twentieth century is both the establishment of Christianity and the persistence of traditional Cherokee religion, especially among the more conservative members of the tribe. The twentieth century brought significant change to the Eastern Band, beginning with an increase in wage labor and a decrease in cultivated acreage. For example, Cherokees farmed 25 percent less land from 1900–1, from 3,953 acres to about 3,000. At the same time, the 290 families that continued to farm averaged little more than ten acres each, which was almost identical to the North Carolina Cherokees in 1835.[6] Cherokee agriculture remained primarily for subsistence, not for the market. Cherokees still possessed their own language, a body of sacred narratives that identified them, a legally defined area of beloved land, and various other customs, traditions, and ways of life that were clearly Cherokee and Native American. Despite Mooney's depiction in 1889 that Cherokees were rapidly losing their customs and traditions, the Cherokee people continued to identify themselves primarily as Cherokee, a term that carried important spiritual meanings, values, and purposes.[7]

While the perception of Cherokees as being Cherokee is paramount to their own identity, it is not enough to define Cherokee self-identity in purely social terms. In other words, Cherokee means much more than social and group identity.[8] Even adaptive Christian Cherokees embody fundamental traits, values, and precepts, which are spiritual in a traditional sense. For example, in 1914, a visiting government physician concluded that the Cherokees had reached a point of education much in advance of most other tribes that he had visited. At the same time, he criticized their apparent lack of knowledge of even the simplest details of hygiene and germ theory and compared them with what he called "the lowliest of the Western tribes."[9]

This clearly derogatory and ethnocentric comment can be viewed in an entirely different way. Cherokees were quite capable intellectually of learning about Western germ theory, but in 1914, Cherokee theories of medicine were still very traditional in nature and a member of the Eastern Band was much more likely to seek the help of a conjuror than a

physician. The same physician who visited in 1914 noted that Cherokees clung as tenaciously to their faith in the medicine man as did Navajos and Pueblos.[10] Given that Pueblos and Navajos are among the most
conservative Native Americans in North America, this statement reflects
the fact that the Eastern Cherokees still inhabited their old religious
view of the world.[11]

1920–1932

Throughout the 1920s, the Indian Office attempted to prohibit Cherokee
dances and ceremonies, which Cherokees continued to perform. The
Cherokee language was still used every day in most households, although
an increasing number of Cherokees could also speak English. Certain traditional ceremonial expressions declined, but nevertheless some Cherokees continued to practice traditional religion.[12] Conservative Cherokees
in Big Cove still felt that menstruating women possessed significant sacred
power, and that they could not eat food prepared by such women or
touch objects that they used.[13] Cherokee medicine men and women found
a functional replacement for menstrual huts. Instead of isolating them in
small structures, they exiled young wives to their grandparents' residence
during menstruation.[14] In 1923, Cherokee mothers still preferred to give
birth in familiar environments, assisted by a midwife, and many still went
to water with medicine men during their fifth month of pregnancy.[15]

Although the material culture of most Cherokees was impossible to
distinguish from that of rural mountain whites, a number of uniquely
Cherokee values and customs remained. For example, there was widespread continuation of the Cherokee language, the persistence of the
ball play, conjuring, various ceremonies, and clan affiliation. In 1931
and 1932, more than half of the people on Cherokee land still had some
clan affiliation, and most spouses belonged to different clans.[16] By 1935–
36, older Indians knew the clans of both their mother and father. However, among Cherokees in their twenties, only 20 percent could identify
even their mother's clan. Thus, it is fair to say that the Cherokee clan
was beginning to fade during the first half of the twentieth century.[17]

Traditionally, each Cherokee village had its own ball play team that
competed against other villages, largely as preparation for war. After
the five Cherokee townships were established in the late 1800s, each
town maintained that tradition by fielding a stickball team. However,
this tradition faded in the 1930s, and after that, only a few townships
maintained a ball team, mainly Big Cove and Wolftown.[18]

PERSISTENCE OF TRADITIONAL RELIGIOUS VALUES

In 1926 and 1927 there were still several active conjurors, and the average Cherokee went to them for traditional medicine and protection from witches. This was true despite that, in the late 1800s, traditional Cherokee religion had fused and competed with Christianity. In his notes, Mooney wrote, "the old religion of the Cherokees is now so beclouded and corrupted by the influence of missionary ideas" that it was hard to uncover traditional beliefs.[19] The North Carolina Cherokees were largely Christian at some level by 1875.[20] At the same time it is clear that, in the 1920s, the majority of Cherokees were not mainstream Christians in terms of worldview. When Cherokees discussed death and the afterlife, Christian concepts rarely appeared; instead, they described the afterlife in traditional Cherokee terms. In fact, only a few Cherokees understood the afterlife modeled on a Christian pattern: "they see our Father calling them and telling them it is time for them to come and join Him."[21] More often, Cherokees in 1926 and 1927 discussed afterlife as "out west" or in the "Night Land."[22]

According to some Cherokee consultants, the soul had its seat in the heart.[23] Interestingly, Cherokees said that people should act properly, not because improper conduct would bring punishment in the next life but because it was the right thing to do. In the Night Land, people lived exactly according to the Cherokee pattern: they went hunting and fishing, played ball games, and performed dances.[24] Cherokee conceptions of the afterlife were "slowly being superseded by hazy beliefs influenced by Christian eschatology."[25] In short, it is clear that, despite widespread Christian influence and conversion to Christianity by many Cherokees, traditional Cherokee religious views were widespread among the Eastern Band of Cherokees in the 1920s. Indeed, conjuring was little changed from 1850 to 1926, a period of relative freedom from outside pressure to change.[26]

The Cherokee government, established around 1870, was about the same in 1932.[27] At the same time, Cherokee ceremonial organization was in decline and a number of aboriginal customs had disappeared.[28] The ancient ceremonial cycle had been reduced to a dozen or so dances that were given irregularly in one or two villages. Some of the dances faded away. The Buffalo Dance disappeared with the buffalo and had not been seen since the Civil War.[29] Some dances were still performed but they had lost some of their meaning. However, the most beloved of all ceremonies, the Green Corn Dance, was still alive and well.[30] At the same time, Native medicine and healing began to decline in the 1930s and 1940s.[31]

To uncover the presence of traditional values, Gilbert studied Cherokee dreams and compared them with dream interpretation from the Payne-Butrick manuscripts based on research in 1836. In 1932, Cherokees interpreted twenty dreams identically to those recorded by Payne and Butrick in 1836, which represented continuity in half of the dreams studied.[32] This significant finding demonstrated the persistence of ancient values and symbols among the Eastern Band. In 1842, several medicine men in Big Cove ritually lit the new fire in a ceremonial context.[33] However, it was very difficult to get information on this topic, which participating conjurors jealously guarded. In contrast to 1836 when the New Fire Rite was associated with public ceremonies, by 1842 it seemed to be a secret rite performed only by medicine men for private purposes. Clan affiliation still controlled choices of spouses in 1932–1942, but that custom was beginning to fade.

In 1956, most Big Cove residents could carry on a basic conversation in English, and more than half of the Big Cove residents continued to speak Cherokee at home and in the presence of other Cherokees. Even in those households where English was spoken for the most part, there was usually at least one member present who could fluently speak Cherokee. In Big Cove, some young children spoke Cherokee exclusively until they began school.[34] The situation was different in Paint Town where Cherokee was never spoken in some 75 percent of the households, although it was used in half of the houses where the head of the household was a full blood.[35] Farming in Big Cove had generally declined in part because a number of younger people had left for unskilled jobs in surrounding areas. Big Cove residents would make frequent trips to Cherokee to sell hand-woven baskets. They also did a little bit of logging and farming and sometimes hired out their labor. Only 54 percent of Big Cove houses had electricity in 1956 and fewer than 50 percent of houses had radios, washing machines, or refrigerators. Wood-burning stoves were prevalent and the day school had the only telephone in the entire Big Cove community. Paint Town, by contrast, had more conveniences: 74 percent of the homes had electricity, 64 percent had refrigerators, 36 percent had television, 26 percent had indoor plumbing, and 10 percent had telephones.[36] About half of the Paint Town households had at least one automobile.

Conjuring was still very common in Big Cove in 1957 and elsewhere on the Qualla Boundary, and there were even some members of the Tribal

Council who practiced traditional Cherokee medicine.[37] Many healers were also practicing Christians who easily reconciled any apparent conflict between the two. Church attendance was very common among Eastern Cherokees during the 1950s.[38] Preaching in Eastern Cherokee churches stressed the sinfulness of humankind and the absolute necessity of faith in Christ in order to gain salvation. In contrast to the surrounding mountain whites, who generally preached in a highly emotional pitch, Eastern Cherokees typically responded in a very passive and quiet manner and were not known to erupt into intense outbursts. Indeed, Gulick, who for the most part took a somewhat negative view of traditional Cherokee values, did note that "the values system which underlies the Indians' quiet and passive social behavior is very powerful indeed."[39]

In 1958, in the Big Cove community, there were four widely separated churches: three Baptist and one Pentecostal Holiness Church.[40] Most members of the Big Cove community were formal members who actually participated in one or more of the four churches. The churches were the most noticeable institutions in the community, and they sponsored the two most important forms of group entertainment: singings and box socials.[41] It appears that the traditional ball play had been largely discontinued before 1940.[42] After 1940, the ball play was done primarily at the Annual Cherokee Fair, later called the Fall Festival. Softball had largely replaced the ball play in the 1950s and each township fielded a team.[43] Gulick incorrectly believed that softball involved no conjuring, except perhaps among conservative Cherokees. In reality, conjurors were employed at softball games, but perhaps only to influence the game's outcome and not to prepare individual players.[44]

In Big Cove it seems that ball play dances and other traditional pregame rituals had declined since the late 1930s, although that seems to have changed in recent years.[45] In Big Cove, the old free labor companies (gadugi) continued to operate, even while not everyone participated. To a certain extent the functions of the gadugi were assumed by the community development clubs created in the late 1940s at the urging of the Bureau of Indian Affairs. It is clear that in the 1950s, Cherokee, Paint Town, Wolf Town, and Bird Town all reflected the influence of modern American society more so than Big Cove and Snowbird.[46] Baptists and Methodists were still dominant, but the Qualla Boundary also contained other religious denominations, including Catholics, Episcopalians, and even Mormons.[47] According to one 1959 report, most families on the Qualla boundary still had gardens and did a small amount of subsistence farming.[48]

Around 1960–61 there were at least two major cultural divisions among the Eastern Cherokees: conservatives/traditionalists and modern Indians. The former emphasized the harmony ethic and passivity as well as some other traits, while the latter subscribed to the Catholic or Protestant Ethic.[49]

HARMONY ETHIC

In the 1950s, Robert Thomas described the behavior of conservative Cherokees in terms of a series of traits that he classified as the harmony ethic.[50] Traits of the harmony ethic are listed below:

1. Nondemonstrative emotionality.
2. A pattern of generosity.
3. Autonomy of the individual linked with low sociopolitical dominance-submission hierarchies.
4. Ability to endure pain, hardships, hunger, and frustration without external evidence of discomfort.
5. A positive valuation on bravery and courage.
6. A generalized fear of the world as dangerous and particularly a fear of witchcraft.
7. Attention to concrete realities rather than to abstract integration in terms of long-range goals.
8. Dependence on supernatural power, which can be acquired through dreams.

Gulick interpreted each of these traits in terms of psychoanalysis, reducing their significance to psychological processes, which he viewed as less than healthy.[51] However, it would be more accurate to say that the traditional spiritual character of their lifeway was reflected by the harmony ethic together with other aspects of Cherokee life: the continued use of the Cherokee language; the recitation of sacred stories, myths, and legends; the gathering of wild plants for medicinal purposes; the Cherokee ball game; hunting; farming; the preservation of basketry and pottery; helping one another according to community tradition (ᏍᏚ, *gadugi*); the continuance of traditional birth customs; obscuring their traditional names; conjuring; going to water; and participating in various rituals and ceremonies.[52] All are part and parcel of ᏍᎦᏓ (*duy-*

ukdv), or "the right path to walk and live," an orientation "that is balanced and in harmony with all the rest of Creation."[53]

According to coauthor Ben Frey, the value of SGAᏋ (*duyukdv*, "the right way") is about behaving in a manner that is forthright and just. It involves being the kind of human being who lives in harmony with all those around them and being in right relationship with people and with nature. The crucial component of *duyukdv* is that it involves having a mind toward relationships and interrelatedness.

The term SGAᏋ (*duyukdv*), "the right way" or "the straight path," to Ben's mind, evokes the concept of being ᎤᏓᏂ (*udanti*)—being the kind of person who is heart led, kind, and sincere. The term ᎤᏓᏂ (*udanti*) shares a root word with ᎠᏓᏂᎬᏯ (*adantogi*, "the heart"), the word ᎠᏓᏂᏖᏗ (*adantedi*, "idea"), and ᎠᏓᏂᏖᎭ (*adanteha*, "he/she is thinking"). These concepts are tightly interwoven and speak to a constellation of meanings that involve forthrightness in the heart and in the mind.

In addition to the principles of SGAᏋ (*duyukdv*) and ᏍᏚᏯ (*gadugi*), Cherokees also adhere to the idea of SGAᏋ ᏔᏗᏊ SᏟᏫᏞᎠᎠᏎᎠᏗ (*duyukdv iditlv detsadasehesdesdi*, "direct one another in the right way, without confining or pushing"). It is not truly SGAᏋ (*duyukdv*), for example, to demand that someone be compensated financially when they lose their lives, because it does not adhere to the spirit of these terms as dealing with interrelatedness rather than financial value.

Other terms like SᏟᏞᏢᏂᎤᎠᏎᏫᎢᏎᏗ (*detsadaligenvdisgesdi*, "you all take responsibility for one another's well-being") apply specifically to Cherokee people in tending to *other* Cherokee people. Traditionally, this would have applied to people who possessed matrilineal clan kinship ties, because those were the ones who were considered to be included in the community. This emphasis on "you all" being addressed toward Cherokee people is even indicated in the language, the word SᏟᏞᏢᏂᎤᎠᏎᏫᎢᎠᏗ (*detsadaligenvdisgesdi*) containing the second person plural ("you all") prefix *its(i)-*, followed by the reflexive *-ada-* prefix, which refers to doing the action of the verb either to oneself or to each other.

Laws such as the ᎠᏍᏚᏯ ᏗᎠᏃᏩᏛᏍᏗ (*sgadugi dikanowadvsdi*, "community laws"), originally articulated by the late Cherokee Nation elder Smithy B. "Benny" Smith of the Nighthawk Keetoowah Society, deal specifically with those within the community of Cherokee people. Indeed, the word ᎠᏍᏚᏯ (*sgadugi*, "community") shares a root with the words ᏈᏏᎤᎢ (*gaduhvi*), or "town," and ᏈᏏᏴ (*gadugi*, "people coming together as one and working to help one another"). The word ᏗᎧᏃᎤᏍᏗ (*dikanowadvsdi*, "laws") refers to a set of guidelines that will benefit a group of people. In fact, it shares a root word with the word ᏅᏬᏗ (*nvwoti*, "medicine") and evokes the idea that these will be medicine to you if you live your life according to these principles.

With regard to Christianity's influence on Cherokees and the Cherokees' influence on Christianity, the story is not simple. Some Cherokees rejected Christianity their entire lives. Some converted at some point in their life's journey but then rejected it later. Some Cherokees embraced Christianity as a form of spirituality that replaced the old Cherokee religion. Still others practiced a religious orientation that fused the two, and this was done in different ways and in differing degrees. Then there are those cases where Cherokees convert to Christianity and make a conscious effort to shed themselves of certain Cherokee old ways that they feel are prohibited by Christianity. Finally, a very few Cherokees, even in the old days, were not religious. There was not and is not one simple Cherokee religion, especially after contact with the English. Cherokee religious experience and expression is multilayered, internally diverse, and flexible enough to accommodate individual differences. Nevertheless, sometimes there are clear distinctions between the Cherokee old ways and Christianity. For example, translating Christian terms into Cherokee is not always easy. The Christian description of the gospel as the "good news" is readily translated into Cherokee as ᎣᏍᏓ ᎧᏃᎮᏓ (*osda kanoheda*). However, other terms are not so easily rendered, and indeed the missionary John Gambald's letter dated April 22, 1809, described (in ethnocentric terms) the main obstacle to converting Indians to Christianity as "the wretched Cherokee language."[54]

The Sequoyan syllabary helped Cherokees access Christian documents. John Arch, a Christian, translated a section of the Gospel According to John into Cherokee in 1824. Later the same year, David Brown, a minister, translated the entire New Testament into Cherokee.[55] Few biblical words could be translated readily into a phonetically identical term. For example, Jesus is translated as Tsisa. Matthew, Mark, Luke, and John are translated Maga, Madu, Luga, and Tsani, respectively.[56] Some concepts were more readily translated; for example, the Christian term for *heaven* is often translated into the traditional Cherokee word for *above*—ᎦᎸᎳᏗ (*galv'ladi*, or *galv'la?di*).[57] However, sometimes one encounters the term *tsosv'i* for *heaven*, which is a very difficult word to translate but may be derived from the Cherokee word

ᏚᏜᎤᎥᎢ (*tsulvsadoi*, "bright rays place").[58] Interestingly, the Cherokee word for *Christian* is ᏚᏋᏁᏥᎥ (*tsunane'l(o)di*), which means "to strive to attain, they." Western Cherokee Alan Kilpatrick observed that this term refers to the convert's active effort to seek salvation rather than denoting a state already achieved. Also, it shows that Cherokees feel that they must convert to Christianity, in contrast to the old ways of the Cherokee, which are experienced as given. Also, the term *Christmas* appears to have no religious significance and refers to a festive occasion when one feasts on birds—ᏞᎯᏜᏞᏢᎯᏍᎢ (*danisdayohihv'i*, "they are shooting them"). Christian elements are sometimes even incorporated into conjuring formula. For example, one Eastern Cherokee conjuror referenced Christian spiritual power when he stated, "you can't over-power the Lord."[59]

Christian and Cherokee concepts are blended in a Western Cherokee burn conjuration from 1885 to 1886. The medicine man asked "angel wizards," ᎷᏔᏲᏣᎥᏙᎯ ᏗᏘᏣᏯᎯ (*dighahnawadidohi anidawehi*), to come and relieve his patient's pain. Prayer is further strengthened by invoking "the Ancient One, His Son, and the Holy Spirit."[60] One perennial problem in translating Christian texts into Cherokee concerns the nature of sin. Traditionally, the Cherokees did not possess a concept comparable to Christian sin. They understood what it meant to stray from proper behavior, but they did not believe people were born in a state of spiritual depravity that required salvation. Indeed, Psalms 1:1, in one translation, defines *sinner* as ᎠᏍᎦᏅᏨᎯ (*asganvtsvhi*, "one who has strayed").

Going to water was once considered by some to be almost synonymous with Christian baptism. However, by the nineteenth century, translators of the Gospel avoided the Cherokee term *going to water* and instead created a word for *baptism* that draws upon the Cherokee term for "to wash, or to bathe an animate creature."[61] Hence, *going to water* is written as ᎠᎼᎯ ᎠᏨᏍᏗ (*amohi atsvsdi*, "water, to go to and return to"), while *baptism* is written ᎠᎦᏬᏓ (*agawoda*, "he/she is baptized").[62]

The harmony ethic may be summed up by stating that a Cherokee "tries to maintain harmonious interpersonal relationships with his fellow Cherokee by avoiding giving offense on the negative side, and by giving of himself to his fellow Cherokee in regard to his time and his material goods on the positive side."[63] Cherokees are slow to punish a violator of the harmony ethic for two interrelated reasons. First, Cherokees feel as though the sacred (Thomas's omnipotent force) will punish the offender in due time. Second, Cherokees feel that the execution of punishment may also violate the harmony ethic because two wrongs do not make a right. Keeping a good heart is of great importance to Cherokees, and they feel that fault originates in the heart, the seat of the soul.[64]

Cherokee generosity, with respect to sharing food, is a concrete demonstration of the harmony ethic and its ancient value among the Cherokees. Assertive individuals are offensive within the Cherokees' lifeway.[65] This applies not only to aggressive behavior but also to any behavior that draws attention to oneself. This is why Cherokee leaders have always sought to gain a consensus regarding any important decision-making. The ability to suffer hardship is related to the Cherokees' lack of preoccupation with oneself and conversely with helping fellow Cherokees. Finally, it is clear that conservative Cherokees continue to perceive witchcraft as a dangerous threat, although it is difficult to say to what extent. However, witchcraft clearly constitutes part of aboriginal Cherokee religion as it does for many Native Americans.

Gulick attempted to account for the apparent conflict between the fear of witchcraft and the harmony ethic by saying that the ethic is not perfect.[66] There is perhaps some truth in that position but the problem is more fundamentally related to the Cherokees' worldview. The harmony ethic presupposes chaos and disorder, and that realm is exemplified by witchcraft. Witchcraft is especially feared by conservatives because it can disrupt the order of the harmony ethic. Witchcraft is practiced by selfish, arrogant individuals who attempt to prolong their own lives through the destruction of others. Such a blatant emphasis on oneself flies in the face of Cherokee religion. Traditional Cherokees understand themselves more as "being oriented" rather than "as becoming oriented."[67] In other words, they feel that the world makes them more than they make the world. Conservative Cherokees do not attempt to better themselves through ambitious future-oriented self-assertion. To be Cherokee means to take one's proper place in a world that makes life possible, to follow the path set before one. Values inherent in the harmony ethic are clearly Indigenous in character and thus link contemporary Cherokees with their ancestors in a religious manner. By embodying the values given to Cherokees in the beginning, Cherokees continue to experience transcendence from historical, sequential time.

Therefore, despite the loss of specific traits such as the clan system, the council house, the warrior society, and various ceremonies, Cherokees have retained many important values and meanings underlying those phenomena. Moreover, the Eastern Band of Cherokees continue to inhabit at least some of their aboriginal lands. The "intrinsic fondness for their mountain habitat" is certainly related to their aboriginal understanding that their world was created by the sacred. Their land, their life, and their religion are interrelated.[68] The symbolism of the center/middle is very much alive among the Cherokees who reacquired Kituwah in 1996.[69]

It has been said that some of the traits embodied by conservative Cherokees have been adapted in the last sixty years and, therefore, are not truly Indian. One observer even suggested that Cherokees should clearly perceive what their Indian traits are so that they can dispose of certain traits that tend to prevent their assimilation into the larger economic culture of the United States. One wonders how Cherokees can enter into a necessarily competitive and aggressive marketplace while simultaneously preserving the values inherent in the harmony ethic, *gadugi*, and *duyuktv*. Perhaps traditionalists will one day "figure out" how to "solve" that problem; or maybe they simply do not wish to do so. Perhaps Cherokee resistance to assimilation is inseparably related to the underlying values of traditional Cherokee spirituality. As for the fact that many conservative traits arose after contact, their meaning is aboriginal. The truth of the matter is that the Cherokees underwent many changes prior to contact with Europeans and Americans. However, according to their experience, their traditional sacred cultural patterns were given to them "in the beginning . . . long years ago, soon after the world was made."[70] Various peoples throughout the world have experienced historical novelty as timeless within only a few generations. Similarly, Fred Eggan observed an example of the mythicization of a specific event among the Hopi Indians.[71] The formulation of the new perception may be recent but its content is archaic and refers to a sacred reality.[72] Such a metamorphic process has arguably occurred among those Eastern Cherokees who today view Stomp Dances as ceremonies that have always been around, rather than as borrowed from other tribes.

Traditions and customs continue to guide Cherokees as they creatively address the issues raised by living as a minority within a dominant society. On the one hand, Cherokees realize that many aspects of the aboriginal culture are lost forever and that they are subject to political and economic forces they cannot control. On the other hand, they have retained some of their traditional land, worldview, and lifeways and have not simply acquiesced to external pressure to assimilate.

Up until the 1950s, several Cherokee traditional dances were conducted at some level. One medicine man who attended the dances until they stopped in the 1950s stated that there was a monthly circuit and that different people hosted the dances at particular times. In an interview at his home on June 14, 2011, William Lossiah told coauthor John Loftin that he regularly attended dances at the home of Leslie Armachain. However, he did make it clear that regular performance of Cherokee traditional dances and ceremonies ended in the 1950s, before being revived.

In 1960, Robert K. Thomas, a Western Cherokee, recorded a speech about Cherokee religion by Stokes Smith, youngest son of Redbird Smith, then chief of the Night Hawk Keetowahs, and took it to the Eastern Cherokee. He played it at Big Cove for a gathering of conservatives and traditionalists. Big Cove traditionalists listened to the tape and discussed it quietly. Then in 1979, Thomas visited the Eastern Cherokee again while doing research on Indians of the Southeast. He talked with a few elders about introducing Oklahoma-style stomp dancing, and while the elders expressed some interest, no action was taken. Thomas returned and brought the Redbird Fire to Big Cove in late September of 1989 to inaugurate the ground with a Stomp Dance.

Walker Calhoun was then appointed chief of the newly installed Raven Rock Ceremonial Grounds. Interestingly, Thomas noted that Walker Calhoun still knew some Eastern Cherokee songs and dances. Calhoun later visited Oklahoma and attended some Night Hawk stomp dances but recognized that these dances were different from the ones he had learned in his youth from Will West Long and others. In 1990, Thomas was enlisted again to work with Walker Calhoun to stage a true four-day Green Corn Ceremony in Big Cove.[73] Thomas introduced the sweat bath in exchange for going to water and taking medicine, which are traditional parts of the Cherokee Green Corn Dance. It is hard to put an exact finger on it, but we are told that the "Walker Calhoun" Stomp Dance Grounds has hosted several Green Corn Dances and Booger Dances since 1990.

Many Cherokees turn to religion in hard times, and, like a lot of folks, they tend to get more religious as they age. Moreover, it is impossible to understand questions related to the identity of the Eastern Cherokee without understanding the fundamental part that spirituality plays in their lives. True, there is an important political, economic, and social dimension to the lives of Eastern Cherokees; but there is also a religious dimension that is constitutive of their mode of being. Indeed, Cherokee spiritual meanings and values are as important to their worldview as any other. Without recognizing that fact, one simply cannot understand these extraordinary people.

It is true that Christianity is widespread among many members of the Eastern Band of Cherokee Indians, including conservatives. However, it is important to realize that Christianity among many Cherokees is understood as being consistent with aboriginal Cherokee values and meanings. For example, there are some parallels between Christian baptism and going to water, both of which attempt to spiritually purify and regenerate the participant, although Alan Kilpatrick suggests that no right-thinking conjuror would "confuse the two."[74]

A Cherokee who is baptized or who goes to water may simultaneously experience rebirth in Christ and the reactualization of the beginning of time when the water beetle first emerged from the water to create the earth. For many Cherokees, these understandings do not ultimately conflict with one another. Indeed, the similarity between the two may help explain why Free Will Baptists have been so successful among the Cherokees.[75] In other words, it is the case for some Cherokees that there is no perceived conflict between Cherokee tradition and Christianity. Additionally, some Cherokees understand Christianity itself as being ancestral to the Cherokee, so their acceptance of Christianity fulfills rather than undermines Cherokee tradition. Similar experiences are, of course, known among other Native Americans.

Much more needs to be written about contemporary Cherokee religion, including a survey of the current Cherokee churches, doctrines, and practices. However, such a study is beyond the scope of this overview and must be left for another day.

Epilogue

John Loftin began researching the old ways of the Eastern Band of Cherokee Indians in 1982 and since 2005 has also done considerable legal work for the People. In 2010, he was fortunate enough to meet a practicing medicine man, William Lossiah. William was born in the Swimmer Branch section in the Qualla Boundary. Growing up speaking Cherokee as a first language, he remained primarily a speaker of Cherokee. He was a celebrated artist and, among other things, made torches for the tribe. Descending from a long line of Cherokee medicine men and women, including his father, William was a very thoughtful and spiritual man. His mother, Betty Lossiah, was a basket maker. Davy Arch, Eastern Cherokee member, storyteller, and traditional artist, knew this "conjure-man," whom he described as being "pretty deep" into the "supernatural aspects" of Cherokee traditional medicine (personal communication, June 2021). William worked for more than a decade at the Oconaluftee Village in Cherokee, and Davy fondly recalls William teaching him as a boy to make arrowheads. Davy says that William was "good to him" but added that he would not speak to Davy in English, only in Cherokee. In earlier drafts of this work, William's anonymity was preserved out of respect for him, and it is only because he passed on to the spirit world in 2021 that Ben and I call him by name. In writing about William, I (John) have made every effort to avoid violating his trust in me. William, of course, never revealed any ceremonial secrets, but he did say some things in confidence, which I have honored in the following pages.[1]

William's parents began to take notice of his spiritual gifts around age seven when he repeatedly had dreams about people dying. Several times William would wake up in the middle of the night after dreaming that a Cherokee had died and then tell his parents, who would try to soothe him by saying that it was only a dream and then send him back to bed. Often the next day, his parents would learn that his dream was, in fact, true. After this happened a handful of times, his formal training to develop his spiritual gifts began.

Cherokee healers spend years learning their craft and continue to share information with one another throughout their lives, so long as they get along. William had an enormous collection of prayers and ritual formulas that he both developed personally and acquired from other healers. Once, William shared with me that he would know when he was going to get sick or die and that, just before, he was going to dig a hole in the ground and bury all his notebooks. Many medicine men follow that custom when they have no chosen successor. I don't know whether he found someone to carry on as a healer. Well into old age, William spent several hours most days climbing mountains looking for medicinal plants—just like the late nineteenth-century medicine men described by Mooney and Olbrechts. Like a lot of Cherokee elders, William was concerned that the traditional ways of Cherokee medicine were in decline, that there were not as many medicine men and women as there used to be, and that the type of knowledge he possessed was rapidly fading.

He grew up subjected to Christianity and attended church regularly, but it is not exactly clear when he became a Christian. However, he told me that he was, indeed, a Christian. He daily read the New Testament in Cherokee syllabary and studied it very closely. When asked if there were special Cherokee meanings that he could glean from reading the New Testament in syllabary as opposed to reading it in English, he said that there were not, as it was the same Bible. It was not clear to me if he sincerely meant that or if he thought that my question pried into Cherokee spirituality more than he was willing to discuss (at least on that day). He did say that since he became a Christian he no longer did "the bad stuff," which I took to mean conjuring that could hurt another person. Apparently, William remained willing to do "love medicine" under certain circumstances. He once said that a Cherokee man asked him to attract a certain woman but he decided after talking to the man that it would not be good "to bring them together."[2] According to William, they were not right for each other and it would have been a mistake to make them a couple.

He told me a number of stories involving spiritual or supernatural power, a few of which I would like to share. I want to note that he relayed each of these events in a very matter-of-fact manner, as though he were, for example, talking about the weather. In considering these medicine man anecdotes, we would do well to remember the words of the renowned Indian theologian and lawyer Vine Deloria Jr. from his final book, completed shortly before he passed away. He wrote: "In regard to the veracity of these accounts, many skeptics abound. People reject the stories and claims (in self-protection) that the demonstration of spiritual powers was delusional or coincidental, that it involved trickery or sleight of hand, that it was not properly reported in the first place. Or they argue that the original story was greatly elaborated to make it sound supernatural. Thus they can easily excuse each story or anecdote describing the exercise of spiritual powers."[3] Or as Cherokee Robert Thomas put it, "Most of the older Cherokee still think in terms of older ideas of disease. And most Cherokees still believe in witches, 'boogers,' bad medicine men who will 'use their medicine' on individuals for various reasons, and the like."[4]

On one occasion, William was gathering medicine in a rocky area near the home of some "Little People" (Yunwi Tsunsdi) when he was suddenly stopped in his tracks. He described it in English as an "invisible force field" and said he had to turn around and continue his walk in the opposite direction. The "Rock Little People," according to Cherokee tradition, can be mischievous or even mean when their privacy is invaded, and this anecdote provides a brief first-hand account of such an encounter.[5] Cherokee Beloved Man Jerry Wolfe (1928–2018) recounted that his father told him that "there were seven clans of the little people. One clan lives in the rhododendron thickets. And one of the clans lives in the rock cliffs. And one clan lives in the bottoms—in the meadows. And one clan lives along the rivers. And then one clan lives on the ridges of the mountains. Not all ridges of the mountains—just in certain areas. And one clan lives in the valleys."[6]

Among the Cherokees, medicine men perform many important functions of practical significance, and William was no exception. He healed a number of very ill people, some having exhausted all Western medical treatments; found lost persons; solved a cold murder case; and battled a number of Raven Mockers, witches, and bad medicine men. Cherokee conjurors and evil witches regularly confront and try to overcome one another. William briefly told me about a few such encounters that he participated in or witnessed. For example, once he was sitting watch over a deathly ill person, as Cherokee healers were often called upon to do. According to Cherokee tradition, witches hover around the dying to steal their livers. On this occasion William sensed the presence of a witch in the room. He began struggling with this "person," and eventually overpowered her. At daybreak, the person became visible and she was identified as an old woman known to the community.[7]

On another occasion, William observed a very powerful medicine man confront what he described as a "young woman." He said the other medicine man shot "red lightning" (his words in English) out of the palm of one hand, which went toward the "young woman," circled her, and then struck the conjuror in the stomach. According to William, the other medicine man, whom he described as being "very good at it," lost all his power as a result.

Once, in broad daylight, while we were talking by the Oconaluftee River, William abruptly turned around and verbally addressed a presence that I could not see. He was clearly agitated. There followed a standoff, I'd say a minute or so, during which William stared ahead silently in deep concentration. He then recovered his composure and resumed our conversation as though nothing had happened. I did not ask him what had just taken place and he did not tell me, but I felt certain that I had just witnessed William "fighting" another medicine man. Oklahoma medicine man John Little Bear told Cherokee author Robert Conley that he got into a "fight" with an old medicine man. "Sometimes . . . it's like two old gunfighters going after each other just to see who is the best."[8]

These few brief examples may seem fantastic to some outsiders, but most Cherokees would readily embrace them as credible and convincing. For example, when discussing the Cherokee winged serpent, Uktena, Sandra Muse Isaacs writes that, "belief in Uktena and other wondrous creatures is as strong today among the People as it ever was."[9]

For most Eastern Cherokees, spiritual power is mysterious but very real. Indeed, it would be fair to say that their natural world simultaneously symbolizes and embodies sacred meaning and essence.

Notes

INTRODUCTION

1. Barre Toelken, "Seeing with a Native Eye: How Many Sheep Will It Hold," in *Seeing with a Native Eye: Essays on Native American Religion*, Walter H. Capps, editor. New York: Harper & Row, 1976, p. 11.

2. Christopher B. Teuton, *Cherokee Stories of the Turtle Island Liars' Club*, with contributions by Hastings Shade, Sammy Still, Sequoyah Guess, and Woody Hansen, and illustrations by America Meredith (Chapel Hill: University of North Carolina Press, 2012); Sara L. Snyder, "Poetics, Performance, and Translation" (PhD. diss., Columbia University, 2016); Sarah Muse Isaacs, *Eastern Cherokee Stories: A Living Oral Tradition and Its Cultural Continuance* (Norman: University of Oklahoma Press, 2019).

3. George Tinker, "Spirituality, Native American Personhood, Sovereignty, and Solidarity," in *Native and Christian: Indigenous Voices on Religious Identity in the United States and Canada*, ed. James Treat (New York: Routledge, 1996), 125. See: Philip P. Arnold, "Indigeneity: The Work of History of Religions and Charles H. Long," in *With This Root about My Person: Charles H. Long and New Directions in the Study of Religion*, ed. Jennifer Reid and David Carrasco (Albuquerque: University of New Mexico Press, 2020), chap. 3.

4. We do not wish to risk the utility of this study by too much generalizing. While we do not argue that Eastern Cherokee community identity is a singular entity or that all Cherokee people experience identity in the same way, we do take issue with the argument that there exists only individual difference. Very few Cherokees take that position, and in this book we are placing emphasis on traditional Cherokee spiritual unity.

CHAPTER 1

1. For an introduction to the Eastern Cherokee, see: Theda Perdue, *The Cherokees* (Philadelphia: Chelsea House, 2005); Joyce C. Dugan and B. Lynn Harlan, *The Cherokee* (Cherokee: Eastern Band of Cherokee Nation, 2002); https://visitcherokeenc.com; https://ebci.com. For a good overview of Eastern Cherokee affairs, see their weekly newspaper: *Cherokee One Feather, Tsalagi Soquo Ugidahli.*

2. Robert K. Thomas, "Culture History of the Eastern Cherokee," typescript. University of North Carolina, 1958, p. 35; G. P. Horsefly, *The History of the True People: The Cherokee Indians* (Detroit: Southwest Oakland Vocational Education Center, 1979).

3. Significantly, some Cherokees ultimately understood that Jesus was in their hearts and minds prior to the arrival of Columbus. Edna Chekelelee, "Jesus before Columbus Time," in *Living Stories of the Cherokee*, ed. Barbara R. Duncan (Chapel Hill: University of North Carolina Press, 1998), 130–31. David Carrasco discusses how some Mesoamericans embody Christian beliefs and practices while transforming the powers of Jesus through myth. David Carrasco, "Jaguar Christians in the Contact Zone: Concealed Narratives in the Histories of Religions in the Americas," in *Beyond Primitivism Indigenous Religious Traditions and Modernity*, ed. Jacob K. Olupona (New York: Routledge, 2002), 128–38.

For a history of Cherokee Christianity, see, for example, William G. McLoughlin, *The Cherokees and Christianity, 1794–1870: Essays on Acculturation and Cultural Persistence*, ed. Walter H. Conser Jr. (Athens: University of Georgia Press, 1994). Throughout the book we will employ the terms *Cherokee* and *Christianity* and recognize that the very terms are subject to criticism. One issue concerns whether identity is inherited or constructed (or both). Some want to delegitimate the concept by saying it is nonsensical and leads to conflict. However, identity is important for Native Americans and other Indigenous peoples, and postmodernism arguably does not solve the problems its proponents claim are caused by essentialism. Cultural identities can occasion transcendence, meaning, and value for communities like the Cherokee. We submit that subjectivity and objective knowledge, difference and similarity, presuppose one another and neither can be reduced to the other. See: Paula M. L. Moya and Michael R. Hames-Garcia, eds., *Reclaiming Identity: Realist Theory and the Predicament of Postmodernism* (Berkeley: University of California Press, 2000); Niigonwedom James Sinclair, "Trickster Reflections: Part 1," in *Troubling Tricksters: Revisioning Critical Conversations*, eds. Deanna Reder and Linda M. Morra (Waterloo, Ontario: Wilfrid Laurier University Press, 2010), 42. For a Cherokee perspective on postmodernism, see: Sean Kicummah Teuton, *Red Land, Red Power: Grounding Knowledge in the American Indian Novel* (Durham, NC: Duke University Press, 2008). Teuton, a Western Cherokee, raises, through Native writer Paula Gunn Allen, an important issue: "How do we explain the Indigenous relationship with the land without appealing to spiritual concepts, which are often mystified yet fundamental to that relationship?" He also notes that European invaders have used essentialist concepts such as the Puritan City on the Hill and the doctrine of Manifest Destiny to justify their presence on Native lands. Our project is different and focuses on Eastern Cherokee religious experience and expression. Sean Teuton argues that postmodernism sometimes trades in "failed categories for indeterminacy." Promising to liberate Native Americans from essentialist definitions, theorists of postcolonialism ironically "cannot support a coherent Native identity nor protect actual Native territories" (p. 14). Therefore, "strategies of essentialization and generalization" and "we-they distinctions" can be useful for Native liberation and sovereignty. Moreover, as Cherokee Thomas King writes, the term *post-colonial* "itself assumes that the starting point for the discussion is the advent of Europeans in North America. . . . And, worst of all, the idea of post-colonial writing effectively cuts us off from our traditions." See: Russell T. McCutcheon, *Manufacturing Religion: The Discourse on Sui Generis Religion and the Politics of Nostalgia* (New York: Oxford University Press, 1997), 191; Thomas King, "Godzilla v. Post-Colonial," *World Literature Written in English* 30 (1990): 10–16.

4. James Mooney, "Myths of the Cherokee," in *19th Annual Report of the Bureau of American Ethnology*, 1897–1898, pt. 1, 3–576 (Washington, DC: US Government Printing Office, 1900), reprinted in *Myths of the Cherokee and Sacred Formulas of the Cherokees* (Nashville, TN: Charles and Randy Elder, 1982), 239–40 (page citations refer to reprint edition; John D. Loftin, "The 'Harmony Ethic' of the Conservative Eastern Cherokees: A Religious Interpretation," *Journal of Cherokee Studies* 8 (1983): 40–45; Sarah H. Hill, *Weaving New Worlds: Southeastern Cherokee Women and Their Basketry* (Chapel Hill: University of North Carolina Press, 1997. James Mooney was a very good listener and chronicler of Eastern Cherokee mythology, legends, and medicinal prayers. Unlike John Payne and Daniel Butrick, who wrote about the Cherokees a few years prior to removal (1818–36), and therefore more than fifty years before Mooney (1887–89, Mooney sought to record the old ways of the Cherokees, devoid of all Christian influence. Still, there are two problems with his otherwise fine work. First, Mooney pushed his way upon the Eastern Cherokees and obtained information that was not always freely given. Therefore, Swimmer, his chief consultant, is reputed to have held back certain ceremonial secrets and other spiritual details, without telling Mooney. Second, Mooney, embodied what Charles Long called the ideology of "primitive/civilized," which, sometimes explicitly, sometimes implicitly, leads to an interpretation of Cherokees as "other than human." See: Charles H. Long, "Primitive/Civilized: The Locus of a Problem," *History of Religions* 20 (1980): 43–61; William L. Anderson, Jane L. Brown, and Anne P. Rogers, eds., *The Payne-Butrick Papers*, 2 vols. (Lincoln: University of Nebraska Press, 2010), xiii–xiv.

5. Heidi Altman and Tom Belt, "Moving Around in the Room," in *Museums and Memory*, ed. Margaret Williamson Huber (Knoxville, TN: Newfound Press, 2008), 232. See: Charles H. Long, *Alpha: The Myths of Creation* (New York: George Braziller, 1963); Vine Deloria Jr., *The World We Used to Live In: Remembering the Powers of The Medicine Men* (Golden, CO: Fulcrum, 2006).

6. Mooney, "Myths of the Cherokee."

7. Mooney, 239–40; See also Barbara R. Duncan, ed., *Living Stories of the Cherokee* (Chapel Hill: University of North Carolina Press, 1998).

8. Charles Long, *Alpha*. Charles Long wrote extensively about theory and method in religious studies and focused much of his attention on African

Americans and Native Americans, peoples clearly oppressed by the colonial West. McCutcheon, oversimplifying Long's subtly complex thought, takes aim at Long's argument that "traditional forms of religious thinking are a potent ground for a radical critique of the hegemony of the modern, white West," (McCutcheon's words, p. 33). Long is surprisingly accused by McCutcheon and Armin Geertz for thinking that "archaic roots" necessarily and solely are spiritual essences unrelated to historical conditions. Long, in fact, has written "we must admit that we know of no religion which is unrelated to the various important dimensions of human life. Such an idea of religion is completely abstract, and even if it could be discovered, could not aid us in our investigations." Geertz (and Jensen) write, "myths about the rule of parrots in the beginning of time do not reflect historical events but legitimate the order in which the world now finds itself" (p. 33). First, cosmogonies are not primarily histories in the Western sense (although they may contain some history), and, second, they may be "disruptive of societal and cultural harmony." Most fundamentally, myths are "true stories" which represent humanity's "initial confrontation with the power of life." Finally, Long knows "roots" are complex issues that might support as well as undermine dominant societies, although arguably not when they relate to an "awareness of an objectivity that lies beyond the social and the existential." Raymond Firth, British anthropologist, argued that "religion is universal in human societies. This is an empirical generalization, an aggregate of a multitude of specific observations." True, inductive reasoning cannot prove an absolute, but the weight of the evidence supports the claim that most humans traditionally understand everything significant in their lives religiously. But J. Z. Smith's point about the lack of a "satisfactory definition of religion" is well taken, and perhaps most of all in an Indigenous context. Indeed, Philip Arnold argues we should drop the term *religion* in favor of *values* in interpreting Indigenous traditions. At the same time, perhaps the lack of a single definition of religion is acceptable. As Charles Long was fond of saying, "some things are best misunderstood in terms of definitional structures." See: Philip P. Arnold, "Indigeneity: The Work of History of Religions and Charles H. Long," in *With This Root about My Person: Charles H. Long and New Directions in the Study of Religion*, eds. Jennifer Reid and David Carrasco (Albuquerque: University of New Mexico Press, 2020), 27; Long, *Alpha*, Introduction; Long, *Significations: Signs, Symbols, and Images in the Interpretation of Religion* (Philadelphia: Fortress Press, 1986); Raymond Firth, *Elements of Social Organization*, 3rd ed. (London: Watts, 1962), 216; Jonathan Z. Smith, *Imagining Religion: From Babylon to Jamestown* (Chicago: University of Chicago Press, 1982), 38; McCutcheon, *Manufacturing Religion*.

9. McCutcheon, *Manufacturing Religion*, 192.

10. Mircea Eliade, *The Forge and the Crucible: The Origins and Structure of Alchemy* (Chicago: University of Chicago Press, 1956).

11. Michael J. Zogry, *Anetso, The Cherokee Ballgame: At the Center of Ceremony and Identity* (Chapel Hill: University of North Carolina Press, 2010), 39.

12. Robert J. Conley, *The Witch of Goingsnake and Other Stories* (Norman: University of Oklahoma Press, 1988), xi; Cherokee Alan Kilpatrick states that Cherokee conjurors "conflate" future and present time to bring about desired

results. See: Alan Kilpatrick, *The Night Has a Naked Soul: Witchcraft and Sorcery among the Western Cherokee* (Syracuse, NY: Syracuse University Press, 1997), 32; Christopher B. Teuton, *Deep Waters: The Textual Continuum in American Indian Literature* (Lincoln: University of Nebraska Press, 2010); Mircea Eliade, *The Myth of the Eternal Return or, Cosmos in History*, trans. Willard R. Trask (Princeton, NJ: Princeton University Press, 1954); Joseph Epes Brown, *The Spiritual Legacy of the American Indian* (New York: Crossroad, 1982), esp. 98–99, 115–21.

13. Altman and Belt, "Moving Around in the Room."

14. Altman and Belt, "Moving Around in the Room"; Kilpatrick, *The Night Has a Naked Soul*; Eliade, *The Myth of the Eternal Return*; Deloria, *The World We Used to Live In*, xix.

15. Thomas M. Hatley, "Cherokee Women Farmers Hold Their Ground," in *Powhatan's Mantle: Indians in the Colonial Southeast*, ed. Gregory A. Waselkov and Peter H. Wood (Lincoln: University of Nebraska Press, 2006), 306. For a discussion of the importance of Kituwah to the Cherokee, see: Brett H. Riggs, M. Scott Shumate, Patti Evans-Shumate, and Brad Bowden, Report Submitted to the Office of Cultural Resources, Eastern Band of Cherokee Indians (Cherokee, North Carolina, 1998), ix; Sandra Muse Isaacs, *Eastern Cherokee Stories: A Living Oral Tradition and Its Cultural Continuance* (Norman: University of Oklahoma Press, 2019), 32–44; Tyler Boulware, *Deconstructing the Cherokee Nation: Town, Region, and Nation among Eighteenth-Century Cherokees* (Gainesville: University of Florida Press, 2011), 12–14, 24–26; John Norton, *The Journal of Major John Norton (Teyoninhokarawen), 1816*, ed. Carl F. Klinck and James J. Talman (Toronto: Champlain Society, 1970), 62.

Interestingly, Mooney says that Kituwah had lost its meaning, which was not an accurate statement. It is likely that Swimmer and the other consultants did not feel comfortable discussing the term with Mooney because it was so sacred. Mooney, "Myths of the Cherokee," 525. For another discussion of Cherokee "center place," see: Christopher B. Rodning, *Center Places and Cherokee Towns: Archaeological Perspectives on Native American Architecture and Landscape in the Southern Appalachians* (Tuscaloosa: University of Alabama Press, 2015), 163–67. The spiritual concept of the center also played a significant role in the Hopi worldview. Hopi emergence cosmogony holds that the Hopi emerged to this fourth world through the *sipaapuni* ("earth navel") located in the world's center. See, John D. Loftin, *Religion and Hopi Life*, 2nd ed. (Bloomington: Indiana University Press, 2001), 48, 66, 135, 142n5. Coauthor John Loftin is forever indebted to the late Emory Sekaquaptewa, ritual participant, cultural interpreter, Chief Justice of the Hopi Supreme Court, and writer of the Hopi language, for his friendship and contribution to Hopi studies. See also: Jonathan Z. Smith, "The Wobbling Pivot," *Journal of Religion* 52 (1972): 134–49. As David Carrasco said in a recent podcast, the ceremonial center is a place of prestige for Indigenous peoples to which they always want to return. Philip Arnold, "The Doctrine of Discovery in the Mesoamerican Context with David Carrasco," June 27, 2022, in *Mapping the Doctrine of Discovery*, podcast, https://podcast.doctrineofdiscovery.org/season1/episode-03/. Professor Cordova (Jicarilla Apache/Hispanic) writes about the importance of

Native Americans "standing 'in the center of the universe.'" V. F. Cordova, *How It Is: The Native American Philosophy of V. F. Cordova*, ed. Kathleen Dean Moore, Kurt Peters, Ted Jojola, and Amber Lacy. (Tucson: University of Arizona Press, 2007), 192.

16. See: https://theonefeather.com/2022/05/21/cherokee-tribes-come-together-to-celebrate-kituwah/. Richard French, EBCI Tribal Council Chairman, at the June 16, 2023, meeting of all three federally recognized Cherokee tribes, emphasized the importance of Kituwah to Cherokee identity and origin. "We're Kituwah. This is where we come from, every one of us, and we are blessed." *Cherokee One Feather*, tsalagi soquo ugidahli, week of dehaluyi 21–27, 2023, 2.

17. Sequoyah v. Tennessee Valley Authority, 620 F.2d 1159 (1980); *Cherokee One Feather*, tsalagi soquo ugidahli, week of kawoni 7–13, 2021, 28.

18. John D. Loftin, "Anglo-American Jurisprudence and the Native American Tribal Quest for Religious Freedom," *American Indian Culture and Research Journal* 13 (1989): 1–52; Loftin, "A Hopi-Anglo Discourse of Myth and History," *Journal of American Academy of Religion* 63 (1996): 677–93; Deloria, "Sacred Lands and Religious Freedom," *American Indian Religions*, 1 (1994): 73–83.

19. Rodning, *Center Places and Cherokee Towns*, 163–67. Payne and Butrick seem to designate the fire hearth as the townhouse "center" in some passages but not in others. The semicircular area encompassing the fire and three white seats for the chief priest and two assistants is called "centre" and "holy place." In another place it is said that the "seventh post and the space around it, holiest of all." Anderson, Brown, and Rogers, *The Payne-Butrick Papers*, 2:53, 55, 58, 224; 1:237. In the case of the sanctity of the council house's seventh pillar, we suggest that it was a symbol that unified the four cardinal directions and the three vertical spaces. In a related vein, Alan Kilpatrick says that a prayer reference to "sunland is not a reference to any point on the compass but to a state of being. Sunland is a metaphor for a metaphysical dwelling place of the spirits." Alan Edwin Kilpatrick, "'Going to the Water': A Structural Analysis of Cherokee Purification Rituals," *American Indian Culture and Research Journal* 15, no. 4 (1991): 55.

20. Mooney, "Myths of the Cherokee," 431; Jack F. Kilpatrick and Anna G. Kilpatrick, *Walk in Your Soul: Love Incantations of the Oklahoma Cherokees* (Dallas: Southern Methodist University Press, 1965), 7, 130. For another discussion of the "middle" see: Teuton, *Cherokee Stories of the Turtle Island Liars' Club*, 34; Christopher B. Teuton and Hastings Shade, *Cherokee Earth Dwellers: Stories and Teachings of the Natural World*, with Loretta Shade and Larry Shade, and illustrated by Mary Beth Timothy (Seattle: University of Washington Press, 2023), pp. 2, 9, 13, 18, 21, 23, 30, 44, 48–51, 60, 70–71, 260. Hastings Shade, respected Cherokee elder, told Chris Teuton of the fundamental importance of this purpose. Ben Frey assisted Chris Teuton with the Cherokee language in *Cherokee Earth Dwellers*.

21. Mooney, "Myths of the Cherokee," 542; Zogry, *Anetso*, 54; James Mooney and Frans M. Olbrechts, *The Swimmer Manuscript: Cherokee Sacred Formulas and Medicinal Prescriptions*, Smithsonian Institution Bureau of

American Ethnology Bulletin 99 (Washington, DC: US Government Printing Office, 1932).

22. Jack F. Kilpatrick and Anna G. Kilpatrick, *Run toward the Nightland: Magic of the Oklahoma Cherokee* (Dallas: Southern Methodist University Press, 1967), 73, 75.

23. Zogry, *Anetso*, 54–56.

24. Henry T. Malone, *Cherokees of the Old South: A People in Transition* (Athens: University of Georgia Press, 1976), 21.

25. Wilhelm Schmidt, *The Origin and Growth of Religion: Facts and Theories* (New York: Dial Press, 1931), 18.

26. Alexander Longe, "A Small Postscript on the ways and manners of the Indians called Cherokees, the contents of the whole so that you may find everything by the pages," ([1725] 1975; transcript of original manuscript from Library of Congress); photostats and "modern version" edited, with an introduction, by David H. Corkran, *Southern Indian Studies* 21 (October 1969): 3, 11, 22–27.

27. Mircea Eliade, *Patterns in Comparative Religion*, trans. Rosemary Sheed (New York: Sheed and Ward, 1958), 52.

28. Eliade, 52.

29. David H. Corkran, "The Nature of the Cherokee Supreme Being," *Southern Indian Studies* 8 (1956): 27–35; Anderson, Brown, and Rogers, *The Payne-Butrick Papers*, vol. 1–3, pp. 7–23, 129–30.

30. Charles Hudson, *The Southeastern Indians* (Knoxville: University of Tennessee Press, 1976), 121.

31. Hudson, 121.

32. Jack Frederick Kilpatrick and Anna Gritts Kilpatrick, *Notebook of a Cherokee Shaman*, Smithsonian Contributions to Anthropology, vol. 2, no. 6 (Washington, DC: Smithsonian Institution Press, 1970), 90.

33. Kilpatrick and Kilpatrick, *Walk in Your Soul*; Jack F. Kilpatrick and Anna G. Kilpatrick, *Friends of Thunder: Folktales of the Oklahoma Cherokees* (Dallas: Southern Methodist University Press, 1964); Kilpatrick and Kilpatrick, *Run toward the Nightland*.

34. Personal communication, 2010, 2011.

35. Charles C. Royce, *The Cherokee Nation of Indians* (Chicago: Aldine, 1975). For a discussion of Cherokee regions, see Boulware, *Deconstructing the Cherokee Nation*.

36. William H. Gilbert Jr., "Eastern Cherokee Social Organization," in *Social Organization of North American Tribes: Essays in Social Organization, Law and Religion*, ed. Fred Eggan, 285–338 (Chicago: University of Chicago Press, 1937), 181.

37. Charles Hudson, *The Juan Pardo Expeditions: Exploration of the Carolinas and Tennessee, 1566–1568*, rev. ed. (Tuscaloosa: University of Alabama Press, 1990); Mooney, "Myths of the Cherokee," 23–29.

38. Hudson, *The Southeastern Indians*, 72.

39. Henry Timberlake, *Lieutenant Henry Timberlake's Memoirs, 1756–1765*. Edited by Samuel Cole Williams (Johnson City, TN: Watauga Press, 1927), 85, 86; Duane H. King, "Cherokee Bows," *Journal of Cherokee Studies* 1 (1976): 92–97.

40. Gilbert, "Eastern Cherokee Social Organization"; John Gulick, *Cherokees at the Crossroads*, rev. ed. with epilogue by Sharlotte Neely Williams (Chapel Hill Institute of Research in Social Science, University of North Carolina, 1973).

41. Theda Perdue, *Cherokee Women: Gender and Culture Change, 1700–1835* (Lincoln: University of Nebraska Press, 1998), 25.

42. See: Anderson, Brown, and Rogers, *The Payne-Butrick Papers*, 1:234, 2:97; Perdue, *Cherokee Women*, 84.

43. Raymond D. Fogelson, "On the 'Petticoat Government' of the Eighteenth-Century Cherokee," in *Personality and the Cultural Construction of Society*, ed. David K. Jordan and Marc J. Swartz (Tuscaloosa: University of Alabama Press, 1990), 173.

44. Fogelson, "On the 'Petticoat Government' of the Eighteenth-Century Cherokee," 174.

45. James Adair, *The History of the American Indians*, 1775, reprinted as *Adair's History of the American Indians*, ed. Samuel Cole Williams (Johnson City, TN: Watauga Press, 1930), 124, 125.

46. William H. Gilbert Jr., *The Eastern Cherokees*, Smithsonian Institution Bureau of American Ethnology Bulletin 133, Anthropological Papers, no. 23, 196–413 (Washington, DC: US Government Printing Office, 1943), reprinted as *The Eastern Cherokees* (New York: AMS Press, 1978), 212 (page citations refer to reprint edition).

47. James Mooney, "Myths of the Cherokees," *Journal of the American Folklore* 1, no. 2 (1888): 98; Mooney, "Myths of the Cherokee," 319–20; Frank G. Speck and Leonard Broom, in collaboration with Will West Long, *Cherokee Dance and Drama*, 1951, reprint, (Norman: University of Oklahoma Press, 1983), 13–16; Jenny James, "The Sacred Feminine in Cherokee Culture: Healing and Identity," in *Under the Rattlesnake: Cherokee Health and Resiliency*, ed. Lisa J. Lefler (Tuscaloosa: University of Alabama Press, 2009), 113–14.

48. Mooney, "Myths of the Cherokees," 98.

49. Mircea Eliade, *The Quest: History of Meaning in Religion* (Chicago: University of Chicago Press, 1969), 86–87; John D. Loftin, *Religion and Hopi Life*, 2nd ed. (Bloomington: Indiana University Press, 2001), p. 141.

50. John Loftin, *The Big Picture: A Short World History of Religions* (Jefferson, NC: McFarland, 2000).

51. Sharlotte Neely, "The Eastern Cherokee: Farmers of the Southeast," in *This Land Was Theirs: A Study of North American Indians*, ed. Wendell Oswalt and Sharlotte Neely, 5th ed. (New York: McGraw Hill, 1995), 439.

52. Perdue, *Cherokee Women*, 18.

53. Perdue, 18.

54. Hatley, "Cherokee Women Farmers Hold Their Ground," 309.

55. Teuton, *Cherokee Stories of the Turtle Island Liars' Club*, 105. Hastings Shade discusses the seven levels of heaven.

56. Perdue, *Cherokee Women*, 18.

57. Gregory Cajete, *Native Science: Natural Laws of Interdependence* (Sante Fe, NM: Clear Light, 2000), 62.

58. Teuton, *Red Land, Red Power*, 141, 168.

CHAPTER 2

1. Jack F. Kilpatrick and Anna G. Kilpatrick, *Walk in Your Soul: Love Incantations of the Oklahoma Cherokees* (Dallas: Southern Methodist University Press, 1965), 19; James Mooney, *Myths of the Cherokee*, 508, 509; Anderson, Brown, and Rogers, *The Payne-Butrick Papers*, vol. 1–3, pp. 86, 221, 349n39, vol. 4–6, p. 65; Perdue, *Cherokee Women*, 207n4; Perdue, *The Cherokees*, 10; John Phillip Reid, *A Law of Blood: The Primitive Law of the Cherokee Nation* (New York: New York University Press, 1970), 37; Hill, *Weaving New Worlds*, 27–31. The following discussion of clan duties, functions and characteristics are taken from various Cherokees.

2. Kilpatrick and Kilpatrick, *Walk in Your Soul*, 19.

3. William H. Gilbert Jr., "The Cherokees of North Carolina: Living Memorials of the Past," in *Annual Report for the Board of Regents of the Smithsonian Institution 1956* (Washington, DC: US Government Printing Office, 1957), 529–55, 203.

4. Mooney, *Myths of the Cherokee*, 264–65.

5. Mooney, 508.

6. Mooney, 08; Gilbert, *The Cherokees of North Carolina*, 203.

7. Reid, *A Law of Blood*, 42.

8. Reid, 37; *Cherokee Phoenix*, February 18, 1829, p. 2, col. 5.

9. Reid, *A Law of Blood*, 37.

10. Fred Gearing, *Priests and Warriors: Social Structures for Cherokee Politics in the 18th Century*, Memoir 93 (Menasha, WI: American Anthropological Association, 1962), 21.

11. Gilbert, *The Cherokees of North Carolina*, 207.

12. Loftin, *Religion and Hopi Life*, chap. 2.

13. Mooney, *Myths of the Cherokee*, 326.

14. Mooney, 326.

15. Mooney, 473.

16. Mooney, 327–29.

17. Eliade, *The Myth of the Eternal Return*; Claude Lévi-Strauss, *The Elementary Structures of Kinship*, ed. Rodney Needham, trans. J.H. Bell, John Richard, Vaughn Stermer, and Rodney Needham (Boston: Beacon Press, 1969).

18. Perdue, *Cherokee Women*, 47.

19. Perdue, 49.

20. Perdue, 49.

21. Reid, *A Law of Blood*, 42.

22. Gilbert, *The Eastern Cherokees*; Reid, *A Law of Blood*; Gearing, *Priests and Warriors*.

23. Gearing, *Priests and Warriors*, 3.

24. Gearing, 2.

25. Gearing, 23. See: Rennard Strickland, *Fire and the Spirits: Cherokee Law from Clan to Court* (Norman: University of Oklahoma Press, 1975), chap. 1–2.

26. Timberlake, *Lieutenant Henry Timberlake's Memoirs*, 59, for a description of Cherokee townhouse.

27. Reid, *A Law of Blood*, 18.

28. Anderson, Brown, and Rogers, *The Payne-Butrick Papers*, vol. 1–3, pp. 86, 221, vol. 4–6, p. 65.

29. Gearing, *Priests and Warriors*, 26.

30. Gearing, 26.

31. Adair, *The History of the American Indians*, 382.

32. John Haywood, *The Natural and Aboriginal History of Tennessee, up to the First Settlements therein by the White People in the Year 1768* (Nashville: George Wils, 1823), 248.

33. Timberlake, *Lieutenant Henry Timberlake's Memoirs*, 94.

34. Dennis L. Isenbarger, *Native Americans in Early North Carolina: A Documentary History*, (Raleigh, NC: Office of Archives and History, 2013), 201.

35. Gilbert, *The Eastern Cherokees*, 355.

36. Haywood, *The Natural and Aboriginal History of Tennessee*, 249.

37. Haywood, 249.

38. Gilbert, *The Eastern Cherokees*, 352.

39. Mooney and Olbrechts, *The Swimmer Manuscript*, 91.

40. Mooney and Olbrechts, 116.

41. Frans M. Olbrechts, "Cherokee Belief and Practice with Regard to Childbirth," *Anthropos* 26 (1931), 19.

42. Olbrechts, 19.

43. Olbrechts, 20.

44. Olbrechts, 21; Mooney and Olbrechts, *The Swimmer Manuscript*, 53.

45. James George Frazer, *The Golden Bough: A Study in Magic and Religion*, abr. ed. (1922; New York: Simon Schuster, 1996), 12.

46. Frazer, *The Golden Bough*.

47. Frazer, 13.

48. Frazer, 12.

49. Frazer, 56–59.

50. Gilbert, *The Eastern Cherokees*, 287.

51. Gilbert, 287.

52. Kilpatrick, *The Night Has a Naked Soul*, 21–23.

53. Kilpatrick, 22.

54. Gilbert, *The Eastern Cherokees*, 286.

55. Kilpatrick, *The Night Has a Naked Soul*, 30, 47, 48, 103, 144. Alan Kilpatrick argues that "an abiding sense of reciprocity underscores all human thought and action in the Cherokee ontology." Kilpatrick, "'Going to the Water,'" 58.

56. Frazer, *The Golden Bough*, 57.

57. John D. Loftin, "Supplication and Participation: The Distance and Relation of the Sacred in Hopi Prayer Rites," *Anthropos* 81 (1986): 177–201, for a discussion of Hopi Indian prayer rite.

58. Maurice Leenhardt, *Do Kamo: Person and Myth in the Melanesian World*, trans. Basia Miller Gulati (Chicago: University of Chicago Press, 1979), 190.

59. Mooney and Olbrechts, *The Swimmer Manuscript*, 21; Gilbert, *The Eastern Cherokees*, 207.

60. Perdue, *Cherokee Women*, 30.

61. Olbrects, "Cherokee Belief and Practice with Regard to Childbirth," 22–23.

62. Olbrects, 29.

63. Olbrects, 24.

64. Olbrects, 27.

65. Olbrects, 27.

66. James Mooney, "The Cherokee River Cult," *Journal of Cherokee Studies* 7, no. 1 (Spring 1982): 30–36. Reprint of article first published in *Journal of American Folklore* 13 (1900). Mooney and Olbrechts, *The Swimmer Manuscript*, 127.

67. Mooney, *Myths of the Cherokee*, 431.

68. Anderson, Brown, and Rogers, *The Payne-Butrick Papers*, vol. 4–6, p. 66.

69. Olbrechts, "Cherokee Belief and Practice with Regard to Childbirth," 31; Mooney and Olbrechts, *The Swimmer Manuscript*, 129–30.

70. Mooney and Olbrechts, *The Swimmer Manuscript*, 32.

71. Mooney and Olbrechts, 33.

72. Anderson, Brown, and Rogers, *The Payne-Butrick Papers*, vol. 4–6, pp. 65, 183.

73. Alexander Longe, *A Small Postscript on the ways and manners of the Indians called Cherokees, the contents of the whole so that you may find everything by the pages* (1725), transcript of original manuscript from Library of Congress, photostats and "modern version" edited and with an introduction by David H. Corkran, *Southern Indian Studies* 21 (October 1969): 3–49.

74. Longe, 32.

75. Reid, *A Law of Blood*, 113–14.

76. Reid, 114.

77. Longe, *A Small Postscript*, Introduction.

78. Gilbert, *The Eastern Cherokees*, 256.

79. Gregory Cajete, *Native Science: Natural Laws of Interdependence* (Sante Fe, NM: Clear Light, 2000), 71; Lévi-Strauss, *The Elementary Structures of Kinship*.

80. Rodning, *Center Places and Cherokee Towns*, 114–115, 138, 163; H. Trawick Ward and R. P. Stephen Davis Jr., *Time Before History: The Archaeology of North Carolina* (Chapel Hill: University of North Carolina Press, 1999), 164–65; Roy S. Dickens Jr., *Cherokee Prehistory: The Pisgah Phase in the Appalachian Summit Region* (Knoxville: University of Tennessee Press, 1976), 14, chap. 3.

81. Dickens, *Cherokee Prehistory*, 107.

82. Mircea Eliade, *Images and Symbols: Studies in Religious Symbolism*, trans. Philip Mairet (New York: Sheed & Ward, 1969), 125.

83. Eliade, 128.

84. Eliade, 135.

85. Adair, *The History of the American Indians*, 133; Mooney and Olbrechts, *The Swimmer Manuscript*, 134.

86. Mooney and Olbrechts, *The Swimmer Manuscript*, 135.

87. Gilbert, *The Eastern Cherokees*, 347.

88. Mooney and Olbrechts, *The Swimmer Manuscript*, 139.

89. Gilbert, *The Eastern Cherokees*, 348.

90. Gilbert, 348.

91. Mooney and Olbrechts, *The Swimmer Manuscript*, 138.

92. Mooney and Olbrechts, 138; personal communication, 2011.

93. Mooney, *Myths of the Cherokee*, 254.

94. John Witthoft, "Cherokee Beliefs Concerning Death," *Journal of Chero-kee Studies* 8 (Fall 1983): 68–72. See also: Raymond D. Fogelson, "Exploring Cherokee Metaphysics of Death and Life," lecture presented at the Michael D. Green Lecture in American Indian Studies, University of North Carolina at Chapel Hill, NC, November 3, 2015.

95. Fogelson, "Exploring Cherokee Metaphysics of Death and Life," 68.

96. Fogelson, 69.

97. Fogelson, 69.

98. Fogelson, 69.

99. Fogelson, 70.

100. Fogelson, 70.

101. Mooney and Olbrechts, *The Swimmer Manuscript*, 144. For discussion of late twentieth-century Cherokee conceptions of afterlife, see: Michelle D. Hamilton, "Adverse Reactions: Practicing Bioarchaeology among the Chero-kee," in *Under the Rattlesnake: Cherokee Health and Resiliency*, ed. Lisa J. Lefler (Tuscaloosa: University of Alabama Press, 2009), 29–60. See comments by Cherokee Tom Belt about the continuing concept of the seventh heaven: Isaacs, *Eastern Cherokee Stories*, 80. Belt says that more traditional Cherokees do not accept the concept of hell for "bad" people. Rather, they understand that the souls of the deceased grow through higher and higher levels of heaven until they reach the seventh heaven, the abode of the Creator.

102. Teuton, *Cherokee Stories of the Turtle Island Liars' Club*, 19.

103. Leenhardt, *Do Kamo*, 189.

CHAPTER 3

1. Anderson, Brown, and Rogers, *The Payne-Butrick Papers*, vol. 4–6, pp. 144–77; Anderson, Brown, and Rogers, *The Payne-Butrick Papers*, vol. 1–3, pp. 34–79; Gilbert, *The Eastern Cherokees*, 327; Gilbert, *The Cherokees of North Carolina*, 540–41; Ruth Wetmore, "The Green Corn Ceremony of the Eastern Cherokees," *Journal of Cherokee Studies* 8 (Spring 1983): 46.

2. Perdue, *Cherokee Women*, 107; William G. McLoughlin, *The Cherokee Ghost Dance: Essays on the Southeastern Indians, 1789–1861* (Macon, GA: Mercer University Press, 1984), 11; Anderson, Brown, and Rogers, *The Payne-Butrick Papers*, vol. 1–3.

3. Perdue, *Cherokee Women*, 56. Gearing says the opposite, that Cherokee villages acted independently beginning in the 1780s. Gearing, *Priests and Warriors*, 103–4.

4. Gearing, *Priests and Warriors*, 104.

5. Anderson, Brown, and Rogers, *The Payne-Butrick Papers*, vol. 1–3, p. 221.

6. John Lame Deer and Richard Erdoes, *Lame Deer: Seeker of Visions* (New York: Simon & Schuster, 1972), 233.

7. R. R. Marett, *The Threshold of Religion* (London: Metheun, 1909), xxxi; Loftin, *The Big Picture*, 21.

8. Longe, "A Small Postscript," 14.

9. Longe, 14.

10. Longe, 16.

11. Speck, Broom, and Long, *Cherokee Dance and Drama*, v-vi.

12. Wetmore, "The Green Corn Ceremony of the Eastern Cherokees," 47.

13. Wetmore, 47.

14. Mooney and Olbrechts, *The Swimmer Manuscript*, 280–81; Lee Irwin, "Cherokee Healing: Myth, Dreams, and Medicine," *American Indian Quarterly* 16 (Spring 1992): 241.

15. Wetmore, "The Green Corn Ceremony of the Eastern Cherokees," 48; John R. Swanton, "Indians of the Southeastern United States," Smithsonian Institution Bureau of American Ethnology Bulletin 137 (Washington, DC: US Government Printing Office, 1946), 771. John Witthoft, "The Cherokee Green Corn Medicine and the Green Corn Festival," *Journal of the Washington Academy of Sciences* 36, no. 7 (1946): 214; John Witthoft, *Green Corn Ceremonialism in the Eastern Woodlands*, Occasional Contributions, University of Michigan Museum of Anthropological Archaeology (Ann Arbor: University of Michigan Press, 1949), 44.

16. Witthoft, *Green Corn Ceremonialism in the Eastern Woodlands*, 44.

17. Anderson, Brown, and Rogers, *The Payne-Butrick Papers*, vol. 1–3, pp. 34–58.

18. Anderson, Brown, and Rogers, vol. 1–3, p. 53.

19. Anderson, Brown, and Rogers, vol. 1–3, p. 61.

20. Anderson, Brown, and Rogers, vol. 1–3, p. 61.

21. Witthoft, *Green Corn Ceremonialism in the Eastern Woodlands*, 46. Anderson, Brown, and Rogers, *The Payne-Butrick Papers*, vol. 1–3, p. 41.

22. Anderson, Brown, and Rogers, *The Payne-Butrick Papers*, vol. 1–3, p. 41.

23. Swanton, "Indians of the Southeastern United States," 771. The Cherokee migration myth is discussed in the following sources: Haywood, *The Natural and Aboriginal History of Tennessee*, 157, 236; Longe, "A Small Postscript," 25, 29–30; Horsefly, *A History of the True People*, esp. 12; George Sahkiyah "Soggy" Sanders, *Red Man's Origin*, trans. William Eubanks, 3rd ed. ([1896] Longmont, CO: Panther's Lodge, 2016); Teuton, *Cherokee Stories of the Turtle Mountain Liars' Club*, 56–60; Howard Meredith and Virginia Milam Sobral, eds., *Cherokee Vision of Elohi*, trans. Wesley Proctor (Oklahoma City, OK: Noksi, 1997; Hastings Shade, "Journey of the Cherokees," in *Myths, Legends and Old Sayings* (Tahlequah, OK: Shade, 1994).

24. Swanton, "Indians of the Southeastern United States," 771.

25. Haywood, *The Natural and Aboriginal History of Tennessee*, 235–37.

26. King, *The Memoirs of Lt. Henry Timberlake: The Story of a Soldier, Adventurer, and Emissary to the Cherokees, 1756–1765* (Chapel Hill: University of North Carolina Press, 2007), 35.

27. Witthoft, *Green Corn Ceremonialism in the Eastern Woodlands*, 34–35.

28. Anderson, Brown, and Rogers, *The Payne-Butrick Papers*, vol. 1–3, p. 6.

29. Longe, "A Small Postscript," 10.

30. Clemens de Baillou, "A Contribution to the Mythology and Conceptual World of the Cherokee Indians," *Ethnohistory* 8, no. 1 (Winter 1961): 97.

31. Baillou, "A Contribution to the Mythology and Conceptual World of the Cherokee Indians," 97; Raymond D. Fogelson, "Who Were the *Ani-Kutani*? An Excursion into Cherokee Historical Thought," *Ethnohistory* 31, no. 4 (1984): 257; John Witthoft, "Notes on a Cherokee Migration Story," *Journal of the Washington Academy of Sciences* 37, no. 9 (1947): 304–5. Western Cherokee citizen and scholar Alan Kilpatrick uses the term *conflation* to talk about the Cherokee experience of timelessness. Kilpatrick, *The Night Has a Naked Soul*, 32.

32. Norton, *The Journal of Major John Norton, 1816*, 80.

33. Fogelson, "Who Were the *Ani-Kutani*?" 257.

34. George E. Lankford, "World on a String: Some Cosmological Components of the Southeastern Ceremonial Complex," in *Hero, Hawk, and the Open Hand: American Indian Art of the Ancient Midwest and South*, ed. Richard F. Townsend (Chicago: Art Institute of Chicago, 2004), 207–18.

35. Mircea Eliade, *The Sacred and the Profane: The Nature of Religion*, trans. Willard R. Trask (New York: Harcourt, Brace & World, 1959), 188–201.

36. Theda Perdue, *Slavery and the Evolution of Cherokee Society: 1540–1866* (Knoxville: University of Tennessee Press, 1979), 13.

37. Rudolf Otto, *The Idea of the Holy: An Inquiry into the Non-rational Factor in the Idea of the Divine and Its Relation to the Rational*, trans. John W. Harvey (Oxford: Oxford University Press, 1923).

38. Mooney and Olbrechts, *The Swimmer Manuscript*, 20.

39. Kilpatrick and Kilpatrick, *Walk in Your Soul*, 72–73.

40. Kilpatrick and Kilpatrick, *Run toward the Nightland*, 73.

41. Jack F. Kilpatrick, ed., "The Wahnenauhi Manuscript: Historical Sketches of the Cherokees, Together with Some of Their Customs, Traditions, and Superstitions," Smithsonian Institution Bureau of American Ethnology Bulletin 196, Paper 77, 175–214 (Washington, DC: US Government Printing Office, 1966), 85.

42. Kilpatrick, "The Wahnenauhi Manuscript," 85.

43. Mooney, *Myths of the Cherokee*, 518.

44. Kilpatrick, *The Night Has a Naked Soul*, 52.

45. Mooney, *Myths of the Cherokee*, 518.

46. Cephas Washburn, *Reminiscences of the Indians* (New York: Johnson Reprint Corp., 1971), 190; *Cherokee Phoenix*, April 29, 1829.

47. *Cherokee Phoenix*, April 29, 1829.

48. Mary Ulmer Chiltoskey, *Cherokee Words with Pictures* (Cherokee, NC: Cherokee Publications, 1972), 13, 33.

49. Prentice Robinson, *Cherokee Dictionary* (Tulsa, OK: Cherokee Language and Culture, 1996), 45.

50. Anderson, Brown, and Rogers, *The Payne-Butrick Papers*, vol. 1–3, p. 286.

51. Anderson, Brown, and Rogers, vol. 1–3, pp. 20, 21, 44, 129–30.

52. Speck, Broom, and Long, *Cherokee Dance and Drama*, 45; Witthoft, *Green Corn Ceremonialism in the Eastern Woodlands*, 44.

53. Witthoft, *Green Corn Ceremonialism in the Eastern Woodlands*, 47. Guns were observed at a Green Corn Dance as early as 1803 by Moravian mis-

sionaries. Edmund Schwarze, *History of the Moravian Missions among the Southern Indian Tribes of the United States*, Transactions of the Moravian Historical Society, Special Series, Vol. 1 (Bethlehem, PA: Moravian Historical Society, 1923), 78.

54. Kilpatrick and Kilpatrick, *Walk in Your Soul*, 32; Mooney, *Myths of the Cherokee*, 248.

55. Mooney, *Myths of the Cherokee*, 248.

56. Longe, "A Small Postscript," 38. See also: Alan Kilpatrick, "A Note on Cherokee Theological Concepts," *American Indian Quarterly* 19 (Summer 1995): 394.

57. Anderson, Brown, and Rogers, *The Payne-Butrick Papers*, vol. 4–6, p. 200.

58. Mooney, *Myths of the Cherokee*, 257.

59. Mooney and Olbrechts, *The Swimmer Manuscript*, 24.

60. Raymond D. Fogelson, "Cherokee Little People Reconsidered," *Journal of Cherokee Studies* 7 (Fall 1982): 95; See also: Kilpatrick and Kilpatrick, *Walk in Your Soul*, 51; Jack F. Kilpatrick and Anna G. Kilpatrick, "Cherokee Rituals Pertaining to Medicinal Roots," *Southern Indian Studies* 16 (1964): 26; Kilpatrick and Kilpatrick, *Friends of Thunder*, 51.

61. Zogry, *Anesto*, 59.

62. Speck, Broom, and Long, *Cherokee Dance and Drama*, 45–53; Gilbert, *The Eastern Cherokees*, 308–309; Olivia S. Rivers, "Two Versions of Cherokee Traditional Dances Compared," *Journal of Cherokee Studies* 19 (1997): 18–45. Rivers' article compares a number of traditional Cherokee dances according to descriptions by Will West Long and Richard "Geet" Crowe. Rivers also observed five traditional dances at the Cherokee Fall Festival from 1983 to 1988.

63. Speck, Broom, and Long, *Cherokee Dance and Drama*, 69.

64. Speck, Broom, and Long, *Cherokee Dance and Drama*, 77.

65. Boulware, *Deconstructing the Cherokee Nation*, 91–92; Gilbert, "The Cherokees of North Carolina," 539.

66. Timberlake, *Lieutenant Henry Timberlake's Memoirs*, 102.

67. Gearing, *Priests and Warriors*.

68. Raymond D. Fogelson, "The Cherokee Ballgame Cycle: An Ethnographer's View," in *Ethnology of the Southeastern Indians: A Source Book*, ed. Charles M. Hudson, 327–38 (New York: Garland, 1985).

69. Fogelson, "The Cherokee Ballgame Cycle," 331; See also: Zogry, *Anetso*.

70. Fogelson, "The Cherokee Ballgame Cycle," 331.

71. Fogelson, "The Cherokee Ballgame Cycle," 332.

72. James Mooney, "The Cherokee Ball Play," *American Anthropologist* 31 (1890): 111.

73. Zogry, *Anetso*, 116.

74. Fogelson, "The Cherokee Ballgame Cycle," 331.

75. Speck, Broom, and Long, *Cherokee Dance and Drama*, 57.

76. Speck, Broom, and Long, 59.

77. Speck, Broom, and Long, 57.

78. Speck, Broom, and Long, 59.

79. Speck, Broom, and Long, 60.

80. Zogry, *Anetso*, 47.

81. Fogelson, "The Cherokee Ballgame Cycle." 333; Lankford, "World on a String."

82. Speck, Broom, and Long, *Cherokee Dance and Drama*, 55.

83. Kilpatrick, "'Going to the Water.'" See also: Gilbert, *The Eastern Cherokees*, 268–69.

84. Kilpatrick, "'Going to the Water,'" 51; James Mooney, *The Sacred Formulas of the Cherokees, 7th Annual Report of the Bureau of American Ethnology, 1885–1886* (Washington, DC: US Government Printing Office, 1891), 301–97, reprinted in *Myths of the Cherokee and Sacred Formulas of the Cherokees* (Nashville, TN: Charles and Randy Elder, 1982), 379 (page citations refer to reprint edition).

85. Kilpatrick, "'Going to the Water,'" 49.

86. Mooney, *Myths of the Cherokee*, 230; See also: Mooney, "The Cherokee Ball Play," 125.

87. Zogry, *Anetso*, 120.

88. Eliade, *Images and Symbols*.

89. Longe, "A Small Postscript," 36.

90. Mooney, *Myths of the Cherokee*, 476.

91. Mooney, "The Cherokee Ball Play," 121–22.

92. Zogry, *Anetso*, 127.

93. Mooney, "The Cherokee Ball Play," 121–26.

94. Mooney, 126.

95. Mooney, 127.

96. Zogry, *Anetso*, 194.

97. Zogry, 198.

98. Loftin, "Supplication and Participation," 177–201.

99. "Seneca Nation Repatriates Booger Masks to the Eastern Band of Cherokee Indians," *The Cherokee One Feather*, August 7, 2019, https://theonefeather.com/2019/08/07/seneca-nation-repatriate-masks-to-the-eastern-band-of-cherokee-indians/.

100. Speck, Broom, and Long, *Cherokee Dance and Drama*, 25.

101. Speck, Broom, and Long, 28.

102. Raymond D. Fogelson and Amelia B. Walker, "Self and Other in Cherokee Booger Masks," *Journal of Cherokee Studies* 5 (1980): 89.

103. Anderson, Brown, and Rogers, *The Payne-Butrick Papers*, vol. 4–6, p. 445.

104. Speck, Broom, and Long, *Cherokee Dance and Drama*, 29.

105. Speck, Broom, and Long, 29.

106. Speck, Broom, and Long, 30.

107. Speck, Broom, and Long, 30, 37–38.

108. Speck, Broom, and Long, 30.

109. Speck, Broom, and Long, 33.

110. Speck, Broom, and Long, 29.

111. Speck, Broom, and Long, 33.

112. Speck, Broom, and Long, 36.

113. Speck, Broom, and Long, 36.

114. Gilbert, *The Eastern Cherokees*, 262.

115. Gilbert, 262.

116. Gilbert, 262.

117. Gilbert, 262.

118. Gilbert, 262.

119. Raymond D. Fogelson and Amelia R. Bell, "Cherokee Booger Mask Tradition," in *The Power of Symbols: Masks and Masquerade in the Americas*, ed. N. Ross Crumrine and Marjorie Halpin (Vancouver: University of British Columbia Press, 1983), 50.

120. Fogelson and Bell, 51.

121. Fogelson and Bell, 52.

122. Fogelson and Bell, 52.

123. Fogelson and Bell, 53.

124. Bernard S. Mason, *Dances and Stories of the American Indian* (New York: Ronald Press, 1944), 194.

125. Carol Johnston, "Burning Beds, Spinning Wheels, and Calico Dresses," *Journal of Cherokee Studies* 19 (1997): 5–6.

126. Loftin, *Religion and Hopi Life*, chap. 6; Speck, Broom, and Long, *Cherokee Dance and Drama*, 38.

127. Fogelson and Bell, "Cherokee Booger Mask Tradition," 64. "Seneca Nation Repatriates Booger Masks to the Eastern Band of Cherokee Indians," *The Cherokee One Feather*, August 7, 2019, https://theonefeather.com/2019/08/07/seneca-nation-repatriate-masks-to-the-eastern-band-of-cherokee-indians/.

128. Johnston, "Burning Beds, Spinning Wheels, and Calico Dresses," 5–6.

129. Speck, Broom, and Long, *Cherokee Dance and Drama*, 38.

130. Speck, Broom, and Long, 38.

CHAPTER 4

1. Hill, *Weaving New Worlds*, 13–14. See: Mooney, *Myths of the Cherokee*, 512.

2. Mooney, *The Sacred Formulas of the Cherokees*, 310.

3. Mooney, 310.

4. Mooney, 311.

5. Mooney, 311.

6. Mooney, 311.

7. Many early English and Americans, intellectually stymied by the novelty of the New World, tried to make sense of the Cherokee by interpreting them as a Lost Tribe of Israel. See: Adair, *The History of the American Indians*; William McLoughlin, *Cherokees and Missionaries, 1789–1839* (New Haven, CT: Yale University Press, 1984).

8. Anderson, Brown and Rogers, *The Payne-Butrick Papers*, vol. 4–6, p. 10.

9. Mooney, *Myths of the Cherokee*, 507.

10. Cherokee wizards were perhaps shamans, and there are arguably shamanic elements present among some medicine men and women. Some Eastern (and Western) Cherokees occasionally use the term *shaman* to describe certain

conjurors and healers, but some do not. See: Mircea Eliade, *Shamanism: Archaic Techniques of Ecstasy*, trans. Willard R. Trask (Princeton, NJ: Princeton University Press, 1964); Loftin, *The Big Picture*, chap. 1; Kilpatrick and Kilpatrick, *Notebook of a Cherokee Shaman*; Kilpatrick, *The Night Has a Naked Soul*, 114.

11. Kilpatrick and Kilpatrick, *Walk in Your Soul*, 9.

12. Mooney and Olbrechts, *The Swimmer Manuscript*, 84.

13. Kilpatrick and Kilpatrick, *Run toward the Nightland*, 4.

14. Kilpatrick and Kilpatrick, 4.

15. Fogelson and Walker, "Self and Other in Cherokee Booger Masks," 60.

16. Kilpatrick, *The Night Has a Naked Soul*, 28.

17. Mooney and Olbrechts, *The Swimmer Manuscript*, 160.

18. Mooney and Olbrechts, 163, 147.

19. Mooney and Olbrechts, 183, 189–190, 242, 376; Kilpatrick and Kilpatrick, *Notebook of a Cherokee Shaman*, 90; Kilpatrick and Kilpatrick, *Run toward the Nightland*, 80.

20. Alan Kilpatrick, "Cherokee War Charms," unpublished manuscript in author's possession, ca. 1992, 25.

21. Heidi M. Altman and Thomas N. Belt, "*Tohi*: The Cherokee Concept of Well-Being," in *Under the Rattlesnake: Cherokee Health and Resiliency*, ed. Lisa J. Lefler (Tuscaloosa: University of Alabama Press, 2009), 14–16.

22. John Witthoft, "An Early Cherokee Ethnobotanical Note," *Journal of the Washington Academy of Sciences* 37 (1947): 73–75; John R. Swanton, "Religious Beliefs and Medical Practices of the Creek Indians," *42nd Annual Report of the Bureau of American Ethnology* (Washington, DC: US Government Printing Office, 1928), 666–70.

23. J. T. Garrett, *The Cherokee Herbal: Native Plant Medicine from the Four Directions* (Rochester, VT: Bean & Co., 2003).

24. Mooney and Olbrechts, *The Swimmer Manuscript*; Kilpatrick and Kilpatrick, *Notebook of a Cherokee Shaman*.

25. Anderson, Brown, and Rogers, *The Payne-Butrick Papers*, vol. 1–3, pp. 45, 55, 70, 226, 290.

26. Anderson, Brown, and Rogers, vol. 4–6, p. 529.

27. Mooney and Olbrechts, *The Swimmer Manuscript*, 18.

28. Mooney and Olbrechts, 44–50.

29. Mooney and Olbrechts, 21; Mooney, *Myths of the Cherokee*, 252.

30. Mooney and Olbrechts, *The Swimmer Manuscript*, 21.

31. Chadwick C. Smith, Rennard Strickland, and Benny Smith, *Building One Fire: Art and Worldview in Cherokee Life* (Talequah, OK: Cherokee Nation, 2010).

32. Mooney and Olbrechts, *The Swimmer Manuscript*, 19–20.

33. Mooney and Olbrechts, 23.

34. Mooney and Olbrechts, 23.

35. Mooney and Olbrechts, 23.

36. Mooney and Olbrechts, 24.

37. Mooney and Olbrechts, 24–25; Mooney, *The Sacred Formulas of the Cherokees*, 342.

38. Mooney and Olbrechts, *The Swimmer Manuscript*, 26, 27.

39. Mooney and Olbrechts, 29. See also the works by Fogelson and the Kilpatricks.

40. Mooney and Olbrechts, *The Swimmer Manuscript*, 30; Raymond D. Fogelson, "An Analysis of Cherokee Society and Witchcraft," in *Four Centuries of Southern Indians*, ed. Charles M. Hudson, 113–31 (Athens: University of Georgia Press, 1975), 120.

41. Mooney and Olbrechts, *The Swimmer Manuscript*, 29.

42. Mooney and Olbrechts, *The Swimmer Manuscript*, 30; Mooney, *Myths of the Cherokee*, 401, 402; Kilpatrick, *The Night Has a Naked Soul*, 10.

43. Kilpatrick, *The Night Has a Naked Soul*, 10. See also: Mooney and Olbrechts, *The Swimmer Manuscript*, 30; Mooney, *Myths of the Cherokee*, 401, 402.

44. Fogelson, "An Analysis of Cherokee Society and Witchcraft," 113.

45. Fogelson, 113.

46. Kilpatrick, *The Night Has a Naked Soul*, 9.

47. Kilpatrick, 9.

48. Raymond D. Fogelson, "The Conjuror in Eastern Cherokee Society," *Journal of Cherokee Studies* 5 (1980): 67.

49. Kilpatrick and Kilpatrick, *Run toward the Nightland*, 170.

50. Mooney, *The Sacred Formulas of the Cherokees*, 256.

51. Fogelson, "An Analysis of Cherokee Society and Witchcraft," 124.

52. John D. Loftin, "'The Harmony Ethic,'" 40–45; Gulick, *Cherokees at the Crossroads*, 135, 337.

53. Fogelson, "An Analysis of Cherokee Society and Witchcraft," 126.

54. Loftin, "Supplication and Participation," 177–201; Christopher B. Rodning, "Cherokee Towns and Calumet Ceremonialism in Eastern North America," *American Antiquity* 79 (2014): 425–43.

55. William Bartram, *Travels through North and South Carolina, Georgia, East and West Florida, the Cherokee Country, the Extensive Territories of the Muscogulges, or Creek Confederacy, and the Country of the Chactaws* [sic], reprinted as *Travels of William Bartram*, ed. Mark Van Doren ([1791]New York: Dover, 1955), 285; Speck, Broom, and Long, *Cherokee Dance and Drama*, 33; Timberlake, *Lieutenant Henry Timberlake's Memoirs*, 69, 91.

56. Mooney, *Myths of the Cherokee*, 424.

57. Mooney, 422.

58. Robbie F. Ethridge, "Tobacco among the Cherokees," *Journal of Cherokee Studies* 3 (1978): 76.

59. Ethridge, 76.

60. Mooney, *Myths of the Cherokee*, 424.

61. Mooney, 254–55.

62. Mooney, 255.

63. Mooney, 254.

64. Ward and Davis, *Time Before History*.

65. Ethridge, "Tobacco among the Cherokees," 77, 78.

66. Ethridge, 79.

67. Ethridge, 79.

68. Ethridge, 79.

69. Ethridge, 79.

70. Ethridge, 80.

71. Ethridge, 80.

72. Gilbert, *The Eastern Cherokees*, 336.

73. Kilpatrick and Kilpatrick, *Notebook of a Cherokee Shaman*, 113.

74. Kilpatrick and Kilpatrick, 91.

75. Frans M. Olbrechts, "Some Cherokee Methods of Divination," *International Congress of Americanists Proceedings* 23 (1930), 550–51.

76. Hudson, *The Southeastern Indians*, 334.

77. Hudson, 369.

78. Hudson, 369.

79. Mooney and Olbrechts, *The Swimmer Manuscript*, 138.

80. Kilpatrick and Kilpatrick, *Walk in Your Soul*, 139.

81. Ethridge, "Tobacco among the Cherokees," 83.

82. Ethridge, 83.

83. Ethridge, 83.

84. Mooney, *The Sacred Formulas of the Cherokees*, 384.

85. Ethridge, "Tobacco among the Cherokees," 84.

86. Ethridge, 84.

87. Loftin, "Supplication and Participation," 177–201.

88. Kilpatrick and Kilpatrick, *Walk in Your Soul*, 39.

89. Kilpatrick and Kilpatrick, *Run toward the Nightland*, 140.

90. Kilpatrick, *The Night Has a Naked Soul*, 75.

91. Ethridge, "Tobacco among the Cherokees," 84.

92. Gilbert, *The Eastern Cherokees*, 336; Kilpatrick and Kilpatrick, *Run toward the Nightland*, 31–33.

93. Loftin, "The 'Harmony Ethic,'" 40–45; Loftin, "Supplication and Participation," 185.

94. See: Loftin, "The 'Harmony Ethic,'" 40–45; Loftin, "Supplication and Participation," 185; Ethridge, "Tobacco among the Cherokees."

95. Kilpatrick, *The Night Has a Naked Soul*, 32–33.

96. Kilpatrick, 32–33.

97. Kilpatrick, 32–33.

98. Kilpatrick, 32–33.

99. Kilpatrick, 32–33.

100. Gilbert, *The Eastern Cherokees*, 345.

101. Mooney and Olbrechts, *The Swimmer Manuscript*, 148–49.

102. Mooney and Olbrechts, 156.

103. Mooney and Olbrechts, 195.

CHAPTER 5

1. James H. Merrell, *The Indians' New World: Catawbas and Their Neighbors from European Contact through the Era of Removal* (Chapel Hill: University of North Carolina Press, 1989), 529.

2. Lewis O. Saum, *The Fur Trader and the Indian* (Seattle: University of Washington Press, 1965); Immanuel Wallenstein, *The Modern World System I:*

Capitalist Agriculture and the Origins of the European World Economy in the Sixteenth Century (New York: Academic Press, 1974).

3. Joel W. Martin, "Southeastern Indians and the English Trade in Skins and Slaves," in *The Forgotten Centuries: Indians and Europeans in the American South, 1521–1704*, ed. Charles Hudson and Carmen Chaves Teaser (Athens: University of Georgia Press, 1994), 305.

4. Jon Bernard Marcoux, "Cherokee Households and Communities in the English Contact Period, 1670–1740" (PhD diss., University of North Carolina at Chapel Hill, 2008), 50.

5. Peter H. Wood, "The Changing Population of the Colonial South," in *Powhatan's Mantle: Indians in the Colonial Southeast*, ed. P. H. Wood, G. A. Waselkov, and M. T. Hatley (Lincoln: University of Nebraska Press, 1989), 63.

6. Alan Gallay, *The Indian Slave Trade: The Rise of the English Empire in the American South, 1670–1717* (New Haven, CT: Yale University Press, 2002), 298–99.

7. Marcoux, "Cherokee Households and Communities," 52.

8. Marcoux, 54.

9. Marcoux, 54.

10. Verner W. Crane, *The Southeastern Frontier, 1670–1732* (Durham, NC: Duke University Press, 1928), 40.

11. Marcoux, "Cherokee Households and Communities," 57.

12. Marcoux, 59.

13. David H. Corkran, *The Creek Frontier, 1540–1783* (Norman: University of Oklahoma Press, 1967), 73–77.

14. Steven J. Oatis, *A Colonial Complex: South Carolina's Frontiers in the Era of the Yamasee War, 1680–1730* (Lincoln: University of Nebraska, 2004), 254.

15. Marcoux, "Cherokee Households and Communities," 72.

16. Marcoux, 75, 76, 78, 83. For a discussion of the "shatter zone" and the effect of the Yamasee War on the Cherokees, see also, Marcoux, with contributions by Kandace D. Hollenbach, Boyce Driskell, Jessica L. Vavrasek, Judith A. Sichler, Jeremy Sweat, Katherine McMillan, Stephen Carmody, Phyllis Rigney, and Erik Johanson, *The Cherokees of Tuckaleechee Cove*, Museum of Anthropology, University of Michigan Memoirs, No. 52 (Ann Arbor, Michigan, 2012), 3–20.

17. Marcoux, "Cherokee Households and Communities," 84.

18. Oatis, *A Colonial Complex*, 238–52.

19. Adair, *The History of the American Indians*, 244.

20. Adair, 244.

21. Charles Hudson, "Introduction," in *The Transformation of the Southeastern Indians, 1540–1760*, ed. Robbie Ethridge and Charles Hudson (Jackson: University of Mississippi Press, 2002), xix.

22. Hudson, "Introduction," xix.

23. Calvin Martin, *Keepers of the Game: Indian-Animal Relationships in the Fur Trade* (Berkeley: University of California Press, 1978), 154.

24. McLoughlin, *Cherokees and Missionaries, 1789–1839*; McLoughlin, *The Cherokees and Christianity, 1794–1870*.

25. McLoughlin, *The Cherokees and Christianity, 1794–1870*, 193.

26. McLoughlin, chap. 7; For a Native discussion of Native American Christianity, see: James Treat, *Native and Christian: Indigenous Voices on Religious Identity in the United States and Canada* (New York: Routledge, 1996).

27. Martin, *Keepers of the Game*, 152.

28. Perdue, *Slavery and the Evolution of Cherokee Society: 1540–1866*, 12–13.

29. Charles Hudson, "Why the Southeastern Indians Slaughtered Deer," in *Indians, Animals and the Fur Trade: A Critique of Keepers of the Game*, ed. Shepherd Krech III (Athens: University of Georgia Press, 1981), 160; Fogelson, "An Analysis of Cherokee Society and Witchcraft," 113–131; Mooney and Olbrechts, *The Swimmer Manuscript*.

30. Mooney and Olbrechts, *The Swimmer Manuscript*, 38.

31. Martin, *Keepers of the Game*, 161.

32. Anderson, Brown, and Rogers, *The Payne-Butrick Papers*, vol. 4, p. 229, vol 1, pp.74–76; In another section, *The Payne-Butrick Papers* claim smallpox is said to be inflicted by male and female spiritual beings: vol. 4, pp. 80–81. See also: Paul Kelton, *Cherokee Medicine, Colonial Germs: An Indigenous Nation's Fight Against Smallpox, 1518–1824* (Norman: University of Oklahoma Press, 2015). Clearly, smallpox was new to the Cherokees and there were multiple views and theories of its origin.

33. Schwarze, *History of the Moravian Missions among the Southern Indian Tribes of the United States*, 174–75.

34. Mooney and Olbrechts, *The Swimmer Manuscript*, 39.

35. Hudson, "Why the Southeastern Indians Slaughtered Deer," 166.

36. Vicki Rozema, *Cherokee Voices: Early Accounts of Cherokee Life in the East* (Winston-Salem, NC: John F. Blair, 2002), 15.

37. Hudson, "Why the Southeastern Indians Slaughtered Deer," 166, 167.

38. Hudson, 167.

39. Hudson, 168.

40. Gallay, *The Indian Slave Trade*; Hudson, "Why the Southeastern Indians Slaughtered Deer," 169; Virginia Anderson, "King Phillip's Herds: Indians, Colonists, and the Problem of Livestock in Early New England," in *American Encounters: Native and Newcomers from European Contact to Indian Removal, 1500–1850*, ed. Peter C. Mancall and James H. Merrell, 2nd ed., 246–68 (London: Routledge, 2007).

CHAPTER 6

1. David H. Corkran, *The Cherokee Frontier, 1740–1762* (Norman: University of Oklahoma Press, 1962), 3.

2. Corkran, 6.

3. Timberlake, *Lieutenant Henry Timberlake's Memoirs*, 51.

4. Corkran, *The Cherokee Frontier, 1740–1762*, 11.

5. Corkran, 14.

6. Corkran, 15.

7. Timberlake, *Lieutenant Henry Timberlake's Memoirs, 1756–1765*, 29n4.

8. Timberlake, 47, 71.

9. John Oliphant, *Peace and War on the Anglo-Cherokee Frontier, 1756–63* (Baton Rouge: Louisiana State University Press, 2001), 2.

10. Corkran, *The Cherokee Frontier, 1740–1762*, 30.

11. There are numerous excellent historical works that deal with the Cherokee war with the British (Anglo-Cherokee War) in 1760–61. We should not repeat the details of those matters in this book, but see Mooney, Woodward, Oliphant, Corkran, Hoig, and Perdue.

12. Norton, *The Journal of Major John Norton (Teyoninhokarawen), 1816*, 62; Oliphant, *Peace and War on the Anglo-Cherokee Frontier, 1756–63*, 140.

13. Perdue, *The Cherokees*, 26.

14. Perdue, 27.

15. Perdue, 27.

16. Boulware, *Deconstructing the Cherokee Nation*, 129; McLoughlin, *The Cherokees and Christianity, 1794–1870*, 3; McLoughlin, *The Cherokee Ghost Dance*, 4.

17. Tom Holm, "Politics Came First: A Reflection on Robert K. Thomas and Cherokee History," in *A Good Cherokee, A Good Anthropologist: Papers in Honor of Robert K. Thomas*, ed. Steve Pavlik, 41–56 (Los Angeles: UCLA American Indian Studies Center, 1998).

18. Holm, 45.

19. Holm, 45.

20. Holm, 46.

21. Holm, 48.

22. Joel W. Martin, *Sacred Revolt: The Muskogees Struggle for a New World* (Boston: Beacon Press, 1991).

23. Anderson, Brown, and Rogers, *The Payne-Butrick Papers*, vol. 1, p. 123. Interestingly, this aged Cherokee did not know the name Selu, or at least would not say it.

24. Holm, "Politics Came First," 50–51.

25. Mooney, *Myths of the Cherokee*, 77.

26. Mooney, 79.

27. McLoughlin, *The Cherokee Ghost Dance*, xvii.

28. Mooney, *Myths of the Cherokee*, 81; Royce, *The Cherokee Nation of Indians*.

29. Mooney, *Myths of the Cherokee*, 82.

30. McLoughlin, *The Cherokee Ghost Dance*, 5–6; Mooney thinks still twenty thousand at the end of the eighteenth century.

31. McLoughlin, 7.

32. McLoughlin, 9.

33. McLoughlin, 10.

34. McLoughlin, *The Cherokees and Christianity, 1794–1870*, 193.

35. Longe, "A Small Postscript," 3–49.

36. Long, "Primitive/Civilized," 43–61.

37. Longe, "A Small Postscript," 8.

38. See: Loftin, *Religion and Hopi Life*, xxi–xxii. Otto, *The Idea of the Holy*.

39. Otto, *The Idea of the Holy*, 12.

40. Longe, "A Small Postscript," 8; Denise I. Bossy, "Spiritual Diplomacy: Reinterpreting the Yamasee Prince's Eighteenth-Century Voyage to England," in *The Yamasee Indians: From Florida to South Carolina*, ed. Denise I. Bossy with foreword by Alan Gallay, 131–62 (Lincoln: University of Nebraska Press, 2018). Bossy employs the term *spiritual diplomacy* to discuss a cultural strategy in which Yamasees sought a spiritual and political connection with the Spanish and British. Yamasees, like other southeastern Indians, understood that political and spiritual power was symbiotic. Some Cherokees may have converted to Christianity in the early nineteenth century to secure political alliances with the Americans but also to gain sacred power. For example, Cherokees understood European and American political and technological power in spiritual terms and desired to share in that strength.

41. Longe, "A Small Postscript," 8.

42. Longe, 8.

43. Longe, 18.

44. Longe, 18.

45. Longe, 20.

46. Longe, 20.

47. Longe, 22.

48. Longe, 24.

49. Longe, 24.

50. James Axtell, *The European and the Indian: Essays in the Ethnohistory of North America* (Oxford: Oxford University Press, 1981), 112.

51. Longe, "A Small Postscript," 26.

52. Timberlake, *Lieutenant Henry Timberlake's Memoirs, 1756–1765*, 90–91.

53. Longe, "A Small Postscript," 28.

54. Longe, 34. .

55. Longe, 34.

56. Longe, 34.

57. Longe, 37.

58. Adair, *The History of the American Indians*, 68, note *.

59. Longe, "A Small Postscript," 38.

60. Longe, 42.

CHAPTER 7

1. *American State Papers: Indian Affairs, Vol. I, Documents, Legends, and Executive of the Congress of the United States*, ed. Walter Lowrie, Walter S. Franklin, and Matthew. Clark (Washington, DC: Gales and Seaton, 1832, 1834), 13, 53, 61; William G. McLoughlin, *Cherokee Renascence in the New Republic* (Princeton, NJ: Princeton University Press, 1986), 35.

2. Loftin, *The Big Picture*, chap. 13.

3. Loftin, 36; *American State Papers*, 53.

4. Schwarze, *History of the Moravian Missions among the Southern Indian Tribes of the United States*.

5. Schwarze, *History of the Moravian Missions among the Southern Indian Tribes of the United States*; Muriel Wright, *Spring Place Moravian Mission and the Ward Family of the Cherokee Nation* (Guthrie, OK: Co-operative Publishing, 1940), 42.

6. Adelaide Lisetta Fries, ed. and trans., "Report of the Brethren Abraham Steiner and Friedrich Christian von Schweinitz of Their Journey to the Cherokee Nation and in the Cumberland Settlements in the State of Tennessee from 28th October to 28th December," *North Carolina Historical Review* 21 (1944): 358–60; Schwarze. *History of the Moravian Missions among the Southern Indian Tribes of the United States*. McLoughlin, for some reason, spells the elder's name Arcowee, instead of Aarcowee (neither of which can be very accurate, as Cherokee contains no letter R), and says he was a former war chief, rather than a Beloved Man. The Moravian report clearly describes him as a Beloved Man, not former war chief, the highest honor the Cherokee (to this day) bestow upon a Cherokee man or woman. It is true that former war chiefs could become Beloved, so it is possible that McLoughlin inferred that. See: McLoughlin, *Cherokees and Missionaries*, 38–39.

7. McLoughlin, *Cherokees and Missionaries*, 38–39.

8. Schwarze, *History of the Moravian Missions among the Southern Indian Tribes of the United States*.

9. Ben Oshel Bridgers, "Red Clay: Cherokee Past and Future," *American Indian Religions* 1 (1994): 88.

10. McLoughlin, *Cherokee Renascence in the New Republic*, 62, 66. Major Norton, whose father was Cherokee, observed in 1809 that honesty was a "prevailing virtue" among the Cherokee and that they had enacted laws only recently for the punishment of thievery. Norton, *The Journal of Major John Norton*, 133.

11. Duane Champagne, *Social Order and Political Change: Constitutional Governments among the Cherokee, the Chickasaws, and the Creek* (Stanford, CA: Stanford University Press, 1992); Wilma A. Dunaway, "Rethinking Cherokee Acculturation: Agrarian Capitalism and Women's Resistance to the Cult of Domesticity, 1800–1838," *American Indian Culture and Research Journal* 21 (1997): 155–92.

12. Perdue, *Cherokee Women*, 107, 122, 146–49.

13. Jedidiah Morse, *The American Universal Geography; or, A View of the Present State of All Kingdoms, States, and Colonies in the Known World* (Boston: Thomas & Andrews, 1812), 574.

14. Perdue, *Cherokee Women*, 130–40.

15. Perdue, 140.

16. McLoughlin, *Cherokee Renascence in the New Republic*, 104–8.

17. Long, *Significations*, 118.

18. Long, 118.

19. Loftin, "A Hopi-Anglo Discourse on Myth and History," 677–93.

20. Eliade, *The Myth of the Eternal Return or, Cosmos and History*, 4, 7, 23.

21. Leenhardt, *Do Kamo*, 214, esp. chap. 12.

22. Long, *Significations*, 129; See also: Kenelm Burridge, *New Heaven, New Earth: A Study of Millenarian Activities* (New York: Schocken Books,

1969); Anthony F. C. Wallace, *The Death and Rebirth of the Seneca* (New York: Vintage Books, 1969); Peter Worsley, *The Trumpet Shall Sound: A Study of "Cargo" Cults in Melanesia,* 2nd ed. (New York: Schocken Books, 1968).

23. McLoughlin, *Cherokee Renascence in the New Republic,* 56–57.

24. McLoughlin, 128.

25. Eliade, *The Quest,* 110, 111.

26. Peter M. Whiteley, *Deliberate Acts: Changing Hopi Culture through the Oraibi Split* (Tucson: University of Arizona Press, 1988).

27. Duane Champagne, "Symbolic Structure and Political Change in Cherokee Society," *Journal of Cherokee Studies* 8 (1983): 87–96; Champagne, "Cherokee Social Movements: A Response to Thornton," *American Sociological Review* 50 (1985): 127–30; Russell Thornton, "Boundary Dissolution and Revitalization Movements: The Case of the Nineteenth-Century Cherokees," *Ethnohistory* 40 (1993); 359–83; Jonathan Hancock, "Shaken Spirits, Cherokees, Moravian Missionaries, and the New Madrid Earthquakes," *Journal of the Early Republic* 33 (2013): 643–73; McLoughlin, *The Cherokee Ghost Dance*; McLoughlin, *Cherokees and Missionaries, 1789–1839.* We agree with Wallace and Thornton (and disagree with McLoughlin): the 1811–12 Cherokee Ghost Dance and White Path's Revival (1824–27), as well as Yunaguska's 1830 movement, all embodied a spiritual element.

28. McLoughlin, *The Cherokee Ghost Dance,* 136.

29. McLoughlin, 137

30. James Mooney, *The Ghost-Dance Religion and Wounded Knee* (New York: Dover, 1973), 667–77.

31. Mooney, 667–77.

32. McLoughlin, *The Cherokee Ghost Dance,* 113, 138–39, 142–47; Thomas L. McKenney and James Hall, *Biographical Sketches and Anecdotes of Ninety-Five of 120 Principal Chiefs from the Indian Tribes of North America* (Washington, DC: US Department of Interior, 1967), 191–92.

33. McLoughlin, *The Cherokee Ghost Dance,* 142.

34. McLoughlin, 142–47.

35. McLoughlin, 142–47.

36. McLoughlin, 143.

37. Burridge, *New Heaven, New Earth*; Worsley, *The Trumpet Shall Sound*; Long, *Significations,* chap. 7–8.

38. Mooney, *Myths of the Cherokee,* 27.

39. Loftin, *The Big Picture,* 45.

40. Eliade, *The Forge and the Crucible,* 81.

41. McLoughlin, *The Cherokee Ghost Dance,* 144.

42. McLoughlin, 145.

43. McLoughlin, *Cherokee Renascence in the New Republic,* 185.

44. McLoughlin, 186. Pesantubbee argues that Tecumseh and his brother influenced the Cherokee prophecies but rightly states they did not begin with Tecumseh. Michelene Pesantubbee, "When the Earth Shakes: The Cherokee Prophecies of 1811–12," *American Indian Quarterly* 17, no. 3 (Summer 1993): 301–17.

CHAPTER 8

1. Ralph Linton, "Nativistic Movements," *American Anthropologist* 45 (1943): 230–40.

2. Mooney, *The Ghost-Dance Religion and Wounded Knee*; Anthony Wallace, "Revitalization Movements," *American Anthropological Association* 58 (1956): 264–81.

3. McLoughlin, *Cherokee Renascence in the New Republic*, 187.

4. McLoughlin, 194.

5. McLoughlin, 194.

6. McLoughlin, 382.

7. McLoughlin, 416–28, 448–49.

8. McLoughlin, 384–85.

9. McLoughlin, 241, 245.

10. McLoughlin, *The Cherokees and Christianity, 1794–1870*.

11. McLoughlin, *The Cherokees and Christianity, 1794–1870*.

12. Joyce B. Phillips and Paul Gary Phillips, eds., *The Brainerd Journal: A Mission to the Cherokees, 1817–1823* (Lincoln: University of Nebraska Press, 1998), 2.

13. Phillips and Phillips, 3.

14. Phillips and Phillips, 5.

15. Phillips and Phillips, 51.

16. Phillips and Phillips, 85.

17. Phillips and Phillips, 31.

18. Phillips and Phillips, 51.

19. McLoughlin, *Cherokees and Missionaries, 1789–1839*, 191.

20. Malone, *Cherokees of the Old South*, 135.

21. Malone, 199.

22. Mooney, *Myths of the Cherokee*, 113–14, 237; Malone, *Cherokees of the Old South*, 213–38.

23. Mooney, *Myths of the Cherokee*, 113–14, 237. White Path lived in Turniptown, near Ellijay. He died on the Trail of Tears and was buried in Kentucky. Featherstonhaugh described White Path in 1837 as an "old chief remarkably cheerful and light of step." G. W. Featherstonhaugh, *A Canoe Voyage of the Minnay Sotor*, 2 vols. (London: Richard Bentley, 1837), 235.

24. McLoughlin, *Cherokees and Missionaries, 1789–1839*, 225.

25. McLoughlin, 225.

26. Isaac Proctor to Jeremiah Evarts, May 19, 1827, *American Board of Commissioners for Foreign Missions Papers*, Microfilm Reel 739, 1824–1831, Cherokee Mission (ABC 18.3.1), Vols. 4 and 5, Cherokee Mission Letters, Houghton Library, Harvard University, Cambridge, MA.

27. Tiya Miles, *Ties That Bind: The Story of an Afro-Cherokee Family in Slavery and Freedom*, 2nd ed. (Oakland: University of California Press, 2015), 123–24; Strickland, *Fire and Spirits*, 78–80; McLoughlin, *Cherokee Renascence in the New Republic*, 174, 328. Cherokees did acquire slaves aboriginally in small numbers and many were adopted into the tribe as full-fledged members. A few were not and had no rights. Perdue, *Slavery and the Evolution of Cherokee Society, 1540–1866*, 11–12, 166n2. Only about 1 percent of North

Carolina Cherokees owned slaves in the 1800s. On the issue of Eastern Cherokee citizenship, see: Mikaela M. Adams, *Who Belongs? Race, Resources, and
Tribal Citizenship in the Native South* (Oxford: Oxford University Press, 2016),
132–68. It is beyond the scope of this book to explore the relationship between
religion and slavery and the more recent lively discussions regarding Western
Cherokee Black Cherokees/freedmen. In any event, Malone is not accurate
when he argues that popular support for the new constitution and the strength
of the mixed-bloods "proved too powerful for White Path." Malone, *Cherokees of the Old South*, 87.

28. Frederick Elsworth to Jeremiah Evarts, February 7, 1827, *American
Board of Commissioners for Foreign Missions Papers*, Microfilm Reel 739,
1824–1831, Cherokee Mission (ABC 18.3.1), Vols. 4 and 5, Cherokee Mission
Letters, Houghton Library, Harvard University, Cambridge, MA. Theda Perdue argues that culture does not follow blood and that "the time has come to
move beyond a history of southern Indians that rests on 'blood' as a primary
category of analysis." Theda Perdue, *Mixed Blood Indians: Racial Construction in the Early South* (Athens: University of Georgia Press, 2003), x. Cherokee
Daniel Heath Justice writes that there are Christian full-blood and mixed-blood
ceremonialists. And even those categories are "just two points along a broad,
complicated, and occasionally contradictory cultural spectrum." Daniel Heath
Justice, *Our Fire Survives the Storm: A Cherokee Literary History* (Minneapolis: University of Minnesota Press, 2006), 47.

29. Perdue, *Cherokee Women*, 149.

30. Perdue, 150.

31. John R. Finger, *The Eastern Band of the Cherokees, 1819–1900*
(Knoxville: University of Tennessee Press, 1984), 15.

CHAPTER 9

1. McLoughlin, *Cherokees and Missionaries, 1789–1839*, 337.

2. Anderson, Brown, and Rogers, *The Payne-Butrick Papers*, vol. 1–3, Introduction.

3. Lee Irwin, "Different Voices Together: Preservation and Acculturation in
Early 19th Century Cherokee Religion," *Journal of Cherokee Studies* 18 (1997):
3–26; Fogelson, "The Conjuror in Eastern Cherokee Society," 60–87.

4. Anderson, Brown, and Rogers, *The Payne-Butrick Papers*, vol. 1–3, Introduction.

5. Personal communication, 2011.

6. Fogelson, "The Conjuror in Eastern Cherokee Society," 60–87; Kilpatrick
and Kilpatrick, *Walk in Your Soul*; Kilpatrick and Kilpatrick, *Notebook of a
Cherokee Shaman*.

7. Anderson, Brown, and Rogers, *The Payne-Butrick Papers*, chap. 1, sec. 1.

8. Denise I. Bossy, "Spiritual Diplomacy," 131–62. Bossy's "spiritual diplomacy" is instructive here in describing a Cherokee strategy to form an alliance
with Americans by adopting at least some aspects of Christianity.

9. Mooney, *Myths of the Cherokee*, 235.

10. Mooney, 235.

11. Mooney, 235–36.

12. Anderson, Brown, and Rogers, *The Payne-Butrick Papers*, vol. 1–3, p. 6; Duane H. King and Laura H. King, "Old Words for New Ideas: Linguistic Acculturation in Modern Cherokee," *Tennessee Anthropologist* 1 (1976): 58–62.

13. Anderson, Brown, and Rogers, *The Payne-Butrick Papers*, vol. 1–3, p. 20.

14. Anderson, Brown, and Rogers, vol. 1–3, p. 41; Irwin, "Different Voices Together."

15. Irwin, "Different Voices Together," 5.

16. Irwin, 6.

17. Irwin, 6.

18. Irwin, 7.

19. Anderson, Brown, and Rogers, *The Payne-Butrick Papers*, vol. 4–6, pp. 2–4.

20. McLoughlin, *The Cherokees and Christianity, 1794–1870*, 157.

21. Anderson, Brown, and Rogers, *The Payne-Butrick Papers*, vol. 4–6, pp. 29–30.

22. Anderson, Brown, and Rogers, vol. 4–6, pp. 29–30, 87–88, 106–7, 177, 449; Anderson, Brown, and Rogers, vol. 1–3, pp. 10–13, 210–14, 216.

23. Anderson, Brown, and Rogers, vol. 1–3, p. xiv.

24. Anderson, Brown, and Rogers, vol. 1–3, p. lxii.

25. James H. Merrell, "The Indians New World: Catawba Experience," in *American Encounters: Native and Newcomers from European Contact to Indian Removal, 1500–1850*, ed. Peter C. Mancall and James H. Merrell, 2nd ed. (London: Routledge, 2007), 149.

26. Merrell, 100–102.

27. Long, *Significations*, 128.

28. Long, 127, 129, 118–19.

29. Anderson, Brown, and Rogers, *The Payne-Butrick Papers*, vol. 4–6, note 1.

30. See Edward H. Spicer, ed., *Perspectives in American Indian Culture Change* (Chicago: University of Chicago Press, 1961).

31. McLoughlin, *The Cherokees and Christianity, 1794–1870*, 166–68.

32. McLoughlin, chap. 6–7.

33. Elizur Butler letter, September 13, 1826, *American Board of Commissioners for Foreign Missions Papers*, Microfilm Reel 739, 1824–1831, Cherokee Mission (ABC 18.3.1), Vols. 4 and 5, Cherokee Mission Letters, Houghton Library, Harvard University, Cambridge, MA.

34. Fries, "Report of the Brethren Abraham Steiner and Friedrich Christian von Schweinitz," 330–75.

35. Haywood, *The Civil and Political History of the State of Tennessee*, 246–47.

36. Evan Jones journal, February 2, 1829, *American Board of Commissioners for Foreign Missions Papers*, Microfilm Reel 739, 1824–1831, Cherokee Mission (ABC 18.3.1), Vols. 4 and 5, Cherokee Mission Letters, Houghton Library, Harvard University, Cambridge, MA.

37. Mooney, *Myths of the Cherokee*, p. 351.

38. Samuel Worcester, *Cherokee Phoenix*, April 1, 1829.

39. *Springplace Diary*, Moravian Mission to the Cherokees, June 1, 1824, Moravian Archives, Winston-Salem, NC.

40. Haywood, *The Civil and Political History of the State of Tennessee*, 248.

41. Phillips and Phillips, *The Brainerd Journal: A Mission to the Cherokees, 1817–1823*.

42. McLoughlin, *The Cherokees and Christianity*, 1794–1870, 19.

43. Anderson, Brown, and Rogers, *The Payne-Butrick Papers*, vol. 1–3, p. 7.

44. Washburn, *Reminiscences of the Indians*, 198, 201.

45. *Springplace Diary*, Moravian Mission to the Cherokees, March 1816, Moravian Archives, Winston-Salem, NC.

CHAPTER 10

1. Theda Perdue and Michael D. Green, eds. *The Cherokee Removal: A Brief History with Documents* (Boston: St. Martin's Press, 1995), 49; Mooney, *Myths of the Cherokee*, 168; Brett Riggs, "Removal Period Cherokee Households in Southwestern North Carolina: Material Perspectives on Ethnicity and Cultural Differentiation" (PhD diss., University of Tennessee, 1999).

2. Perduc and Green, *The Cherokee Removal*, 59.

3. Johnson v. McIntosh, 21 U.S. (8 Wheat.) 543, L.Ed. 681 (1823).

4. Loftin, "Anglo-American Jurisprudence and the Native American Tribal Quest for Religious Freedom," 14. See the following books about Indian law and the Cherokee: Jill Norgren, *The Cherokee Cases: Two Landmark Federal Decisions in the Fight for Sovereignty* (Norman: University of Oklahoma Press, 2004); David E. Wilkins and Kimberly Tsianina Lomawaima, *Uneven Ground: American Indian Sovereignty and Federal Law* (Norman: University of Oklahoma Press, 2002); Andrew Denson, *Demanding the Cherokee Nation: Indian Autonomy and American Culture* (Lincoln: University of Nebraska Press, 2015); Tim Alan Garrison, *The Legal Ideology of Removal: The Southern Judiciary and the Sovereignty of Native Americans Nations* (Athens: University of Georgia Press, 2009); Steve Russell, "The Jurisprudence of Colonialism," in *American Indian Thought: Philosophical Essays*, ed. Anne Waters, 217–28 (Malden, MA: Blackwell, 2001).

5. Loftin, "Anglo-American Jurisprudence and the Native American Tribal Quest for Religious Freedom," 13.

6. Loftin, 13.

7. Loftin, 13.

8. Cherokee Nation v. Georgia, 30 U.S. (5 Pet.) 1, 8l L.Ed. 25 (1831).

9. Perdue and Green, *The Cherokee Removal*, 84.

10. McLoughlin, *Cherokee Renascence in the New Republic*, 442.

11. McLoughlin, 444.

12. Perdue and Green, *The Cherokee Removal*, 84.

13. McLoughlin, *Cherokees and Missionaries, 1789–1839*, 397–422.

14. Worcester v. Georgia, 31 U.S. (6 Pet.) 515, 8 L.Ed. 483 (1832).

15. McLoughlin, *Cherokees and Missionaries*, 397–422.

16. McLoughlin, 397–422.

17. Horace Greely, *The American Conflict: The Great Rebellion in the United States of America 1860–1864* (Ann Arbor: University of Michigan Scholarly Publishing Office, 2006), 106.

18. Malone, *Cherokees of the Old South*, 179.

19. Malone, 180.

20. Perdue and Green, *The Cherokee Removal*, 110.

21. Mooney, *Myths of the Cherokee*, 122.

22. McLoughlin, *Cherokee Renascence in the New Republic*, 450.

23. Mooney, *Myths of the Cherokee*, 122.

24. Mooney, 129.

25. Perdue and Green, *The Cherokee Removal*, 134.

26. Perdue, *The Cherokees*.

27. Finger, *The Eastern Band of the Cherokees, 1819–1900*, 17.

28. Finger, 18.

29. R. Paul Kutsche Jr., "The Tsali Legend: Culture Heroes and Historiography," *Ethnohistory* 10 (1963): 329–57.

30. Eliade, *The Myth of the Eternal Return or, Cosmos and History*, 37–48.

31. Eliade, *The Myth of the Eternal Return or, Cosmos and History*, 37–48; Loftin, "A Hopi-Anglo Discourse on Myth and History." Among the Hopi Indians, Fred Eggan has shown how a historical event was mythologized as a sacred event in only a couple of generations, and Mircea Eliade has shown how various archaic societies metamorphosize historical events into sacred narratives after only a few generations.

32. William G. McLoughlin and Walter H. Conser Jr. "The Cherokees in Transition: A Statistical Analysis of the Federal Cherokee Census of 1835," *Journal of American History* 64 (1977): 689.

33. William G. McLoughlin, "Cherokees and Methodists, 1824–1834." *Church History* 50, no. 1 (March 1981): 62–63.

34. McLoughlin, *The Cherokees and Christianity, 1794–1870*, 189.

35. Kilpatrick, "A Note on Cherokee Theological Concepts," 398.

36. Kilpatrick, 396.

37. Jack F. Kilpatrick and Anna G. Kilpatrick, eds. and trans., *The Shadow of Sequoyah: Social Documents of the Cherokees, 1862–1964* (Norman: University of Oklahoma Press, 1965), 97, 105.

38. Margaret Bender, *Signs of Cherokee Culture: Sequoyah's Syllabary in Eastern Cherokee Life* (Chapel Hill: University of North Carolina Press, 2002), 84.

39. Bender, 92.

40. Bender, 94.

41. Treat, *Native and Christian*, 10, 34, 185–90.

42. Charles Lanman, *Letters from the Alleghany Mountains* (New York, 1849), 109.

43. Catherine L. Albanese, "Exploring Regional Religion: A Case Study of the Eastern Cherokee," *History of Religions* 23 (May 1984): 355; Gulick, *Cherokees at the Crossroads*, 14.

44. Tyler B. Howe, "'The Ancient Customs of Their Fathers': Cherokee Generational Townhouse Politics of Mid-19th Century Western North Carolina," *Journal of Cherokee Studies* 29 (Reprint 2011): 3–14.

CHAPTER 11

1. Perdue, *The Cherokees*, 77.

2. Stanley W. Hoig, *The Cherokees and Their Chiefs in the Wake of Empire* (Fayetteville: University of Arkansas Press, 1998), 265.

3. Hoig, 265.

4. Hoig, 265.

5. Lanman, *Letters from the Alleghany Mountains*, 94.

6. Lanman, 95.

7. Lanman, 95.

8. Lanman, 95.

9. Thomas Donaldson, *Eastern Band of Cherokees of North Carolina*, Eleventh Census of the United States, 1890 (Washington, DC: US Census Printing Office, 1892), 715.

10. Lanman, *Letters from the Alleghany Mountains*, 96.

11. John R. Finger, "The North Carolina Cherokees, 1838–1866: Traditionalism, Progressivism and the Affirmation of State Citizenship," *Journal of Cherokee Studies* 5 (1980): 20.

12. George E. Frizzell, "The Quallatown Cherokees in the 1840s: Accounts of their Condition and Lives," *Journal of Cherokee Studies* 23 (2002): 28.

13. Finger, "The North Carolina Cherokees, 1838–1866," 21.

14. Lanman, *Letters from the Alleghany Mountains*, 96.

15. Lanman, 97.

16. Lanman, 97.

17. Lanman, 99.

18. Lanman, 99.

19. Lanman, 100. For a religious interpretation of the Eastern Cherokee ball play today, see: Zogry, *Anetso*.

20. Lanman, 101.

21. Lanman, 104.

22. Lanman, 105.

23. Lanman, 109.

24. Lanman, 110.

25. Lanman, 111.

26. Lanman, 113.

27. Finger, *The Eastern Band of the Cherokees, 1819–1900*, 68; McLoughlin and Conser, "The Cherokees in Transition," table 7; Dunaway, "Rethinking Cherokee Acculturation," 155–92.

28. For discussion of persistence of Cherokee women's gender roles, see: Hatley, "Cherokee Women Farmers Hold Their Ground."

29. Finger, *The Eastern Band of the Cherokees, 1819–1900*, 69.

30. Finger, 69.

31. Lanman, *Letters from the Alleghany Mountains*, 95.

32. Finger, *The Eastern Band of the Cherokees, 1819–1900*, 70.

33. *Eastern Cherokee Census Rolls, 1835–1884*, National Archives and Records Administration, Washington, DC, 2005.

34. Finger, *The Eastern Band of Cherokees, 1819–1900*, 82.

35. Finger, 84.

36. Mooney, *Myths of the Cherokee*, 170.

37. Vernon H. Crowe, *Storm in the Mountains: Thomas' Confederate Legion of Cherokee Indians and Mountaineers* (Cherokee, NC: Museum of the Cherokee Indian, 1982), 138.

38. Mooney, *Myths of the Cherokee*, 170; Anne F. Rogers and Barbara R. Duncan, eds., *Culture, Crisis and Conflict: Cherokee British Relations, 1756–1765* (Cherokee, NC: Museum of the Cherokee Indian Press, 2009), 108.

39. Mooney, *Myths of the Cherokee*, 396.

40. Perdue, *The Cherokees*, 77.

41. Finger, *The Eastern Band of the Cherokees, 1819–1900*, 82–83.

42. Finger, 90.

43. Finger, 92.

44. Crowe, *Storm in the Mountains*, 59.

45. Crowe, 59.

46. This is difficult to date, and this conclusion is based largely on the following sources: Robert K. Thomas, "Cherokee Values and World View" (research paper, Cross-Cultural Laboratory, Institute for Research in Social Science, North Carolina Collection, Wilson Library, University of North Carolina, Chapel Hill, 1958), 27; Thomas, "Culture History of the Eastern Cherokee," 17; Thomas, "Report on Cherokee Social and Community Organization," typescript, University of North Carolina, 1958, p. 14; Thomas, "The Present 'Problem' of the Eastern Cherokees," typescript, University of North Carolina, 1958, p. 35; Thomas, "Eastern Cherokee Acculturation," typescript, University of North Carolina, 1958, p. 42; Thomas, "Culture History of the Eastern Cherokee," typescript, University of North Carolina, 1958, p. 35; Thomas, *Getting to the Heart of the Matter: Collected Letters and Papers* (Vancouver: Native Ministries Consortium, 1990); Raymond D. Fogelson, "Change, Persistence, and Accommodation in Cherokee Medico-Magical Beliefs," in *Symposium on Cherokee and Iroquois Culture*, Smithsonian Institution Bureau of American Ethnology Bulletin 180, ed. William N. Fenton and John Gulick, 213–26 (Washington, DC: US Government Printing Office, 1961); Finger, *The Eastern Band of the Cherokees, 1819–1900*; Finger, "The North Carolina Cherokees, 1838–1866," 17–29; Gilbert, *The Eastern Cherokees*; Lanman, *Letters from the Alleghany Mountains*; Donaldson, *Eastern Band of Cherokees of North Carolina*; McLoughlin, *Cherokees and Missionaries, 1789–1839*; McLoughlin, *Cherokee Renascence in the New Republic*; McLoughlin, *The Cherokees and Christianity, 1794–1870*; Perdue, *The Cherokees*; Mooney and Olbrechts, *The Swimmer Manuscript*; Mooney, *Myths of the Cherokee*; Horsefly, *A History of the True People*.

47. Catherine L. Albanese, *A Republic of Mind and Spirit: A Cultural History of American Metaphysical Religion* (New Haven, CT: Yale University Press, 2007); Robert S. Cox, *Body and Soul: A Sympathetic History of American Spiritualism* (Charlottesville: University of Virginia Press, 2003).

48. Thomas, "Cherokee Values and World View."

49. David H. Getches, Charles F. Wilkinson, Robert A. Williams Jr., and Matthew L. M. Fletcher, *Federal Indian Law*, 6th ed. (St. Paul, MN: West Academic Publishing, 2011), 147.

50. Getches et al., 148.

51. Getches et al., 149.

52. Getches et al., 150.

53. Adams, *Education for Extinction*; John Demos, *The Heathen School: A Story of Hope and Betrayal in the Age of the Early Republic* (New York: Knopf, 2014).

54. Finger, *The Eastern Band of the Cherokee Indians, 1819–1900*, 138.

55. Finger, 140.

56. Horsefly, *A History of the True People*, 20.

57. Michael Zogry, "Interview of Mr. Goingback Chiltoskey, November 3, 1997," typescript, Fading Voices, 7–8; Zogry, "Interview of Robert Bushyhead, November 2, 1997," typescript, Fading Voices, 4–5; Finger, *The Eastern Band of the Cherokees, 1819–1900*, 197.

58. Finger, *The Eastern Band of the Cherokees, 1819–1900*, 198.

59. Finger, 190. For a discussion of allotment among Oklahoma Cherokees and the way they used extended family bonds to retain a sense of collectivity to resist assimilation, see: Rose Stremlau, *Sustaining the Cherokee Family: Kinship and the Allotment of an Indigenous Nation* (Chapel Hill: University of North Carolina Press, 2011).

60. Mooney, *Myths of the Cherokee*, 181.

CHAPTER 12

1. Perdue, *Slavery and the Evolution of Cherokee Society*, 44.

2. Steve Pavlik, *A Good Cherokee, A Good Anthropologist: Papers in Honor of Robert K. Thomas* (Los Angeles: UCLA American Indian Study Center, 1998), 110–11.

3. Speck, Broom, and Long, *Cherokee Dance and Drama*, xxi.

4. Pavlik, *A Good Cherokee, A Good Anthropologist*, 105.

5. Pavlik, 105.

6. John R. Finger, *Cherokee Americans: The Eastern Band of Cherokees in the Twentieth Century* (Lincoln: University of Nebraska Press, 1991), 7.

7. Finger, 7.

8. Finger, 16.

9. William M. Colby, *Routes to Rainy Mountain: A Biography of James Mooney* (PhD diss., University of Wisconsin at Madison, 1977), 90–91.

10. Colby, 30.

11. Loftin, *The Big Picture*, 248.

12. Mooney and Olbrechts, *The Swimmer Manuscript*, 10; Gilbert, *The Eastern Cherokees*, 199.

13. Finger, *Cherokee Americans*, 64; Fogelson, "The Conjuror in Eastern Cherokee Society," 70.

14. Fogelson, "The Conjuror in Eastern Cherokee Society," 70.

15. Finger, *Cherokee Americans*, 65.

16. Finger, 67, 68.

17. Leonard Bloom, "The Cherokee Clan: A Study in Acculturation," *American Anthropologist* 41 (1939), 266–8; Gilbert, *The Eastern Cherokees*; Thomas, "Culture History of the Eastern Cherokee," 35.

18. Gulick, *Cherokees at the Crossroads*, 113–14.

19. Mooney and Olbrechts, *The Swimmer Manuscripts*, 27.

20. Gulick, *Cherokees at the Crossroads*, 147; Horsefly, *A History of the True People*, 137.

21. Mooney and Olbrechts, *The Swimmer Manuscripts*, 132.

22. Mooney and Olbrechts, 141.

23. Mooney and Olbrechts, 141.

24. Mooney and Olbrechts, 142.

25. Mooney and Olbrechts, 142.

26. Fogelson, "The Conjuror in Eastern Cherokee Society," 60.

27. Gilbert, *The Eastern Cherokees*, 366.

28. Gilbert, 367; Horsefly, *A History of the True People*, 137.

29. Gilbert, *The Eastern Cherokees*, 367.

30. Gilbert, 367.

31. Gilbert, 367.

32. Gilbert, 369.

33. Gilbert, 369.

34. Gulick, *Cherokees at the Crossroads*, 140.

35. Gulick, 140.

36. Gulick, 141.

37. Fogelson, "Change, Persistence, and Accommodation in Cherokee Medico-Magical Beliefs"; Fogelson, "The Conjuror in Eastern Cherokee Society," 60–87.

38. Gulick, *Cherokees at the Crossroads*, 118, 119.

39. Gulick, 119.

40. Gulick, 66.

41. Gulick, 66.

42. Gulick, 113, 114; John Gulick, "Language and Passive Resistance among the Eastern Cherokee," *Ethnohistory* 5, no. 1 (Winter 1958): 69.

43. Fogelson, "The Conjuror in Eastern Cherokee Society," 82; Gulick, *Cherokees at the Crossroads*, 114.

44. Fogelson, "The Conjuror in Eastern Cherokee Society," 82.

45. Zogry, *Anetso*, 142; Finger, *Cherokee Americans*, 142.

46. Finger, *Cherokee Americans*, 147.

47. Finger, 143.

48. Finger, 143.

49. Thomas, "Eastern Cherokee Acculturation," 19–42; Harriet Jane Kupferer, "The Principal People, 1960: A Study of Cultural and Social Groups of the Eastern Cherokee," Smithsonian Institution Bureau of American Ethnology Bulletin 196 (Washington, DC: US Government Printing Office, 1966), 308–17.

50. Thomas, "Cherokee Values and World View," 27; See also: Kupferer, "The Principal People, 1960."

51. Gulick, *Cherokees at the Crossroads*, 135–69.

52. Loftin, "The 'Harmony Ethic' of the Conservative Eastern Cherokees" 40–45; John D. Loftin and Benjamin E. Frey, "Eastern Cherokee Creation and Subsistence Narratives: A Cherokee and Religious Interpretation," *American Indian Culture and Research Journal* 43 (2019): 83–98.

53. Sandra Muse Isaacs, *Eastern Cherokee Stories*, 28. The following Cherokee interpretation of *duyuktv* and other related Cherokee concepts dovetails nicely with Rennard Strickland's work on traditional law. Strickland, *Fire and the Spirits*. See also a Cherokee medicine man's discussion of *duyuktv*: Barbara R. Duncan, ed., *Living Stories of the Cherokee* (Chapel Hill: University of North Carolina Press, 1998), 25–27.

54. Kilpatrick, "A Note on Cherokee Theological Concepts," 391; The quote is from McLoughlin, *Cherokees and Missionaries, 1789–1839*, 66.

55. Kilpatrick, "A Note on Cherokee Theological Concepts."

56. Kilpatrick, 392.

57. Kilpatrick, 395.

58. Kilpatrick, 395.

59. Fogelson, "The Conjuror in Eastern Cherokee Society," 71.

60. Kilpatrick, "A Note on Cherokee Theological Concepts," 396.

61. Kilpatrick, 398.

62. Kilpatrick, 398.

63. Thomas, "Cherokee Values and World View," 1.

64. Mooney and Olbrechts, *The Swimmer Manuscripts*, 139.

65. Gulick, *Cherokees at the Crossroads*, 139.

66. Gulick, 145.

67. Gulick, 146.

68. Loftin, "The 'Harmony Ethic' of the Conservative Eastern Cherokees."

69. Scott McKie, "Coming Home to Kituwah," *Cherokee One Feather*, May 31, 2012: 5.

70. Mooney, *Myths of the Cherokee*, 240, 242.

71. Fred R. Eggan, "From History to Myth: A Hopi Example," in *Studies in Southwestern Ethnolinguistics*, ed. Dell H. Hymes and William E. Bittle (Paris: Mouton & Co., 1967).

72. See also: Loftin, "A Hopi-Anglo Discourse on Myth and History."

73. Raymond D. Fogelson, "Bringing Home the Fire: Bob Thomas and Cherokee Studies," in *A Good Cherokee, A Good Anthropologist: Papers in Honor of Robert K. Thomas*, ed. Steve Pavlik (Los Angeles: UCLA American Indian Studies Center, 1998), 110. Gulick, *Cherokees at the Crossroads*, 160; See also: Loftin, "The 'Harmony Ethic' of the Conservative Eastern Cherokees," 41; Fogelson, "Change, Persistence, and Accommodation in Cherokee Medico-Magical Beliefs," 220; Fogelson, "The Conjuror in Eastern Cherokee Society," 83.

In a book entitled *Cherokee Psalms*, there are multiple translations of the Psalms in Cherokee. Published in 1991, the book was edited by J. Ed Sharpe, who lived among the Eastern Cherokee for many years. In Psalm 103, "Lord" was translated as *yihowa*, just as was done in the *Payne-Butrick Papers* in 1838. However, Samuel Worcester in 1829 said that "Yehowah" was known only to those Cherokees "who learned it by means of Christian missionaries." A number of Eastern Cherokee elders—especially Shirley Oswalt and Mary Brown, with help from Janie Brown, Mary's mother, and Western Cherokee Anna Sixkiller—translated an 1829 Cherokee hymnbook into English.

"Creator" is translated as *unehlanvhi*, while *yihowa* is translated as "Jehovah." See: *Cherokee Hymn Book: New Edition for Everyone* (Cherokee, NC: Museum of the Cherokee Indian, 2014). See also: Fogelson, "Change, Persistence, and Accommodation in Cherokee Medico-Magical Beliefs," 64; Gulick, *Cherokees at the Crossroads*, 60; J. Ed Sharpe, ed., *Cherokee Psalms: A Collection of Hymns in the Cherokee Language*, trans. Daniel Scott (Cherokee, NC: Cherokee Publications, 1991), 35; Jack Frederick Kilpatrick and Anna Gritts Kilpatrick, eds., *New Echota Letters: Contributions of Samuel A. Worcester to the Cherokee Phoenix* (Dallas: Southern University Press, 1968), 51.

74. Kilpatrick, "'Going to the Water,'" 52. Loftin, "The 'Harmony Ethic' of the Conservative Eastern Cherokees." A clean-up event along Cherokee waterways occurred on October 20, 2021. Called "Honoring Long Man Day," the occasion was more than a river cleaning. As tribal member Juanita Wilson said, the event will also be "a cultural awakening and/or re-awakening. The Cherokees have always viewed the river as 'Long Man' (*gunahita asgaya*) whose head lay in the mountains and the feet in the sea." *Cherokee One Feather*, tsalagi soquo ugadahli, week of dulisdi 29–duninodi 5, 2021, 6.

75. Thomas, "Cherokee Values and World View," 20.

EPILOGUE

1. Prolific Cherokee author Robert Conley told Cherokee scholar Sean Teuton that he is comfortable writing about Cherokee medicine, "up to a certain point. . . . If I know exactly how, say, a Cherokee medicine man prepares his tobacco or whatever medicine, and if I know the words he says, then I shouldn't write that. That's not my business. In fact, I don't know those details, but I don't want to find them out. I don't think that's my business. I don't mind describing a scene in which an Indian doctor takes some tobacco and goes into his room and does something and says something, to have such and such an effect." Ben and John agree with Conley and have written about Cherokee spirituality and medicine without violating any ceremonial secrets. Cherokee author Alan Kilpatrick writes that conjuror texts, in and of themselves, are "ritually" dead and must be purified through a secret ritual to be effective. Sean Teuton and Robert Conley, "Writing Home: An Interview with Robert J. Conley, " *Wicazo Sa Review* 16 (2001): 126; Kilpatrick, *The Night Has a Naked Soul*, xviii.

2. Lisa J. Lefler and Roseanna Belt, "Historical Trauma, Stress, and Diabetes: A Modern Model among the Eastern Cherokees," in *Under the Rattlesnake: Cherokee Health and Resiliency*, ed. Lisa J. Lefler with a foreword by Susan Leading Fox (Tuscaloosa; University of Alabama Press, 2009), 78. Lefler's field notes make it clear the conjurors counseled their patients and did not just issue prescriptions like many Western physicians.

3. Deloria, *The World We Used to Live In*, xix–xx.

4. Thomas, "Culture History of the Eastern Cherokees," 24–25.

5. Jeannie Reed, ed., *Stories of the Yunwi Tsunsdi: The Cherokee Little People*, A Western Carolina University English 102 Class Project, March 1991. Isaacs, *Eastern Cherokee Stories*, 122. See also: Lynn King Lossiah, *The Secrets and Mysteries of the Cherokee Little People: Yunwi Tsunsdi* (Cherokee, NC: Cherokee Publications, 1998).

6. Barbara R. Duncan and Brett H. Riggs, *Cherokee Heritage Trails Guidebook* (Chapel Hill: University of North Carolina Press, 2003), 66.

7. Ray Fogelson repeats a story told to him by John Witthoft regarding a medicine man who was guarding the grave of a recently departed Cherokee. (Witches were also known to steal the liver of the recently deceased.) On a clear, moonlit night, the conjuror was seated near the grave when the sky darkened and a raven dove into the ground and disappeared, seeking the liver of the corpse. The medicine man was gripped in fear and lost consciousness. When he awoke, he could not speak for a time. Fogelson, "Exploring Cherokee Metaphysics of Death and Life." Cherokee elder Hastings Shade said his aunt told a story of an elderly woman who was struggling to breathe one night. Some women who were assisting her summoned an elderly man (healer) who came in smoking a pipe. He blew smoke around the sick woman, and it revealed three people (Raven Mockers) that had been invisible. Christopher B. Teuton and Hastings Shade, with Loretta Shade and Larry Shade and illustrated by Mary-Beth Timothy, *Cherokee Earth Dwellers: Stories and Teachings of the Natural World* (Seattle: University of Washington Press, 2023), 254–55.

8. In another case, Little Bear described a two-year battle in which someone was using "bad medicine" to hurt another Cherokee. One time, "he felt the thing get in her house." A long fight followed, and the patient called Little Bear and said the opposing "old man" was found dead in his front yard. Robert J. Conley, *Cherokee Medicine Man: The Life and Work of a Modern-Day Healer* (Norman: University of Oklahoma Press, 2005), 109.

9. Isaacs, *Eastern Cherokee Stories*, 96, 115.

Bibliography

Adair, James. *The History of the American Indians*. 1775. Reprinted as *Adair's History of the American Indians*. Edited by Samuel Cole Williams. Johnson City, TN: Watauga Press, 1930.

Adams, David Wallace. *Education for Extinction: American Indians and the Boarding School Experience*. Lawrence: University of Kansas Press, 1995.

Adams, Mikaela M. *Who Belongs? Race, Resources, and Tribal Citizenship in the Native South*. Oxford: Oxford University Press, 2016.

Albanese, Catherine L. "Exploring Regional Religion: A Case Study of the Eastern Cherokee." *History of Religions* 23 (May 1984): 344–81.

———. *A Republic of Mind and Spirit: A Cultural History of American Metaphysical Religion*. New Haven, CT: Yale University Press, 2007.

Altman, Heidi M., and Thomas N. Belt. "*Tohi*: The Cherokee Concept of Well-Being." In *Under the Rattlesnake: Cherokee Health and Resiliency*, edited by Lisa J. Lefler with foreword by Susan Leading Fox, 9–22. Tuscaloosa: University of Alabama Press, 2009.

———. "Moving Around in the Room." In *Museums and Memory*, edited by Margaret Williamson Huber, 227–34. Knoxville, TN: Newfound Press, 2008.

American Baptist Foreign Mission Society Correspondence, Baptist Missionary Records. MSS 93–11, Folders 13–14 (photocopies). Museum of the Cherokee Indian Archives, Cherokee, NC.

American Board of Commissioners for Foreign Missions Papers. Microfilm Reel 739. 1824–1831, Cherokee Mission (ABC 18.3.1), Vols. 4 and 5, Cherokee Mission Letters. Houghton Library, Harvard University, Cambridge, MA.

American State Papers: Indian Affairs, Vols. I and II, Documents, Legislative, and Executive of the Congress of the United States, edited by Walter Lowrie,

Walter S. Franklin, and Matthew Clark. Washington, DC: Gales and Seaton, 1832, 1834.

Anderson, Virginia. "King Phillip's Herds: Indians, Colonists, and the Problem of Livestock in Early New England." In *American Encounters: Native and Newcomers from European Contact to Indian Removal, 1500–1850*, edited by Peter C. Mancall and James H. Merrell, 2nd ed., 246–68. London: Routledge, 2007.

Anderson, William L. "Editor's Note." *Journal of Cherokee Studies* 19 (1997): 18–19.

———, ed. *Cherokee Removal: Before and After*. Athens: University of Georgia Press, 1991.

Anderson, William L., Jane L. Brown, and Anne P. Rogers, eds. *The Payne-Butrick Papers*. 2 vols. Lincoln: University of Nebraska Press, 2010.

Andrew, John A., III. *From Revivals to Removal: Jeremiah Evarts, The Cherokee Nation and the Search for the Soul of America*, Athens: University of Georgia Press, 1992.

Anonymous. Review of "The Cherokee Ball Play" and "Cherokee Theory and Practice of Medicine." *American Journal of Psychology* 3, no. 2 (April 1890): 271.

Appalshop Archive. "Headwaters: Amoneeta Sequoyah and Kate Sturgill." Audio Visual Interview of Cherokee Amoneeta Sequoyah, 1981. Produced by Native Americans in Media. Approximately 10 minutes.

Apter, Andrew. *Black Critic and Kings: The Hermeneutics of Power in Yoruba Society*, Chicago: University of Chicago Press. 1992.

Arneach, Lloyd. With illustrations by Lydia G. Halverson. *The Animals' Ballgame: A Cherokee Story from the Eastern Band*. N.p.: Lake Book Mfg., 1992. Children's book with audiocassette.

———. *Long Ago Stories of the Eastern Cherokee*. Boston: History Press, 2008.

Arnold, Philip P. "The Doctrine of Discovery in the Mesoamerican Context with David Carrasco." Podcast. Mapping the Doctrine of Discovery, June 27, 2022. https://podcast.doctrineofdiscovery.org/season1/episode-03/.

———. "Indigeneity: The Work of History of Religions and Charles H. Long." In *With This Root about My Person: Charles H. Long and New Directions in the Study of Religion*, edited by Jennifer Reid and David Carrasco, 24–38. Albuquerque: University of New Mexico Press, 2020.

Axtell, James. "Ethnohistory: A Historian's Viewpoint." *Ethnohistory* 26 (1979): 1–13.

———. *The European and the Indian: Essays in the Ethnohistory of North America*. Oxford: Oxford University Press, 1981.

———. *Natives and Newcomers: The Cultural Origins of North America*. New York: Oxford University Press, 2001.

Badders, Hurely E. *Broken Path: The Cherokee Campaign of 1776*. Pendleton, GA: Pendleton District Historical and Recreational Commission, 1976.

Baillou, Clemens de. "A Contribution to the Mythology and Conceptual World of the Cherokee Indians." *Ethnohistory* 8, no. 1 (Winter 1961): 93–102.

Banks, William H. *Plants of the Cherokee: Medicinal, Edible, and Useful Plants of the Eastern Cherokee Indians.* Gatlinburg, TN: Great Smoky Mountains Association, 2004.

Barkun, Michael. "Religion and Secrecy after September 11." *Journal of the American Academy of Religion* 74, no. 2 (June 2006): 275–301.

Bartram, William. *Travels through North and South Carolina, Georgia, East and West Florida, the Cherokee Country, the Extensive Territories of the Muscogulges, or Creek Confederacy, and the Country of the Chactaws* [sic]. Philadelphia: James & Johnson, 1791. Reprinted as *Travels of William Bartram*, edited by Mark Van Doren. New York: Dover, 1955.

Basso, Keith. *Western Apache Language and Culture: Essays in Linguistic Anthropology.* Tucson: University of Arizona Press, 1990.

———. *Wisdom Sits in Place: Landscape and Language among the Western Apache.* Albuquerque: University of New Mexico Press, 1996.

Beckwith, Christopher I. *Empires of the Silk Road.* Princeton, NJ: Princeton University Press, 2009.

Bender, Ernest. "Cherokee II." *International Journal of American Linguistics* 15, no. 4 (October 1949): 223–28.

Bender, Margaret. "The Gendering of *Langue* and *Parole*: Literacy in Cherokee." In *Southern Indians and Anthropologists: Culture, Politics, and Identity*, edited by Lisa J. Lefler and Frederic W. Gleach. Athens: University of Georgia Press, 2002, 77–88.

———. *Signs of Cherokee Culture: Sequoyah's Syllabary in Eastern Cherokee Life.* Chapel Hill: University of North Carolina Press, 2002.

Benitez-Rojo, Antonio. *The Repeating Island: The Caribbean and the Postmodern Perspective.* Translated by James E. Maraniss. Durham, NC: Duke University Press. 1996.

Berkhofer, Robert. *Salvation and the Savage.* New York: Atheneum, 1976.

Bird, Solomon. "Solomon Bird Interview." *Journal of Cherokee Studies* 14 (Special Edition, 1989): 10–16.

Blanchard, Kendall. "Stick Ball and the American Southeast." In *Forms of Play of Native North Americans*, 1977 Proceedings of the American Ethnological Society, edited by Edward Norbeck and Claire Farrer, 189–207. St. Paul, MN: West Publishing Co., 1979.

Bloom, Leonard. "The Acculturation of the Eastern Cherokee." PhD diss., Duke University, 1937.

———. "The Cherokee Clan: A Study in Acculturation." *American Anthropologist* 41 (1939): 266–8.

Board of Commissioners of Indian Trade of South Carolina. Minutes, May 4, 1714–May 6, 1714. *Journals of the Commissioners of the Indian Trade: September 20, 1710–August 29, 1718.* Colonial Records of South Carolina, edited by W. L. McDowell, 53–56. Columbia: South Carolina Archives Department, 1955.

Bossy, Denise I. "Spiritual Diplomacy: Reinterpreting the Yamasee Prince's Eighteenth-Century Voyage to England." In *The Yamasee Indians: from Florida to South Carolina*, edited by Denise I. Bossy with foreword by Alan Gallay, 131–62. Lincoln: University of Nebraska Press, 2018.

Boulware, Tyler. *Deconstructing the Cherokee Nation: Town, Region, and Nation among Eighteenth-Century Cherokees.* Gainesville: University of Florida Press, 2011.

Bridgers, Ben Oshel. "An Historical Analysis of the Legal Status of the North Carolina Cherokees." *North Carolina Law Review* 58 (1980): 1075–131.

———. "Red Clay: Cherokee Past and Future." *American Indian Religions* 1 (1994): 85–92.

Brown, Joseph Epes. *The Spiritual Legacy of the American Indian.* New York: Crossroad, 1982.

Brown, Michael F. *Who Owns Native Culture?* Cambridge, MA: Harvard University Press, 2003.

Bureau of Indian Affairs Record Group 75 (75.19.7). Records of the Cherokee Indian Agency, NC, 1886–1952. National Archives, Southeast Region, Morrow, GA.

Burkhart, Brian Yazzie. "What Coyote and Thales Can Teach Us." In *American Indian Thought: Philosophical Essays*, edited by Anne Waters, 15–26. Malden, MA: Blackwell, 2001.

Burridge, Kenelm. *New Heaven, New Earth: A Study of Millenarian Activities.* New York: Schocken Books, 1969.

Burt, Jesse, and Robert Ferguson. *Indians of the Southeast: Then and Now.* Nashville, TN: Abingdon Press, 1973.

Buttrick [Butrick], Daniel S. *Antiquities of the Cherokee Indians.* Vinita, Indian Territory: Indian Chieftain, 1884. Reprinted in *Journal of Cherokee Studies* 18 (1997): 27–51.

Bynum, Caroline W. "Avoiding the Tyranny of Morphology: or, Why Compare?" *History of Religions* 53 (2014): 341–68.

Cajete, Gregory. *Native Science: Natural Laws of Interdependence.* Foreword by Leroy Little Bear. Sante Fe, NM: Clear Light, 2000.

Capps, Walter H. *Seeing with a Native Eye: Essays on Native American Religion.* New York: Harper & Row, 1976.

Carrasco, David. "Codex Charles Long: The Scholar Who Traveled to Many Places to Understand Others." In *With This Root about My Person: Charles H. Long and New Directions in the Study of Religion*, edited by Jennifer Reid and David Carrasco, 296–314. Albuquerque: University of New Mexico Press, 2020.

———. "Jaguar Christians in the Contact Zone: Concealed Narratives in the Histories of Religions in the Americas." In *Beyond Primitivism Indigenous Religious Traditions and Modernity*, edited by Jacob K. Olupona, 128–38. New York: Routledge, 2002.

———. "Proem." Charles H. Long. *Significations: Signs, Symbols and Images in the Interpretation of Religion.* Philadelphia: Fortress Press, 1986.

Carroll, Clint. *Roots of Our Renewal: Ethnobotany and Cherokee Environmental Governance.* Minneapolis: University of Minnesota Press, 2015.

"A Catechism of the Ten Commandments in Cherokee and English." Cherokee, NC: Big Cove Baptist Church and Global Bible Society, n.d.

Caterine, Darryl. "The Haunted Grid: Nature, Electricity, and Indian Spirits in the American Metaphysical Tradition." *Journal of the American Academy of Religion* 82 (2014): 371–97.

Chamberlain, Kathleen Egan. "Competition for the Native American Soul: The Search for Religious Freedom in Twentieth-Century New Mexico." In *Religion in Modern New Mexico*, edited by Ferenc M. Szasz and Richard W. Etulain, 81–99. Albuquerque: University of New Mexico Press, 1997.

Champagne, Duane. "Cherokee Social Movements: A Response to Thornton." *American Sociological Review* 50 (1985): 127–30.

———. "Institutional and Cultural Order in Early Cherokee Society." *Journal of Cherokee Studies* 15 (1990): 3–23.

———. *Social Order and Political Change: Constitutional Governments among the Cherokee, the Chickasaw, and the Creek.* Stanford, CA: Stanford University Press, 1992.

———. "Social Structure, Revitalization Movements and State Building: Social Change in Four Native American Societies." *American Sociological Review* 48 (1983): 754–63.

———. "Symbolic Structure and Political Change in Cherokee Society." *Journal of Cherokee Studies* 8 (1983): 87–96.

Chekelelee, Edna. "Jesus before Columbus Time." In *Living Stories of the Cherokee*, edited by Barbara R. Duncan. Chapel Hill: University of North Carolina Press, 1998.

Cherokee Documents in Foreign Archives. Microfilm Collection. Fading Voices MSS 87–16. Museum of the Cherokee Indian Archives, Cherokee, NC.

Cherokee Hymn Book: New Edition for Everyone. Cherokee, NC: Museum of the Cherokee Indian, 2014.

Cherokee Phoenix. February 18, 1829.

Cherokee Phoenix. April 29, 1829.

Cherokee Progress and Challenge. Cherokee, NC: Cherokee Tribal Government, 1972.

Chiltoskey, Mary Ulmer, ed. *Cherokee Fair and Festival: A History thru 1978.* Cherokee Indian Fall Festival Association, 1979.

———. *Cherokee Words with Pictures.* Cherokee, NC: Cherokee Publications, 1972.

Chinnery, E. W. P., and A. C. Hadden. "Five New Religious Cults in British New Guinea." *Hibbert Journal* 15 (1917): 448–63.

Churchill, Mary C. "Purity and Pollution: Unearthing an Oppositional Paradigm in the Study of Cherokee Religious Traditions." In *Native American Spirituality*, edited by Lee Irwin, 205–35. Lincoln: University of Nebraska Press, 2000. First published as "The Oppositional Paradigm of Purity versus Pollution in Charles Hudson's *The Southeastern Indians*." *American Indian Quarterly* 20 (Fall 1996): 563–93.

Colby, William M. "Routes to Rainy Mountain: A Biography of James Mooney." PhD diss., University of Wisconsin at Madison, 1977.

Conley, Robert J. *A Cherokee Encyclopedia.* Albuquerque: University of New Mexico Press, 2007.

———. *Cherokee Medicine Man: The Life and Worth of a Modern-Day Healer.* Norman: University of Oklahoma Press, 2005.

———. *The Witch of Goingsnake and Other Stories.* Norman: University of Oklahoma Press, 1988.

Cordova, V. F. *How It Is: The Native American Philosophy of V. F. Cordova,* edited by Kathleen Dean Moore, Kurt Peters, Ted Jojola, and Amber Lacy with a foreword by Linda Hogan. Tucson: University of Arizona Press, 2007.

Corkran, David H. *The Cherokee Frontier, 1740–1762.* Norman: University of Oklahoma Press, 1962.

———. "A Cherokee Migration Fragment." *Southern Indian Studies* 4 (1952): 27–28.

———. "Cherokee Sun and Fire Observances." *Southern Indian Studies* 7 (1955): 33–38.

———. *The Creek Frontier, 1540–1783.* Norman: University of Oklahoma Press, 1967.

———. "The Nature of the Cherokee Supreme Being." *Southern Indian Studies* 8 (1956): 27–35.

———. "The Sacred Fire of the Cherokees." *Southern Indian Studies* 5 (1953): 21–26.

Corman, Catherine A. Review of *Writing Indians: Literacy, Christianity, and Native Community in Early America,* by Hilary E. Wyss, and *The Brainerd Journal: A Mission to the Cherokees, 1817–1823,* by Joyce B. Phillips and Paul Gary Phillips. *William and Mary Quarterly* 58 (July 2001): 742–45.

Cox, Robert S. *Body and Spirit: A Sympathetic History of American Spiritualism.* Charlottesville: University of Virginia Press, 2003.

Crane, Verner W. *The Southern Frontier, 1670–1732.* Durham, NC: Duke University Press, 1928.

Crowe, Vernon H. *Storm in the Mountains: Thomas' Confederate Legion of Cherokee Indians and Mountaineers.* Cherokee, NC: Museum of the Cherokee Indian, 1982.

Cushman, Ellen. *The Cherokee Syllabary: Writing a People's Perseverance.* Norman: University of Oklahoma Press, 2011.

Davis, Hester A. "Social Interaction and Kinship in Big Cove Community, Cherokee, N.C." Unpublished master's thesis, University of North Carolina, 1957.

Deloria, Vine, Jr. "Afterword." In *The World of the Indian Peoples before the Arrival of Columbus,* edited by Alvin M. Josephy Jr., 429–44. New York: Vintage Books. 1991.

———. *Custer Died for Your Sins: An Indian Manifesto.* 1969. Reprint. Norman: University of Oklahoma Press, 1988.

———. *This Land: Writings on Religion in America.* Introduction by James Treat. New York: Routledge, 1999.

———. "Is Religion Possible? An Evaluation of Present Efforts to Revive Traditional Tribal Religions." In *For This Land: Writings on Religion in America,* 261–68. New York: Routledge, 1999.

———. *We Talk, You Listen: New Tribes, New Turf.* 1970. Reprint. Lincoln: University of Nebraska Press, 2007.

———. *The World We Used to Live In: Remembering the Powers of the Medicine Men.* Golden, CO: Fulcrum, 2006.

Demos, John. *The Heathen School: A Story of Hope and Betrayal in the Age of the Early Republic.* New York: Knopf, 2014.

Denson, Andrew. *Demanding the Cherokee Nation: Indian Autonomy and American Culture.* Lincoln: University of Nebraska Press, 2015.

Diary of the Mission in Spring Place among the Cherokee Indians 1825, Spring Place Diary, 1823–29, M 406 D, Spring Place Correspondence 1808, M 411:6:19 Spring Place Correspondence 1825, M 413:24–27. Moravian Archives. Winston-Salem, NC.

Dickens, Roy S., Jr., *Cherokee Prehistory: The Pisgah Phase in the Appalachian Summit Region.* Knoxville: University of Tennessee Press, 1976.

Dilworth, Leah. *Imagining Indians in the Southeast: Persistent Visions of a Primitive Past.* Washington, DC: Smithsonian Institution Press, 1996.

Dobyns, Henry F. "Demographics of Native American History." In *The American Indian and the Problem of History,* edited by Calvin Martin, 67–74. New York: Oxford University Press, 1987.

Donaldson, Thomas. *Eastern Band of Cherokees of North Carolina.* Eleventh Census of the United States, 1890. Washington, DC: US Census Printing Office, 1892.

Doniger, Wendy. "Foreword." Mircea Eliade. *Shamanism: Archaic Techniques of Ecstasy,* translated by Willard R. Trask, xi–xv. Princeton, NJ: Princeton University Press, 2004.

Dowd, Gregory Evans. "Renewing Sacred Power in the South." In *A Spirited Resistance: The North American Struggle for Unity, 1745–1815,* 167–90. Baltimore: Johns Hopkins University Press, 1992.

Drinnon, Richard. *Facing West: The Metaphysics of Indian-Hating and Empire-Building.* Minneapolis: University of Minnesota Press, 1980.

Dubuisson, Daniel. *The Invention of Religions.* Translated by Martha Cunningham. Bristol, CT: Equinox, 2019.

Dugan, Joyce C., and B. Lynn Harlan. *The Cherokee.* Cherokee, NC: Eastern Band of Cherokee Nation, 2002.

Duggan, Betty J. "Being Cherokee in a White World: Ethnic Identity in a Post-Removal American Indian Enclave." PhD diss., University of Tennessee, 1998.

Dunaway, Wilma A. "Rethinking Cherokee Acculturation: Agrarian Capitalism and Women's Resistance to the Cult of Domesticity, 1800–1838." *American Indian Culture and Research Journal* 21 (1997): 155–92.

Duncan, Barbara R., ed. *Living Stories of the Cherokee.* Chapel Hill: University of North Carolina Press, 1998.

———. *The Origin of the Milky Way and Other Living Stories of the Cherokee.* Chapel Hill: University of North Carolina Press, 2008.

Duncan, Barbara R., and Brett H. Riggs. *Cherokee Heritage Trails Guidebook.* Chapel Hill: University of North Carolina Press, 2003.

Eastern Cherokee Census Rolls, 1835–1884. National Archives and Records Administration, Washington, DC, 2005.

Echo Hawk, Roger C., and Walter R. Echo Hawk. *Battlefields and Burial Grounds: The Indian Struggle to Protect Ancestral Graves in the United States.* Minneapolis: Learner Publications, 1994.

Eggan, Fred R. "From History to Myth: A Hopi Example." In *Studies in Southwestern Ethnolinguistics*, edited by Dell H. Hymes and William E. Bittle. Paris: Mouton & Co., 1967.

Eliade, Mircea. *The Forge and the Crucible: The Origins and Structure of Alchemy.* Chicago: University of Chicago Press, 1956.

———. *History of Religious Ideas, Volume I.* Translated Willard R. Trask. Chicago: University of Chicago Press, 1978.

———. *Images and Symbols: Studies in Religious Symbolism.* Translated by Philip Mairet. New York: Sheed & Ward, 1969.

———. *The Myth of the Eternal Return or, Cosmos and History.* Translated by Willard R. Trask. Princeton, NJ: Princeton University Press, 1954.

———. *Patterns in Comparative Religion.* Translated by Rosemary Sheed. New York: Sheed & Ward, 1958.

———. *The Quest: History of Meaning in Religion.* Chicago: University of Chicago Press, 1969.

———. *The Sacred and the Profane: The Nature of Religion.* Translated by Willard R. Trask. New York: Harcourt, Brace & World, 1959.

———. *Shamanism: Archaic Techniques of Ecstasy.* Translated by Willard R. Trask. Princeton, NJ: Princeton University Press, 1964.

Elliot, J. H. *The Old World and the New: 1492–1650.* Cambridge: Cambridge University Press, 1970.

Erdoes, Richard, and Alfonso Ortiz, eds. *American Indian Myths and Legends.* New York: Pantheon Books, 1984.

Ethridge, Robbie F. "Tobacco among the Cherokees." *Journal of Cherokee Studies* 3 (1978): 76–85.

Fariello, M. Anna. *Cherokee Carving: From the Hands of Our Elders.* Cullowhee, NC: Western Carolina University, 2017.

Faulkner, Charles H. "Origin and Evolution of the Cherokee Winter House." *Journal of Cherokee Studies* 3, no. 2 (1978): 87–93.

Featherstonhaugh, G. W. *A Canoe Voyage of the Minnay Sotor.* 2 vols. London: Richard Bentley, 1837.

Feeling, Durbin, William Pulte, and Gregory Pulte. *Cherokee Narratives: A Linguistic Study.* Norman: University of Oklahoma Press, 2018.

Fenton, William N. "Cherokee and Iroquois Connection Revisited." *Journal of Cherokee Studies* 3 (Fall 1978): 239–49.

Fine-Dare, Kathleen S. *Grave Injustice: The American Indian Repatriation Movement and NAGPRA.* Lincoln: University of Nebraska Press, 2002.

Finger, John R. *Cherokee Americans: The Eastern Band of Cherokees in the Twentieth Century.* Lincoln: University of Nebraska Press, 1991.

———. *The Eastern Band of the Cherokees, 1819–1900.* Knoxville: University of Tennessee Press, 1984.

———. "The North Carolina Cherokees, 1838–1866: Traditionalism, Progressivism and the Affirmation of State Citizenship." *Journal of Cherokee Studies* 5 (1980): 17–29.

Firth, Raymond. *Elements of Social Organization*. 3rd ed. London: Watts, 1962

Fixico, Donald L. *The American Indian Mind in a Linear World: American Indian Studies and Traditional Knowledge*. New York: Routledge, 2009.

Fogelson, Raymond D. "An Analysis of Cherokee Society and Witchcraft." In *Four Centuries of Southern Indians*, edited by Charles M. Hudson, 113–31. Athens: University of Georgia Press, 1975.

———. "Bringing Home the Fire: Bob Thomas and Cherokee Studies." In *A Good Cherokee, A Good Anthropologist: Papers in Honor of Robert K. Thomas*, edited by Steve Pavlik. Los Angeles: UCLA American Indian Studies Center, 1998.

———. "Change, Persistence, and Accommodation in Cherokee Medico-Magical Beliefs." In *Symposium on Cherokee and Iroquois Culture*, Smithsonian Institution Bureau of American Ethnology Bulletin 180, edited by William N. Fenton and John Gulick, 213–26. Washington, DC: US Government Printing Office, 1961.

———. "The Cherokee Ballgame Cycle: An Ethnographer's View." In *Ethnology of the Southeastern Indians: A Source Book*, edited by Charles M. Hudson, 327–38. New York: Garland, 1985.

———. "The Cherokee Ball Game: A Study in Southeastern Ethnology." PhD diss., University of Pennsylvania, 1962.

———. "Cherokee Little People Reconsidered." *Journal of Cherokee Studies* 7 (Fall 1982): 92–97.

———. "Cherokee Notions of Power." In *The Anthropology of Power: Ethnographic Studies from Asia, Oceania, and the New World*, edited by Raymond D. Fogelson and Richard M. Adams, 185–94. New York: Academic Press, 1977.

———. *The Cherokees: A Critical Bibliography*. Newberry Library Center for the History of the American Indian Bibliographical Series. Bloomington: Indiana University Press, 1978.

———. "The Conjuror in Eastern Cherokee Society." *Journal of Cherokee Studies* 5 (1980): 60–87.

———. "The Ethnohistory of Events and Nonevents." *Ethnohistory* 36, no. 2 (1989): 133–47.

———. "Exploring Cherokee Metaphysics of Death and Life." Lecture presented at the Michael D. Green Lecture in American Indian Studies, University of North Carolina at Chapel Hill, NC, November 3, 2015.

———. "Major John Norton as Ethno-ethnologist." *Journal of Cherokee Studies* 3 (Fall 1978): 250–55.

———. "On the 'Petticoat Government' of the Eighteenth-Century Cherokee." *Personality and the Cultural Construction of Society*, edited by David K. Jordan and Marc J. Swartz, 161–81. Tuscaloosa: University of Alabama Press, 1990.

———. "Person, Self, and Identity: Some Anthropological Retrospects, Circumspects, and Prospects." In *Psychological Theories of the Self*, edited by Benjamin Lee, 67–109. New York: Plenum Press, 1979.

———. "A Study of the Conjuror in Eastern Cherokee Society." Master's thesis, University of Pennsylvania, 1958.

———. "Who Were the *An:Kutani*? An Excursion into Cherokee Historical Thought." *Ethnohistory* 31, no. 4 (1984): 255–63.

———. "Windigo Goes South: Stoneclad among the Cherokees." In *Manlike Monsters on Trial: Early Records and Modern Evidence*, edited by Marjorie Halpin and Michael M. Ames. Vancouver: University of British Columbia Press, 1980.

Fogelson, Raymond D., and Amelia R. Bell. "Cherokee Booger Mask Tradition." In The Power of Symbols: Masks and Masquerade in the Americas, edited by N. Ross Crumrine and Marjorie Halpin, 48–69. Vancouver: University of British Columbia Press, 1983.

Fogelson, Raymond D., and Amelia B. Walker. "Self and Other in Cherokee Booger Masks." *Journal of Cherokee Studies* 5 (Fall 1980): 88–102.

Fogelson, Raymond D., and Paul Kutsche, "Cherokee Economic Cooperatives: The Gadugi." In *Symposium on Cherokee and Iroquois Culture*, Smithsonian Institution Bureau of American Ethnology Bulletin 180, edited by William N. Fenton and John Gulick, 83–124. Washington, DC: US Government Printing Office, 1961.

Foucault, Michel. *Madness and Civilization: A History of Insanity in the Age of Reason.* Translated by Richard Howard. London: Tavistock, 1967.

Fradkin, Arlene. *Cherokee Folk Zoology: The Animal World of a Native American People, 1700–1838.* New York: Garland, 1990.

Frazer, James George. *The Golden Bough: A Study in Magic and Religion.* 1922. Abr. ed. New York: Simon & Schuster, 1996.

French, Laurence. "Missionaries among the Eastern Cherokees: Religion as a Means of Interethnic Communication." In *Interethnic Communication*, Southern Anthropological Society Proceedings, No. 12, edited by E. Lamar Ross, 100–112. Athens: University of Georgia Press, 1978.

French, Laurence, and Jim Hornbuckle, eds. *The Cherokee Perspective.* Boone, NC: Appalachian Consortium Press, 1981.

Frey, Benjamin E., and John D. Loftin. "Eastern Cherokee Creation and Subsistence Narratives: A Cherokee and Religious Interpretation." *American Indian Culture and Research Journal* 43 (2019): 83–98.

Fries, Adelaide Lisetta, ed. and trans. "Report of the Brethren Abraham Steiner and Friedrich Christian von Schweinitz of Their Journey to the Cherokee Nation and in the Cumberland Settlements in the State of Tennessee from 28th October to 28th December." *North Carolina Historical Review* 21 (1944): 330–75.

Frizzell, George E. "The Quallatown Cherokees in the 1840s: Accounts of Their Condition and Lives." *Journal of Cherokee Studies* 23 (2002): 27–34.

Gallay, Alan. *The Indian Slave Trade: The Rise of the English Empire in the American South, 1670–1717.* New Haven, CT: Yale University Press, 2002.

Galloway, Mary. *Aunt Mary, Tell Me a Story: A Collection of Cherokee Legends and Tales as Told by Mary Ulmer Chiltoskey.* Cherokee, NC: Cherokee Communications, 1990.

Gardner, Annie Cofield. "Social Organization and Community, Solidarity in Painttown, Cherokee, N.C." Unpublished master's thesis, University of North Carolina, 1958.

Gardner, Robert G. *Cherokees and Baptists in Georgia*. Atlanta, GA: Georgia Baptist Historical Society, 1989.

Garrett, J. T. *The Cherokee Herbal: Native Plant Medicine from the Four Directions*. Rochester, VT: Bean & Co., 2003.

———. *Meditations with the Cherokee: Prayers, Songs and Stories of Healing and Harmony*. Rochester, VT: Bean & Co., 2001.

Garrison, Tim Alan. *The Legal Ideology of Removal: The Southern Judiciary and the Sovereignty of Native Americans Nations*. Athens: University of Georgia Press, 2009.

Gearing, Fred. *Priests and Warriors: Social Structures for Cherokee Politics in the 18th Century*. Memoir 93. Menasha, WI: American Anthropological Association, 1962.

———. "The Structural Poses of 18th Century Cherokee Villages." *American Anthropologist*, 60 (1958): 1148–57.

Geertz, Clifford. *The Interpretation of Cultures*. New York: Basic Books, 1973.

Getches, David H., Charles F. Wilkinson, Robert A. Williams Jr., and Matthew L. M. Fletcher. *Federal Indian Law*. 6th ed. St. Paul, MN: West Academic Publishing, 2011.

Gilbert, William H., Jr. "The Cherokees of North Carolina: Living Memorials of the Past." In *Annual Report for the Board of Regents of the Smithsonian Institution 1956*, 529–55. Washington, DC: US Government Printing Office, 1957.

———. *The Eastern Cherokees*. Smithsonian Institution Bureau of American Ethnology Bulletin 133, Anthropological Papers, no. 23, 169–413. Washington, DC: US Government Printing Office, 1943. Reprinted as *The Eastern Cherokees*. New York: AMS Press, 1978. Page citations refer to reprint edition.

———. "Eastern Cherokee Social Organization." In *Social Organization of North American Tribes: Essays in Social Organization, Law and Religion*, edited by Fred Eggan, 285–338. Chicago: University of Chicago Press, 1937.

Gill, Sam D. *Native American Religions: An Introduction*. Belmont, CA: Wadsworth, 1983.

Gillespie, John D. "Some Eastern Cherokee Dances Today." *Southern Indian Studies* 13 (October 1961): 29–43.

Godbold, E. Stanley, Jr., and Mattie U. Russell. *Confederate Colonel and Cherokee Chief: The Life of William Holland Thomas*. Knoxville: University of Tennessee Press, 1990.

Gould, Stephen Jay. *The Mismeasure of Man*. New York: W. W. Norton, 1996.

Grant, John L. "Behavioral Premises in the Culture of Conservative Eastern Cherokee Indians." Unpublished master's thesis, University of North Carolina, 1957.

Greely, Horace. *The American Conflict: The Great Rebellion in the United States of America, 1860–1864*. Ann Arbor: University of Michigan Scholarly Publishing Office, 2006.

Greenblatt, Stephen. *Marvelous Possessions: The Wonder of the New World*. Chicago: University of Chicago Press, 1991.

Gulick, John. "The Acculturation of Eastern Cherokee Community Organization." *Social Forces* 36, no. 3 (March 1958): 246–50.

———. *Cherokees at the Crossroads*. Revised edition with epilogue by Sharlotte Neely Williams. Chapel Hill Institute of Research in Social Science, University of North Carolina, 1973.

———. "Language and Passive Resistance among the Eastern Cherokee." *Ethnohistory* 5, no. 1 (Winter 1958): 60–81.

———. "Problems of Cultural Communication: The Eastern to Cherokees." *The American Indian* 8 (1958): 20–30.

———. "The Self-Corrective Circuit and Trait-Persistence in Conservative Eastern Cherokee Culture." *Research Previews* 6, no. 3 (March 1959): 1–10.

Hackett, David G., ed. *Religion and American Culture*. 2nd ed. New York: Routledge, 2003.

Hagar, Stansbury. "Cherokee Star Lore." In *Boas Anniversary Volume: Papers Written in Honor of Franz Boas*, edited by Berthold Laufer. New York: G. E. Stechert, 1906.

Hallowell, A. Irving. "Ojibwa Ontology, Behavior, and World View." In *Teachings from the American Earth: Indian Religion and Philosophy*, edited by Dennis Tedlock and Barbara Tedlock, 141–78. New York: Liveright, 1975. Originally published in Stanley Diamond, ed., *Culture in History: Essays in Honor of Paul Radin*. New York: Columbia University Press, 1960.

Halpin, Marjorie, and Michael M. Ames, eds. *Manlike Monsters on Trial: Early Records and the Modern Evidence*. Vancouver: University of British Columbia Press, 1980.

Hamel, Paul B., and Mary U. Chiltoskey. *Cherokee Plants and Their Uses: A 400 Year History*. Sylva, NC: Herald Publishing, 1975.

Hamilton, Michelle D. "Adverse Reactions: Practicing Bioarchaeology among the Cherokee." In *Under the Rattlesnake: Cherokee Health and Resiliency*, edited by Lisa J. Lefler with foreword by Susan Leading Fox, 29–60. Tuscaloosa: University of Alabama Press, 2009.

Hancock, Jonathan. "Shaken Spirits, Cherokees, Moravian Missionaries, and the New Madrid Earthquakes." *Journal of the Early Republic* 33 (2013): 643–73

Harkin, Michael. "Staged Encounters: Postmodern Tourism and Aboriginal People." *Ethnohistory* 50, no. 3 (Summer 2003): 575–85.

Hatley, M. Thomas. "Cherokee Women Farmers Hold Their Ground." In *Powhatan's Mantle: Indians in the Colonial Southeast*, edited by Gregory A. Waselkov and Peter H. Wood, 339–44. Lincoln: University of Nebraska Press, 2006.

Haywood, John. *The Civil and Political History of the State of Tennessee: From Its Earliest Settlement up to the Year 1796*. Nashville, TN: Methodist Episcopal Church, South, 1891.

———. *The Natural and Aboriginal History of Tennessee, up to the First Settlements therein by the White People in the Year 1768*. Nashville, TN: George Wils, 1823.

Herndon, Marcia. "The Cherokee Ballgame Cycle: An Ethnomusicologist's View." In *Ethnology of the Southeastern Indians: A Source Book*, edited by Charles M. Hudson, 339–52. New York: Garland, 1985.

Hicks, Charles. "Manners and Customs of the Cherokees." *Raleigh Register and North Carolina Gazette*, vol. 19, November 6, 1818, p. 1. North

Carolina Collection, University of North Carolina at Chapel Hill. Chapel Hill, NC.

Hill, Jonathan D., ed. *Rethinking History and Myth: Indigenous South American Perspectives on the Past.* Urbana: University of Illinois Press, 1988.

Hill, Sarah H. *Weaving New Worlds: Southeastern Cherokee Women and Their Basketry.* Chapel Hill: University of North Carolina Press, 1997.

Hoig, Stanley W. *The Cherokees and Their Chiefs in the Wake of Empire.* Fayetteville: University of Arkansas Press, 1998.

Holm, Tom. "Politics Came First: A Reflection on Robert K. Thomas and Cherokee History." In *A Good Cherokee, A Good Anthropologist: Papers in Honor of Robert K. Thomas,* edited by Steve Pavlik, 41–56. Los Angeles: UCLA American Indian Studies Center, 1998.

Holman, Harriet R. "Cherokee Dancing Remembered: Why the Eastern Band Abjured the Old Eagle Dance." *North Carolina Folklore Journal* 26 (1976): 101–6.

Holmes, Jack D. L. "Spanish Policy toward the Southern Indians." In *Four Centuries of Southern Indians,* edited by Charles M. Hudson, 65–82. Athens: University of Georgia Press, 1975.

Holmes, Ruth Bradley. *The Four Gospels and Selected Psalms in Cherokee.* Norman: University of Oklahoma Press, 2004.

Holzinger, Charles H. *The Eastern Cherokee and the Hypothesized Core Traits of American Indians.* Paper presented at the 56th Annual Meeting of the American Anthropological Association, 1957, Chicago, Illinois.

Horsefly, G. P. *A History of the True People: The Cherokee Indians.* Detroit: Southwest Oakland Vocational Education Center, 1979.

Howe, Tyler B. "'The Ancient Customs of Their Fathers': Cherokee Generational Townhouse Politics of Mid-19th Century Western North Carolina." *Journal of Cherokee Studies* 29 (Reprint 2011): 3–14.

Hoxie, Frederick, ed. *Talking Back to Civilization: Indian Voices from the Progressive Era.* Boston: St. Martin's Press, 2001.

Huddleston, Lee E. *Origins of the American Indians: European Concepts 1492–1729.* Austin: University of Texas Press, 1967.

Hudson, Charles, ed. *Ethnology of the Southeastern Indians: A Source Book.* New York: Garland, 1985.

———, ed. *Four Centuries of Southern Indians.* Athens: University of Georgia Press, 1975.

———. "Introduction." In *The Transformation of the Southeastern Indians, 1540–1760,* edited by Robbie Ethridge and Charles Hudson, xi–xxxix. Jackson: University of Mississippi Press, 2002.

———. *The Juan Pardo Expeditions: Exploration of the Carolinas and Tennessee, 1566–1568.* Revised edition. Tuscaloosa: University of Alabama Press, 1990.

———. "North American Indians: Indians of the Southeast Woodlands." In *The Encyclopedia of Religion,* edited by Mircea Eliade, vol. 10, 485–90. New York: Macmillan, 1987.

———. "Reply to Mary Churchill." *American Indian Quarterly* 24 (Summer 2000): 494–502.

————. *The Southeastern Indians.* Knoxville: University of Tennessee Press, 1976.

————. "Uktena: A Cherokee Anomalous Monster." *Journal of Cherokee Studies* 3 (Spring 1978): 62–73.

————. "Why the Southeastern Indians Slaughtered Deer." In *Indians, Animals, and the Fur Trade: A Critique of Keepers of the Game,* edited by Shepard Krech III, 157–76. Athens: University of Georgia Press, 1981.

Hughes, L.H. "Cherokee Death Customs." Master's thesis, University of Tennessee, 1982.

Hymes, William J., and William G. Doty, eds. *Mythical Trickster Figures: Contours, Contexts, and Criticisms.* Tuscaloosa: University of Alabama Press, 1993.

Ireland, Emilienne. "Cerebral Savage: The White Man's Symbol of Cleverness and Savagery in Warà Myth." In *Rethinking History and Myth: Indigenous South American Perspectives on the Past,* edited by Jonathan D. Hill. Urbana: University of Illinois Press, 1988.

Irwin, Lee. "Cherokee Healing: Myth, Dreams, and Medicine." *American Indian Quarterly* 16 (Spring 1992): 237–57.

————. "Different Voices Together: Preservation and Acculturation in Early 19th Century Cherokee Religion." *Journal of Cherokee Studies* 18 (1997): 3–26.

————. "Freedom, Law, and Prophecy: A Brief History of Native American Religious Resistance," *American Indian Quarterly* 21 (1997): 35–55.

————, ed. *Native American Spirituality.* Lincoln: University of Nebraska Press, 2000.

Isaacs, Sandra Muse. *Eastern Cherokee Stories: A Living Oral Tradition and Its Cultural Continuance.* Foreword by Joyce Dugan. Norman: University of Oklahoma Press, 2019.

Isenbarger, Dennis L. *Native Americans in Early North Carolina: A Documentary History.* Raleigh, NC: Office of Archives and History, 2013.

Jackson, Gilliam. "Cultural Identity for the Modern Cherokees." *Appalachian Journal* 2 (1975): 280–83.

James, Jenny. "The Sacred Feminine in Cherokee Culture: Healing and Identity." In *Under the Rattlesnake: Cherokee Health and Resiliency,* edited by Lisa J. Lefler with foreword by Susan Leading Fox, 113–14. Tuscaloosa: University of Alabama Press, 2009.

Jennings, Francis. *The Invasion of America: Indians, Colonialism, and the Cant of Conquest.* Chapel Hill: University of North Carolina Press, 1973.

Johnston, Carol. "Burning Beds, Spinning Wheels, and Calico Dresses." *Journal of Cherokee Studies* 19 (1997): 3–17.

Jones, David S. "Virgin Soils Revisited." In *American Encounters: Natives and Newcomers from European Contact to Indian Removal, 1500-1850,* edited by Peter C. Mancall and James H. Merrell, 2nd ed., 51–83. London: Routledge, 2007.

Josephy, Alvin M., Jr., ed. *America in 1492: The World of the Indian Peoples Before the Arrival of Columbus.* New York: Vintage Books, 1993.

Justice, Daniel Heath. *Our Fire Survives the Storm: A Cherokee Literary History.* Minneapolis: University of Minnesota Press, 2006.

Kehoe, Alice B. "Eliade and Hultkrantz: The European Primitivist Tradition."
American Indian Quarterly 20, no. 3 (Summer 1996): 377–92.

Kelton, Paul. "Avoiding the Smallpox Spirits: Colonial Epidemics and Southeastern Indian Survival." *Ethnohistory* 51 (2004): 45–71.

———. *Cherokee Medicine, Colonial Germs: An Indigenous Nation's Fight against Smallpox, 1518–1824.* Norman: University of Oklahoma Press, 2015.

Kilpatrick, Alan Edwin. "Cherokee War Charms." Unpublished manuscript in author's possession, ca. 1992.

———. "'Going to the Water': A Structural Analysis of Cherokee Purification Rituals." *American Indian Culture and Research Journal* 15, no. 4 (1991): 49–58.

———. *The Night Has a Naked Soul: Witchcraft and Sorcery among the Western Cherokee.* Syracuse, NY: Syracuse University Press, 1997.

———. "A Note on Cherokee Theological Concepts." *American Indian Quarterly* 19 (Summer 1995): 389–405.

———. "On Translating Magical Texts." *Wicazo Su Review* 14. No. 2 (Autumn 1999): 25–31.

Kilpatrick, Jack F. "Christian Motifs in Cherokee Healing Rituals." *Perkins School of Theology Journal* 18 (1965): 33–36.

———, ed. "The Wahnenauhi Manuscript: Historical Sketches of the Cherokees, together with Some of Their Customs, Traditions, and Superstitions." Smithsonian Institution Bureau of American Ethnology Bulletin 196, Paper 77, 175–214. Washington, DC: US Government Printing Office, 1966.

Kilpatrick, Jack F., and Anna G. Kilpatrick. "Cherokee Rituals Pertaining to Medicinal Roots." *Southern Indian Studies* 16 (1964): 24–28.

———. "Chronicles of Wolftown: Social Documents of the North Carolina Cherokees, 1850–1862." Smithsonian Institution Bureau of American Ethnology Bulletin 196, Paper 75, 1–111. Washington, DC: US Government Printing Office, 1966.

———. *Friends of Thunder: Folktales of the Oklahoma Cherokees.* Dallas: Southern Methodist University Press, 1964.

———, eds. *New Echota Letters: Contributions of Samuel A. Worcester to the Cherokee Phoenix.* Dallas: Southern University Press, 1968.

———. *Notebook of a Cherokee Shaman.* Smithsonian Contributions to Anthropology, vol. 2, no. 6. Washington, DC: Smithsonian Institution, 1970.

———. *Run toward the Nightland: Magic of the Oklahoma Cherokee.* Dallas: Southern Methodist University Press, 1967.

———, eds. and trans. *The Shadow of Sequoyah: Social Documents of the Cherokees, 1862–1964.* Norman: University of Oklahoma Press, 1965.

———. *Walk in Your Soul: Love Incantations of the Oklahoma Cherokees.* Dallas: Southern Methodist University Press, 1965.

King, Duane H. "Cherokee." In the *Encyclopedia of North American Indians*, edited by Frederick E. Hoxie, 105–8. New York: Houghton Mifflin Company, 1996.

———. "Cherokee Bows." *Journal of Cherokee Studies* 1 (1976): 92–97.

———, comp. "Eastern Cherokee Government since 1827." In *Cherokee Heritage: Official Guidebook to the Museum of the Cherokee Indian.* Cherokee, NC: Cherokee Communications, 1988.

———. "A Grammar and Dictionary of the Cherokee Language." PhD diss., University of Georgia, 1975.

———, ed. *The Memoirs of Lt. Henry Timberlake: The Story of a Soldier, Adventurer, and Emissary to the Cherokees, 1756–1765.* Chapel Hill: University of North Carolina Press, 2007.

———. "The Origin of the Eastern Cherokee as a Social and Political Entity." In *The Cherokee Indian Nation: A Troubled History,* edited by Duane H. King, 164–80. Knoxville: University of Tennessee Press, 1979.King, Duane H., and Laura H. King. "The Mythico-Religious Origin of the Cherokees." *Appalachian Journal* 2 (1975): 258–64.

———. "Old Words for New Ideas: Linguistic Acculturation in Modern Cherokee." *Tennessee Anthropologist* 1 (1976): 58–62.

King, Laura H. "The Cherokee Story Teller: The Raven Mocker." *Journal of Cherokee Studies* 2 (1977): 190–94.

King, Richard. *Orientalism and Religion: Postcolonial Theory, India, and "The Mystic East."* London: Routledge, 1999.

King, Thomas. "Godzilla v. Post-Colonial." *World Literature Written in English* 30 (1990): 10–16.

Kitagawa, Joseph M., and Charles H. Long, eds. *Myths and Symbols: Studies in Honor of Mircea Eliade.* Chicago: University of Chicago Press, 1969.

Krech, Shepherd, III. *Indians, Animals, and the Fur Trade: A Critique of "Keepers of the Game."* Athens: University of Georgia Press, 1981.

Kugel, Rebecca. "Of Missionaries and Their Cattle: Ojibwa Perceptions of the Missionary as Evil Conjuror." In *American Encounters: Native and Newcomers from European Contact to Indian Removal, 1500–1850,* edited by Peter C. Mancall and James H. Merrell, 2nd ed., 201–15. London: Routledge, 2007.

Kupferer, Harriet Jane. "Belief in Immanent Justice among Eastern Cherokee and Neighboring Non-Indian Children." Typescript. University of North Carolina, 1958.

———. "The Isolated Eastern Cherokee." In *The American Indian Today,* edited by Stuart Levine and Nancy Oestreich Lurie, 87–97. Deland, FL: Everett/Edwards, 1968.

———. "The Principal People, 1960: A Study of Cultural and Social Groups of the Eastern Cherokee." Smithsonian Institution Bureau of American Ethnology Bulletin 196, Anthropological Paper No. 78, 75–80. Washington, DC: US Government Printing Office, 1966.

———. "A Tentative Analysis of Social Structure among the Eastern Cherokees." Typescript. University of North Carolina, 1959.

Kutsche, R. Paul, Jr. *The Decline of the Importance of the Clan among the Eastern Cherokees.* Paper presented at the 56th Annual Meeting of the American Anthropological Association, 1957, Chicago, Illinois.

———. "Preliminary Summary of Personality: Big Cove, Cherokee, North Carolina." Typescript. University of North Carolina, 1957.

———. "Report of a Summer Field Project in Cherokee, North Carolina." *Bulletin of the Philadelphia Anthropological Society* 10, no. 1 (December 1956): 8–11.

———. "The Tsali Legend: Culture Heroes and Historiography." *Ethnohistory* 10 (1963): 329–57.

Lambert, Leonard Carson, Jr. *Up from These Hills: Memories of a Cherokee Boyhood*. Lincoln: University of Nebraska Press, 2011.

Lame Deer, John, and Richard Erdoes. *Lame Deer: Seeker of Visions*. New York: Simon & Schuster, 1972.

Lankford, George E. "World on a String: Some Cosmological Components of the Southeastern Ceremonial Complex." In *Hero, Hawk, and the Open Hand: American Indian Art of the Midwest and South*, edited by Richard F. Townsend, 207–18. Chicago: Art Institute of Chicago, 2004.

———. *Looking for Lost Lore*. Tuscaloosa: University of Alabama Press, 2008.

Lanman, Charles. "Cherokee Customs." Chap. 23 in *Adventures in the Wilds of North America*, edited by Charles Richard Weld. London: Longman, Brown, Green and Longmans, 1854.

———. *Letters from the Alleghany Mountains*. New York, 1849.

Laughlin, Jay. "Songs of Power and Appeasement: The Magic/Religion Distinction in Cherokee Songs and Prayers." *Annual Review of Undergraduate Research at the College of Charleston* 1 (2002): 1–18.

Leenhardt, Maurice. *Do Kamo: Person and Myth in the Melanesian World*. Translated by Basia Miller Gulati. Chicago: University of Chicago Press, 1979.

———. *The Savage Mind*. Chicago: University of Chicago Press, 1966. Originally published in French as *La Pensée sauvage* (Paris: Librairie Plon, 1962).

Lefler, Lisa J., ed. *Under the Rattlesnake: Cherokee Health and Resiliency*. Foreword by Susan Leading Fox. Tuscaloosa: University of Alabama Press, 2009.

Lefler, Lisa J., and Frederic W. Gleach, eds. *Southern Indians and Anthropologists: Culture, Politics, and Identity*. Athens; University of Georgia Press, 2002.

Lefler, Lisa J., and Roseanna Belt. "Historical Trauma, Stress, and Diabetes: A Modern Model among the Eastern Cherokees." In *Under the Rattlesnake: Cherokee Health and Resiliency*, edited by Lisa J. Lefler with a foreword by Susan Leading Fox, 61–78. Tuscaloosa; University of Alabama Press, 2009.

Lefler, Lisa J., and Thomas N. Belt. Sounds of Tohi: Health and Well-Being in Cherokee Southern Appalachia. Foreword by T. J. Holland. Foreword by Pamela Duncan. Afterword by Tom Hatley. Tuscaloosa: University of Alabama Press, 2022.

Lenoir, Thomas. Papers. David M. Rubenstein Rare Book and Manuscript Library, Duke University, Durham, NC.

Lévi-Strauss, Claude. *The Elementary Structures of Kinship*. Edited by Rodney Needham. Translated by J. H. Bell, John Richard, Vaughn Stermer, and Rodney Needham. Boston: Beacon Press, 1969.

Lévy-Bruhl, Lucien. *Primitive Mentality*. Boston: Beacon Press, 1923.

Lewis, Courtney. *Cherokee Entrepreneurs: Cherokee Small Business Owners and the Making of Cherokee Sovereignty.* Chapel Hill: University of North Carolina Press, 2019.

Lewis, T. M. N., and Madeline Kneberg. "The Cherokee 'Hothouse.'" *Tennessee Archaeologist* 9, no. 1 (1953): 224–27.

Lincoln, Bruce. "A Lakota Sun Dance and the Problematics of Sociocosmic Reunion." *History of Religions* 34, no. 1 (1994): 1–14.

Linton, Ralph. "Nativistic Movements." *American Anthropologist* 45 (1943): 230–40.

Loftin, John D. "Anglo-American Jurisprudence and the Native American Tribal Quest for Religious Freedom." *American Indian Culture and Research Journal* 13 (1989): 1–52.

———. *The Big Picture: A Short World History of Religions.* Jefferson, NC: McFarland, 2000.

———. "The 'Harmony Ethic' of the Conservative Eastern Cherokees: A Religious Interpretation." *Journal of Cherokee Studies* 8 (Spring 1983): 40–45.

———. "A Hopi-Anglo Discourse on Myth and History." *Journal of American Academy of Religion* 63 (1996): 677–93.

———. *Religion and Hopi Life.* 2nd ed. Bloomington: Indiana University Press, 2001.

———. "Supplication and Participation: The Distance and Relation of the Sacred in Hopi Prayer Rites." *Anthropos* 81 (1986): 177–201.

Loftin, John D., and Benjamin E. Frey. "Eastern Cherokee Creation and Subsistence Narratives: A Cherokee and Religious Interpretation." *American Indian Culture and Research Journal* 43 (2019): 83–98.

Long, Charles H. *Alpha: The Myths of Creation.* New York: George Braziller, 1963.

———. "The Chicago School: An Academic Mode of Being." In *With This Root about My Person: Charles H. Long and New Directions in the Study of Religion*, edited by Jennifer Reid and David Carrasco, 283–95. Albuquerque: University of New Mexico Press, 2020).

———. "Indigenous People, Materialities, and Religion: Outline for a New Orientation to Religious Meaning." In *Religion and Global Culture: New Terrain in the Study of Religion and the Work of Charles H. Long*, edited by Jennifer I. M. Reid, 167–180. Oxford: Lexington Books, 2003.

———. "A Post-Colonial Meaning of Religion: Some Reflections from the Indigenous World." In *Beyond Primitivism Indigenous Religious Traditions and Modernity*, edited by Jacob K. Olupona, 89–98. New York: Routledge, 2002.

———. "Primitive/Civilized: The Locus of a Problem." *History of Religions* 20 (1980): 43–61.

———. *Significations: Signs, Symbols, and Images in the Interpretation of Religion.* Philadelphia: Fortress Press, 1986.

Longe, Alexander. *A Small Postscript on the ways and manners of the Indians called Cherokees, the contents of the whole so that you may find everything by the pages* (1725). Transcript of original manuscript from Library of Congress. Photostats and "modern version" edited and with an introduction by David H. Corkran. *Southern Indian Studies* 21 (October 1969): 3–49.

Lossiah, Lynn King. *The Secrets and Mysteries of the Cherokee Little People: Yunwi Tsunsdi*. Cherokee, NC: Cherokee Publications, 1998.

Louis Philippe, King of the French, 1830–1848. *Diary of My Travels in America*. Translated by Stephen Becker. New York: Delacorte Press, 1978.

Malone, Henry T. *Cherokees of the Old South: A People in Transition*. Athens: University of Georgia Press, 1976.

Mancall, Peter C., and James H. Merrell, eds. *American Encounters: Natives and Newcomers from European Contact to Indian Removal, 1500–1850*. 2nd ed. London: Routledge, 2007.

Marcoux, Jon Bernard. "Cherokee Households and Communities in the English Contact Period, 1670–1740." PhD diss., University of North Carolina at Chapel Hill, 2008.

———. With contributions by Kandace D. Hollenbach, Boyce Driskell, Jessica L. Vavrasek, Judith A. Sichler, Jeremy Sweat, Katherine McMillan, Stephen Carmody, Phyllis Rigney, and Erik Johanson. *The Cherokees of Tuckaleechee Cove*. Museum of Anthropology, University of Michigan Memoirs, No. 52. Ann Arbor, Michigan, 2012.

Marett, R. R. *The Threshold of Religion*. London: Methuen, 1909.

Martin, Calvin, ed. *The American Indian and the Problem of History*. New York: Oxford University Press, 1987.

———. *Keepers of the Game: Indian-Animal Relationships in the Fur Trade*. Berkeley: University of California Press, 1978.

———. "The Metaphysics of Writing Indian-White History." In *The American Indian and the Problem of History*, edited by Calvin Martin, 27–34. New York: Oxford University Press, 1987.

Martin, Joel W. "Before and Beyond the Sioux Ghost Dance." *Journal of the American Academy of Religion* 59 (Winter 1991): 677–701.

———. "From Middle Ground to 'Underground': Southeastern Indians and the Early Republic." In *Religion and American Culture: A Reader*, edited by David G. Hackett, 129–45. New York: Routledge, 1995.

———. *Sacred Revolt: The Muskogees Struggle for a New World*. Boston: Beacon Press, 1991.

———. "Southeastern Indians and the English Trade in Skins and Slaves." In *The Forgotten Centuries: Indians and Europeans in the American South, 1521–1704*, edited by Charles Hudson and Carmen Chaves Teaser, 304–24. Athens: University of Georgia Press, 1994.

———. "Visions of Revitalization in the Eastern Woodlands: Can a Middle-Aged Theory Stretch to Embrace the First Cherokee Converts?" In *Reassessing Revitalization Movements: Perspectives from North America and the Pacific Islands*, edited by Michael E. Harkin, 61–87. Lincoln: University of Nebraska Press, 2004.

Martin, J. Matthew. *The Cherokee Supreme Court: 1823–1835*. Durham, NC: Carolina Academic Press, 2021.

Mason, Bernard S. *Dances and Stories of the American Indian*. New York: Ronald Press, 1944.

Mathewes, Charles. "Religion and Secrecy." Editor's Introduction. *Journal of the American Academy of Religion* 74, no. 2 (June 2006): 273–74.

McClinton, Rowena, ed. *The Moravian Springplace Mission to the Cherokees.* Abr. ed. Lincoln: University of Nebraska Press, 2010.

McCutcheon, Russell. *Manufacturing Religion: The Discourse on Sui Generis Religion and the Politics of Nostalgia.* New York: Oxford University Press, 1997.

———. "Relating Smith." Review of *Relating Religion: Essays in the Study of Religion* by Jonathan Z. Smith. *Journal of Religion* 86, no. 2 (April 2006): 287–97.

McKenney, Thomas L., and James Hall. *Biographical Sketches and Anecdotes of Ninety-Five of 120 Principal Chiefs from the Indian Tribes of North America.* Washington, DC: US Department of Interior, 1967.

McKie, Scott. "Coming Home to Kituwah." *Cherokee One Feather*, May 31, 2012.

McLoughlin, William G. "Cherokee Anti-Mission Sentiment, 1824–1828." *Ethnohistory* 21, no. 4 (Fall 1974): 361–70.

———. *The Cherokee Ghost Dance: Essays on the Southeastern Indians, 1789–1861.* Macon, GA: Mercer University Press, 1984.

———. *Cherokee Renascence in the New Republic.* Princeton, NJ: Princeton University Press, 1986.

———. *The Cherokees and Christianity, 1794–1870: Essays on Acculturation and Cultural Persistence.* Edited by Walter H. Conser. Athens: University of Georgia Press, 1994.

———. "Cherokees and Methodists, 1824–1834." *Church History* 50, no. 1 (March 1981): 44–63.

———. *Cherokees and Missionaries, 1789–1839.* New Haven, CT: Yale University Press, 1984.

———. "Ghost Dance Movements: Some Thoughts on Definition Based on Cherokee History." *Ethnohistory* 37 (Winter 1990): 25–44.

———. "New Angles of Vision on the Cherokee Ghost Dance Movement of 1811–1812," *American Indian Quarterly* 5 (1979): 317–45.

———. "Thomas Jefferson and the Rise of Cherokee Nationalism, 1806–1809." *William and Mary Quarterly*, 3rd ser., 32 (1975): 77–78.

McLoughlin, William G., and Walter H. Conser Jr. "The Cherokees in Transition: A Statistical Analysis of the Federal Cherokee Census of 1835." *Journal of American History* 64 (1977): 678–703.

McPherson, Orlando M. *Indians of North Carolina: Letter from the Secretary of the Interior, transmitting in response to a Senate resolution of June 30, 1914, a report on the condition and tribal rights of the Indians of Robeson and adjoining counties of North Carolina.* Washington, DC: US Government Printing Office, 1915.

Meek, Ronald. *Social Science and the Ignoble Savage.* Cambridge: Cambridge University Press, 1976.

Meredith, Howard, and Virginia Milam Sobral, eds. *Cherokee Vision of Elohi.* Translated by Wesley Proctor. Oklahoma City, OK: Noksi, 1997.

Merrell, James H. "The Indians New World: Catawba Experience." In *American Encounters: Native and Newcomers from European Contact to Indian*

Removal, 1500–1850, edited by Peter C. Mancall and James H. Merrell, 2nd ed., 25–50. London: Routledge, 2007.

———. *The Indians' New World: Catawbas and Their Neighbors from European Contact through the Era of Removal.* Chapel Hill: University of North Carolina Press, 1989.

Michelson, Truman. *The Owl Sacred Pack of the Fox Indians.* Smithsonian Institution Bureau of American Ethnology Bulletin 72. Washington, DC: US Government Printing Office, 1921.

———. "Notes on Fox Mortuary Customs and Beliefs." In *40th Annual Report of the Bureau of American Ethnology, 1918–1919,* 351–496. Washington, DC: US Government Printing Office, 1925.

Miles, Tiya. *Ties That Bind: The Story of an Afro-Cherokee Family in Slavery and Freedom.* 2nd ed. Oakland: University of California Press, 2015.

Milling, Chapman J. *Red Carolinians.* Chapel Hill: University of North Carolina Press, 1940.

Mol, Hans, ed. *Identity and Religion: International, Cross-Cultural Approaches.* London: Sage, 1978.

Momaday, N. Scott. "The Becoming of the Native: Man and America before Columbus." In *America in 1492: The World of the Indian Peoples Before the Arrival of Columbus,* edited by Alvin M. Josephy Jr., 13–20. New York: Vintage Books. 1993.

Mooney, James. "The Cherokee Ball Play." *American Anthropologist* 31 (1890): 105–32.

———. "The Cherokee River Cult." *Journal of Cherokee Studies* 7, no. 1 (Spring 1982): 30–36. Reprint of article first published in *Journal of American Folklore* 13 (1900).

———. "The Cherokee Sacred Formulas: Statement of Mr. Mooney's Researches, Submitted Feb. 8, 1916." *Journal of Cherokee Studies* 7 (Spring 1982): 47–48.

———. *The Ghost-Dance Religion and Wounded Knee.* New York: Dover, 1973.

———. "Myths of the Cherokee." In *19th Annual Report of the Bureau of American Ethnology, 1897–1898,* pt. 1, 3–576. Washington, DC: US Government Printing Office, 1900. Reprinted in *Myths of the Cherokee and Sacred Formulas of the Cherokees.* Nashville, TN: Charles and Randy Elder, 1982. Page citations refer to reprint edition.

———. "Myths of the Cherokees." *Journal of American Folklore* 1, no. 2 (1888): 97–108.

———. Original manuscripts of Cherokee stories published in the *19th Annual Report of the Bureau of American Ethnology, 1897–1898,* no. 1905. Smithsonian Institution Bureau of American Ethnology, Catalogue of Manuscripts, National Anthropological Archives. Washington, DC.

———. *The Sacred Formulas of the Cherokees, 7th Annual Report of the Bureau of American Ethnology, 1885–1886,* 301–97. Washington, DC: US Government Printing Office, 1891. Reprinted in *Myths of the Cherokee and Sacred Formulas of the Cherokees.* Nashville, TN: Charles and Randy Elder, 1982. Page citations refer to reprint edition.

Mooney, James, and Frans M. Olbrechts. *The Swimmer Manuscript: Cherokee Sacred Formulas and Medicinal Prescriptions*. Smithsonian Institution Bureau of American Ethnology Bulletin 99. Washington, DC: US Government Printing Office, 1932.

Morison, Samuel Elliot. *The European Discovery of America: The Northern Voyages*. New York: Oxford University Press, 1971.

Morse, Jedidiah. *The American Universal Geography; or, A View of the Present State of All Kingdoms, States, and Colonies in the Known World*. Boston: Thomas & Andrews, 1812.

Moya, Paula M.L., and Michael R. Hames-Garcia, eds. *Reclaiming Identity: Realist Theory and the Predicament of Postmodernism*. Berkeley: University of California Press, 2000.

Muller, Jon. "The Southern Cult." In *The Southeastern Ceremonial Complex: Artifacts and Analysis; The Cottonlandia Conference*, edited by Patricia Galloway, 11–26. Lincoln: University of Nebraska Press, 1989.

Nabokov, Peter. *A Forest or Time: American Indian Ways of History*. Cambridge: Cambridge University Press, 2002.

———. *Indian Running: Native American History and Tradition*. Santa Fe, NM. Ancient City Press, 1981.

———. "Native Views of History." In *The Cambridge History of the Native Peoples of the Americas, Vol. I, North America, Part 1*, edited by Bruce G. Trigger and Wiltham D. Washburn, 1–60. Cambridge: Cambridge University Press, 1996.

Neely, Sharlotte. "The Eastern Cherokee: Farmers of the Southeast." In *This Land Was Theirs: A Study of North American Indians*, edited by Wendell Oswalt and Sharlotte Neely, 5th ed., 435–66. New York: McGraw Hill, 1995.

———. *Snowbird Cherokees: People of Persistence*. Athens: University of Georgia Press, 1991.

Nelson, Joshua R. *Progressive Traditions: Identity in Cherokee Literature and Culture*. Norman: University of Oklahoma Press, 2014.

The New Oxford Annotated Bible: New Revised Standard Version with the Apocrypha. 3rd ed. New York: Oxford University Press, 1981.

Norgren, Jill. *The Cherokee Cases: Two Landmark Federal Decisions in the Fight for Sovereignty*. Norman: University of Oklahoma Press, 2004.

Norton, John. *The Journal of Major John Norton (Teyoninhokarawen), 1816*. Edited by Carl F. Klinck and James J. Talman. Toronto: Champlain Society, 1970.

Oatis, Steven J. *A Colonial Complex: South Carolina's Frontiers in the Era of the Yamasee War, 1680–1730*. Lincoln: University of Nebraska Press, 2004.

Olbrechts, Frans M. "Cherokee Belief and Practice with Regard to Childbirth." *Anthropos* 26 (1931): 17–33.

———. "Some Cherokee Methods of Divination." *International Congress of Americanists Proceedings* 23 (1930): 547–52.

Oliphant, John. *Peace and War on the Anglo-Cherokee Frontier, 1756–63*. Baton Rouge: Louisiana State University Press, 2001.

Olupona, Jacob K. "Bands, Boundaries, and Bondage of Faith." *Harvard Divinity Bulletin* 41 (2013): 20–33.

———, ed. *Beyond Primitivism: Indigenous Religious Traditions and Modernity*. New York: Routledge, 2004.

Orr, Joan Greene, and Lois Calonehuskie. "Fading Voices Project Introduction." *Journal of Cherokee Studies* 14 (Special Edition, 1989): 5–6.

Oswalt, Wendell H., and Sharlotte Neely, eds. *This Land Was Theirs: A Study of North American Indians*. 5th ed. London: Mayfield, 1996.

Otto, Rudolf. *The Idea of the Holy: An Inquiry into the Non-rational Factor in the Idea of the Divine and Its Relation to the Rational*. Translated by John W. Harvey. Oxford: Oxford University Press, 1923.

Owl, W. David. "The Big Ball Game." In *Stories from a Wise Old Owl: As Told by Rev. W. David Owl of the Great Smoky Mountain Eastern Band of Cherokees*, 6–8. Versailles, NY: W. David Owl and Jean Owl Huff, 1972. Museum of the Cherokee Indian Archives, Cherokee, NC.

Pagden, Anthony. *The Fall of Natural Man: The American Indian and the Origins of Comparative Ethnology*. Cambridge: Cambridge University Press, 1982.

Parris, John. *The Cherokee Story*. Asheville, NC: Stephen Press, 1950.

Pavlik, Steve. *A Good Cherokee, A Good Anthropologist: Papers in Honor of Robert K. Thomas*. Los Angeles: UCLA American Indian Study Center, 1998.

Pearce, Roy Harvey. *Savagism and Civilization: A Study of the Indian and the American Mind*. Baltimore: Johns Hopkins University Press, 1965.

Perdue, Theda, ed. *Cherokee Editor: The Writings of Elias Boudinot*. Athens: University of Georgia Press, 1996.

———. *The Cherokees*. Philadelphia: Chelsea House, 2005.

———. *Cherokee Women: Gender and Culture Change, 1700–1835*. Lincoln: University of Nebraska Press, 1998.

———. *Mixed Blood Indians: Racial Construction in the Early South*. Athens: University of Georgia Press, 2003.

———. *Slavery and the Evolution of Cherokee Society, 1540–1866*. Knoxville: University of Tennessee Press, 1979.

———. "Traditionalism in the Cherokee Nation: Resistance to the Constitution of 1827." *Georgia Historical Quarterly* 66 (1982): 159–70.

Perdue, Theda, and Michael D. Green, eds. *The Cherokee Removal: A Brief History with Documents*. Boston: St. Martin's Press, 1995.

Pesantubbee, Michelene. "When the Earth Shakes: The Cherokee Prophecies of 1811–12." *American Indian Quarterly* 17, no. 3 (Summer 1993): 301–17.

Phillips, Joyce B., and Paul Gary Phillips, eds. *The Brainerd Journal: A Mission to the Cherokees, 1817–1823*. Lincoln: University of Nebraska Press, 1998.

Photographs, 1937–1949. Files of the North Carolina Department of Conservation and Development, Travel Information Division. North Carolina Division of Archives and History, Raleigh, NC.

Piker, Joshua A. "'White & Clean' & Contested: Creek Towns and Trading Paths in the Aftermath of the Seven Years' Wars." In *American Encounters: Native and Newcomers from European Contact to Indian Removal, 1500–1850*, edited by Peter C. Mancall and James H. Merrell, 2nd ed., 336–60. London: Routledge, 2007.

Plott, Bob. *Colorful Characters of the Great Smoky Mountains.* Charleston, SC: History Press, 2011.

Poirier, Lisa. "Opacity in Native American Visions." In *With This Root about My Person: Charles H. Long and New Directions in the Study of Religion,* edited by Jennifer Reid and David Carrasco, 85–96. Albuquerque: University of New Mexico Press, 2020.

Powers, William K. *Sacred Language: The Nature of Supernatural Discourse in Lakota.* Normal: University of Oklahoma Press. 1986.

Prucha, Francis Paul. *The Great Father: The United States Government and the American Indians.* Abr. Ed. Lincoln: University of Nebraska Press, 1986.

———. *The Indians in American Society from the Revolutionary War to the Present.* Berkeley: University of California Press, 1985.

Purrington, Burton L. "Introduction: Reassessing Cherokee Studies." *Appalachian Journal* 2 (1975): 252–57.

Quinn, David Beers. *Set Fair for Roanoke, Voyages and Colonies, 1584–1606.* Chapel Hill: University of North Carolina Press, 1985.

Radin, Paul. *The Trickster: A Study in American Indian Mythology.* Introduction by Stanley Diamond with commentaries by Karl Kerenyi and C. G. Jung. New York: Schocken Books, 1972.

Random House Webster's College Dictionary. New York: Random House, 1992.

Reder, Deanna, and Linda M. Morra, eds. *Troubling Tricksters: Revisioning Critical Conversations.* Waterloo, Ontario: Wilfrid Laurier University Press, 2010.

Reed, Jeannie, ed. *Stories of the Yunwi Tsunsdi: The Cherokee Little People.* A Western Carolina University English 102 Class Project, March 1991.

Reed, Marcelina. *Seven Clans of the Cherokee Society.* Cherokee, NC: Cherokee Publications, 1993.

Reed, Mark. "Reflections on Cherokee Stickball." *Journal of Cherokee Studies* 2 (Winter 1977): 195–200.

Reid, Jennifer, and David Carrasco, eds. *With This Root about My Person: Charles H. Long and New Directions in the Study of Religion.* Albuquerque: University of New Mexico Press, 2020.

Reid, John Phillip. "A Bare Board: The Failure of Law." Chap. 5 in *A Better Kind of Hatchet: Law, Trade, and Diplomacy in the Cherokee Nation during the Early Years of European Contact.* University Park: Pennsylvania State University Press, 1976.

———. *A Law of Blood: The Primitive Law of the Cherokee Nation.* New York: New York University Press, 1970.

Riggs, Brett. "The Christie Cabin Site: Historical and Archaeological Evidence of the Life and Times of a Cherokee *Metis* Household (1835–1838)." In *May We All Remember: A Journal of the History and Cultures of Western North Carolina,* edited by Robert S. Brunk, vol. 1, 228–48. Asheville, NC: Robert S. Brunk Auction Services, 1997.

———. "In the Service of Native Interests: Archaeology for, of, and by Cherokee People." In *Southern Indians and Anthropology: Culture, Politics, and Identity,* edited by Lisa J. Lefler and Frederic W. Gleach, 19–30. Athens: University of Georgia Press, 2002.

———. "Removal Period Cherokee Households in Southwestern North Carolina: Material Perspectives on Ethnicity and Cultural Differentiation." PhD diss., University of Tennessee, 1999.

Riggs, Brett H., and M. Scott Shumate. *Archaeological Testing at Kituhwa: 2001 Investigations at Sites 31Sw1, 31Sw2, 31Sw287, 31Sw316, 31Sw317, 31Sw318, and 31Sw320, Report Prepared for the Eastern Band of Cherokee Indians Cultural Resource Program.* Chapel Hill: University of North Carolina, 2003.

Riggs, Brett H., M. Scott Shumate, Patti Evans-Shumate, and Brad Bowden. *Report Submitted to the Office of Cultural Resources, Eastern Band of Cherokee Indians.* Cherokee, NC, 1998.

Rivers, Olivia S. "Two Versions of Traditional Cherokee Dances Compared." *Journal of Cherokee Studies* 19 (1997): 18–45.

Rivers, W. H. R. "The Primitive Conception of Death." *Hibbert Journal* 10 (1912): 393–407.

Robinson, Prentice. *Cherokee Dictionary.* Tulsa, OK: Cherokee Language and Culture, 1996.

Rodning, Christopher B. *Center Places and Cherokee Towns: Archaeological Perspectives on Native American Architecture and Landscape in the Southern Appalachians.* Tuscaloosa: University of Alabama Press, 2015.

———. "Cherokee Towns and Calumet Ceremonialism in Eastern North America." *American Antiquity* 79 (2014): 425–43.

———. "Reconstructing the Coalescence of Cherokee Communities in Southern Appalachia." In *The Transformation of Southeastern Indians: 1540–1760*, edited by Robbie Ethridge and Charles Hudson, 155–76. Jackson: University of Mississippi Press, 2002.

Rogers, Anne F., and Barbara R. Duncan, eds. *Culture, Crisis and Conflict: Cherokee British Relations, 1756–1765.* Cherokee, NC: Museum of the Cherokee Indian Press, 2009.

Royce, Charles C. *The Cherokee Nation of Indians.* Chicago: Aldine, 1975.

Rozema, Vicki. *Cherokee Voices: Early Accounts of Cherokee Life in the East.* Winston-Salem, NC: John F. Blair, 2002.

———. *Footsteps of the Cherokees: A Guide to the Eastern Homelands of the Cherokee Nation.* Winston-Salem, NC: John F. Blair, 1995.

Russell, Steve. "The Jurisprudence of Colonialism." In *American Indian Thought: Philosophical Essays*, edited by Anne Waters, 217–28. Malden, MA: Blackwell, 2001.

Sahlins, Marshall. *How "Natives" Think about Captain Cook, for Example.* Chicago: University of Chicago Press, 1995.

Salisbury, Neal. "The Indians' Old World: Native Americans and the Coming of the Europeans." In *American Encounters: Native and Newcomers from European Contact to Indian Removal, 1500–1850*, edited by Peter C. Mancall and James H. Merrell, 2nd ed., 3–24. London: Routledge, 2007.

Sanders, George "Soggy" Sakhiyah. *Red Man's Origin.* Translated by William Eubanks. 3rd ed. Longmont, CO: Panther's Lodge, 2016. First published 1896.

Saum, Lewis O. *The Fur Trader and the Indian.* Seattle: University of Washington Press, 1965.

Saunt, Claudio. "Taking Account of Property: Stratification among the Creek Indians in the Early Nineteenth Century." In *American Encounters: Native and Newcomers from European Contact to Indian Removal, 1500–1850*, edited by Peter C. Mancall and James H. Merrell, 2nd ed., 609–36. London: Routledge, 2007.

———. " Telling Stories: The Political Uses of Myth and History in the Cherokee and Creek Nations," *Journal of American History* 93 (2006): 673–98.

Schmidt, Wilhelm. *Origin and Growth of Religion*. New York: Dial Press, 1931.

Schwarze, Edmund. *History of the Moravian Missions among the Southern Indian Tribes of the United States*. Transactions of the Moravian Historical Society, Special Series, vol. 1. Bethlehem, PA: Moravian Historical Society, 1923.

Segal, Robert A. "Relativism and Rationality in the Social Sciences." *Journal of Religion* 67 (1987): 353–62.

Sekaquaptewa, Emory. "Hopi Indian Ceremonies." In *Seeing with a Native Eye: Essays on Native American Religion*, edited by Walter H. Capps, 35–43. New York: Harper & Row, 1976.

Sekaquaptewa, Emory, and Dorothy Washburn. "They Go Along Singing: Reconstructing the Hopi Past from Ritual Metaphors in Song and Image." *American Antiquity* 69 (2004): 457–86.

Sequoyah v Tennessee Valley Authority, 620 F. 2d 1159 (1980).

Shade, Hastings. "Journey of the Cherokees." In *Myths, Legends and Old Sayings*. Tahlequah, OK: Shade, 1994.

Sharpe, J. Ed, ed. *Cherokee Psalms: A Collection of Hymns in the Cherokee Language*. Translated by Daniel Scott. Cherokee, NC: Cherokee Publications, 1991.

Shepherd Photo Collection. Photographs, 1921–1923. MSS 99–04. Museum of the Cherokee Indian Archives, Cherokee, NC.

Sider, Gerald M. *Lumbee Indian Histories: Race, Ethnicity, and Indian Identity in the Southern United States*. Cambridge: Cambridge University Press, 1993.

Silver, Timothy. *A New Face on the Countryside: Indians, Colonists and Slaves in South Atlantic Forests 1500–1800*. Cambridge: Cambridge University Press, 1990.

Sinclair, Niigonwedom James. "Trickster Reflections: Part 1." In *Troubling Tricksters: Revisioning Critical Conversations*, edited by Deanna Reder and Linda M. Morra, 21–58. Waterloo, Ontario: Wilfrid Laurier University Press.

Sleeper-Smith, Susan. "Women, Kin, and Catholicism: New Perspectives on the Fur Trade." In *American Encounters: Native and Newcomers from European Contact to Indian Removal, 1500–1850*, edited by Peter C. Mancall and James H. Merrell, 2nd ed., 107–30. London: Routledge, 2007.

Smith, Chadwick C., Rennard Strickland, and Benny Smith. *Building One Fire: Art and Worldview in Cherokee Life*. Tahlequah, OK: Cherokee Nation, 2010.

Smith, Crosslin Fields. *Stand as One: Spiritual Teachings of Keetoowah*. Edited under Crosslin Smith's guidance by Clint Carrol from manuscript provided by Marial Martyn. Ranchos de Taos, NM: Dog Soldier Press, 2018.

Smith, Jonathan Z. *Imagining Religion: From Babylon to Jamestown*. Chicago: University of Chicago Press, 1982.

———. *Relating Religion: Essays in the Study of Religion*. Chicago: University of Chicago Press, 2004.

———. "The Wobbling Pivot." *Journal of Religion* 52 (1972): 134–49.

Smith, Linda Tuhiwai. *Decolonizing Methodologies: Research and Indigenous Peoples*. London: Zed Books, 1999.

Snyder, Sara L. "Poetics, Performance, and Translation." PhD diss., Columbia University, 2016.

Southern Historical Collection, Manuscripts Department, Wilson Library, University of North Carolina at Chapel Hill. Chapel Hill, NC.

Speck, Frank G. *Ethnology of the Yuchi Indians*. Anthropological Publications of the University Museum, vol. 1, no. 1. Philadelphia: University of Pennsylvania Museum, 1909.

Speck, Frank G., and Leonard Broom, in collaboration with Will West Long. *Cherokee Dance and Drama*, 1951. Reprint with a foreword by Leonard Broom. Norman: University of Oklahoma Press, 1983.

Speck, Frank G., and C. E. Schaeffer. "The Mutual Aid and Volunteer Company of the Eastern Cherokee." *Journal of the Washington Academy of Sciences* 35 (1951): 169–79.

Spicer, Edward H., ed. *Perspectives in American Indian Culture Change*. Chicago: University of Chicago Press, 1961.

Spray, Henry W. "Report of Superintendent in Charge of Eastern Cherokee Agency, August 27, 1900." In *Annual Reports of the Department of the Interior for the Fiscal Year ended June 30, 1900, Indian Affairs, Report of Commissioner and Appendixes*, 306–8. Washington, DC: US Government Printing Office, 1900.

Stanton, William. *The Leopard's Spots: Scientific Attitudes towards Race in America, 1815–59*. Chicago: University of Chicago Press, 1960.

Starkey, Marion L. *The Cherokee Nation*. Reprint. New York: Russell and Russell, 1972. First published 1946 by Knopf (New York).

Starr, Emmet. *Early History of the Cherokees: Aboriginal Customs, Religion, Laws, Folklore, and Civilization*. N.p., 1917.

———. *History of the Cherokee Indians*. Oklahoma City, OK: Warden Co., 1921.

———. *History of the Cherokee Indians and Their Legends and Folk Lore*. Oklahoma City, OK: Warden Co., 1922.

Staunt, Claudio. "Telling Stories: The Political Uses of Myth and History in the Cherokee and Creek Nations." *Journal of American History* 93 (2006): 673–97.

Stremlau, Rose. *Sustaining the Cherokee Family: Kinship and the Allotment of an Indigenous Nation*. Chapel Hill: University of North Carolina Press, 2011.

Strickland, Rennard. "Emmet Starr." In *Encyclopedia of North American Indians*, edited by Frederick E. Hoxie, 609–10. New York: Houghton Mifflin, 1996.

———. *Fire and the Spirits: Cherokee Law from Clan to Court*. Norman: University of Oklahoma Press, 1975.

Stutley, Margaret. *Shamanism: An Introduction*. New York: Routledge, 2003.

Sullivan, Winnifred Fallers. "American Religion in Naturally Comparative." In *A Magic Still Dwells: Comparative Religion in the Postmodern Age*, edited by Kimberly C. Patton and Benjamin C. Ray, 117–30. Berkeley: University of California Press, 2000.

Superintendents' Annual Narrative and Statistical Reports from Field Jurisdiction of the Bureau of Indian Affairs, 1907–1938. National Archives Microfilm Publication M1011, Roll 12. Cherokee Orphan Training School, 1912–24. Cherokee School, 1910–1928. National Archives, Central Plains Region, Kansas City, MO.

Swanton, John R. "Indians of the Southeastern United States." Smithsonian Institution Bureau of American Ethnology Bulletin 137. Washington, DC: US Government Printing Office, 1946.

———. "Religious Beliefs and Medical Practices of the Creek Indians." *42nd Annual Report of the Bureau of American Ethnology.* Washington, DC: US Government Printing Office, 1928.

Taussig, Michael. *Defacement: Public Secrecy and the Labor of the Negative.* Stanford, CA: Stanford University Press. 1999.

———. *The Devil and Commodity Fetishism in South America.* Chapel Hill: University of North Carolina Press. 1980.

Tedlock, Dennis, and Barbara Tedlock, eds. *Teachings from the American Earth: Indian Religion and Philosophy.* New York: Liveright, 1975.

Teuton, Christopher B. *Cherokee Stories of the Turtle Island Liars' Club.* With contributions by Hastings Shade, Sammy Still, Sequoyah Guess, and Woody Hansen. Illustrations by America Meredith. Chapel Hill: University of North Carolina Press, 2012.

———. *Deep Waters: The Textual Continuum in American Indian Literature.* Lincoln: University of Nebraska Press, 2010.

———. "Literature, Education, and *The Return of the Whippoorwill*: A Conversation with Freeman Owle." *Appalachian Journal* 34 (2007): 194–205.

Teuton, Christopher B., and Hastings Shade. *Cherokee Earth Dwellers: Stories and Teachings of the Natural World.* With Loretta Shade and Larry Shade. Illustrated by MaryBeth Timothy. Seattle: University of Washington Press, 2023.

Teuton, Sean Kicummah. *Red Land, Red Power: Grounding Knowledge in the American Indian Novel.* Durham, NC: Duke University Press, 2008.

Teuton, Sean Kicummah, and Robert J. Conley. "Writing Home: An Interview with Robert J. Conley." *Wicazo Sa Review* 16 (2001): 115–28.

Thomas, Robert K. "Cherokee Values and World View." Research paper. Cross-Cultural Laboratory, Institute for Research in Social Science, North Carolina Collection, Wilson Library, University of North Carolina, Chapel Hill, 1958.

———. "Culture History of the Eastern Cherokee." Typescript. University of North Carolina, 1958.

———. "Eastern Cherokee Acculturation." Typescript. University of North Carolina, 1958.

———. *Getting to the Heart of the Matter: Collected Letters and Papers.* Vancouver: Native Ministries Consortium, 1990.

———. "The Present 'Problem' of the Eastern Cherokees." Typescript. University of North Carolina, 1958.

———. "Report on Cherokee Social and Community Organization." Typescript. University of North Carolina, 1958.

Thomas, William H. Notice, May 27, 1867. Inoli Letters, no. 22413, National Anthropological Archives, Washington, DC. Reprinted in Jack F. Kilpatrick. "Two Notices by Will Thomas." *Southern Indian Studies* 14 (1962): 27–28.

———. Papers. David M. Rubenstein Rare Book and Manuscript Library, Duke University, Durham, NC.

Thornton, Russell. "Boundary Dissolution and Revitalization Movements: The Case of the Nineteenth-Century Cherokees." *Ethnohistory* 40, no. 3 (Summer 1993): 359–83.

———. *The Cherokees: A Population History*. With the assistance of C. Matthew Snipp and Nancy Breen. Lincoln: University of Nebraska Press, 1990.

Thorp, Daniel B. *The Moravian Community in Colonial North Carolina: Pluralism on the Southern Frontier*. Knoxville: University of Tennessee Press, 1989.

Timberlake, Henry. *Lieutenant Henry Timberlake's Memoirs, 1756–1765*. Edited by Samuel Cole Williams. Johnson City, TN: Watauga Press, 1927.

Tinker, George E. *Missionary Conquest: The Gospel in Native American Cultural Genocide*. Minneapolis, MN: Fortress Press, 1993.

———"Spirituality, Native American Personhood, Sovereignty, and Solidarity." In *Native and Christian: Indigenous Voices on Religious Identity in the United States and Canada*, edited by James Treat, 115–31. New York: Routledge, 1996.

Todorov, Tzvetan. *The Conquest of America: The Question of the Arbor*. Norman: University of Oklahoma Press, 1999.

Toelken, Barre. "Seeing with a Native Eye: How Many Sheep Will It Hold." In *Seeing with a Native Eye: Essays on Native American Religion*, edited by Walter H. Capps, 9–24. New York: Harper & Row, 1976.

"Trail of Tears." In the *Encyclopedia of North American Indians*, edited by Frederick E. Hoxie, 639–40. New York: Houghton Mifflin Company, 1996.

Treat, James. *Native and Christian: Indigenous Voices on Religious Identity in the United States and Canada*. New York: Routledge, 1996.

Tuan, Yi-Fu. *Space and Place: The Perspective of Experience*. Minneapolis: University of Minnesota Press, 1977.

Turner, Terence. "History, Myth, and Social Consciousness among the Kayapoó of Central Brazil." In *Rethinking History and Myth: Indigenous South American Perspectives on the Past*, edited by Jonathan D. Hill, 195–213. Urbana: University of Illinois Press, 1988.

Underwood, Tom B. *The Story of the Cherokee People*. Cherokee, NC: Cherokee Publications, 1990.

Uneg, I. M. "Tracing Your Hysterical Roots." N.p., [1998?].

Urban, Hugh. "The Torment of Secrecy: Ethical and Epistemological Problems in the Study of Esoteric Traditions." *History of Religions* 37, no. 3 (February 1998): 209–48.

Van Der Leeuw, Gerardus. *Religion in Essence and Manifestation*. Vol. I. Gloucester, MA: Peter Smith, 1967.

Van Gennep, Arnold. *The Rites of Passage*. Translated by Monika B. Vizedom and Gabrielle L. Caffee. Chicago: University of Chicago Press, 1960.

Vecsey, Christopher, ed. *Handbook of American Religious Freedom.* New York: Crossroad, 1991.

Vocabularies and Miscellaneous Papers Pertaining to Indian Languages, 1784–1828. Manuscripts, 497.V85, pt. 1. American Philosophical Society. Philadelphia, PA.

Von Hendy, Andrew. *The Modern Construction of Myth.* Bloomington: Indiana University Press, 2002.

Walker, Robert Sparks. *Torchlights to the Cherokees: The Brainerd Mission.* Johnson City, TN: Overmountain Press, 1993.

Walker, Willard. "The Twentieth-Century Conservators of the Cherokee Sacred Formulas." In *Southern Indians and Anthropologists: Culture, Politics, and Identity*, edited by Lisa J. Lefler and Frederic W. Gleach, 107–23. Athens: University of Georgia Press, 2002.

Wallace, Anthony F. C. *The Death and Rebirth of the Seneca.* New York: Vintage Books, 1969.

———. "Revitalization Movements." *American Anthropological Association* 58 (1956): 264–81.

Wallenstein, Emmanuel. *The Modern World System I: Capitalist Agriculture and the Origins of the European World Economy in the Sixteenth Century.* New York: Academic Press, 1974.

Ward, H. Trawick, and R. P. Stephen Davis Jr. *Time Before History: The Archeology of North Carolina.* Chapel Hill: University of North Carolina Press, 1999.

Washburn, Cephas. *Reminiscences of the Indians.* New York: Presbyterian Committee of Publication, Johnson Reprint Corp., 1971.

Washburn, Wilcomb E., ed. *The Indian and the White Man.* New York: Anchor Books, 1964.

Waters, Anne, ed. *American Indian Thought: Philosophical Essays.* Malden, MA: Blackwell, 2001.

Wax, Murray L. "The Ethics of Research in American Indian Communities." *American Indian Quarterly* 15, no. 2 (1991): 431–56.

Wetmore, Ruth. "The Green Corn Ceremony of the Eastern Cherokees." *Journal of Cherokee Studies* 8, no. 1 (Spring 1983): 46–56.

White, Bruce M. "Encounters with Spirits: Ojibwa and Dakota Theories about the French and Their Merchandise." In *American Encounters: Native and Newcomers from European Contact to Indian Removal, 1500–1850*, edited by Peter C. Mancall and James H. Merrell, 2nd ed., 216–45. London: Routledge, 2007.

White, George. *Historical Collections of Georgia.* New York, 1855.

Whiteley, Peter M. *Deliberate Acts: Changing Hopi Culture through the Oraibi Split.* Tucson: University of Arizona Press, 1988.

Whiteman, Henrietta. "White Buffalo Woman." In *The American Indian and the Problem of History*, edited by Calvin Martin, 162–70. New York: Oxford University Press, 1987.

Wilkins, David E., and Kimberly Tsianina Lomawaima. *Uneven Ground: American Indian Sovereignty and Federal Law.* Norman: University of Oklahoma Press, 2002.

Williams, Patrick, and Laura Chrisman, eds. *Colonial Discourse and Post-Colonial Theory: A Reader.* New York: Columbia University Press, 1994.

Williams, Samuel C. "An Account of the Presbyterian Mission to the Cherokees, 1757–1759." *Tennessee Historical Magazine* ser. 2, vol. 1, no. 2 (January 1931): 125–38.

———. "William Tatum, Wataugan." *Tennessee Historical Magazine* 7 (1921): 176–78.

Williams, Samuel Cole, ed. "The Tour of Duke of Orleans, Later Louis Philippe, King of the French (1797)." In *Early Travels in the Tennessee Country, 1549–1800,* 433–41. Johnson City, TN: Watauga Press, 1928.

Witthoft, John. "Ceremonies, pt. 1." Audiotape of remarks, John Witthoft Collection, 87–171. Audiocassette no. 4, side 2 (cassette no. 5 in original master). 1968. Museum of the Cherokee Indian Archives, Cherokee, NC.

———. "Cherokee Beliefs Concerning Death." *Journal of Cherokee Studies* 8 (Fall 1983): 68–72.

———. "The Cherokee Green Corn Medicine and the Green Corn Festival." *Journal of the Washington Academy of Sciences* 36, no. 7 (1946): 213–19.

———. "Cherokee Village Activities." Typescript. John Witthoft Collection, MSS 87–171.1. 1958. Museum of the Cherokee Indian Archives, Cherokee, NC.

———. "An Early Cherokee Ethnobotanical Note." *Journal of the Washington Academy of Sciences* 37 (1947): 73–75.

———. "Eastern Woodland Community Typology and Acculturation." In *Symposium on Cherokee and Iroquois Culture,* Smithsonian Institution Bureau of American Ethnology Bulletin 180, edited by William N. Fenton and John Gulick, 67–76. Washington, DC: US Government Printing Office, 1961.

———. *Green Corn Ceremonialism in the Eastern Woodlands.* Occasional Contributions. University of Michigan Museum of Anthropological Archaeology. Ann Arbor: University of Michigan Press, 1949.

———. "Notes on a Cherokee Migration Story." *Journal of the Washington Academy of Sciences* 37, no. 9 (1947): 304–5.

———. "Notes on Death." Typescript, July 1977. VF Culture File, "Death, Burial," 1977. Museum of the Cherokee Indian Archives, Cherokee, NC.

———. "Stone Pipes of the Historic Cherokee." *Southern Indian Studies* 1 (1949): 43–62.

———. "Will West Long, Cherokee Informant." *American Anthropologist* 50, no. 2 (April–June 1948): 355–59.

Witthoft, John, and Wendell S. Hadlock. "Cherokee-Iroquois Little People." *Journal of American Folklore* 59 (1946): 413–22.

Wood, Peter H. "The Changing Population of the Colonial South." In *Powhatan's Mantle: Indians in the Colonial Southeast,* edited by P. H. Wood, G. A. Waselkov, and M. T. Hatley, 35–103. Lincoln: University of Nebraska Press, 1989.

Wood, William W., Jr. "War and the Eastern Cherokee." *Southern Indian Studies* 2 (1950): 47–53.

Woodward, Grace Steele. *The Cherokees.* Norman: University of Oklahoma Press, 1963.

Worsley, Peter. *The Trumpet Shall Sound: A Study of "Cargo" Cults in Melanesia*. 2nd ed. New York: Schocken Books, 1968.

Wright, Muriel. *Spring Place Moravian Mission and the Ward Family of the Cherokee Nation*. Guthrie, OK: Co-operative Publishing, 1940.

Wyss, Hilary E. *Writing Indians: Literacy, Christianity, and Native Community in Early America*. Amherst: University of Massachusetts Press, 2000.

Yountae, An. "A Decolonial Theory of Religion: Race, Coloniality, and Secularity in the Americas," *Journal of the American Academy of Religion* 88 (2020): 947–80.

Zogry, Michael J. *Anetso, The Cherokee Ballgame: At the Center of Ceremony and Identity*. Chapel Hill: University of North Carolina Press, 2010.

———. "Ballgames: North American Indian Ballgames." In *The Encyclopedia of Religion*, edited by Lindsey Jones, 2nd ed., vol. 2, 752–56. New York: Macmillan, 2005.

———. Enduring Voices Project Collection. Interviews, 1997–1998. Videocassettes and transcriptions. Southern Folklife Collection No. 20339, Wilson Library, University of North Carolina at Chapel Hill, Chapel Hill, NC.

———, interviewer. "Interview of Mr. Goingback Chiltoskey, November 3, 1997." Typescript. Fading Voices Project. Southern Folklife Collection No. 20339, Wilson Library, University of North Carolina at Chapel Hill, Chapel Hill, NC. Same material as in the Enduring Voices Project Collection.

———, interviewer. "Interview of Robert Bushyhead, November 2, 1997." Typescript. Fading Voices Project. Southern Folklife Collection No. 20339, Wilson Library, University of North Carolina at Chapel Hill, Chapel Hill, NC. Same material as in the Enduring Voices Project Collection.

Index

Aarcowee (Beloved Man), on Christianity, 123–24, 223n6

Adair, James, 19, 105; on lunar eclipses, 121; on wounded warriors, 22

Adams, John Quincy, 138

adulthood, transition to, 43, 44, 64

afterlife, Eastern Cherokee, 48, 115, 210n101; association of tobacco with, 91; punishment in, 183; twentieth century beliefs, 183; visions of, 154

agriculture, Eastern Cherokee, 3, 23–26; avoidance of men in, 22; corn/beans/squash crops, 23; crops cultivated, 25; Eastern Band's, 181; harvest rituals, 25; miraculous, 24; old methods in, 178; origin story of, 23; supplementing of gathering, 23; unskilled jobs and, 184; women's practice of, 12, 13, 20, 22–24. *See also* subsistence, Eastern Cherokee

agriculture, white, 132; US encouragement of, 138, 176

Allen, Paula Gunn, 200n3

Altman, Heidi, 13

American Board of Commissioners for Foreign Missions (ABCFM), 124; Butrick with, 148; calls for removal of, 142; mission statement of, 140

American Revolution: attacks on Cherokee during, 110; Cherokee religious life following, 111–14; decimation of Cherokees, 113

Anawaggia (Cherokee woman), killing of soldiers, 163

ancestors, primordial. *See* Kanati; Nvyunuwi; sacred beings; Selu; Thunder Beings

Anglo-Cherokee War, 107, 109–10; histories of, 221n11; loss of unity during, 111

animals: in ball game ritual, 65–66, 67; in Booger Dance, 74; defense against humans, 83–84; in Green Corn Dance, 60; inflicting of disease, 84, 104; killing rituals, 20; masks, 70; narratives of, 10, 11; paradise of, 31; prayers to spirits of, 82–83, 141; primordial, 83; symbols of the sacred, 84. *See also* bears; deer; hunting

Anitsaguhi clan, ancient: transformation into bears, 30–31

Appalachia. *See* Great Smoky Mountains

Arch, Davy, 51, 77, 195; in Booger Dance, 69

Arch, John: translation of Gospel, 188

arks, sacred: fire in, 35

Armachain, Leslie, 192

Arnold, Philip, 202n8

assimilation: advocates of, 137; Great Spirit on, 129; opponents of, 141; postponement of, 106; resistance to, 111, 112, 136, 138–42, 157, 163, 191; through boarding schools, 177. *See also* civilization; contact, European

Founded in 1893,
UNIVERSITY OF CALIFORNIA PRESS
publishes bold, progressive books and journals
on topics in the arts, humanities, social sciences,
and natural sciences—with a focus on social
justice issues—that inspire thought and action
among readers worldwide.

The UC PRESS FOUNDATION
raises funds to uphold the press's vital role
as an independent, nonprofit publisher, and
receives philanthropic support from a wide
range of individuals and institutions—and from
committed readers like you. To learn more, visit
ucpress.edu/supportus.